尾田栄一郎

Birds sure have it good, don't they? They can fly around freely in the sky... According to one scholar's calculations, if humans built up their chest muscles to a thickness of two meters, we'd be able to fly too! Scholars say some crazy things sometimes, huh? Okay, go. Volume 39 is starting!!

-Eiichiro Oda, 2005

Eiichiro Oda begins his manga career at the age of 17, when his one-shot cowboy manga **Wanted!** won second place in the coveted Tezuka manga awards. Oda went on to work as an assistant to some of the biggest manga artists in the industry, including Nobuhiro Watsuki, before winning the Hop Step Award for new artists. His pirate adventure **One Piece**, which debuted in **Weekly Shonen Jump** in 1997, quickly became one of the most popular manga in Japan.

ONE PIECE VOL. 39
WATER SEVEN PART 8

SHONEN JUMP Manga Edition

STORY AND ART BY EIICHIRO ODA

English Adaptation/Jake Forbes
Translation/Taylor Eagle, HC Language Solutions
Touch-up Art & Lettering/HudsonYards
Design/Sean Lee
Supervising Editor/Yuki Murashige
Editor/Megan Bates

VP, Production/Alvin Lu
VP, Sales & Product Marketing/Gonzalo Ferreyra
VP, Creative/Linda Espinosa
Publisher/Hyoe Narita

Printed in the U.S.A.

Published by VIZ Media, LLC
P.O. Box 77010
San Francisco, CA 94107

10 9 8 7 6 5 4 3 2 1
First printing, April 2010

SHONEN JUMP MANGA

ONE PIECE

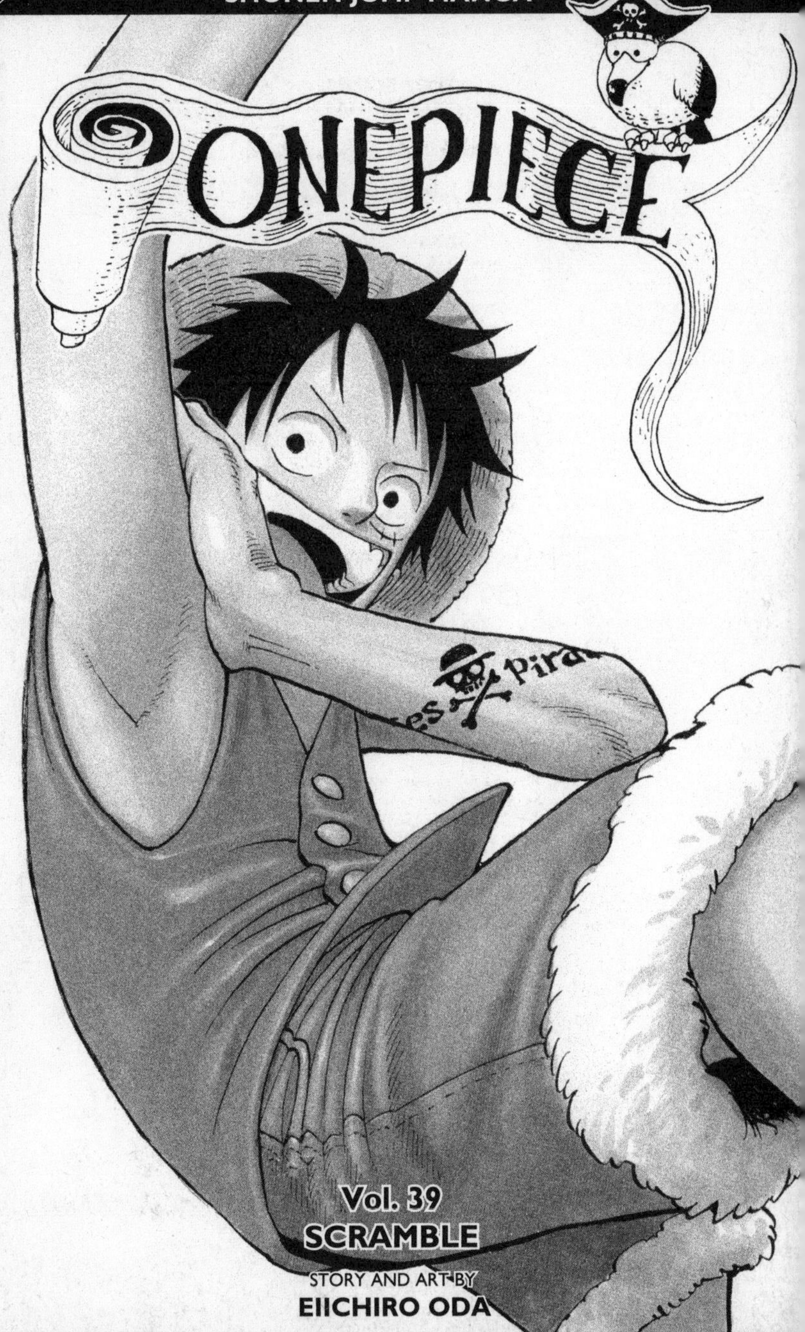

Vol. 39
SCRAMBLE

STORY AND ART BY
EIICHIRO ODA

The Franky Family

Professional ship dismantlers, they moonlight as bounty hunters.

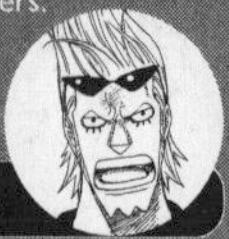

The master builder and an apprentice of Tom, the legendary shipwright.

Franky (Cutty Flam)

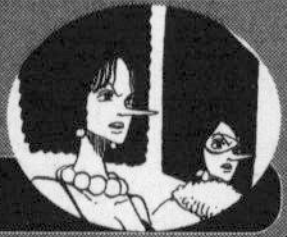

The Square Sisters

Kiwi & Mozu

Cipher Pol No. 9

A covert intelligence agency under the direct supervision of the World Government. They have been granted the license to kill uncooperative citizens.

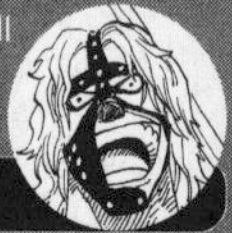

Director

Spandam

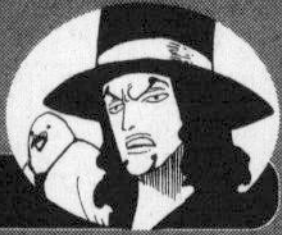

Rob Lucci & Hattori

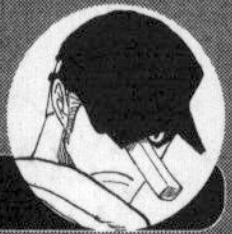

Kaku

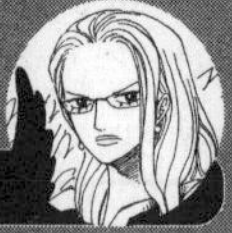

Kalifa

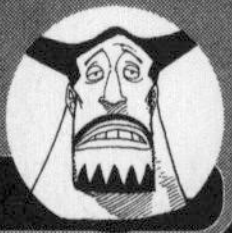

Blueno

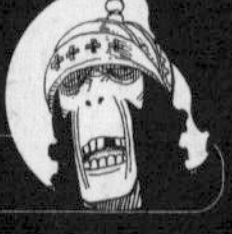

Navy Headquarters

Captain T-Bone

The Straw Hats

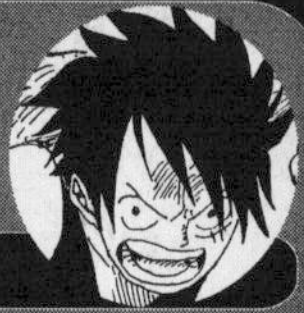

Boundlessly optimistic and able to stretch like rubber, he is determined to become King of the Pirates.

Monkey D. Luffy

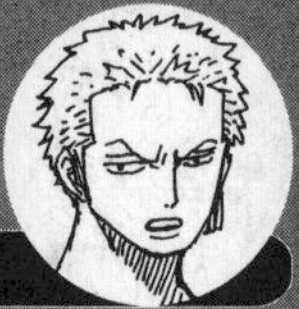

A former bounty hunter and master of the "three-sword" style. He aspires to be the world's greatest swordsman.

Roronoa Zolo

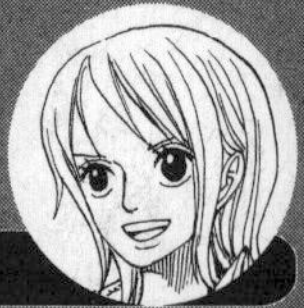

A thief who specializes in robbing pirates. Nami hates pirates, but Luffy convinced her to be his navigator.

Nami

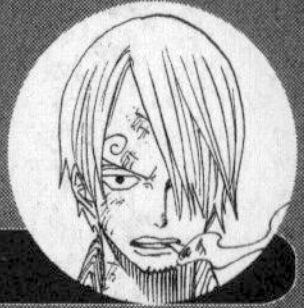

The bighearted cook (and ladies' man) whose dream is to find the legendary sea, the "All Blue."

Sanji

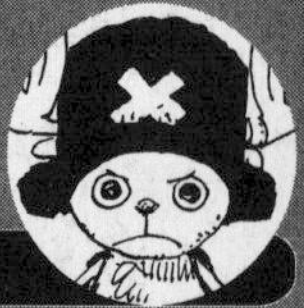

A blue-nosed man-reindeer and the ship's doctor.

Tony Tony Chopper

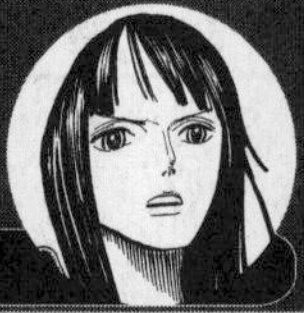

A mysterious woman in search of the Ponegliff on which true history is recorded.

Nico Robin

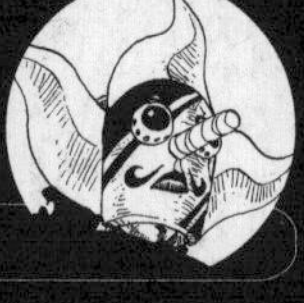

A "good friend" of former crewmate Usopp and a superhero who's come to save Luffy and crew...or at least that's what he says.

Sniper King

THE STORY OF ONE PIECE

Volume 39

Monkey D. Luffy started out as just a kid with a dream—to become the greatest pirate in history! Stirred by the tales of pirate "Red-Haired" Shanks, Luffy vowed to become a pirate himself. That was before the enchanted Devil Fruit gave Luffy the power to stretch like rubber, at the cost of being unable to swim—a serious handicap for an aspiring sea dog. Undeterred, Luffy set out to sea and recruited some crewmates—master swordsman Zolo; treasure-hunting thief Nami; lying sharpshooter Usopp; the high-kicking chef Sanji; Chopper, the walkin' talkin' reindeer doctor; and the mysterious archaeologist Robin.

After many adventures, the Straw Hats' ship, the *Merry Go*, is less than seaworthy. In order to get her repaired, they head to Water Seven, home of the best shipwrights. When told that *Merry* is damaged beyond repair, Luffy makes the agonizing decision to get a new ship. Furious at Luffy's decision, Usopp leaves the crew. And when Robin is linked to an assassination attempt on Mayor Iceberg, her betrayal and then desertion leave them flabbergasted. When the Straw Hats are blamed for the crime, they set out to learn the truth. But what they find out uncovers more deception—the other assassins are the agents of CP9, a covert agency working directly for the World Government! Their real motive is to secure the blueprints of the Pluton, the destructive ancient weapon, believed to be in Iceberg's hands. But when they come up empty-handed, they focus their attention on another possibility—that Franky's got the blueprints!

Galley-La Company

A top shipbuilding company. They are purveyors to the World Government.

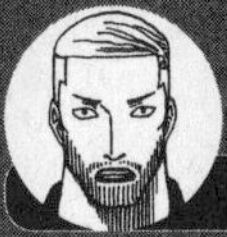

Mayor of Water Seven and president of Galley-La Company

Iceberg

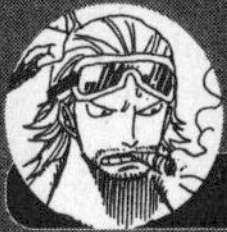

Rigging and Mast Foreman

Paulie

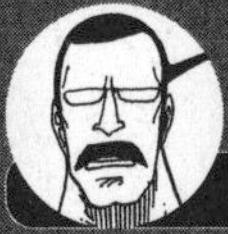

Pitch, Blacksmithing and Block-and-Tackle Foreman

Peepley Lulu

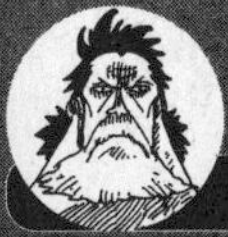

Cabinetry, Caulking and Flag-Making Foreman

Tilestone

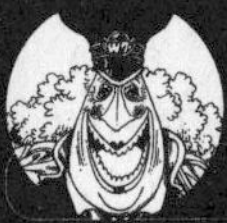

Formerly the beautiful secretary of Tom's Workers. Now stationmaster of Shift Station.

Kokoro

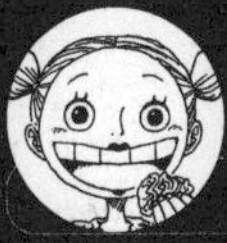

Kokoro's granddaughter

Chimney

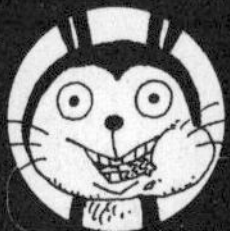

Cat (but actually a rabbit)

Gonbe

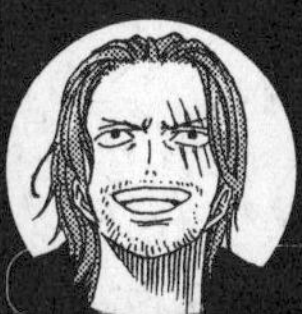

A pirate that Luffy idolizes. Shanks gave Luffy his trademark straw hat.

"Red-Haired" Shanks

WATER SEVEN

ONE PIECE

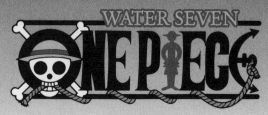

Vol. 39
Scramble

CONTENTS

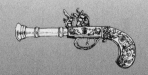

Chapter 368:
SEA TRAIN BATTLE GAME

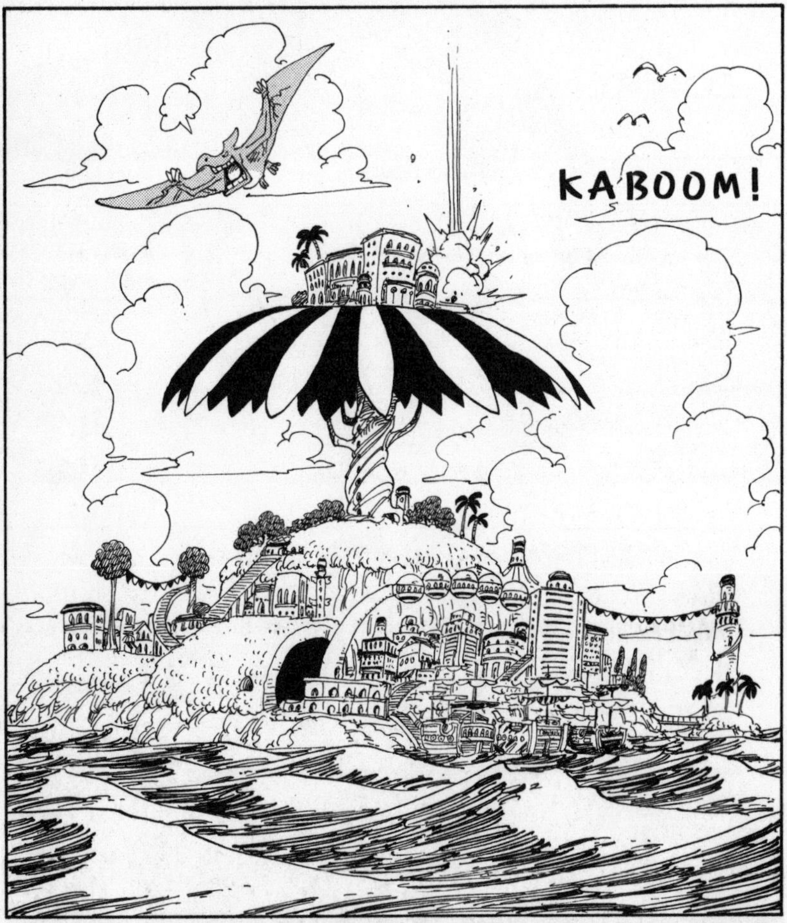
KABOOM!

MS. GOLDEN WEEK'S BIG PLAN, A BAROQUE REUNION, VOL. 8:
"THE FALL TO VACATION ISLAND"

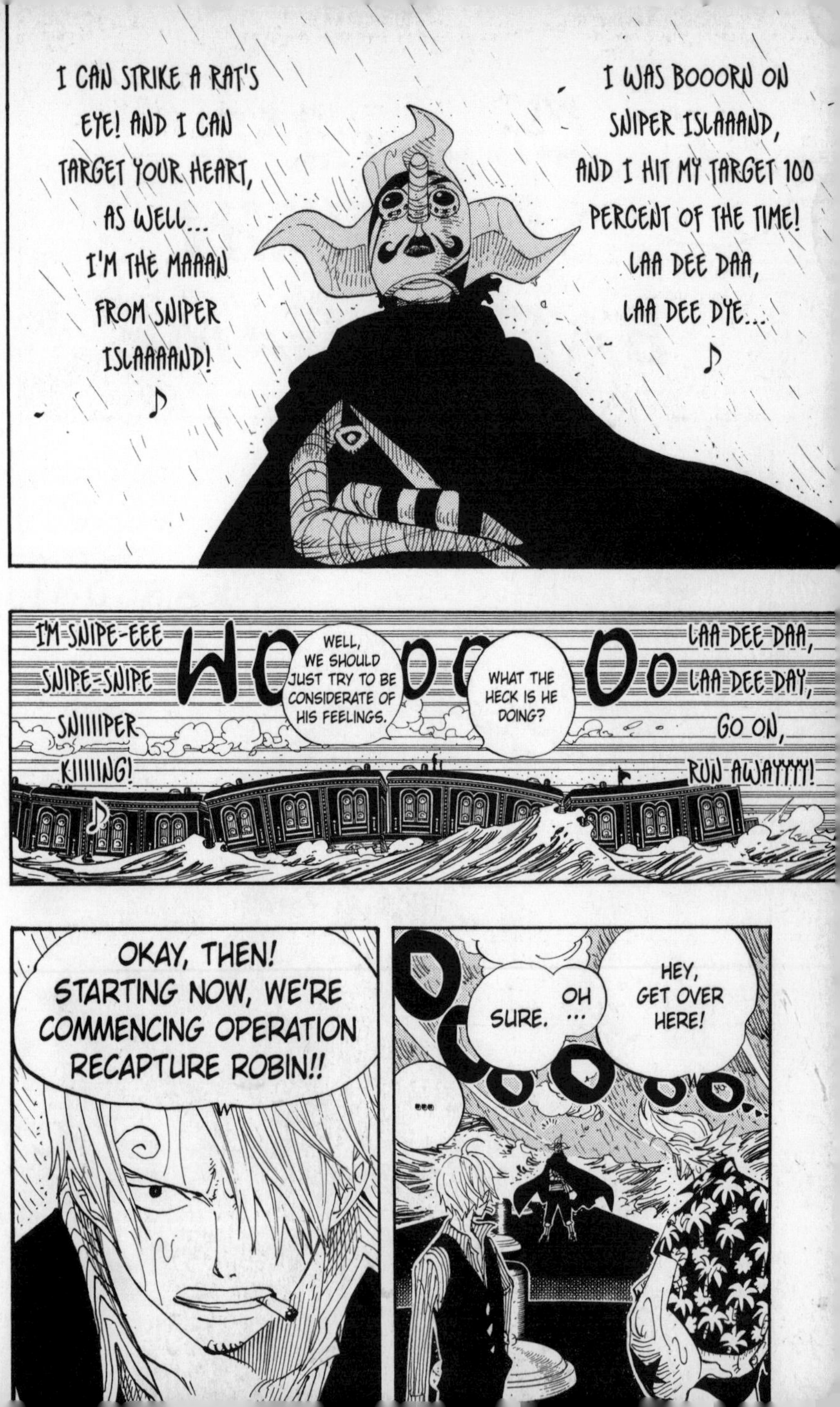
I WAS BOOORN ON SNIPER ISLAAAND, AND I HIT MY TARGET 100 PERCENT OF THE TIME! LAA DEE DAA, LAA DEE DYE... ♪
I CAN STRIKE A RAT'S EYE! AND I CAN TARGET YOUR HEART, AS WELL... I'M THE MAAAN FROM SNIPER ISLAAAAND! ♪
LAA DEE DAA, LAA DEE DAY, GO ON, RUN AWAYYYY!
WHAT THE HECK IS HE DOING?
WELL, WE SHOULD JUST TRY TO BE CONSIDERATE OF HIS FEELINGS.
I'M SNIPE-EEE SNIPE-SNIPE SNIIIIPER KIIIIING! ♪
HEY, GET OVER HERE!
OH ... SURE.
...
OKAY, THEN! STARTING NOW, WE'RE COMMENCING OPERATION RECAPTURE ROBIN!!

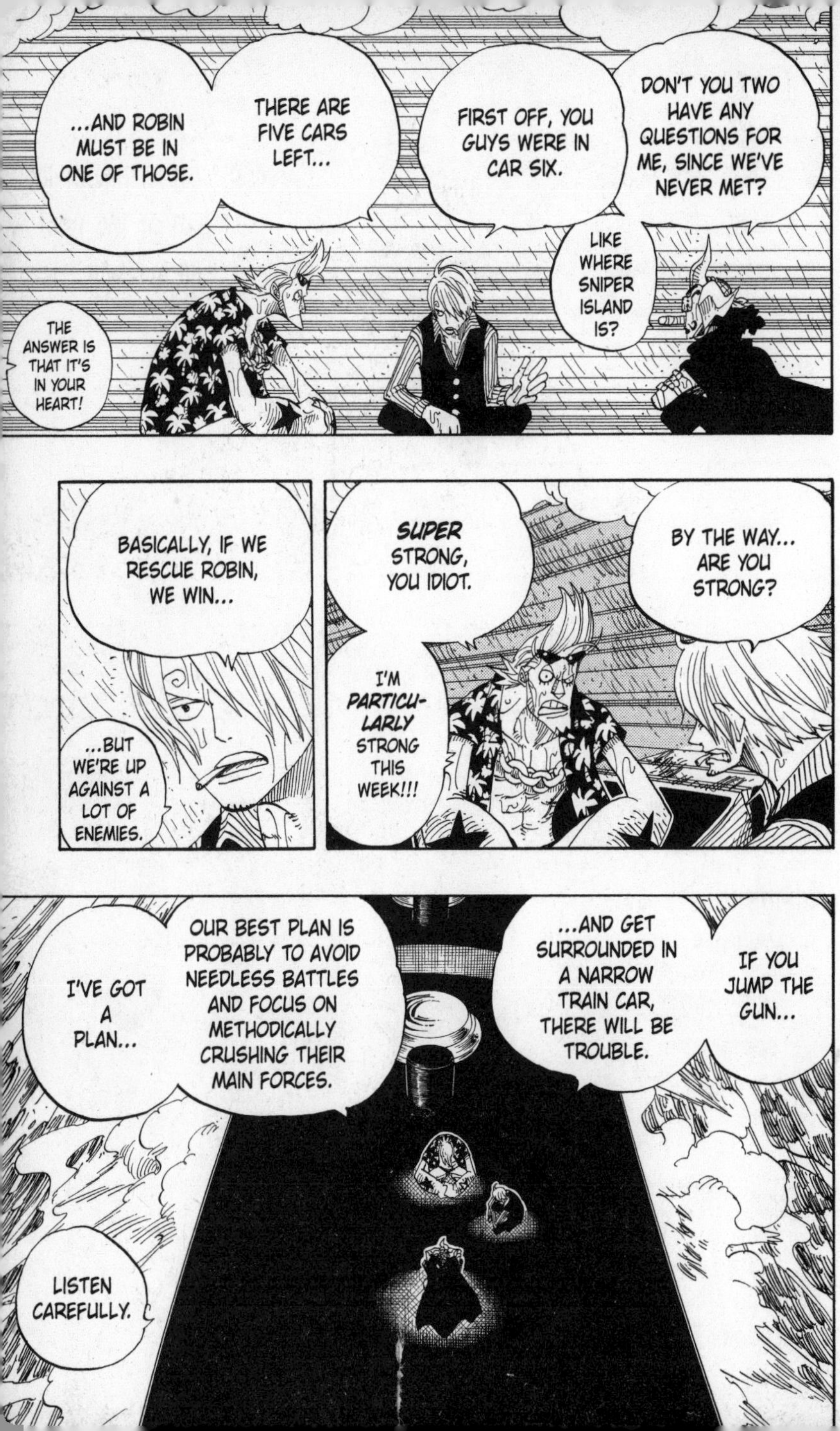
DON'T YOU TWO HAVE ANY QUESTIONS FOR ME, SINCE WE'VE NEVER MET?
LIKE WHERE SNIPER ISLAND IS?
FIRST OFF, YOU GUYS WERE IN CAR SIX.
THERE ARE FIVE CARS LEFT...
...AND ROBIN MUST BE IN ONE OF THOSE.
THE ANSWER IS THAT IT'S IN YOUR HEART!
BY THE WAY... ARE YOU STRONG?
SUPER STRONG, YOU IDIOT.
I'M PARTICU-LARLY STRONG THIS WEEK!!!
BASICALLY, IF WE RESCUE ROBIN, WE WIN...
...BUT WE'RE UP AGAINST A LOT OF ENEMIES.
IF YOU JUMP THE GUN...
...AND GET SURROUNDED IN A NARROW TRAIN CAR, THERE WILL BE TROUBLE.
OUR BEST PLAN IS PROBABLY TO AVOID NEEDLESS BATTLES AND FOCUS ON METHODICALLY CRUSHING THEIR MAIN FORCES.
I'VE GOT A PLAN...
LISTEN CAREFULLY.

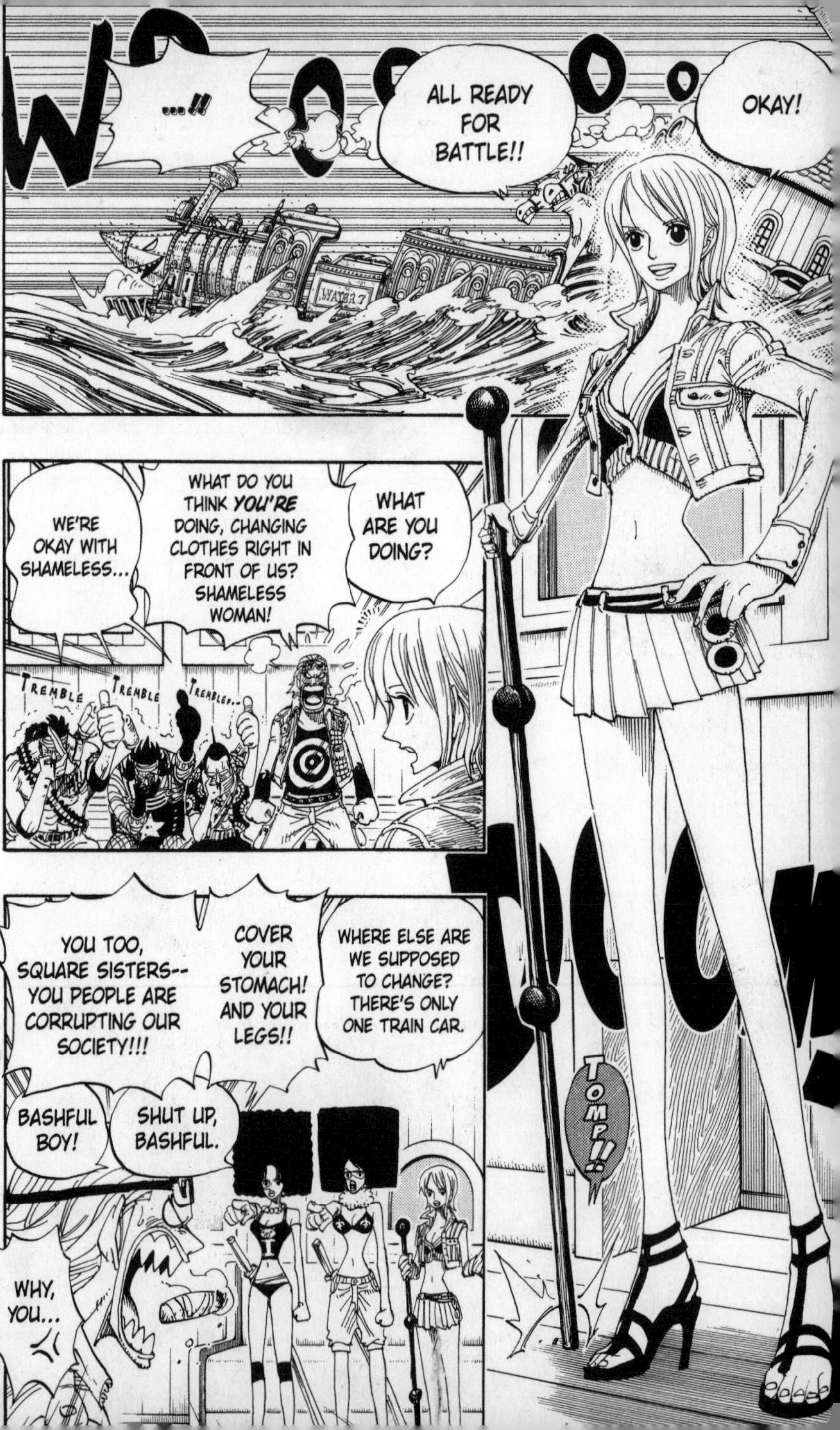
OKAY!
ALL READY FOR BATTLE!!
...!!
WATER 7
DOOM!
TOMP!!
WHAT ARE YOU DOING?
WHAT DO YOU THINK *YOU'RE* DOING, CHANGING CLOTHES RIGHT IN FRONT OF US? SHAMELESS WOMAN!
WE'RE OKAY WITH SHAMELESS...
TREMBLE
TREMBLE
TREMBLE...
WHERE ELSE ARE WE SUPPOSED TO CHANGE? THERE'S ONLY ONE TRAIN CAR.
COVER YOUR STOMACH! AND YOUR LEGS!!
YOU TOO, SQUARE SISTERS-- YOU PEOPLE ARE CORRUPTING OUR SOCIETY!!!
SHUT UP, BASHFUL.
BASHFUL BOY!
WHY, YOU...

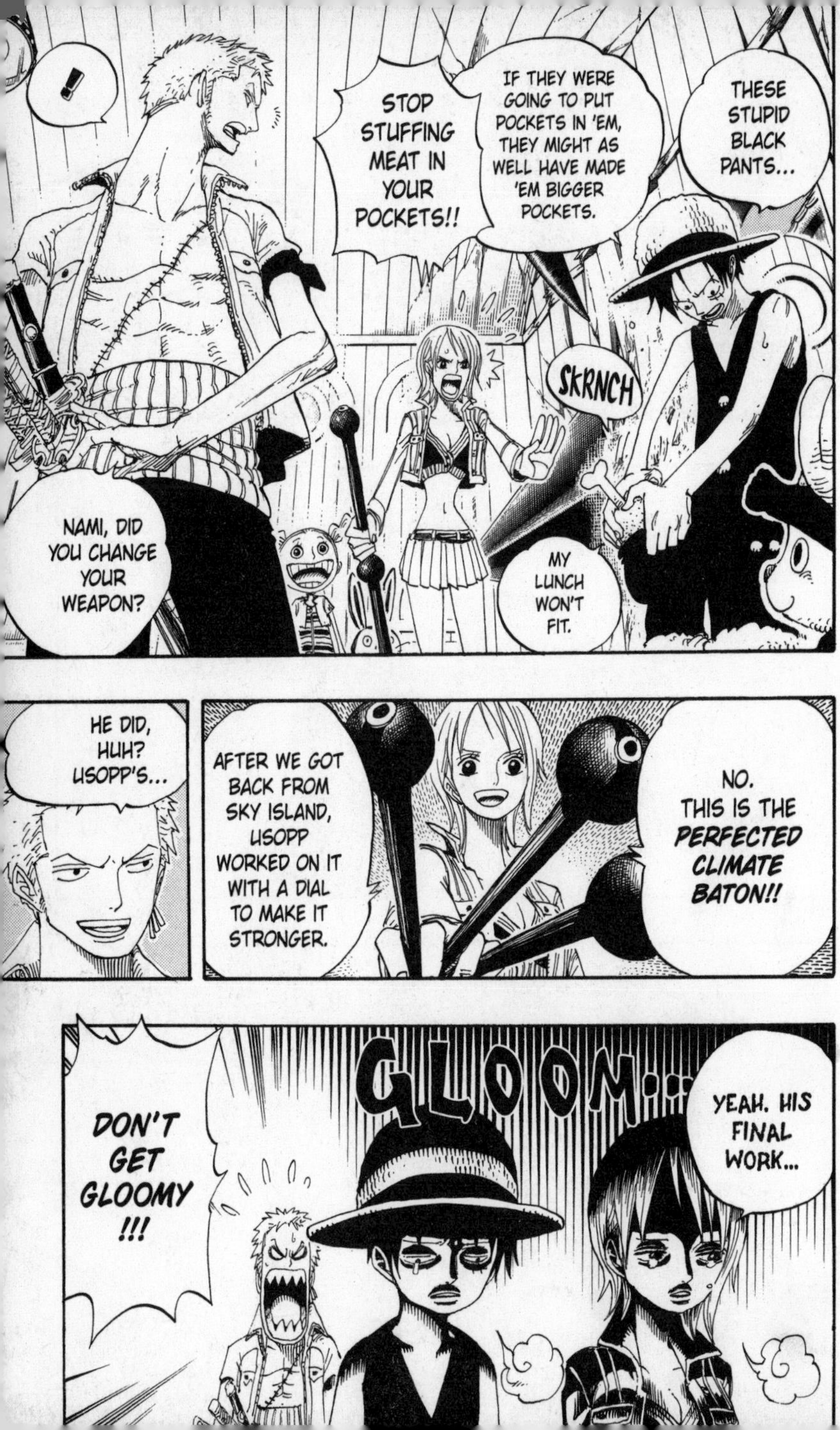
THESE STUPID BLACK PANTS...
IF THEY WERE GOING TO PUT POCKETS IN 'EM, THEY MIGHT AS WELL HAVE MADE 'EM BIGGER POCKETS.
STOP STUFFING MEAT IN YOUR POCKETS!!
!
SKRNCH
MY LUNCH WON'T FIT.
NAMI, DID YOU CHANGE YOUR WEAPON?
NO. THIS IS THE PERFECTED CLIMATE BATON!!
AFTER WE GOT BACK FROM SKY ISLAND, USOPP WORKED ON IT WITH A DIAL TO MAKE IT STRONGER.
HE DID, HUH? USOPP'S...
YEAH. HIS FINAL WORK...
GLOOM...
DON'T GET GLOOMY !!!

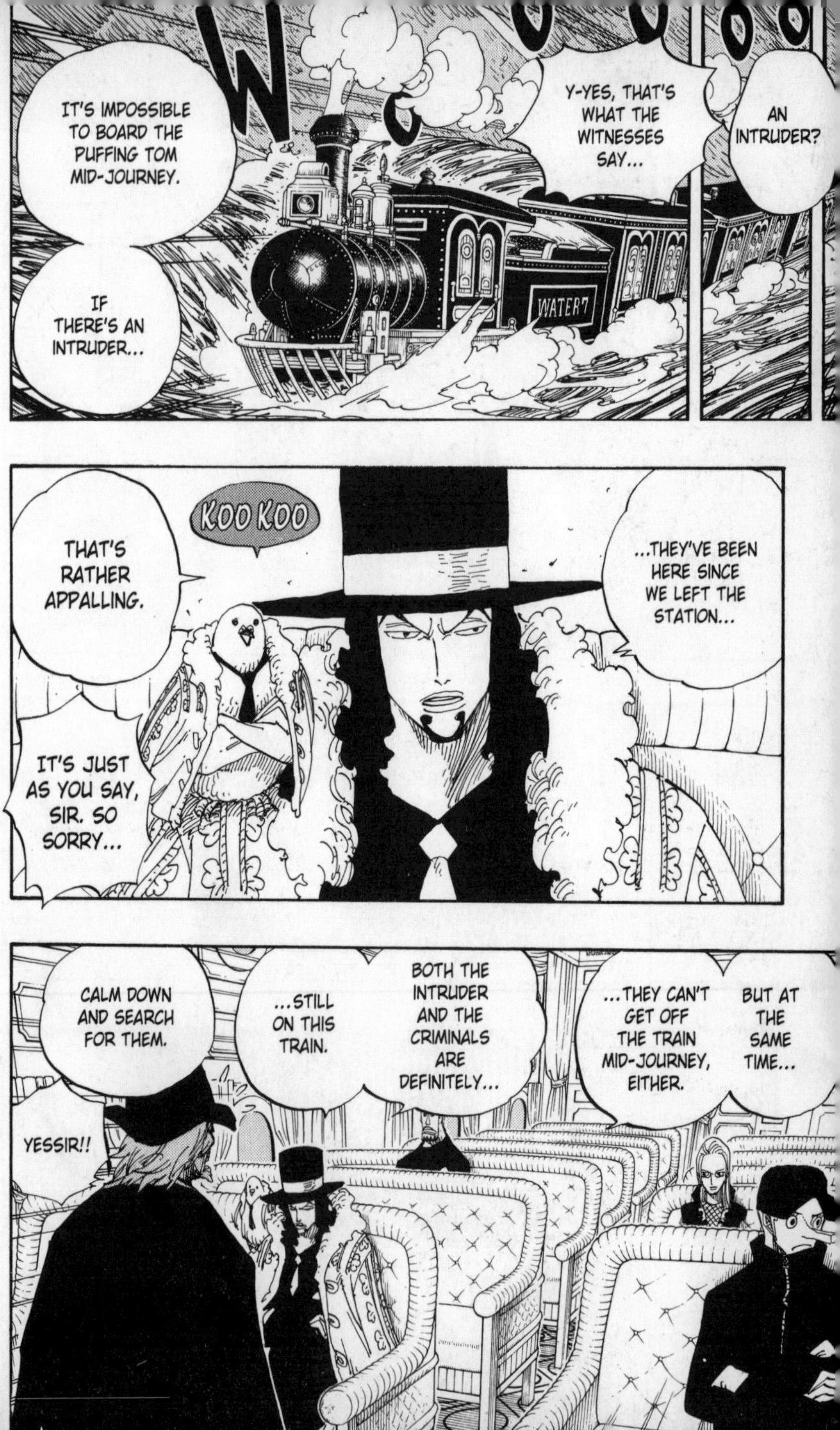
AN INTRUDER?
Y-YES, THAT'S WHAT THE WITNESSES SAY...
WATER7
IT'S IMPOSSIBLE TO BOARD THE PUFFING TOM MID-JOURNEY.
IF THERE'S AN INTRUDER...
...THEY'VE BEEN HERE SINCE WE LEFT THE STATION...
KOO KOO
THAT'S RATHER APPALLING.
IT'S JUST AS YOU SAY, SIR. SO SORRY...
BUT AT THE SAME TIME...
...THEY CAN'T GET OFF THE TRAIN MID-JOURNEY, EITHER.
BOTH THE INTRUDER AND THE CRIMINALS ARE DEFINITELY...
...STILL ON THIS TRAIN.
CALM DOWN AND SEARCH FOR THEM.
YESSIR!!

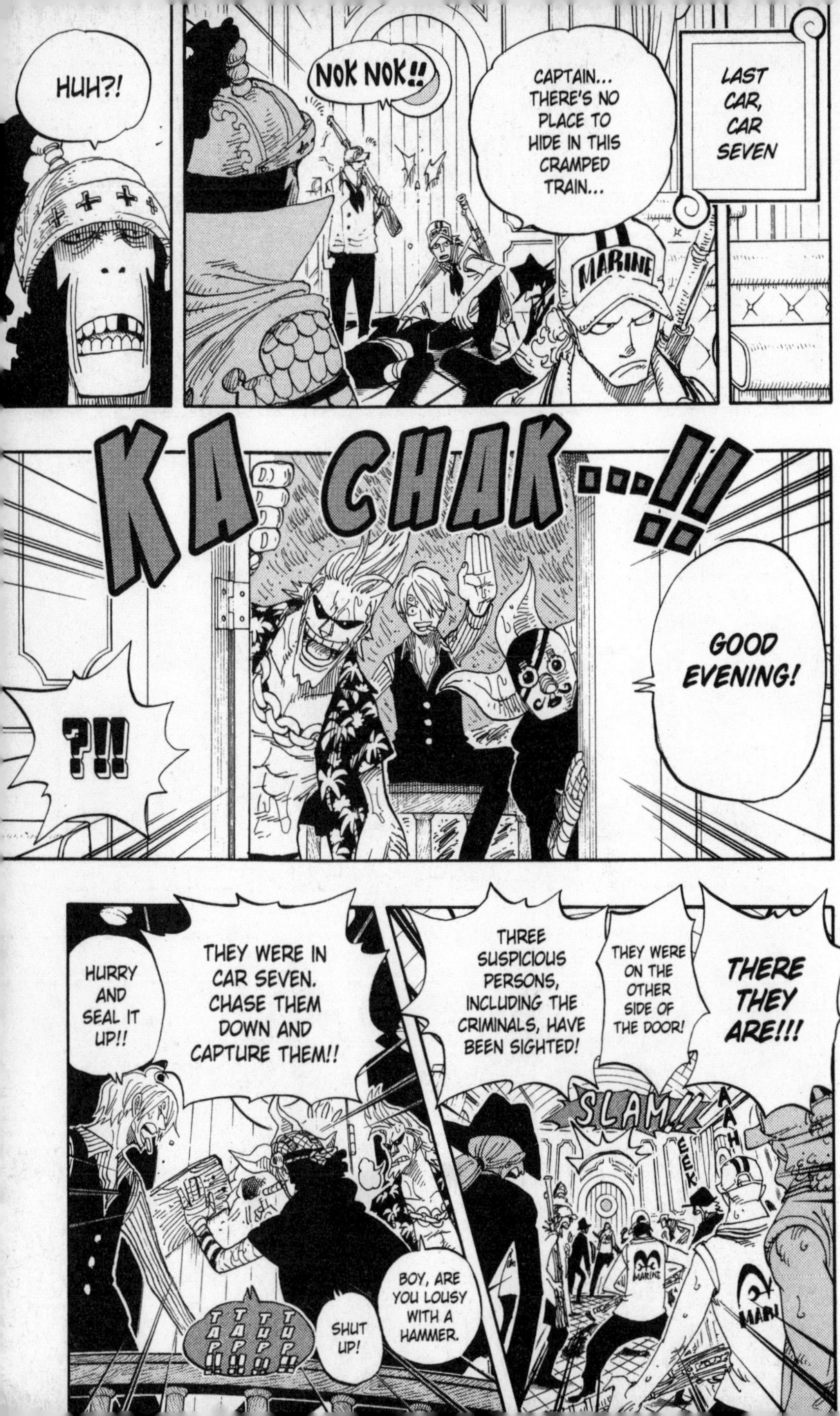
LAST CAR, CAR SEVEN
CAPTAIN... THERE'S NO PLACE TO HIDE IN THIS CRAMPED TRAIN...
NOK NOK!!
HUH?!
KA CHAK...!!
GOOD EVENING!
?!!
THERE THEY ARE!!!
THEY WERE ON THE OTHER SIDE OF THE DOOR!
THREE SUSPICIOUS PERSONS, INCLUDING THE CRIMINALS, HAVE BEEN SIGHTED!
SLAM!!
AAH
EEK
THEY WERE IN CAR SEVEN. CHASE THEM DOWN AND CAPTURE THEM!!
HURRY AND SEAL IT UP!!
BOY, ARE YOU LOUSY WITH A HAMMER.
SHUT UP!
TUPP!! TUPP!! TAPP!! TAP!!

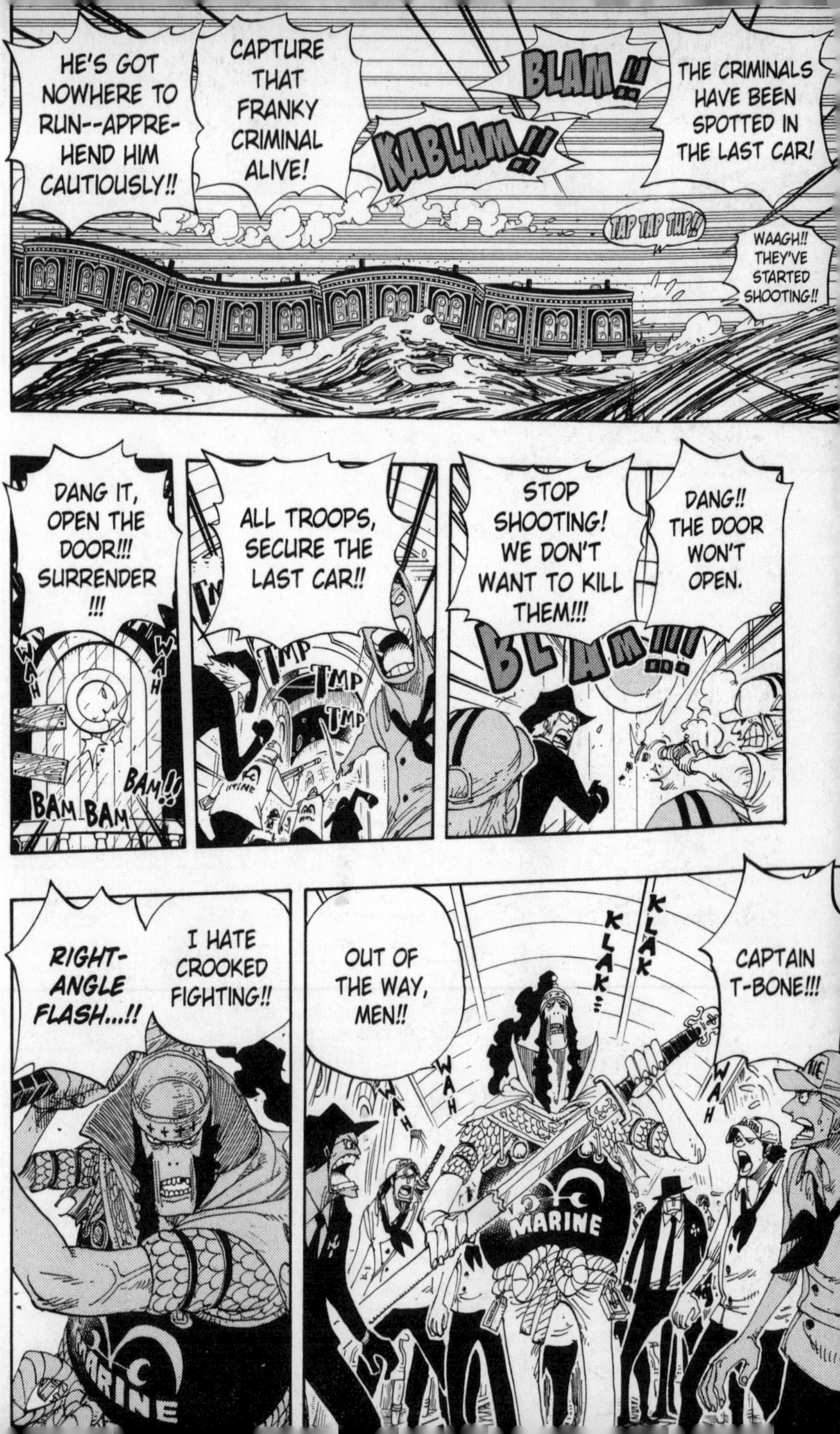
THE CRIMINALS HAVE BEEN SPOTTED IN THE LAST CAR!
BLAM!!
CAPTURE THAT FRANKY CRIMINAL ALIVE!
KABLAM!!
HE'S GOT NOWHERE TO RUN--APPRE-HEND HIM CAUTIOUSLY!!
WAAGH!! THEY'VE STARTED SHOOTING!!
TAP TAP TUP!!
DANG!! THE DOOR WON'T OPEN.
STOP SHOOTING! WE DON'T WANT TO KILL THEM!!!
BLAM!!!
ALL TROOPS, SECURE THE LAST CAR!!
TMP TMP TMP
DANG IT, OPEN THE DOOR!!! SURRENDER !!!
WAH WAH
BAM!!
BAM BAM
CAPTAIN T-BONE!!!
KLAK KLAK
WAH
OUT OF THE WAY, MEN!!
WAH
MARINE
I HATE CROOKED FIGHTING!!
RIGHT-ANGLE FLASH...!!
MARINE

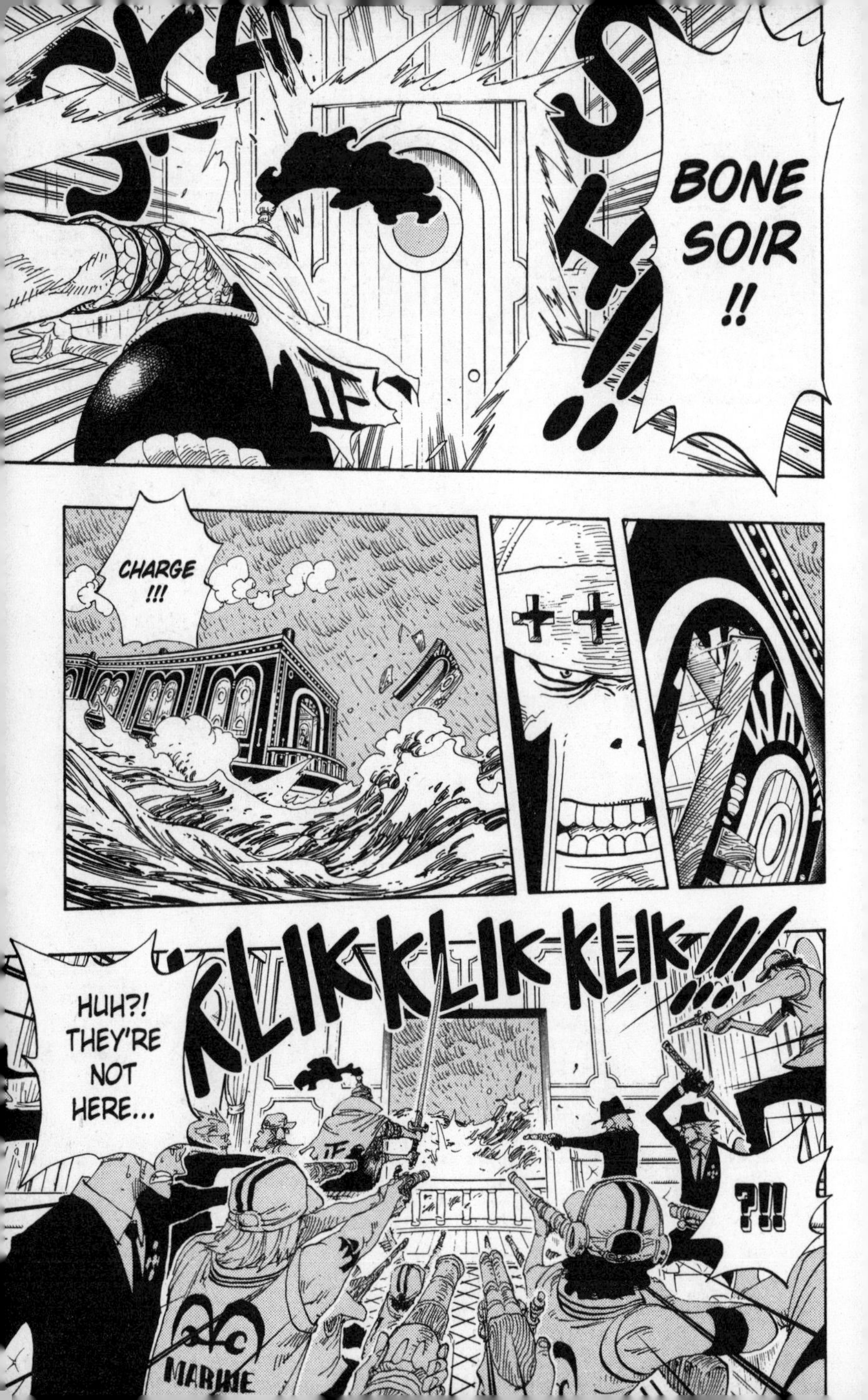
BONE SOIR !!
CHARGE !!!
KLIK KLIK KLIK!!!
?!!
HUH?! THEY'RE NOT HERE...
MARINE

HYOOO

...

WAH   WAH

MARINE

ON THE ROOF?!

THE ENEMIES ARE IN THE LAST CAR!!

TMP TMP TMP TMP...

NO... THEY COULDN'T HAVE!!!

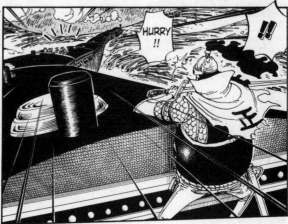

HURRY !!

!!

?!!!

MARINE   MARINE   INE

WAH

MEN, RETREAT TO THE FORWARD CARS!!

THIS IS A TRAP!!!

A TRAP?!

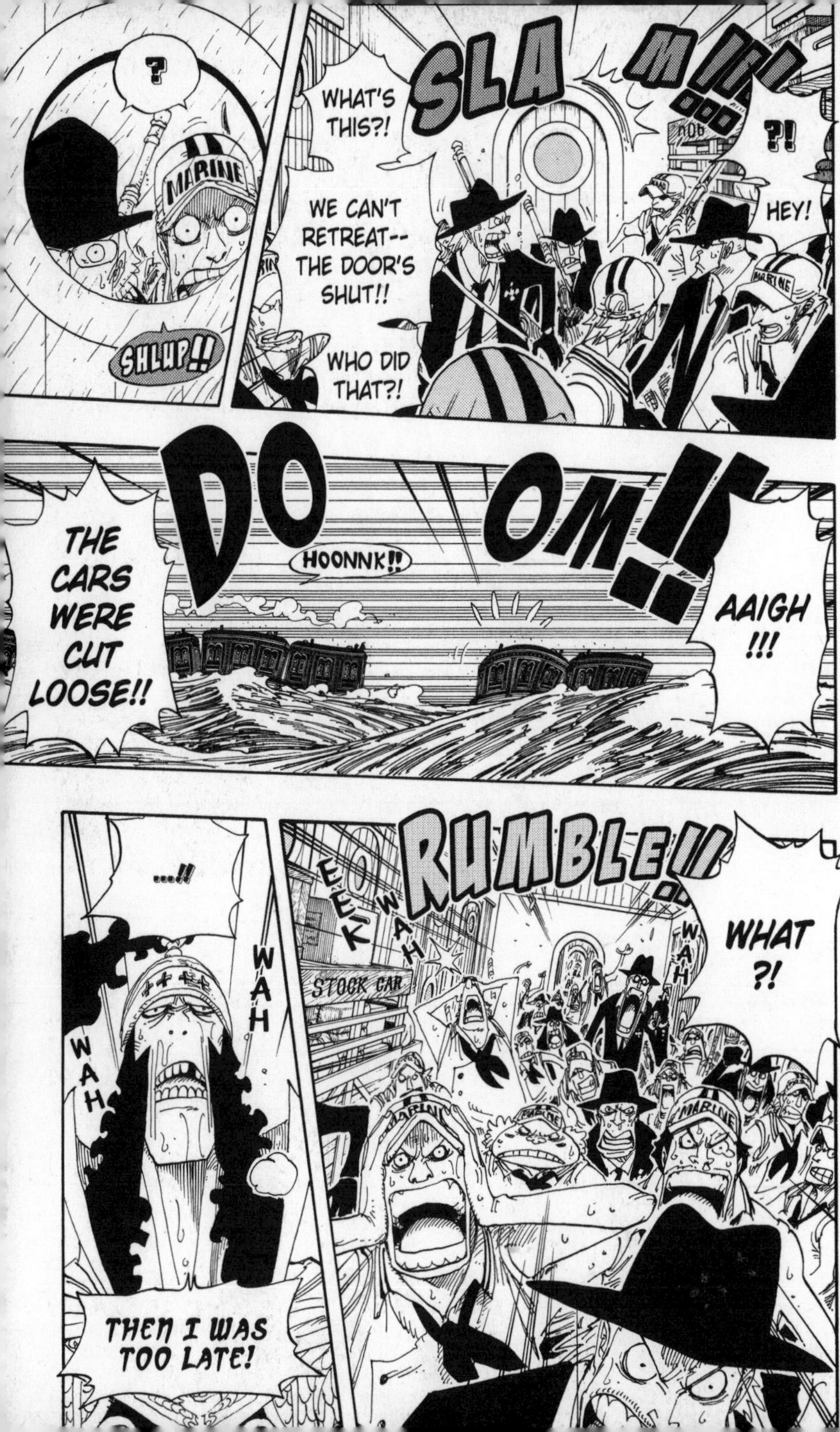
SLAM!!
?!
HEY!
WHAT'S THIS?!
WE CAN'T RETREAT-- THE DOOR'S SHUT!!
WHO DID THAT?!
?
SHLUP!!
DOOM!!
AAIGH!!!
HOONNK!!
THE CARS WERE CUT LOOSE!!
WHAT?!
RUMBLE!!
WAH WAH
WAH WAH
EEEK
STOCK CAR
...!!
WAH WAH
WAH WAH
THEN I WAS TOO LATE!

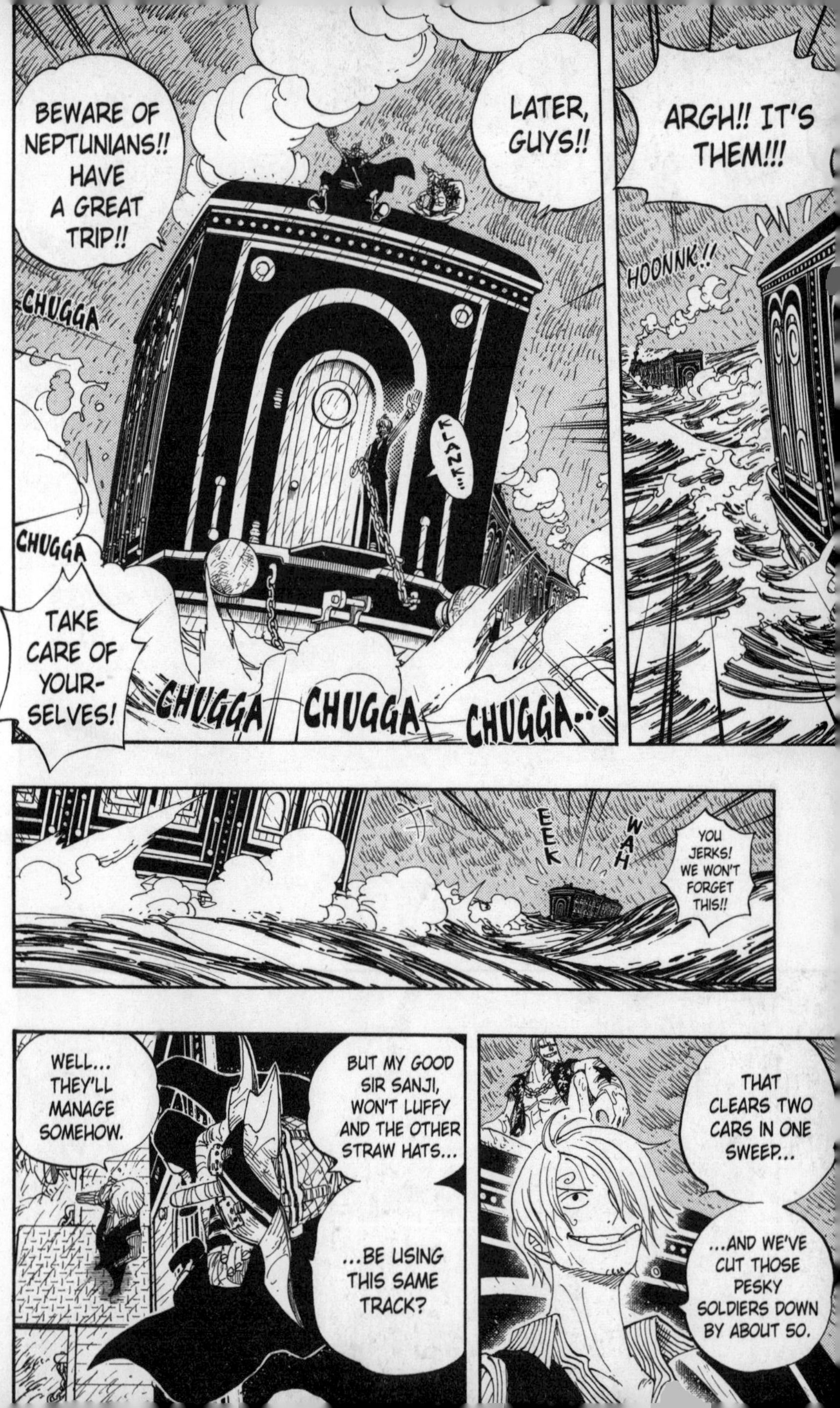
ARGH!! IT'S THEM!!!
HOONNK!!
LATER, GUYS!!
BEWARE OF NEPTUNIANS!! HAVE A GREAT TRIP!!
CHUGGA
KLANK...
CHUGGA
TAKE CARE OF YOUR-SELVES!
CHUGGA CHUGGA CHUGGA...
WAH
EEK
YOU JERKS! WE WON'T FORGET THIS!!
THAT CLEARS TWO CARS IN ONE SWEEP...
...AND WE'VE CUT THOSE PESKY SOLDIERS DOWN BY ABOUT 50.
BUT MY GOOD SIR SANJI, WON'T LUFFY AND THE OTHER STRAW HATS...
...BE USING THIS SAME TRACK?
WELL... THEY'LL MANAGE SOMEHOW.

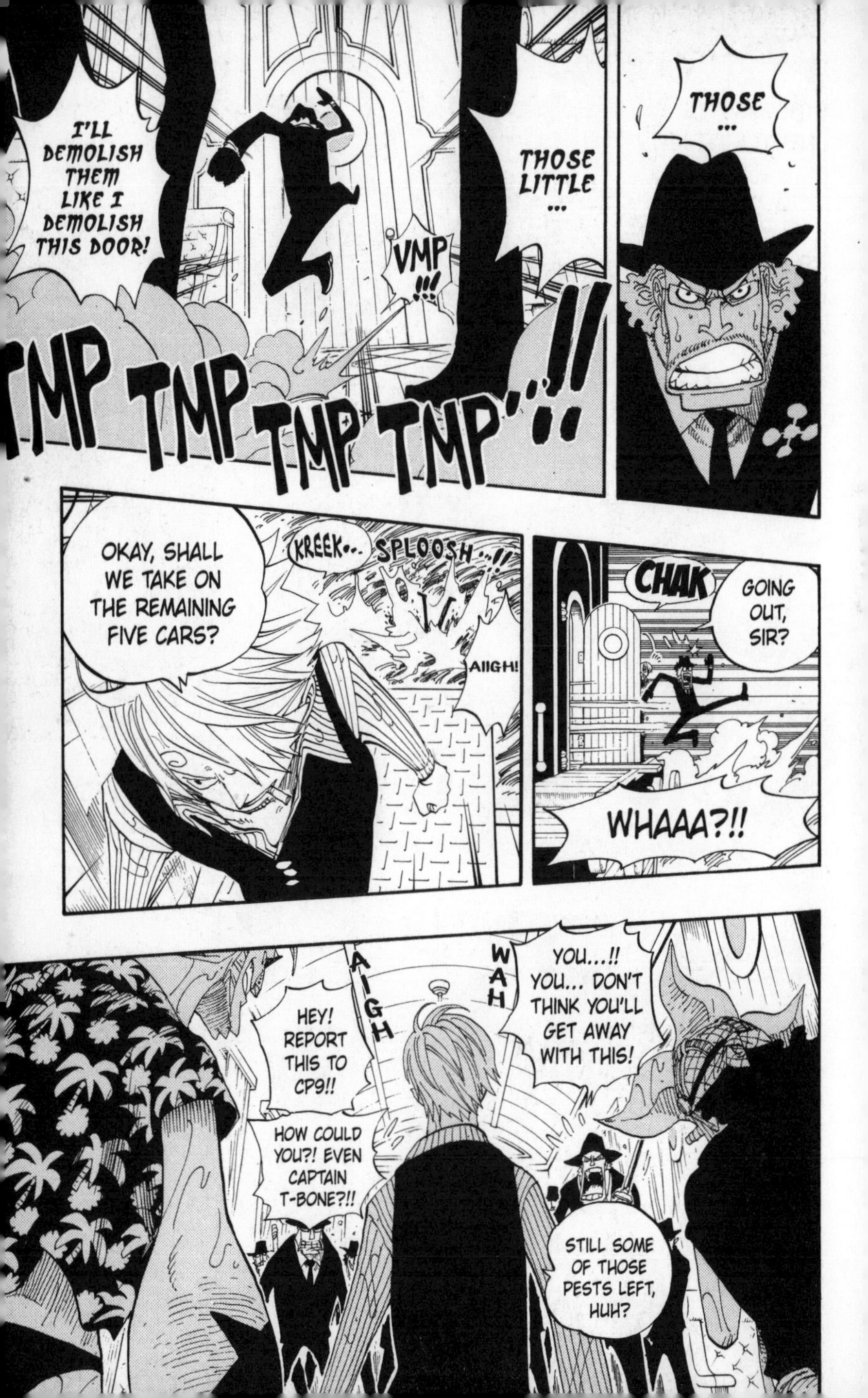
THOSE ...
THOSE LITTLE ...
I'LL DEMOLISH THEM LIKE I DEMOLISH THIS DOOR!
VMP !!!
TMP TMP TMP TMP!!
GOING OUT, SIR?
CHAK
WHAAA?!!
SPLOOSH ...!!
KREEK...
OKAY, SHALL WE TAKE ON THE REMAINING FIVE CARS?
AIIGH!
YOU...!! YOU... DON'T THINK YOU'LL GET AWAY WITH THIS!
WAH
AIGH
HEY! REPORT THIS TO CP9!!
HOW COULD YOU?! EVEN CAPTAIN T-BONE?!!
STILL SOME OF THOSE PESTS LEFT, HUH?

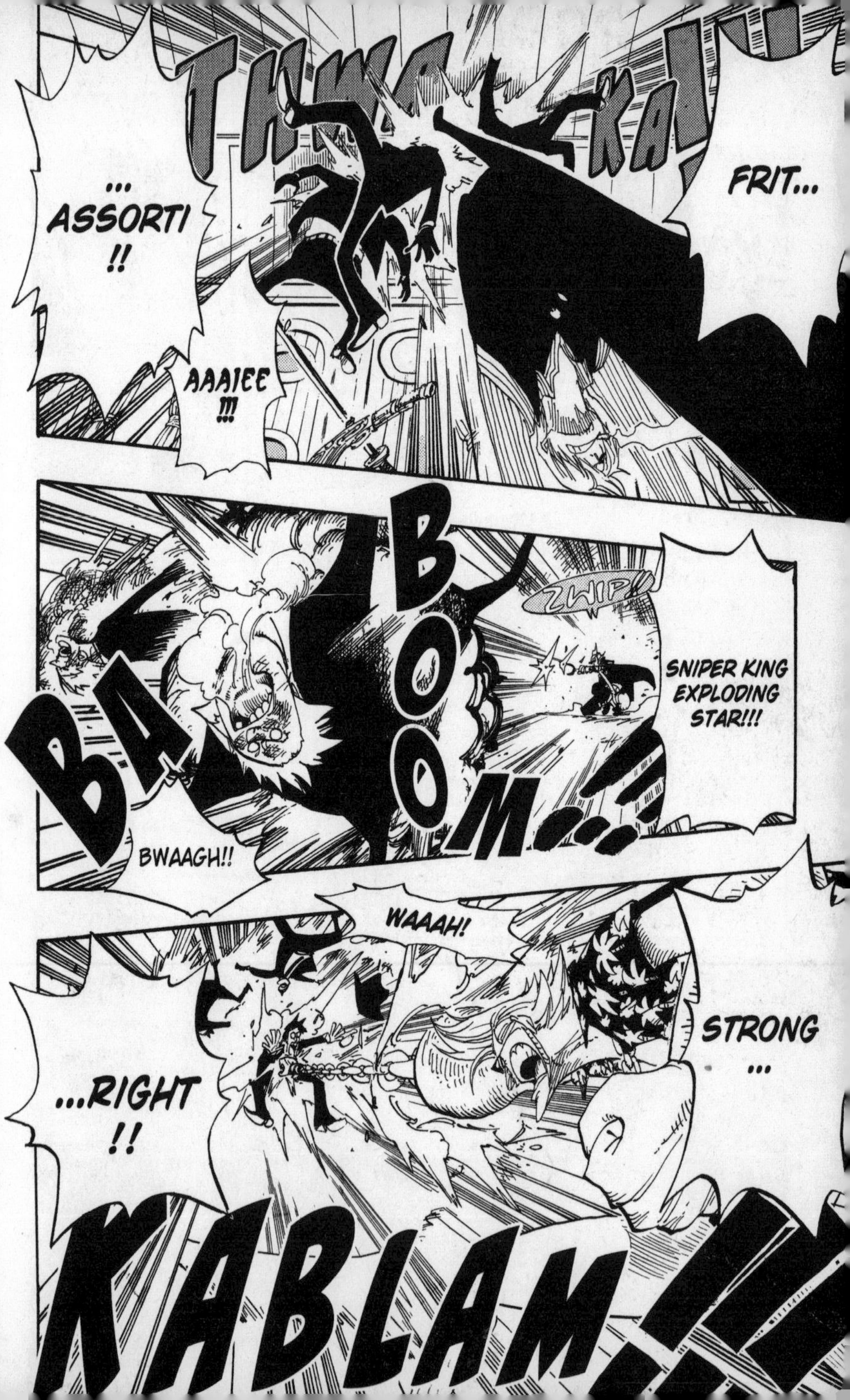
FRIT...
... ASSORTI !!
AAAIEE !!!
ZWIP!!
SNIPER KING EXPLODING STAR!!!
BABOOM...!!
BWAAGH!!
WAAAH!
STRONG ...
...RIGHT !!
KABLAM!!

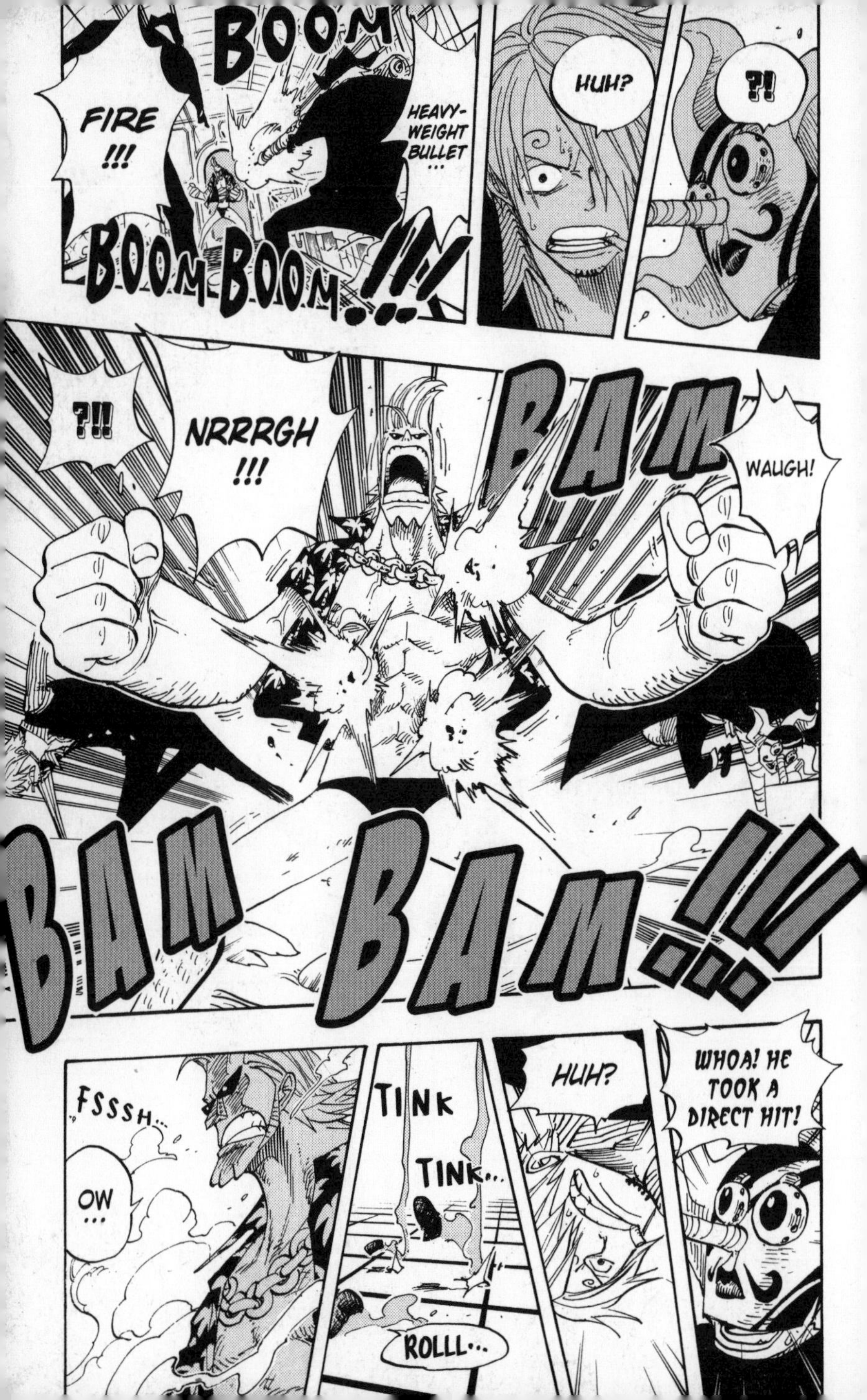
?!
HUH?
BOOM
HEAVY-WEIGHT BULLET...
FIRE!!!
BOOM BOOM!!!
WAUGH!
BAM
NRRRGH!!!
?!!
BAM BAM!!!
WHOA! HE TOOK A DIRECT HIT!
HUH?
TINK
TINK...
ROLLL...
FSSSH...
OW...

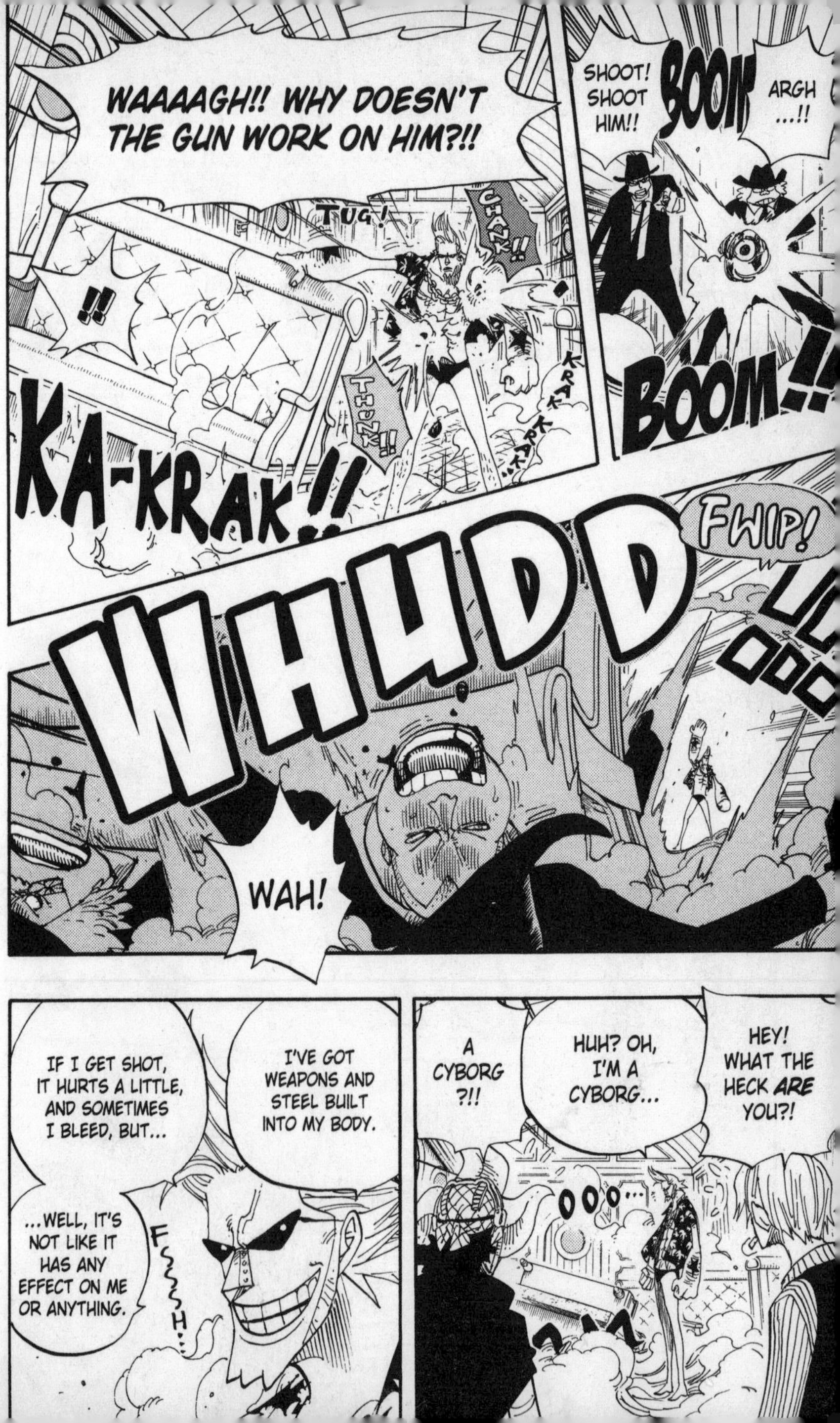
ARGH ...!!
BOOM
SHOOT! SHOOT HIM!!
BOOM!!
WAAAAGH!! WHY DOESN'T THE GUN WORK ON HIM?!!
TUG!
CHAK!!
!!
THUNK!!
KRAK KRAK KRAK
KA-KRAK!!
FWIP!
WHUDD
WAH!
HEY! WHAT THE HECK ARE YOU?!
HUH? OH, I'M A CYBORG...
A CYBORG ?!!
OOO...
I'VE GOT WEAPONS AND STEEL BUILT INTO MY BODY.
IF I GET SHOT, IT HURTS A LITTLE, AND SOMETIMES I BLEED, BUT...
...WELL, IT'S NOT LIKE IT HAS ANY EFFECT ON ME OR ANYTHING.
FSSSH...

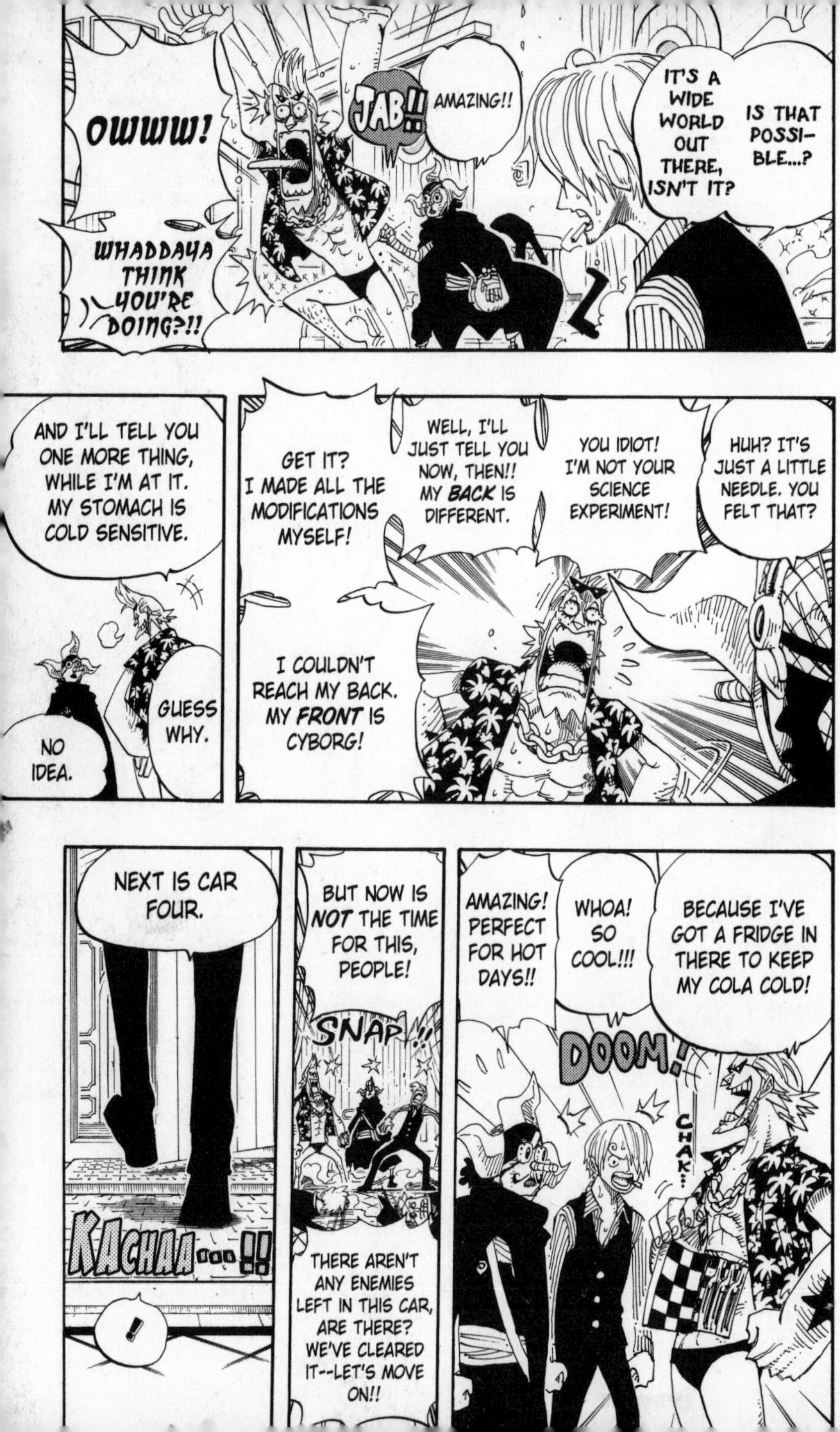
IS THAT POSSIBLE...?
IT'S A WIDE WORLD OUT THERE, ISN'T IT?
AMAZING!!
JAB!!
OWWW!
WHADDAYA THINK YOU'RE DOING?!!
HUH? IT'S JUST A LITTLE NEEDLE. YOU FELT THAT?
YOU IDIOT! I'M NOT YOUR SCIENCE EXPERIMENT!
WELL, I'LL JUST TELL YOU NOW, THEN!! MY BACK IS DIFFERENT.
GET IT? I MADE ALL THE MODIFICATIONS MYSELF!
I COULDN'T REACH MY BACK. MY FRONT IS CYBORG!
AND I'LL TELL YOU ONE MORE THING, WHILE I'M AT IT. MY STOMACH IS COLD SENSITIVE.
GUESS WHY.
NO IDEA.
BECAUSE I'VE GOT A FRIDGE IN THERE TO KEEP MY COLA COLD!
WHOA! SO COOL!!!
AMAZING! PERFECT FOR HOT DAYS!!
DOOM!
CHAK..
BUT NOW IS NOT THE TIME FOR THIS, PEOPLE!
SNAP!!
THERE AREN'T ANY ENEMIES LEFT IN THIS CAR, ARE THERE? WE'VE CLEARED IT--LET'S MOVE ON!!
NEXT IS CAR FOUR.
KACHAA...!!
!

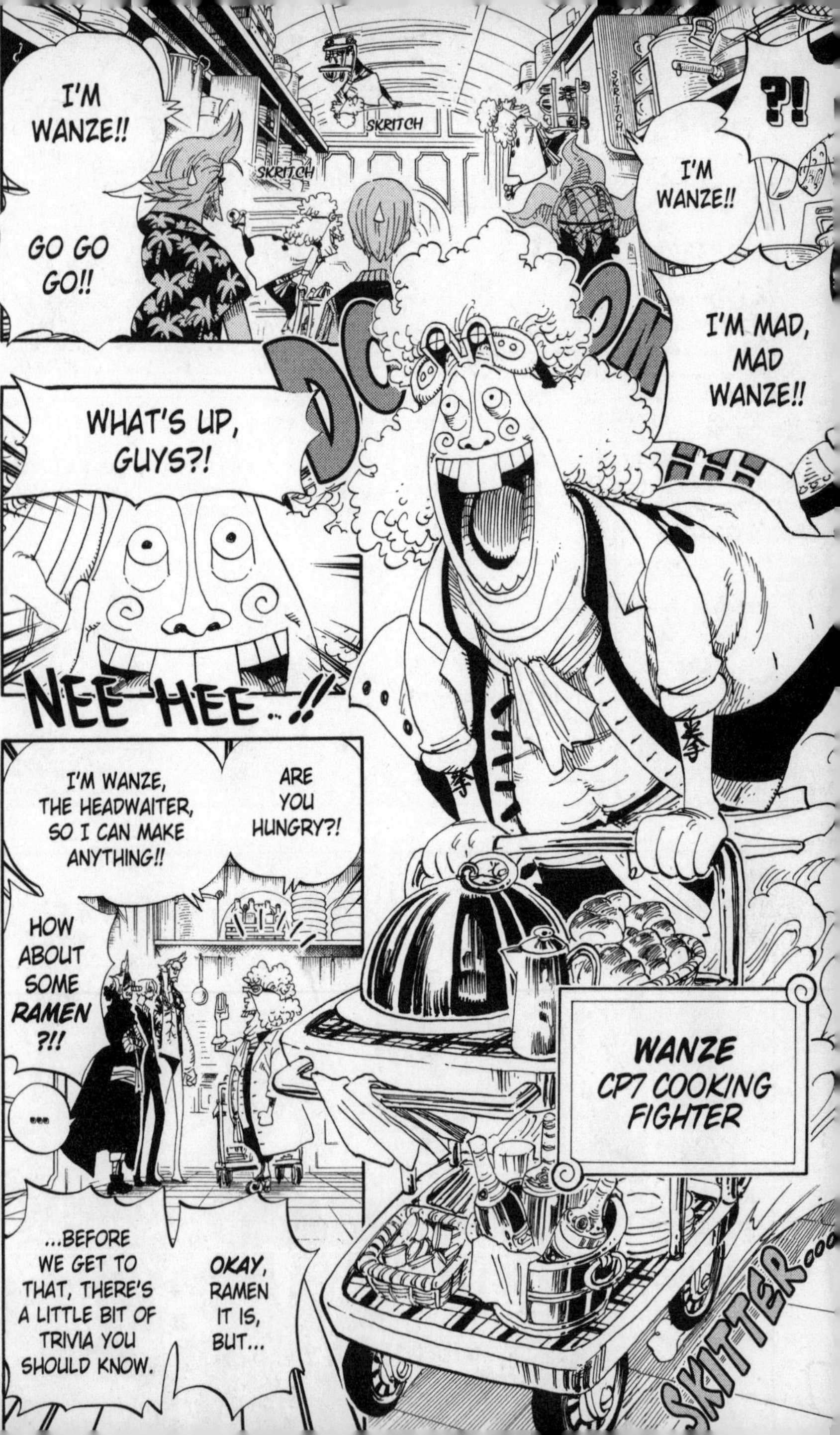
?!
I'M WANZE!!
SKRITCH
SKRITCH
SKRITCH
I'M WANZE!!
GO GO GO!!
DOOM
I'M MAD, MAD WANZE!!
WANZE CP7 COOKING FIGHTER
SKITTER...
WHAT'S UP, GUYS?!
NEE HEE..!!
ARE YOU HUNGRY?!
I'M WANZE, THE HEADWAITER, SO I CAN MAKE ANYTHING!!
HOW ABOUT SOME RAMEN ?!!
...
OKAY, RAMEN IT IS, BUT...
...BEFORE WE GET TO THAT, THERE'S A LITTLE BIT OF TRIVIA YOU SHOULD KNOW.

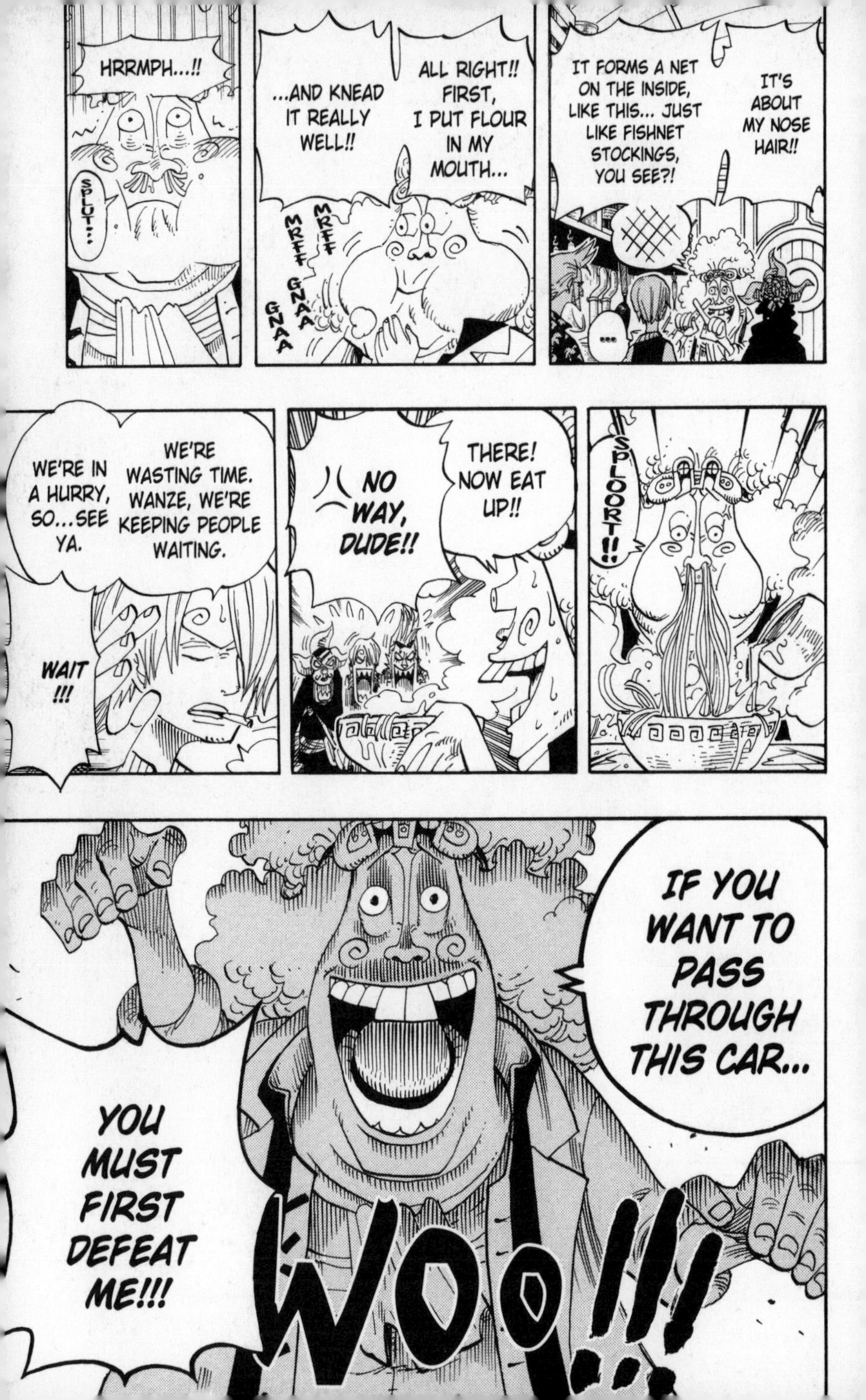
IT'S ABOUT MY NOSE HAIR!!
IT FORMS A NET ON THE INSIDE, LIKE THIS... JUST LIKE FISHNET STOCKINGS, YOU SEE?!
...
ALL RIGHT!! FIRST, I PUT FLOUR IN MY MOUTH...
...AND KNEAD IT REALLY WELL!!
MRFF MRFF
GNAA GNAA
HRRMPH...!!
SPLUT...
SPLOORT!!
THERE! NOW EAT UP!!
NO WAY, DUDE!!
WE'RE WASTING TIME. WANZE, WE'RE KEEPING PEOPLE WAITING.
WE'RE IN A HURRY, SO...SEE YA.
WAIT!!!
IF YOU WANT TO PASS THROUGH THIS CAR...
YOU MUST FIRST DEFEAT ME!!!
WOO!!!

Chapter 369: RAMEN KUNG FU

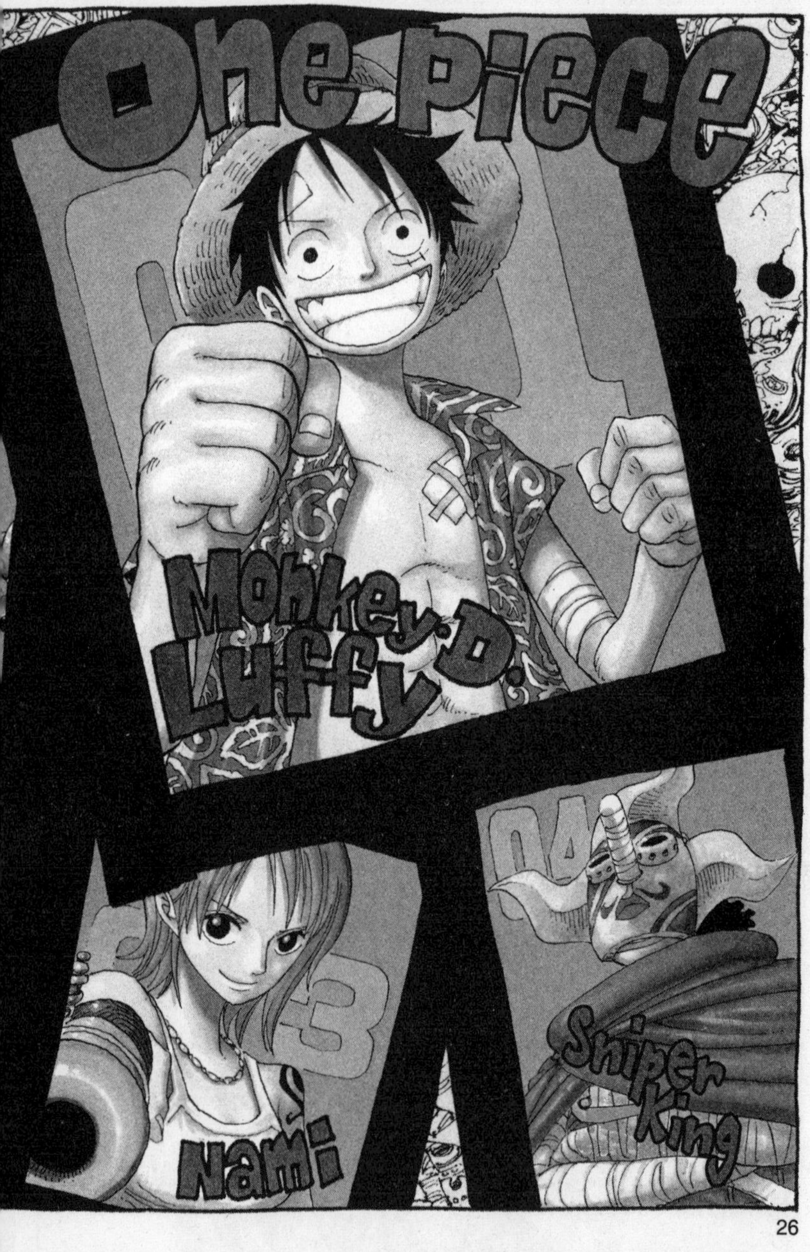
One piece
Monkey.D.Luffy
Nami
Sniper King

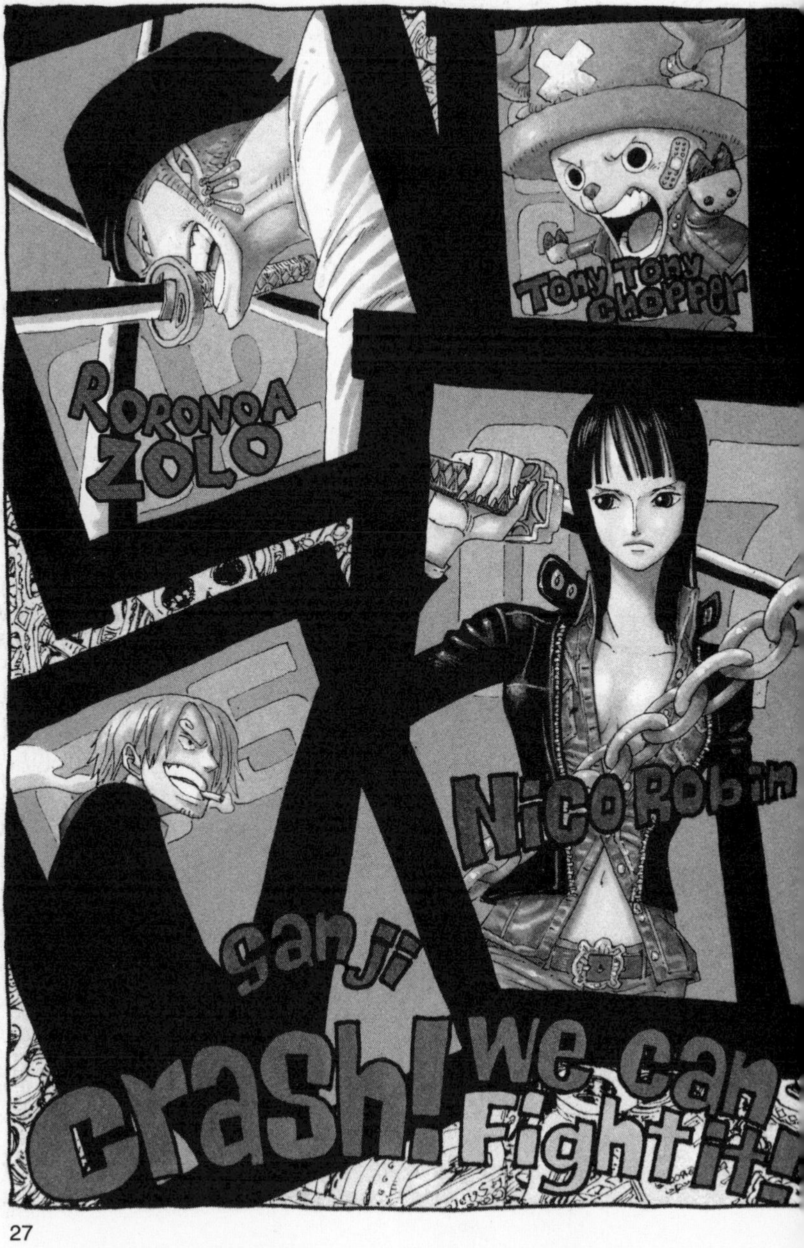
Tony Tony Chopper
RORONOA ZOLO
Nico Robin
Sanji
Crash! We can Fight it!

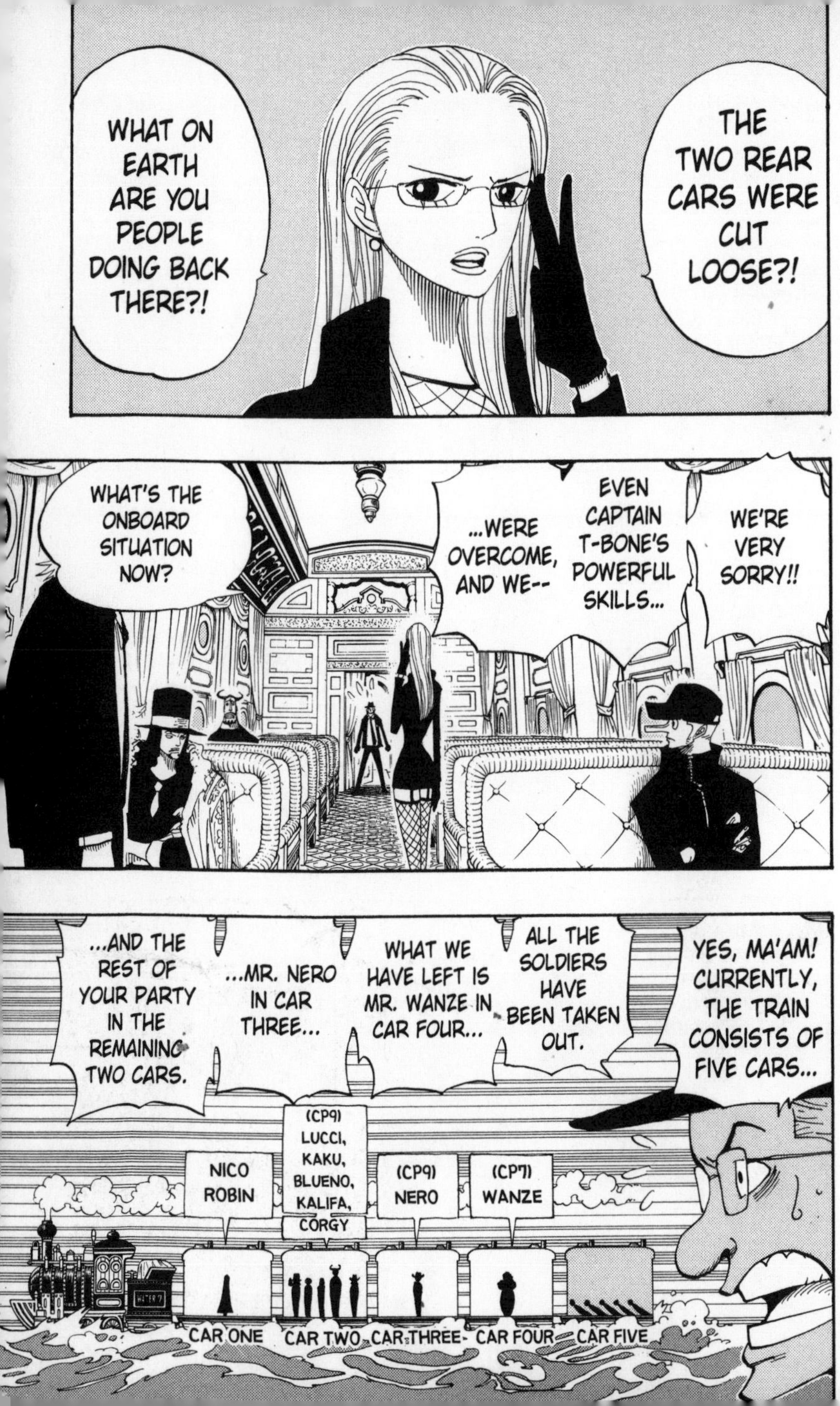
THE TWO REAR CARS WERE CUT LOOSE?!
WHAT ON EARTH ARE YOU PEOPLE DOING BACK THERE?!
WE'RE VERY SORRY!!
EVEN CAPTAIN T-BONE'S POWERFUL SKILLS...
...WERE OVERCOME, AND WE--
WHAT'S THE ONBOARD SITUATION NOW?
YES, MA'AM! CURRENTLY, THE TRAIN CONSISTS OF FIVE CARS...
ALL THE SOLDIERS HAVE BEEN TAKEN OUT.
WHAT WE HAVE LEFT IS MR. WANZE IN CAR FOUR...
...MR. NERO IN CAR THREE...
...AND THE REST OF YOUR PARTY IN THE REMAINING TWO CARS.
(CP7) WANZE
(CP9) NERO
(CP9) LUCCI, KAKU, BLUENO, KALIFA, CORGY
NICO ROBIN
CAR ONE
CAR TWO
CAR THREE
CAR FOUR
CAR FIVE

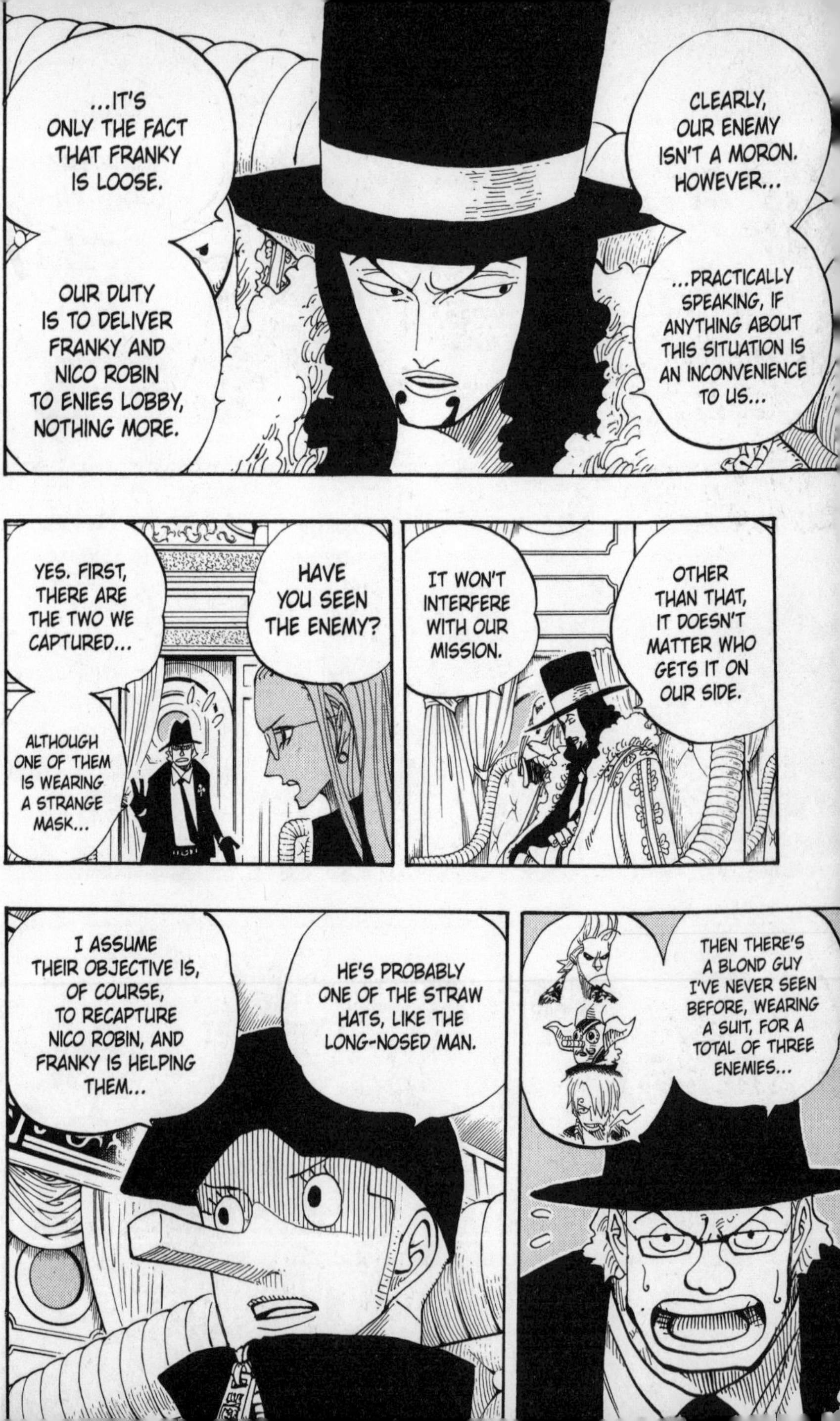
CLEARLY, OUR ENEMY ISN'T A MORON. HOWEVER...
...PRACTICALLY SPEAKING, IF ANYTHING ABOUT THIS SITUATION IS AN INCONVENIENCE TO US...
...IT'S ONLY THE FACT THAT FRANKY IS LOOSE.
OUR DUTY IS TO DELIVER FRANKY AND NICO ROBIN TO ENIES LOBBY, NOTHING MORE.
OTHER THAN THAT, IT DOESN'T MATTER WHO GETS IT ON OUR SIDE.
IT WON'T INTERFERE WITH OUR MISSION.
HAVE YOU SEEN THE ENEMY?
YES. FIRST, THERE ARE THE TWO WE CAPTURED...
ALTHOUGH ONE OF THEM IS WEARING A STRANGE MASK...
THEN THERE'S A BLOND GUY I'VE NEVER SEEN BEFORE, WEARING A SUIT, FOR A TOTAL OF THREE ENEMIES...
HE'S PROBABLY ONE OF THE STRAW HATS, LIKE THE LONG-NOSED MAN.
I ASSUME THEIR OBJECTIVE IS, OF COURSE, TO RECAPTURE NICO ROBIN, AND FRANKY IS HELPING THEM...

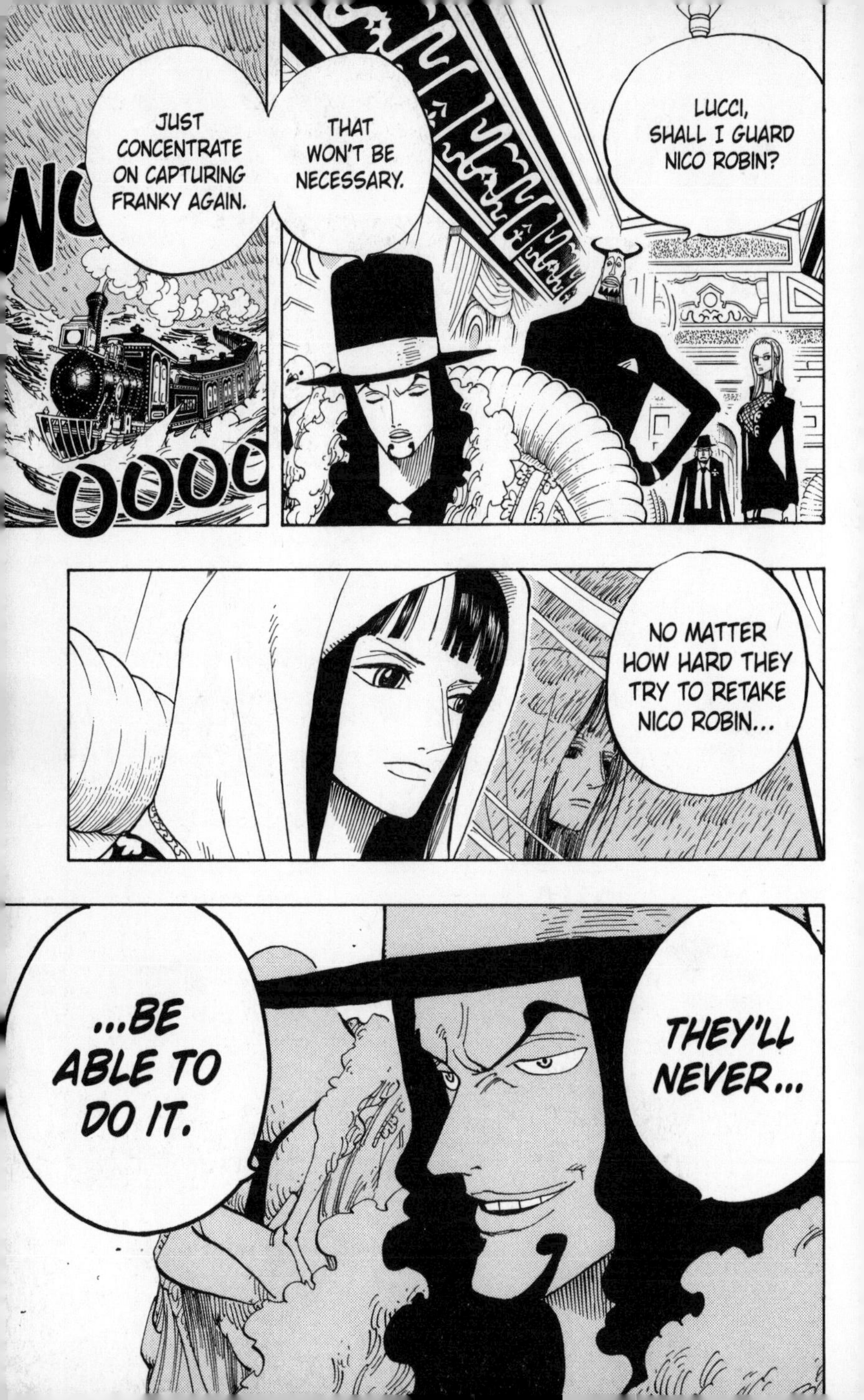
LUCCI, SHALL I GUARD NICO ROBIN?
THAT WON'T BE NECESSARY.
JUST CONCENTRATE ON CAPTURING FRANKY AGAIN.
NOOOO
NO MATTER HOW HARD THEY TRY TO RETAKE NICO ROBIN...
THEY'LL NEVER...
...BE ABLE TO DO IT.

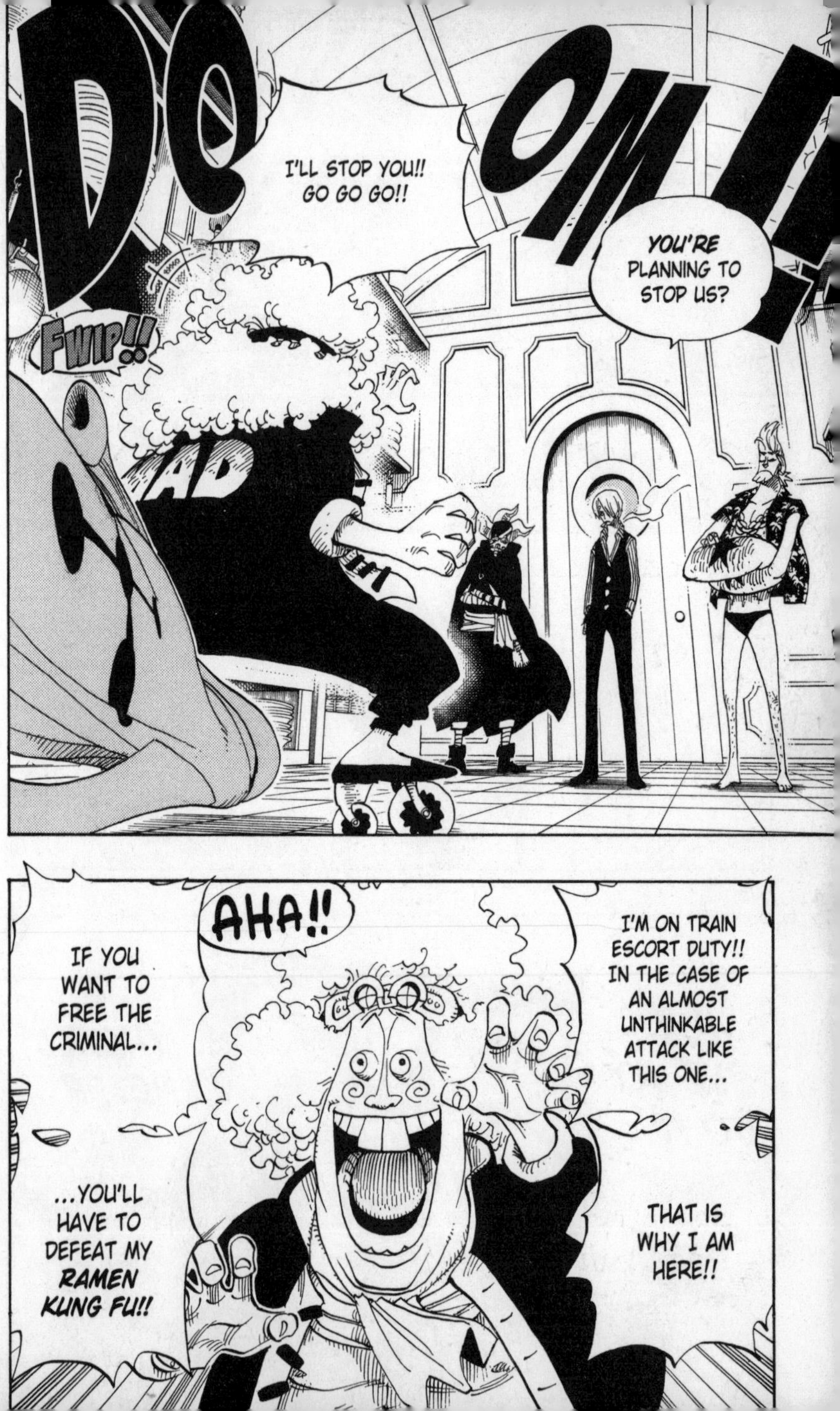

YOU'RE PLANNING TO STOP US?
I'LL STOP YOU!! GO GO GO!!
FWIP!!
AHA!!
I'M ON TRAIN ESCORT DUTY!! IN THE CASE OF AN ALMOST UNTHINKABLE ATTACK LIKE THIS ONE...
THAT IS WHY I AM HERE!!
IF YOU WANT TO FREE THE CRIMINAL...
...YOU'LL HAVE TO DEFEAT MY *RAMEN KUNG FU!!*

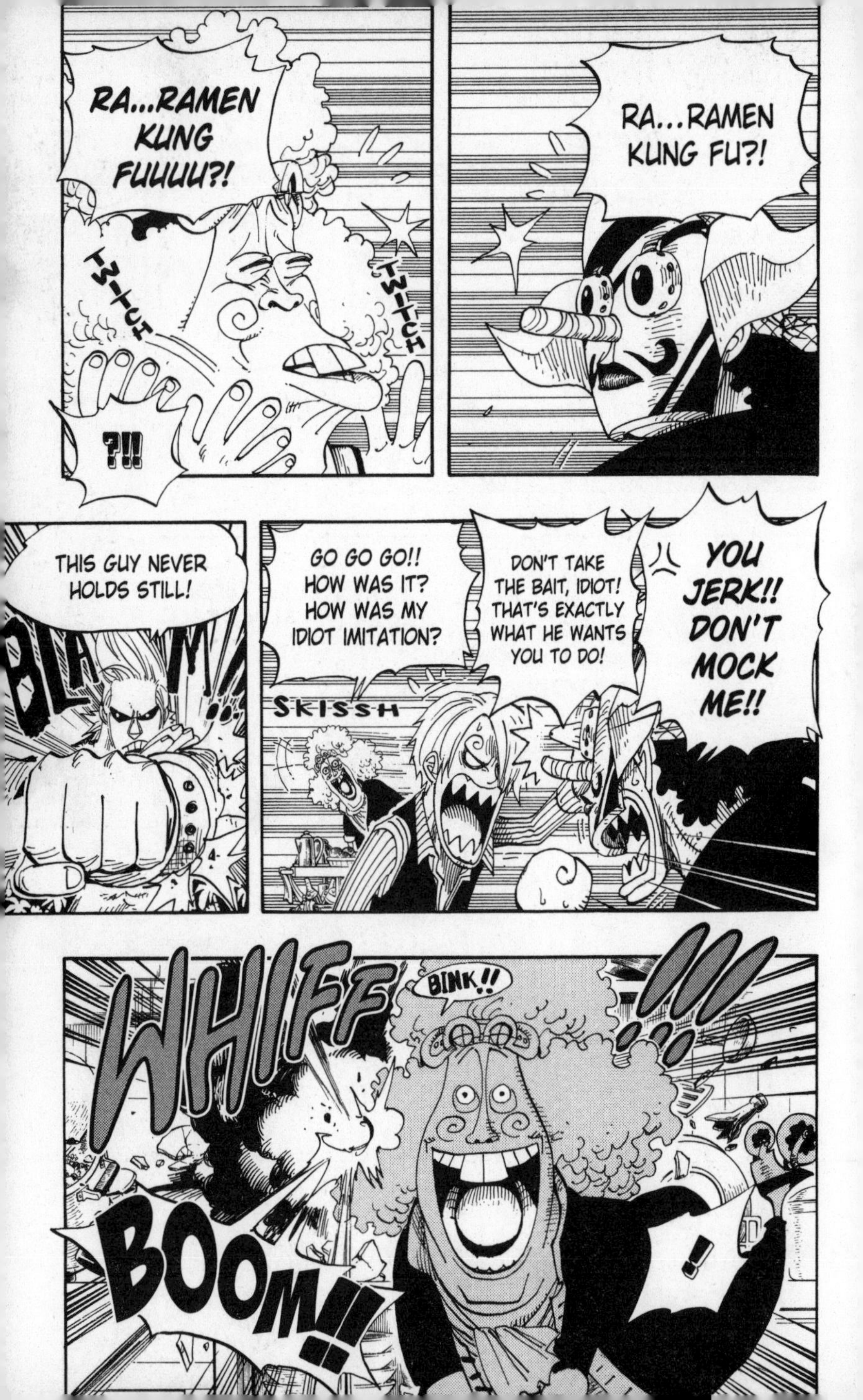
RA...RAMEN KUNG FU?!
RA...RAMEN KUNG FUUUU?!
TWITCH
TWITCH
?!!
YOU JERK!! DON'T MOCK ME!!
DON'T TAKE THE BAIT, IDIOT! THAT'S EXACTLY WHAT HE WANTS YOU TO DO!
GO GO GO!! HOW WAS IT? HOW WAS MY IDIOT IMITATION?
SKISSH
THIS GUY NEVER HOLDS STILL!
BINK!!
!!!
WHIFF
BOOM!!
!

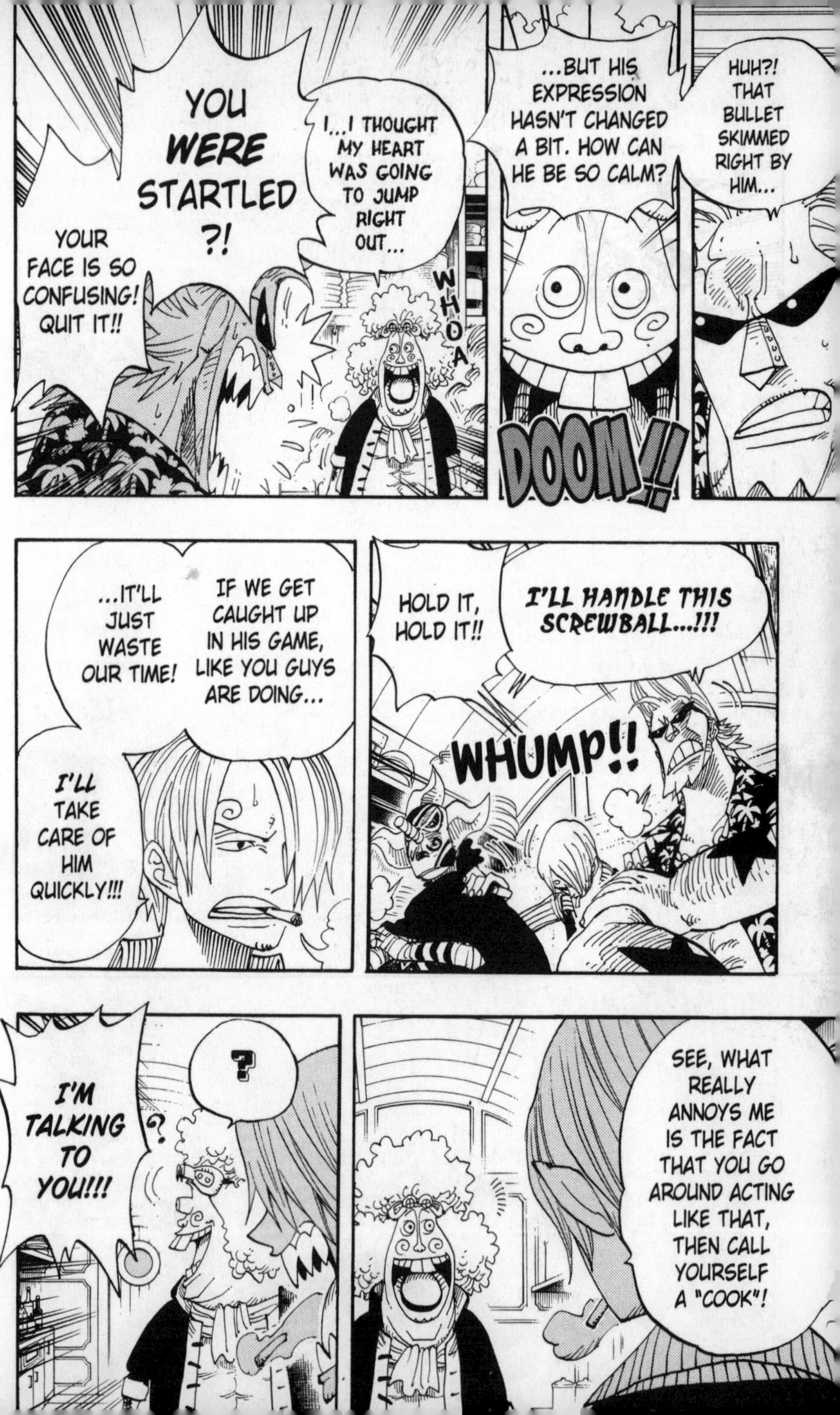
HUH?! THAT BULLET SKIMMED RIGHT BY HIM...
...BUT HIS EXPRESSION HASN'T CHANGED A BIT. HOW CAN HE BE SO CALM?
DOOM!!
I...I THOUGHT MY HEART WAS GOING TO JUMP RIGHT OUT...
WHOA
YOU WERE STARTLED?!
YOUR FACE IS SO CONFUSING! QUIT IT!!
I'LL HANDLE THIS SCREWBALL...!!!
HOLD IT, HOLD IT!!
WHUMP!!
IF WE GET CAUGHT UP IN HIS GAME, LIKE YOU GUYS ARE DOING...
...IT'LL JUST WASTE OUR TIME!
I'LL TAKE CARE OF HIM QUICKLY!!!
SEE, WHAT REALLY ANNOYS ME IS THE FACT THAT YOU GO AROUND ACTING LIKE THAT, THEN CALL YOURSELF A "COOK"!
?
?
I'M TALKING TO YOU!!!

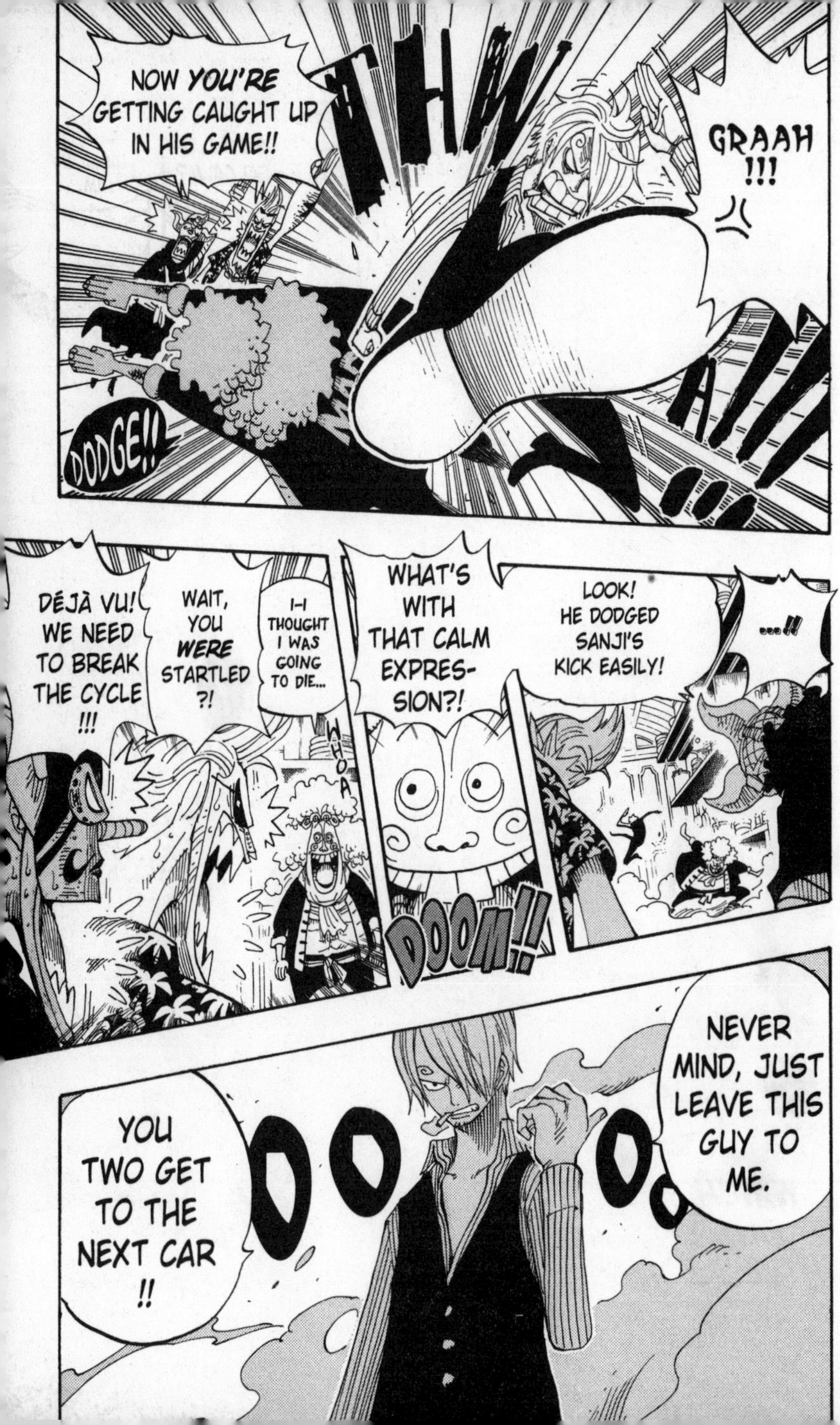
GRAAH!!!
THW
NOW YOU'RE GETTING CAUGHT UP IN HIS GAME!!
AM!!
DODGE!!
...!!
LOOK! HE DODGED SANJI'S KICK EASILY!
WHAT'S WITH THAT CALM EXPRESSION?!
DOOM!!
I-I THOUGHT I WAS GOING TO DIE...
WHOA
WAIT, YOU WERE STARTLED?!
DÉJÀ VU! WE NEED TO BREAK THE CYCLE!!!
NEVER MIND, JUST LEAVE THIS GUY TO ME.
YOU TWO GET TO THE NEXT CAR!!

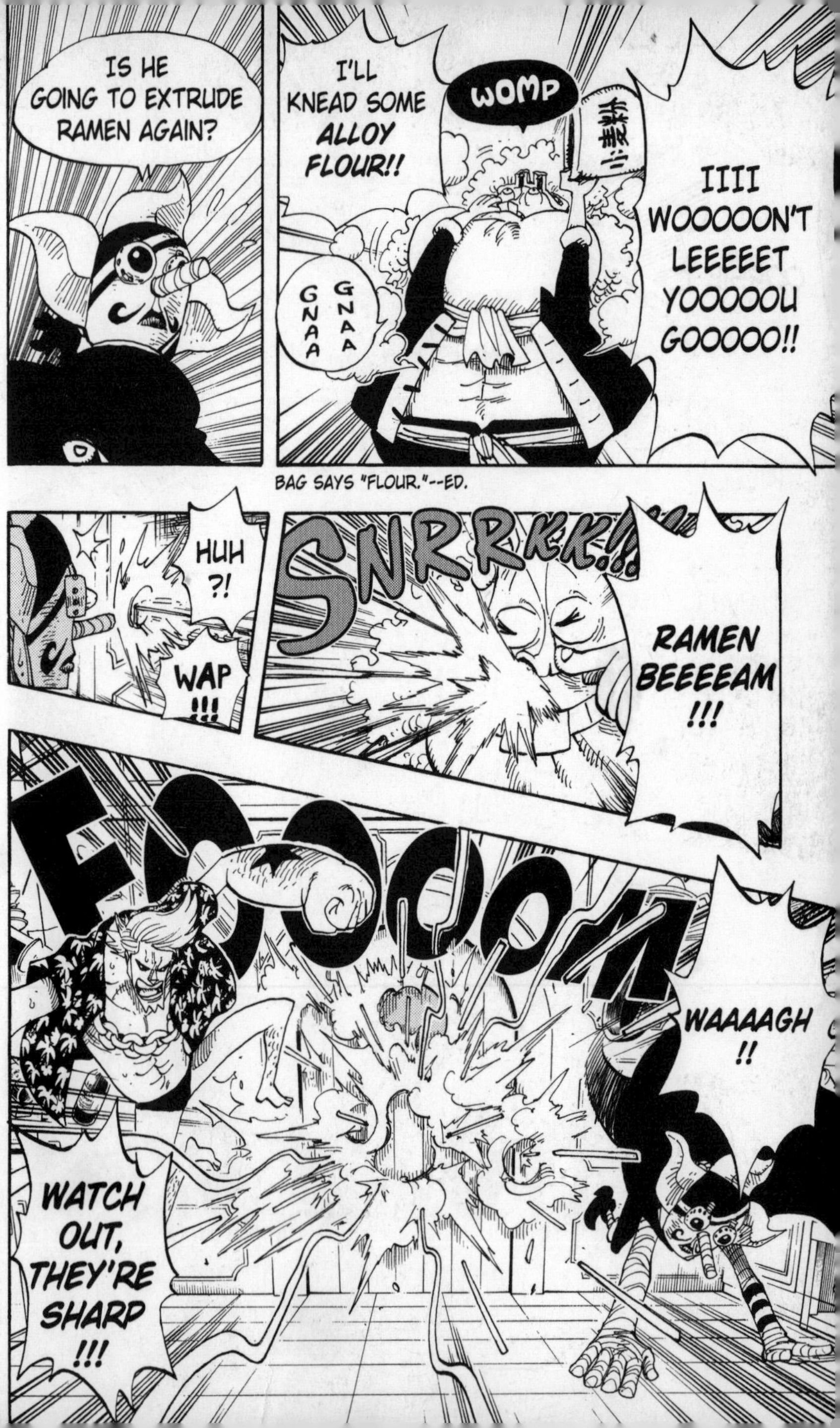
I'LL KNEAD SOME ALLOY FLOUR!!
WOMP
GNAA GNAA
IIII WOOOOON'T LEEEEET YOOOOOU GOOOOO!!
IS HE GOING TO EXTRUDE RAMEN AGAIN?
SNRRKK!!
RAMEN BEEEEAM!!!
HUH?!
WAP!!!
FOOOOM
WAAAAGH!!
WATCH OUT, THEY'RE SHARP!!!
BAG SAYS "FLOUR."--ED.

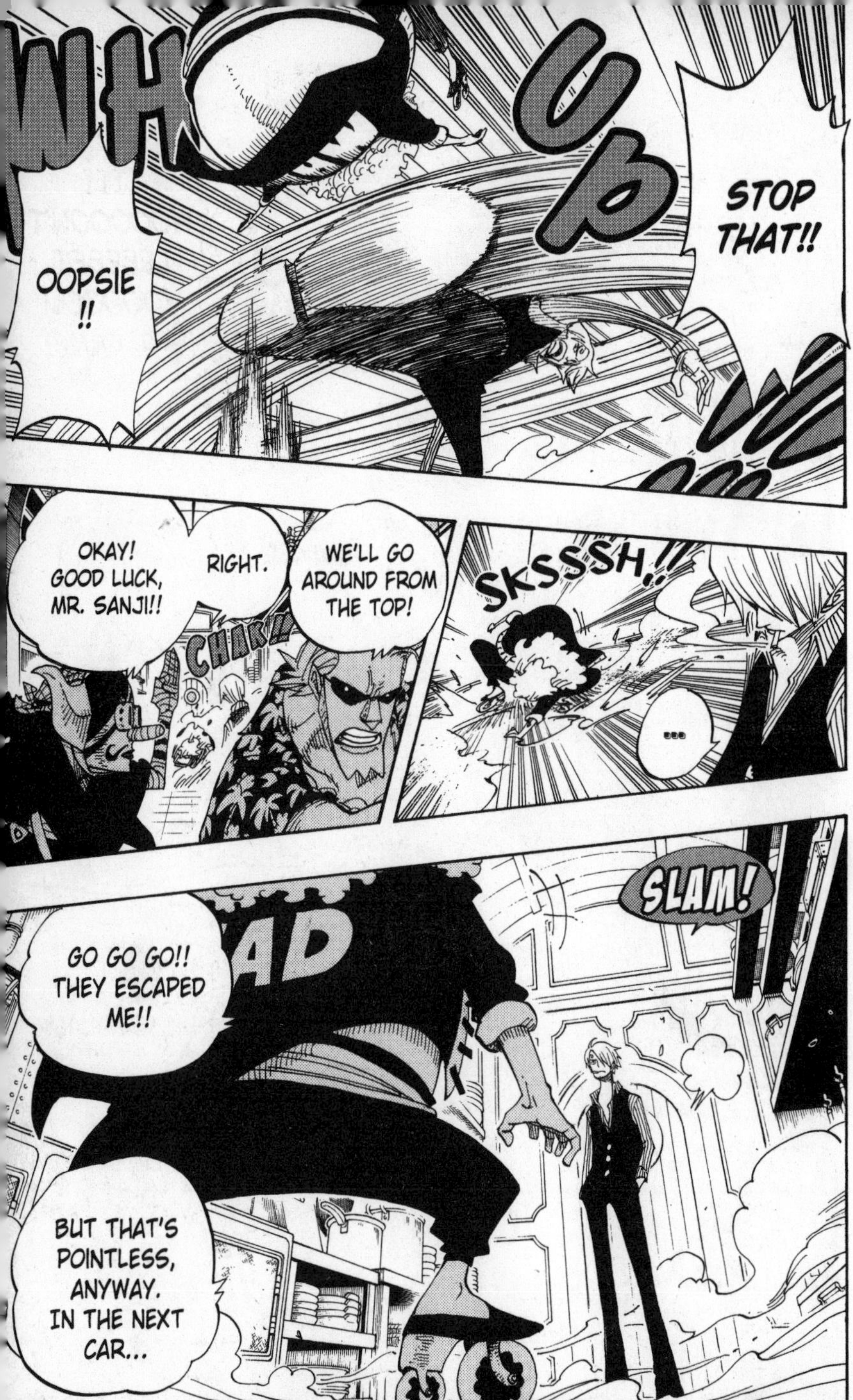
STOP THAT!!
WHUP
OOPSIE!!
SKSSSH!!
...
WE'LL GO AROUND FROM THE TOP!
RIGHT.
OKAY! GOOD LUCK, MR. SANJI!!
CHAK!!
SLAM!
GO GO GO!! THEY ESCAPED ME!!
BUT THAT'S POINTLESS, ANYWAY. IN THE NEXT CAR...

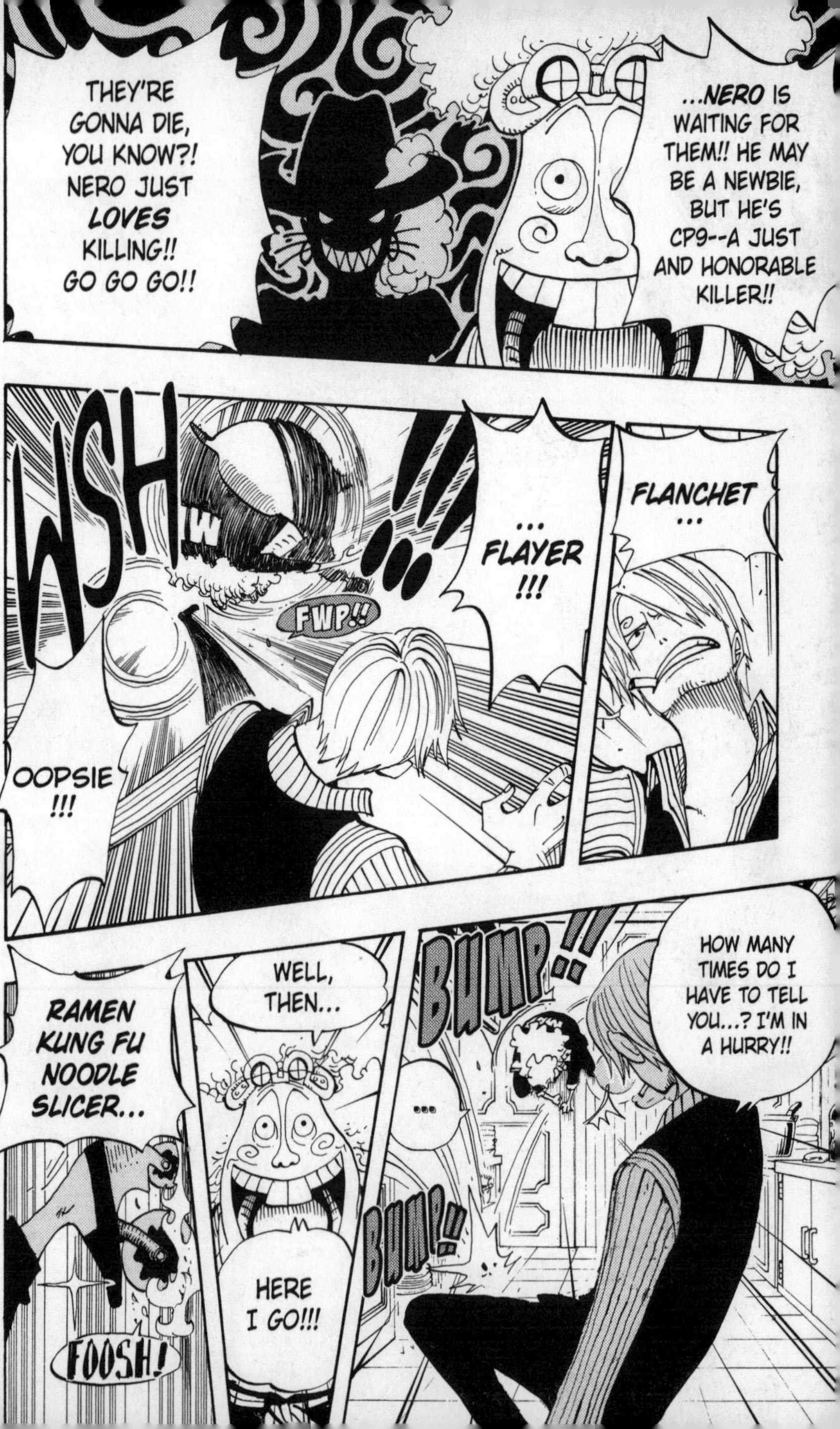
...NERO IS WAITING FOR THEM!! HE MAY BE A NEWBIE, BUT HE'S CP9--A JUST AND HONORABLE KILLER!!
THEY'RE GONNA DIE, YOU KNOW?! NERO JUST LOVES KILLING!! GO GO GO!!
FLANCHET ...
... FLAYER !!!
WSHW
FWP!!
OOPSIE !!!
HOW MANY TIMES DO I HAVE TO TELL YOU...? I'M IN A HURRY!!
BUMP!!
...
BUMP!!
WELL, THEN...
HERE I GO!!!
RAMEN KUNG FU NOODLE SLICER...
FOOSH!

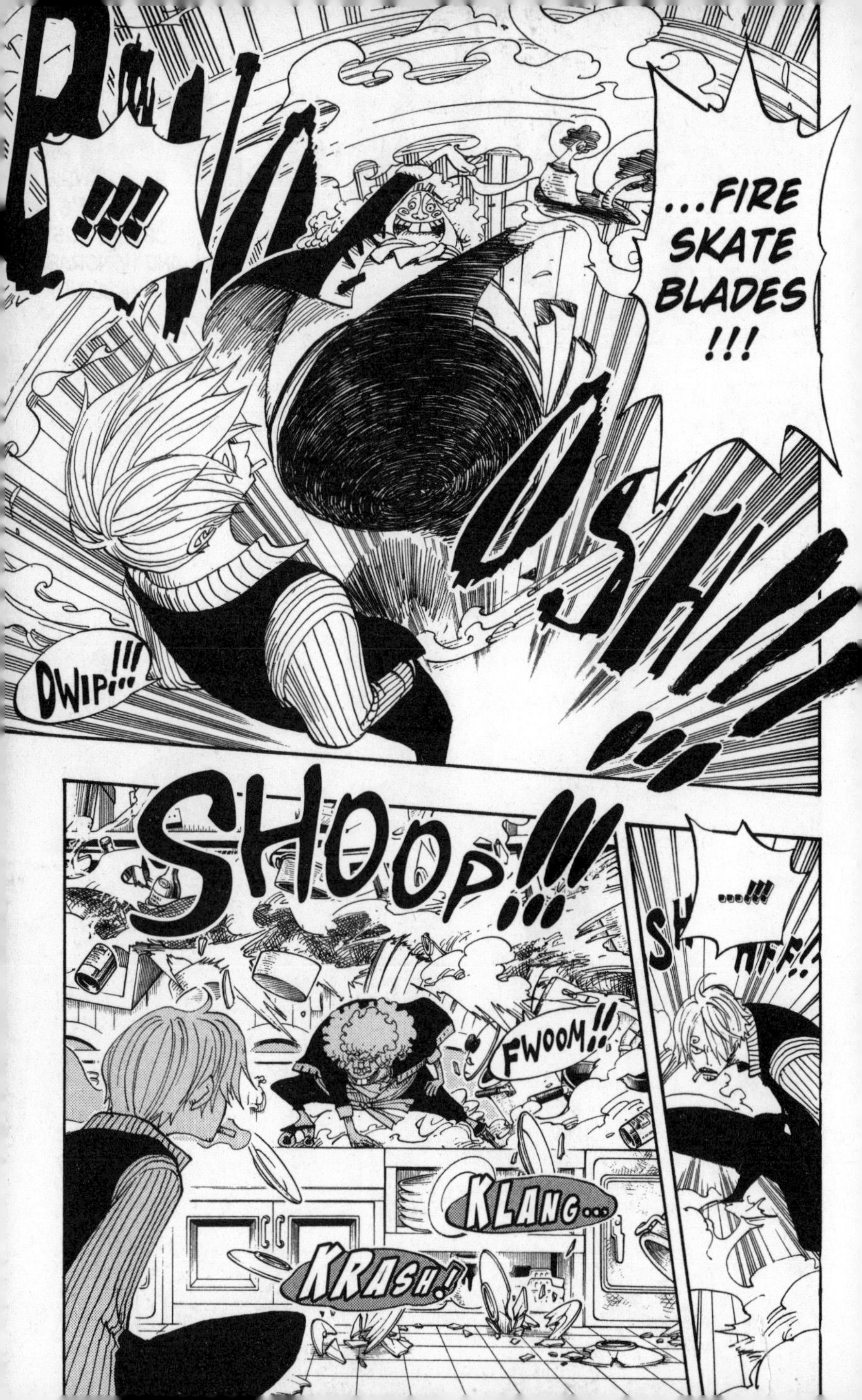
...FIRE SKATE BLADES!!!
DWIP!!!
...!!!
SHOOOP!!!
FWOOM!!
KLANG...
KRASH!

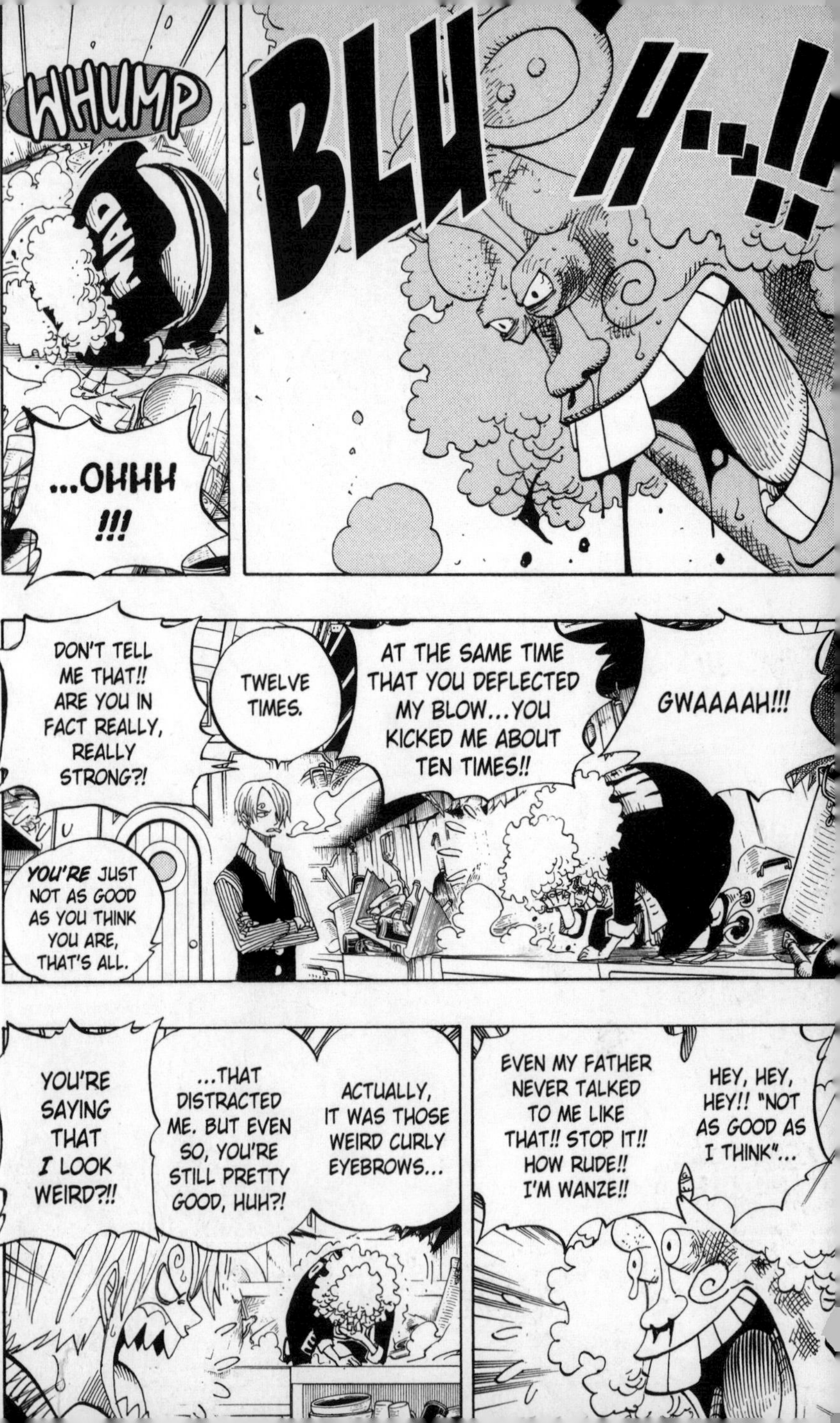
BLUH..!!!
WHUMP
MAD
...OHHH !!!
GWAAAAH!!!
AT THE SAME TIME THAT YOU DEFLECTED MY BLOW...YOU KICKED ME ABOUT TEN TIMES!!
TWELVE TIMES.
DON'T TELL ME THAT!! ARE YOU IN FACT REALLY, REALLY STRONG?!
YOU'RE JUST NOT AS GOOD AS YOU THINK YOU ARE, THAT'S ALL.
HEY, HEY, HEY!! "NOT AS GOOD AS I THINK"...
EVEN MY FATHER NEVER TALKED TO ME LIKE THAT!! STOP IT!! HOW RUDE!! I'M WANZE!!
ACTUALLY, IT WAS THOSE WEIRD CURLY EYEBROWS...
...THAT DISTRACTED ME. BUT EVEN SO, YOU'RE STILL PRETTY GOOD, HUH?!
YOU'RE SAYING THAT *I* LOOK WEIRD?!!

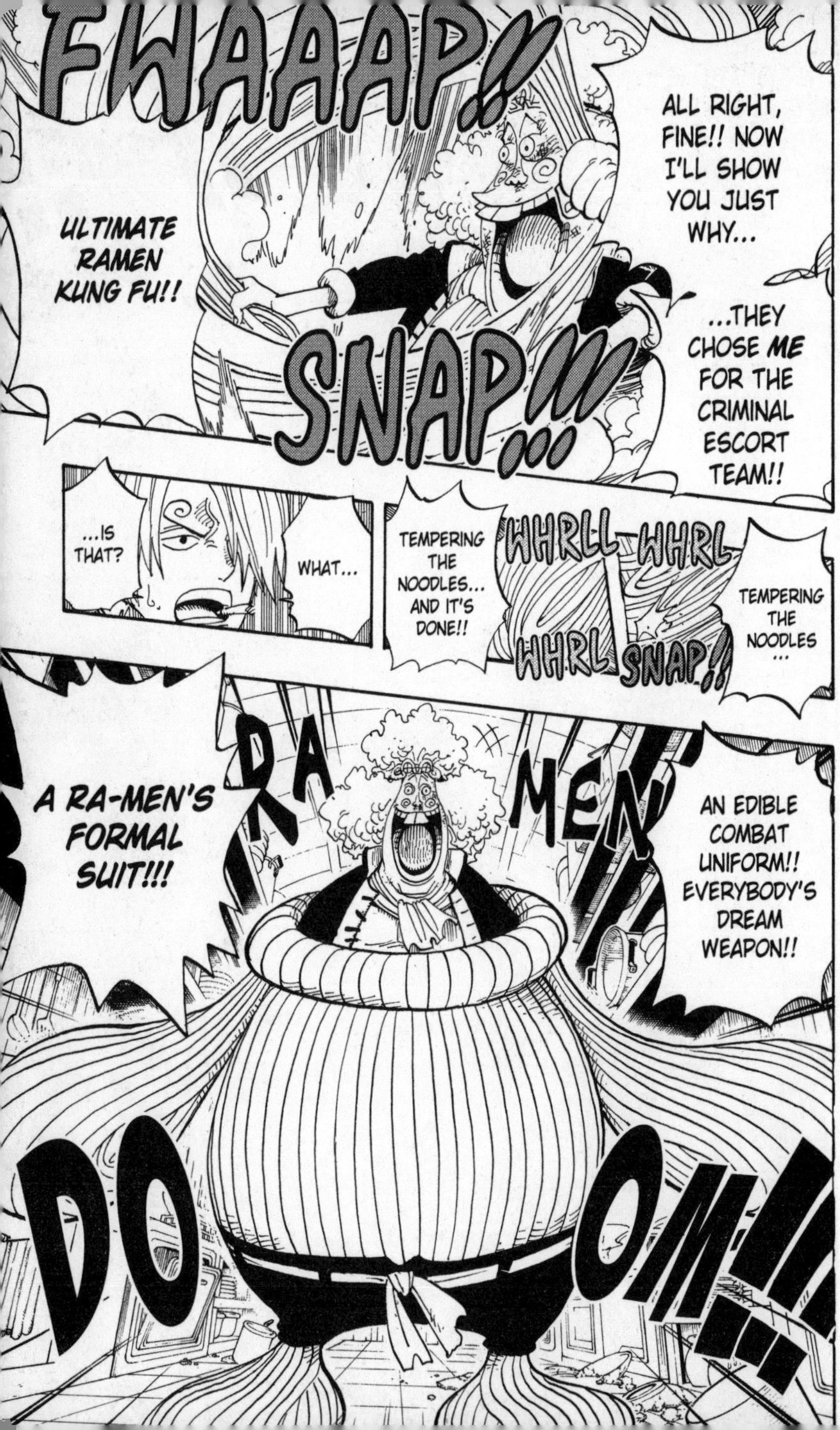
ALL RIGHT, FINE!! NOW I'LL SHOW YOU JUST WHY...
FWAAAP!!
...THEY CHOSE ME FOR THE CRIMINAL ESCORT TEAM!!
ULTIMATE RAMEN KUNG FU!!
SNAP!!!
TEMPERING THE NOODLES ...
WHRLL WHRL
WHRL SNAP!!
TEMPERING THE NOODLES... AND IT'S DONE!!
WHAT...
...IS THAT?
AN EDIBLE COMBAT UNIFORM!! EVERYBODY'S DREAM WEAPON!!
RA
MEN
A RA-MEN'S FORMAL SUIT!!!
DO
OM!!!

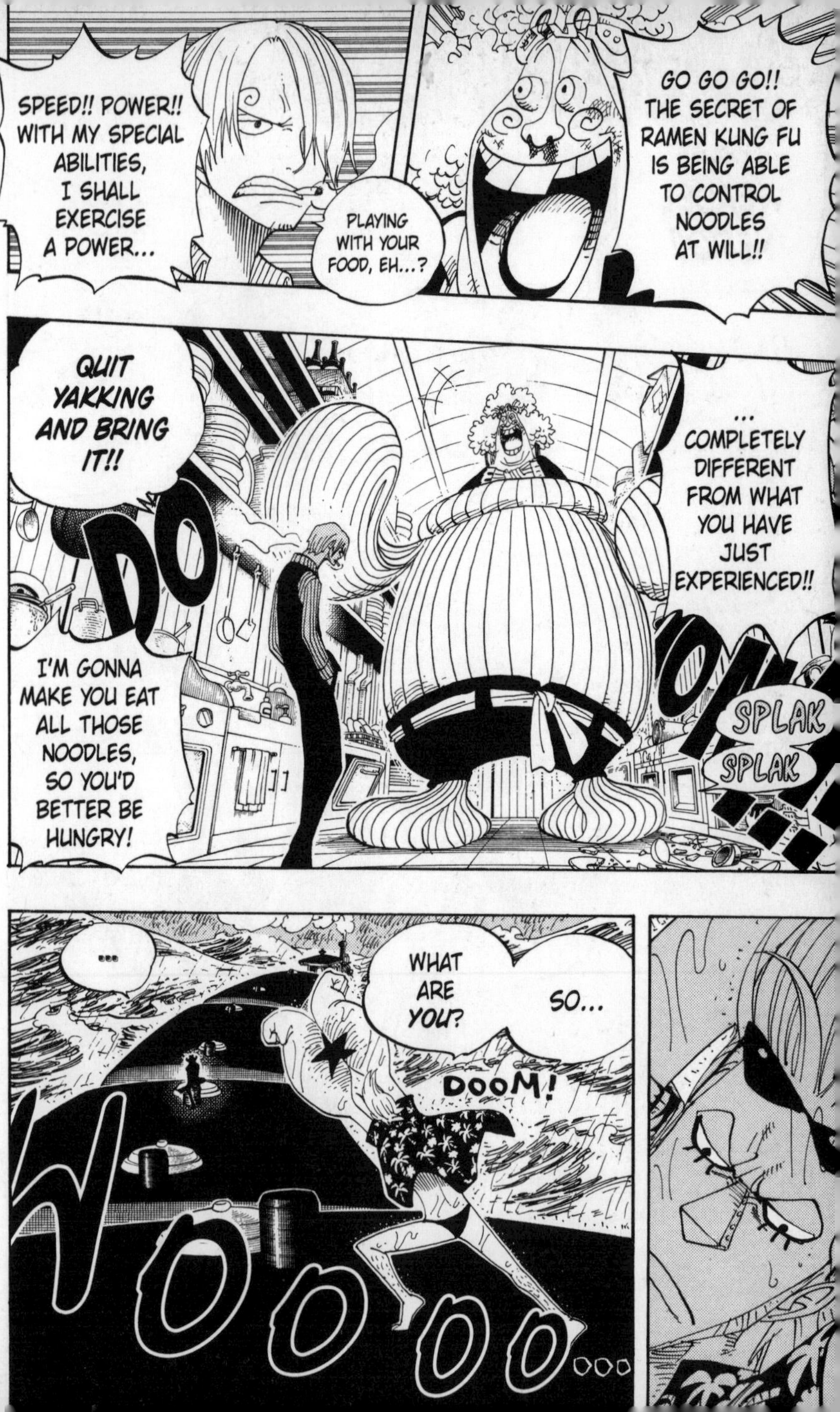
GO GO GO!! THE SECRET OF RAMEN KUNG FU IS BEING ABLE TO CONTROL NOODLES AT WILL!!
SPEED!! POWER!! WITH MY SPECIAL ABILITIES, I SHALL EXERCISE A POWER...
PLAYING WITH YOUR FOOD, EH...?
... COMPLETELY DIFFERENT FROM WHAT YOU HAVE JUST EXPERIENCED!!
SPLAK
SPLAK
QUIT YAKKING AND BRING IT!!
I'M GONNA MAKE YOU EAT ALL THOSE NOODLES, SO YOU'D BETTER BE HUNGRY!
SO...
WHAT ARE YOU?
...
DOOM!
WOOOOO...

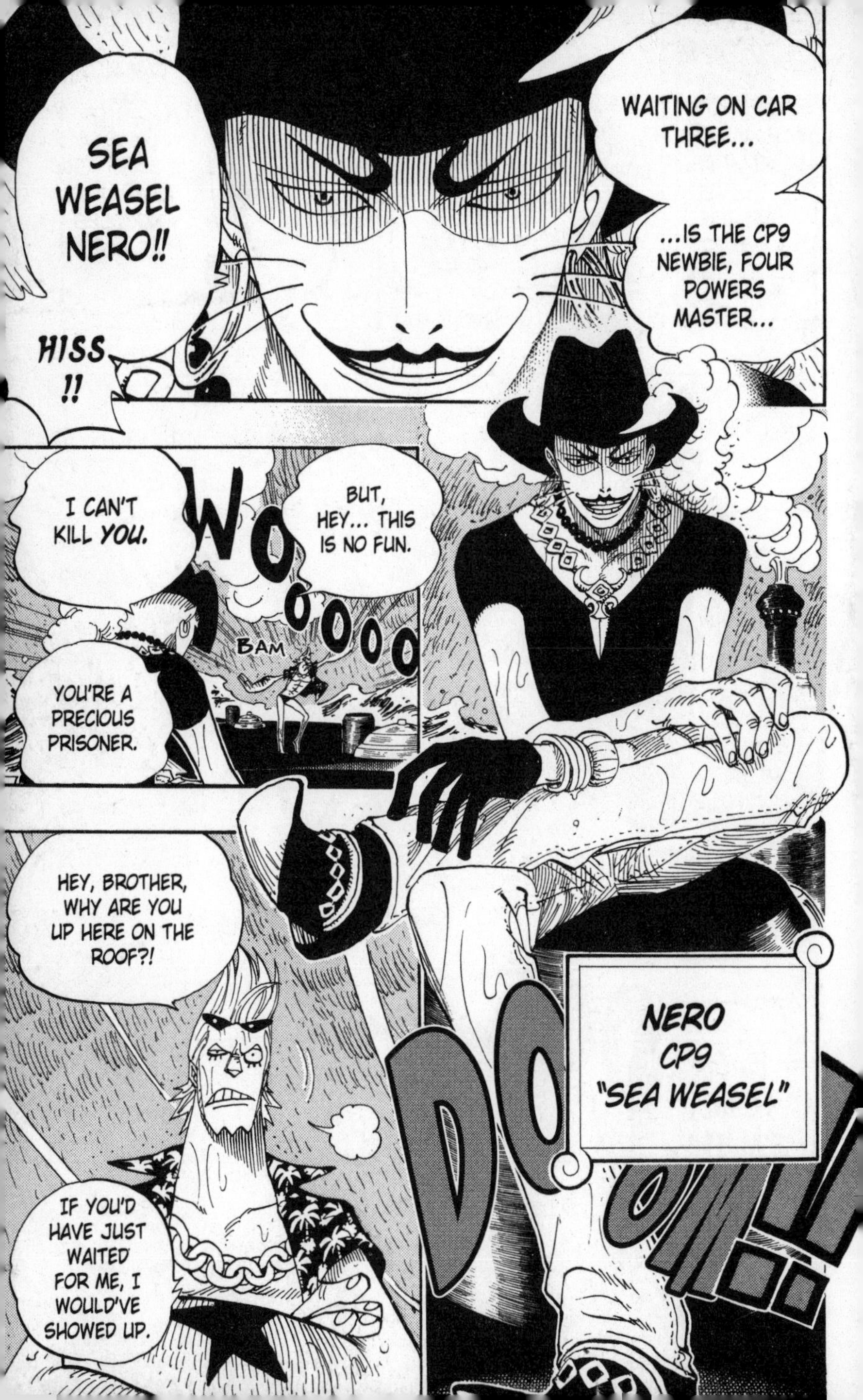
WAITING ON CAR THREE...
...IS THE CP9 NEWBIE, FOUR POWERS MASTER...
SEA WEASEL NERO!!
HISS !!
NERO CP9 "SEA WEASEL"
DOOM!!
BUT, HEY... THIS IS NO FUN.
I CAN'T KILL *YOU.*
WOOOOO
BAM
YOU'RE A PRECIOUS PRISONER.
HEY, BROTHER, WHY ARE YOU UP HERE ON THE ROOF?!
IF YOU'D HAVE JUST WAITED FOR ME, I WOULD'VE SHOWED UP.

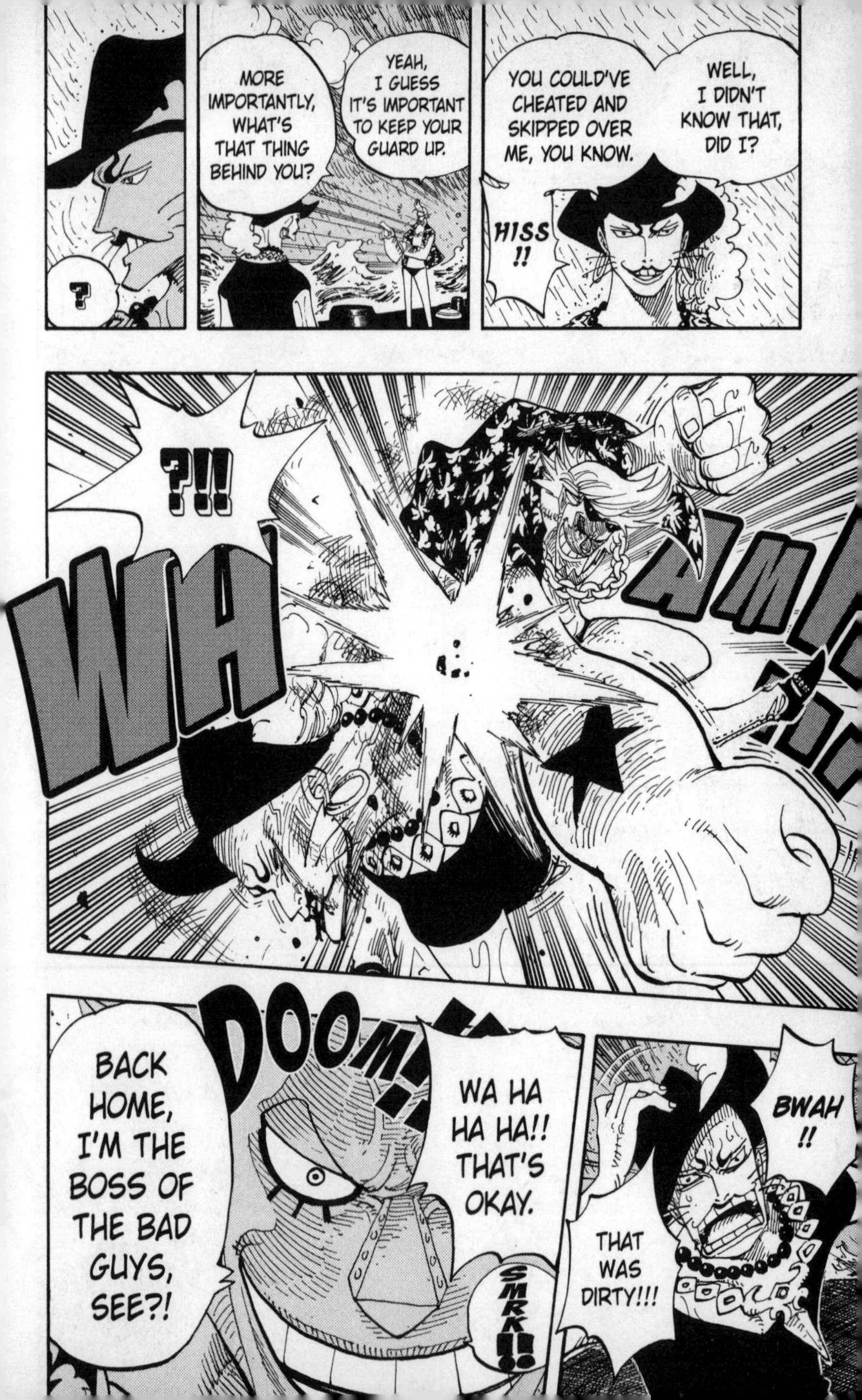
WELL, I DIDN'T KNOW THAT, DID I?
YOU COULD'VE CHEATED AND SKIPPED OVER ME, YOU KNOW.
HISS !!
YEAH, I GUESS IT'S IMPORTANT TO KEEP YOUR GUARD UP.
MORE IMPORTANTLY, WHAT'S THAT THING BEHIND YOU?
?
?!!
WHAM!!
BWAH !!
THAT WAS DIRTY!!!
DOOM!!
WA HA HA HA!! THAT'S OKAY.
BACK HOME, I'M THE BOSS OF THE BAD GUYS, SEE?!
SMRK!!

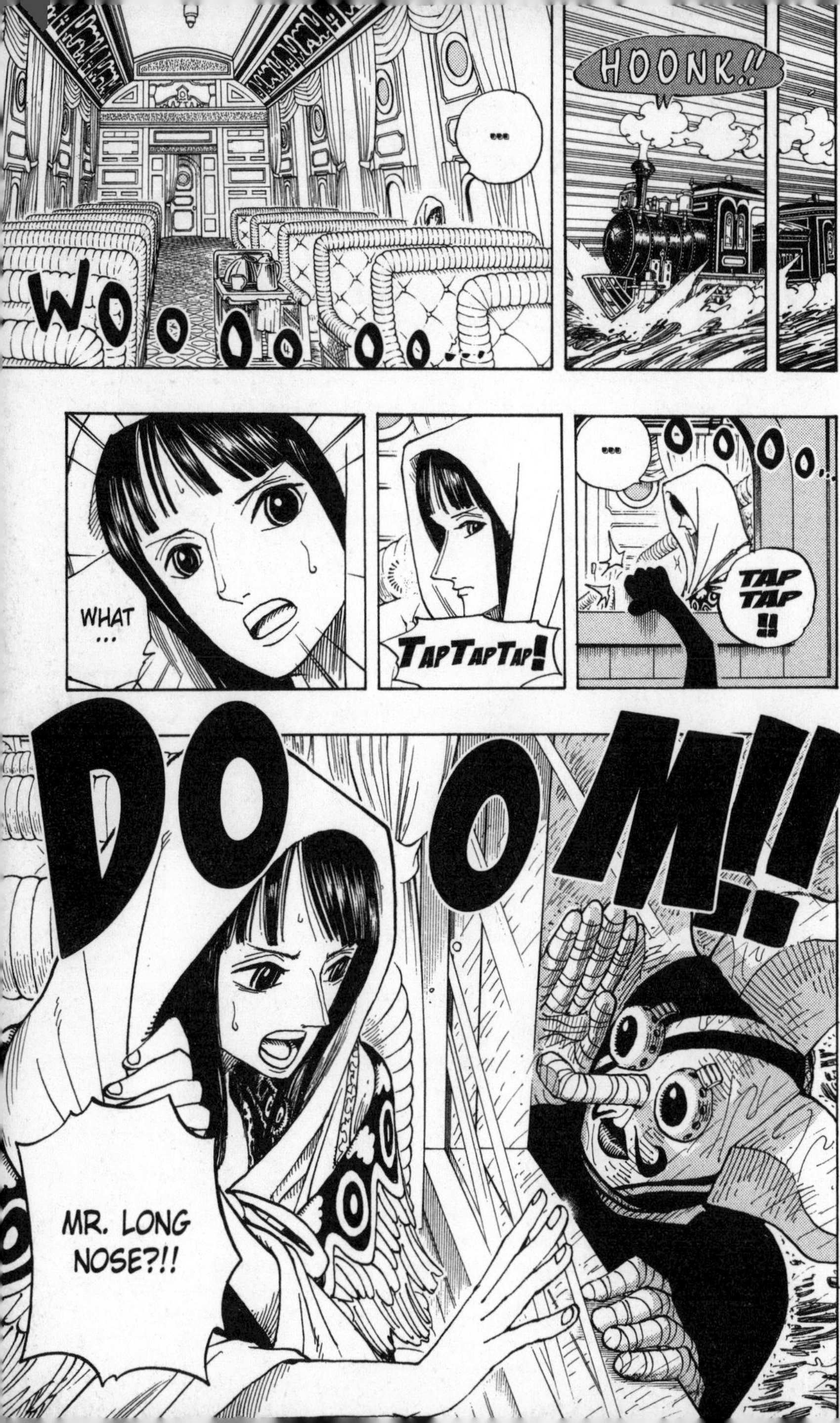
HOONK!!
...
WOOOOOO..
...
OOOO..
TAP TAP !!
TAPTAPTAP!
WHAT ...
DOOM!!
MR. LONG NOSE?!!

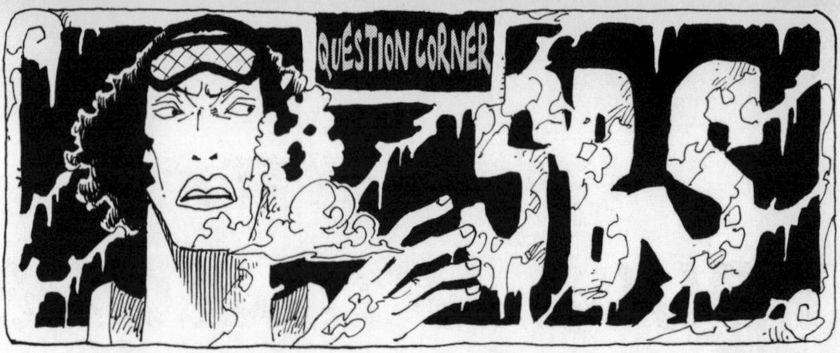
QUESTION CORNER

Reader: Good day, Sir Eiichiro Oda. Please forgive my calling on you in a bathing suit… Huh?! Mr. Oda! What are you wearing?! Uh, what are you doing?! Eeeeek!! Noooooo!! Tmp tmp tmp! (running far away) The Question Corner is starting!!

--Roronoa Robin

Oda: Hi, thanks. Hello everybody. This is the author, who placed a swan-shaped training potty on his head, dressed as a ballerina, and had just salvaged some pasta alla carbonara when he carelessly allowed a reader in Parisian garb to begin the corner. Well then, let's go!!

Q: What would happen if you got goosed with the Finger Pistol?

--Pacchon the Third

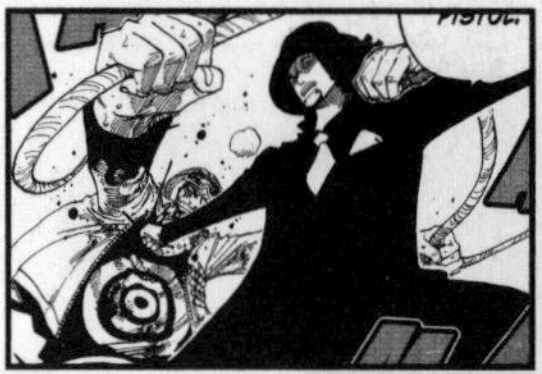
PISTOL.

A: You'd die.

Q: Does Nami wear a strapless bra? Or does she just not wear one at all?

--Tasshii

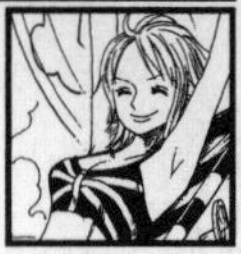

A: I'm rooting for "no bra at all," personally.

Q: Hello, Oda Sensei!! Um, so, where does Paulie pull that rope of his from? And how do you decide the names of his tricks, like Rope Action "Half Knot"? D-Don't tell me…that you just randomly pick something! Please let me know!

--Pig-chan

A: Paulie's rope comes snaking out from under his sleeve. There's apparently a lot of rope rigged up inside the lining of that coat of his! And I don't just make up the names of his tricks, really! Sailing ships have an absolute ton of rope on 'em, and being in charge of them is an important job--lives can hinge on what kind of knot is used! So the names of his tricks are taken from among the many knotting methods. (There are more than 200 knots!) But if there isn't a knotting method that works with the situation…then I just make up the name!

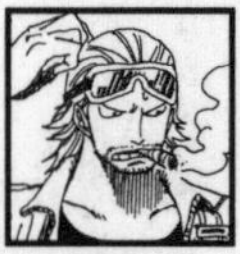

Chapter 370:

YOU'RE NOT ALONE

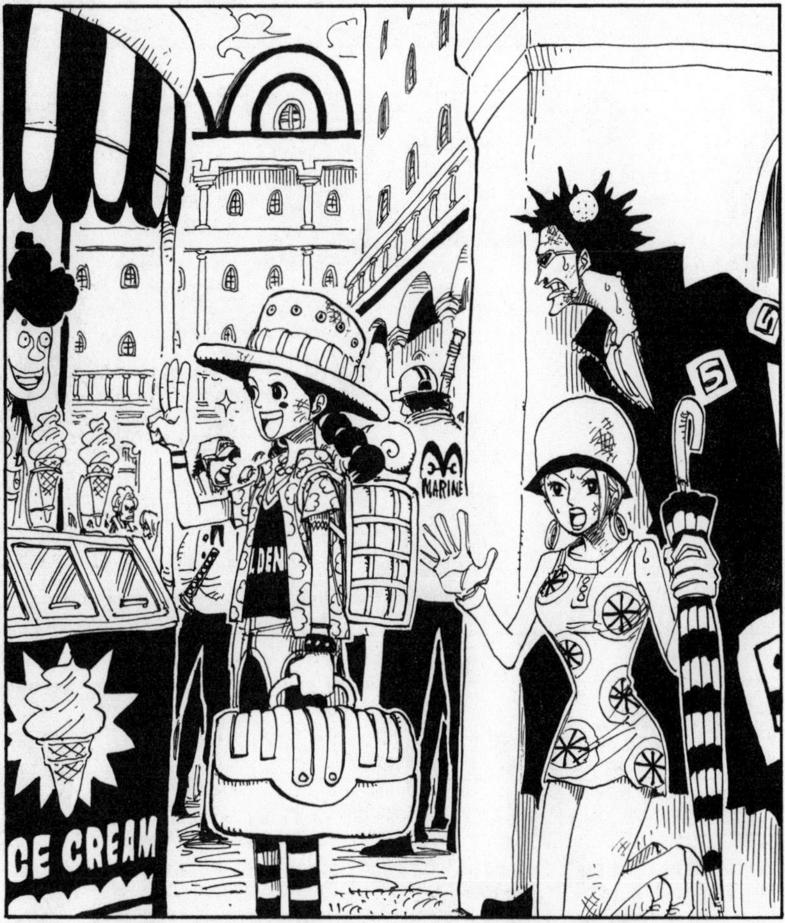

MARINE
LDEN
CE CREAM

MS. GOLDEN WEEK'S BIG PLAN, A BAROQUE REUNION, VOL. 9:
"THE NAVY WAS ON VACATION ISLAND"

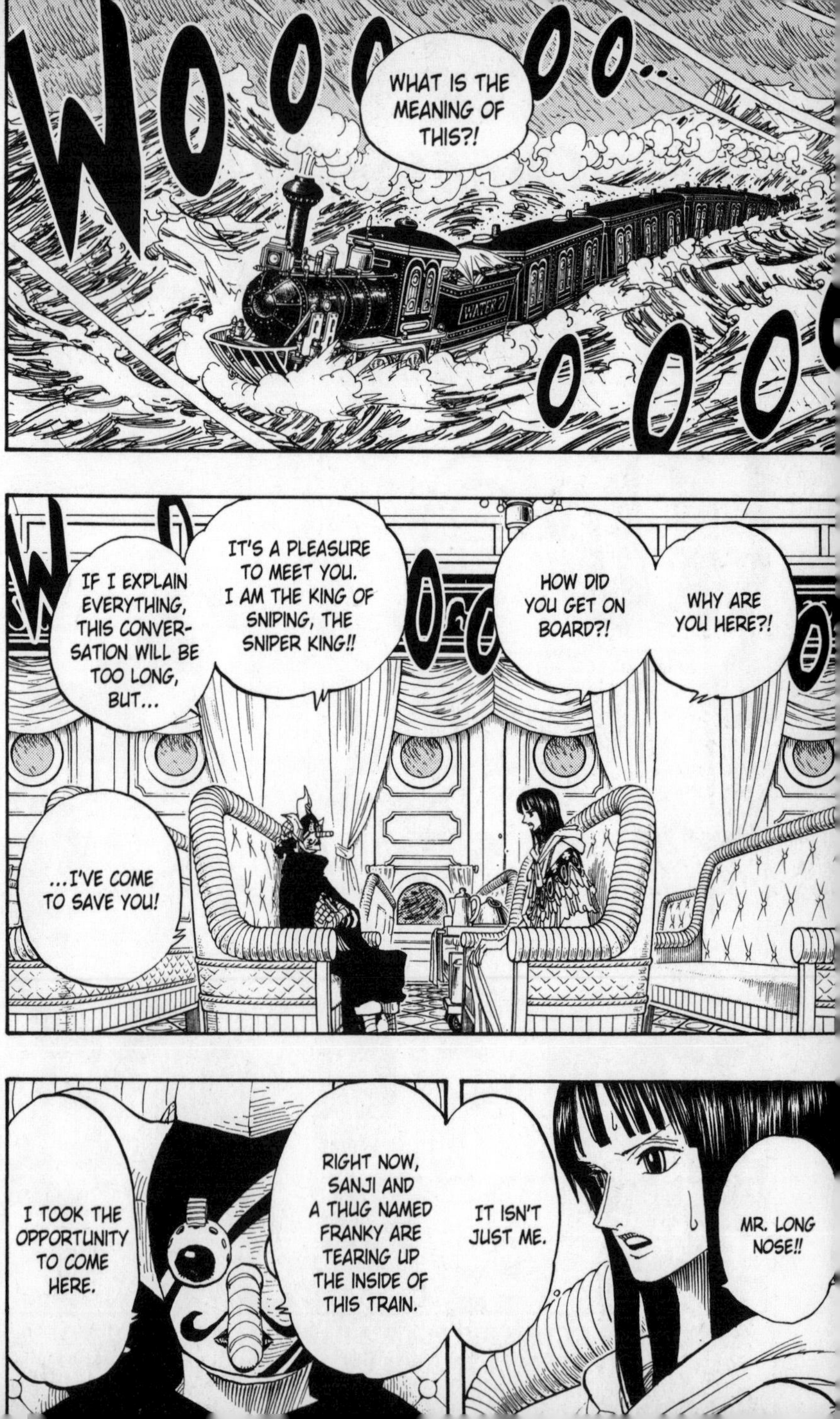
WOOOOO...
WHAT IS THE MEANING OF THIS?!
OOOO
WHY ARE YOU HERE?!
HOW DID YOU GET ON BOARD?!
IT'S A PLEASURE TO MEET YOU. I AM THE KING OF SNIPING, THE SNIPER KING!!
IF I EXPLAIN EVERYTHING, THIS CONVER-SATION WILL BE TOO LONG, BUT...
...I'VE COME TO SAVE YOU!
MR. LONG NOSE!!
IT ISN'T JUST ME.
RIGHT NOW, SANJI AND A THUG NAMED FRANKY ARE TEARING UP THE INSIDE OF THIS TRAIN.
I TOOK THE OPPORTUNITY TO COME HERE.

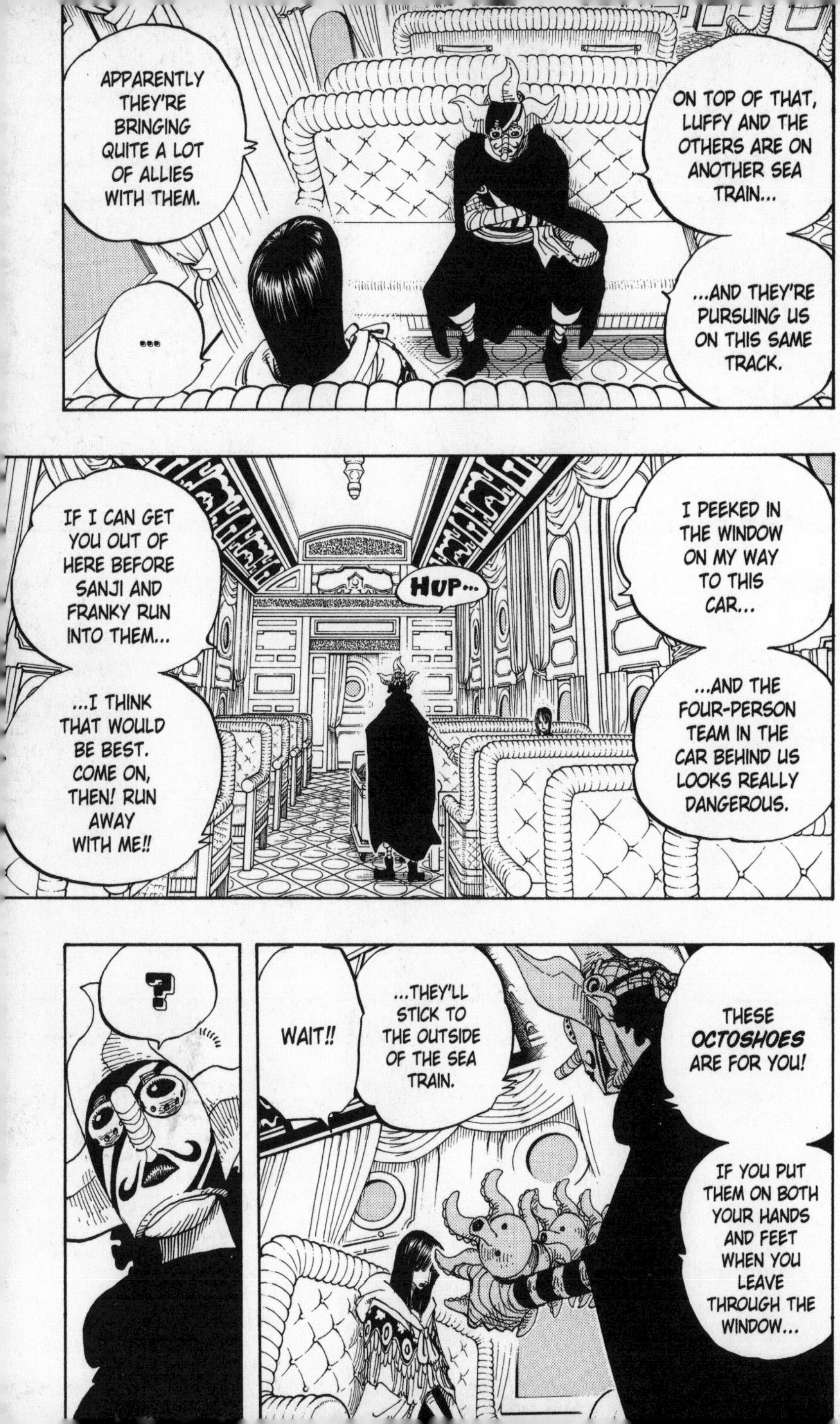
ON TOP OF THAT, LUFFY AND THE OTHERS ARE ON ANOTHER SEA TRAIN...
...AND THEY'RE PURSUING US ON THIS SAME TRACK.
APPARENTLY THEY'RE BRINGING QUITE A LOT OF ALLIES WITH THEM.
...
I PEEKED IN THE WINDOW ON MY WAY TO THIS CAR...
...AND THE FOUR-PERSON TEAM IN THE CAR BEHIND US LOOKS REALLY DANGEROUS.
HUP...
IF I CAN GET YOU OUT OF HERE BEFORE SANJI AND FRANKY RUN INTO THEM...
...I THINK THAT WOULD BE BEST. COME ON, THEN! RUN AWAY WITH ME!!
THESE *OCTOSHOES* ARE FOR YOU!
IF YOU PUT THEM ON BOTH YOUR HANDS AND FEET WHEN YOU LEAVE THROUGH THE WINDOW...
...THEY'LL STICK TO THE OUTSIDE OF THE SEA TRAIN.
WAIT!!
?

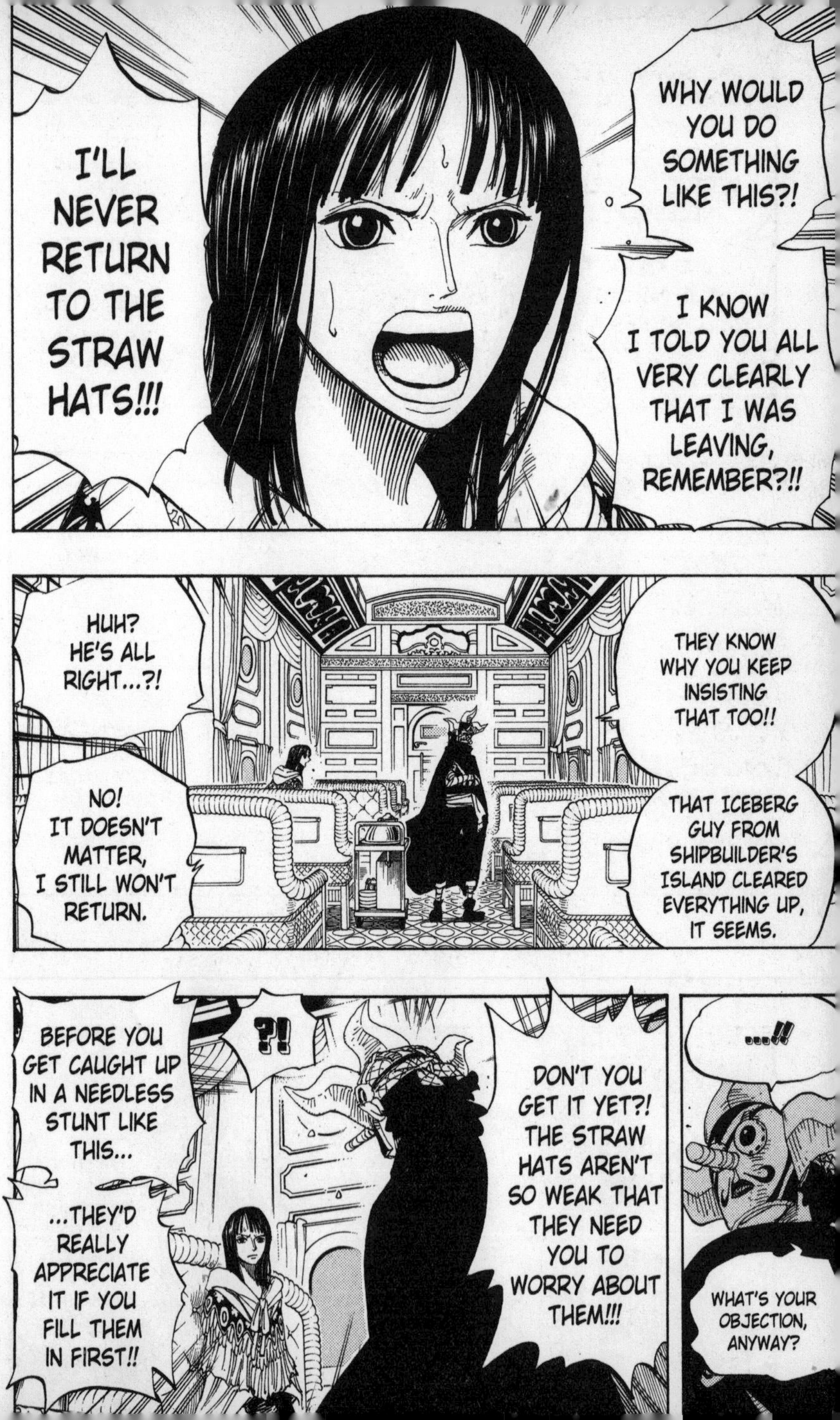
WHY WOULD YOU DO SOMETHING LIKE THIS?!
I KNOW I TOLD YOU ALL VERY CLEARLY THAT I WAS LEAVING, REMEMBER?!!
I'LL NEVER RETURN TO THE STRAW HATS!!!
THEY KNOW WHY YOU KEEP INSISTING THAT TOO!!
THAT ICEBERG GUY FROM SHIPBUILDER'S ISLAND CLEARED EVERYTHING UP, IT SEEMS.
HUH? HE'S ALL RIGHT...?!
NO! IT DOESN'T MATTER, I STILL WON'T RETURN.
...!!
WHAT'S YOUR OBJECTION, ANYWAY?
DON'T YOU GET IT YET?! THE STRAW HATS AREN'T SO WEAK THAT THEY NEED YOU TO WORRY ABOUT THEM!!!
?!
BEFORE YOU GET CAUGHT UP IN A NEEDLESS STUNT LIKE THIS...
...THEY'D REALLY APPRECIATE IT IF YOU FILL THEM IN FIRST!!

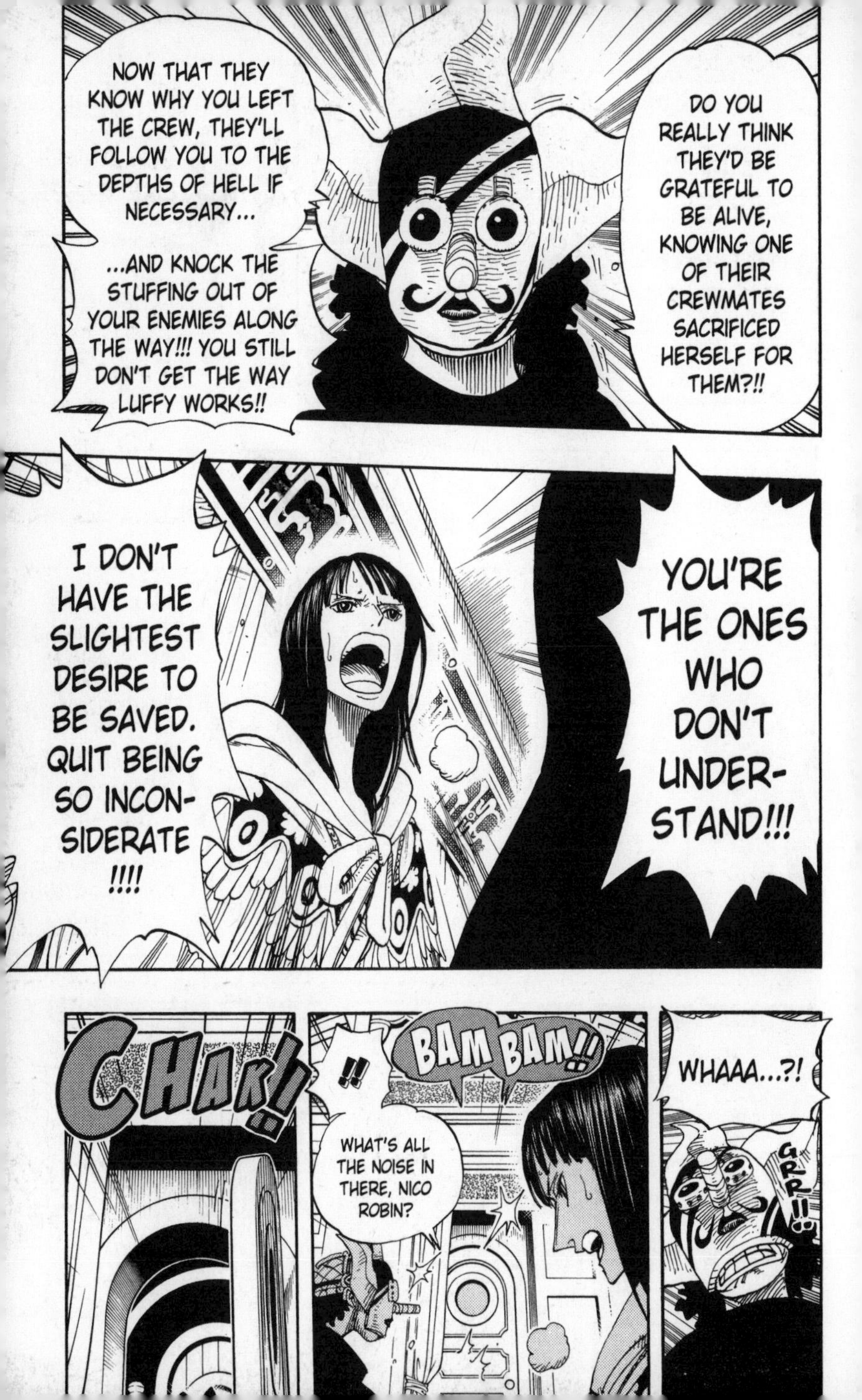
DO YOU REALLY THINK THEY'D BE GRATEFUL TO BE ALIVE, KNOWING ONE OF THEIR CREWMATES SACRIFICED HERSELF FOR THEM?!!
NOW THAT THEY KNOW WHY YOU LEFT THE CREW, THEY'LL FOLLOW YOU TO THE DEPTHS OF HELL IF NECESSARY...
...AND KNOCK THE STUFFING OUT OF YOUR ENEMIES ALONG THE WAY!!! YOU STILL DON'T GET THE WAY LUFFY WORKS!!
YOU'RE THE ONES WHO DON'T UNDER-STAND!!!
I DON'T HAVE THE SLIGHTEST DESIRE TO BE SAVED. QUIT BEING SO INCON-SIDERATE !!!!
WHAAA...?!
GRR!!
BAM BAM!!
!!
WHAT'S ALL THE NOISE IN THERE, NICO ROBIN?
CHAK!!

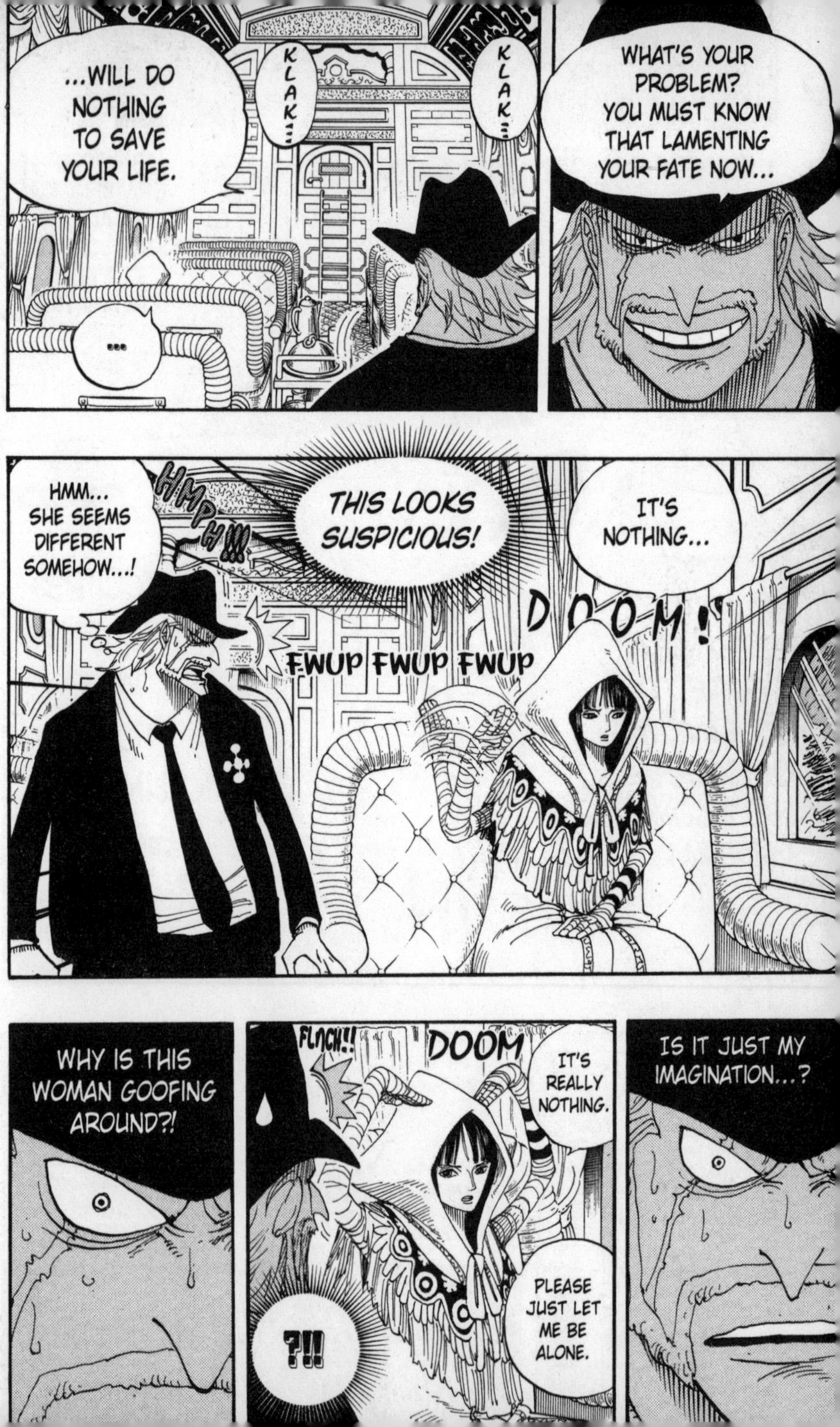
WHAT'S YOUR PROBLEM? YOU MUST KNOW THAT LAMENTING YOUR FATE NOW...
KLAK
KLAK
...WILL DO NOTHING TO SAVE YOUR LIFE.
...
IT'S NOTHING...
DOOM!
THIS LOOKS SUSPICIOUS!
HMPH!!!
HMM... SHE SEEMS DIFFERENT SOMEHOW...!
FWUP FWUP FWUP
IS IT JUST MY IMAGINATION...?
IT'S REALLY NOTHING.
DOOM
FLINCH!!
PLEASE JUST LET ME BE ALONE.
?!!
WHY IS THIS WOMAN GOOFING AROUND?!

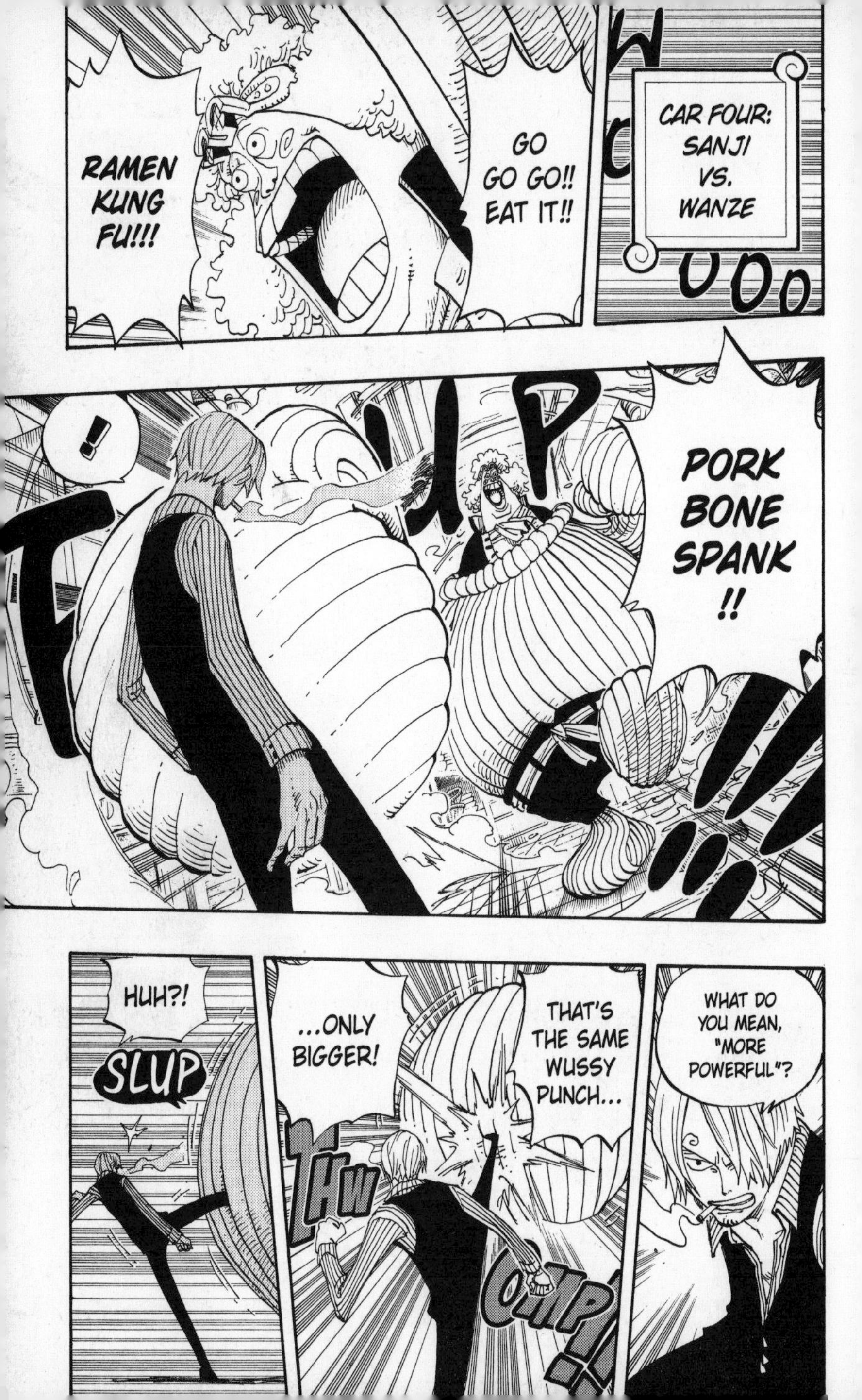

CAR FOUR: SANJI VS. WANZE
GO GO GO!! EAT IT!!
RAMEN KUNG FU!!!
PORK BONE SPANK !!
!
WHAT DO YOU MEAN, "MORE POWERFUL"?
THAT'S THE SAME WUSSY PUNCH...
...ONLY BIGGER!
THW
OMP!!
HUH?!
SLUP

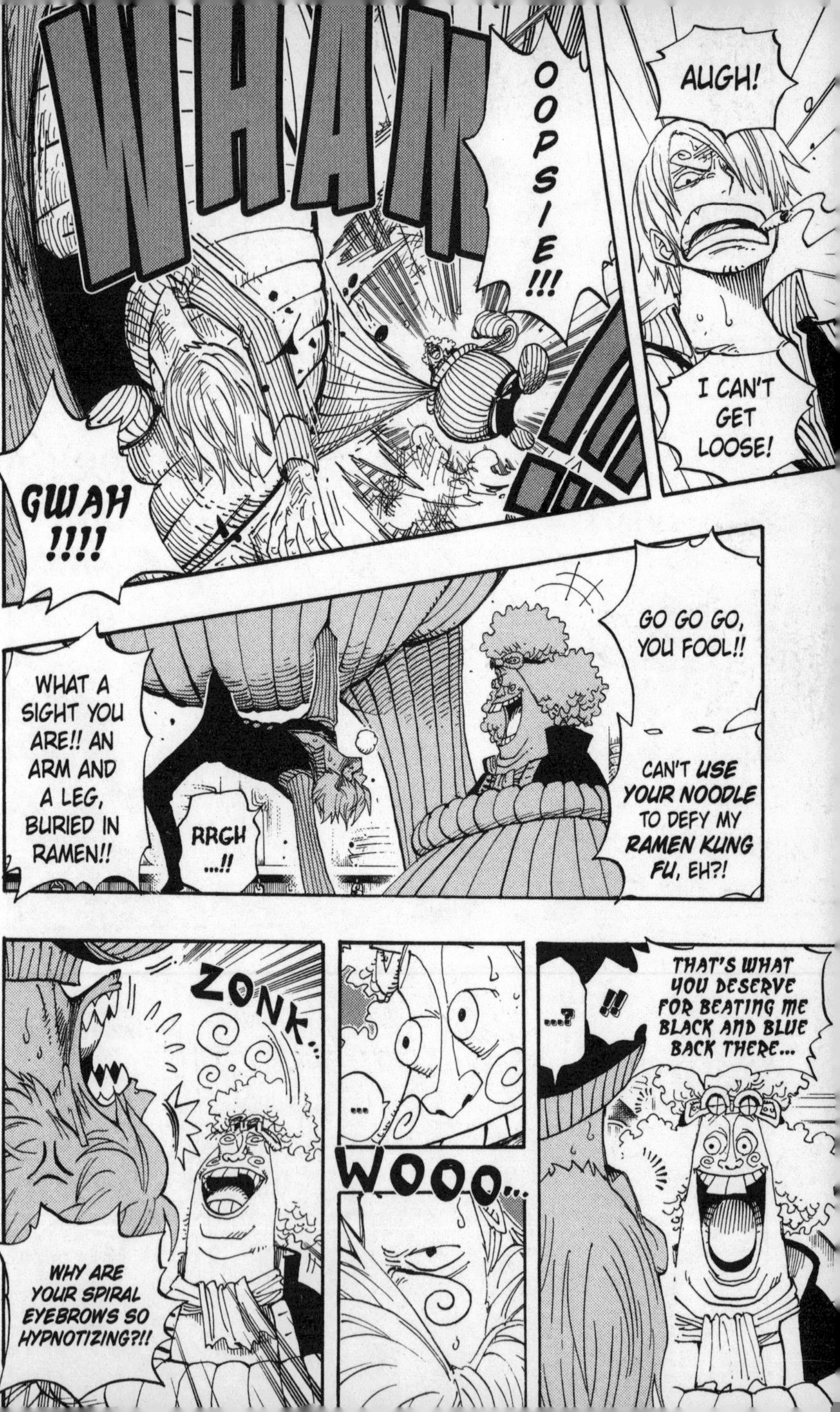
AUGH!
I CAN'T GET LOOSE!
OOPSIE!!!
WHAM
GWAH!!!!
GO GO GO, YOU FOOL!!
CAN'T USE YOUR NOODLE TO DEFY MY RAMEN KUNG FU, EH?!
RRGH ...!!
WHAT A SIGHT YOU ARE!! AN ARM AND A LEG, BURIED IN RAMEN!!
THAT'S WHAT YOU DESERVE FOR BEATING ME BLACK AND BLUE BACK THERE...
...?
!!
...
WOOO...
ZONK...
WHY ARE YOUR SPIRAL EYEBROWS SO HYPNOTIZING?!!

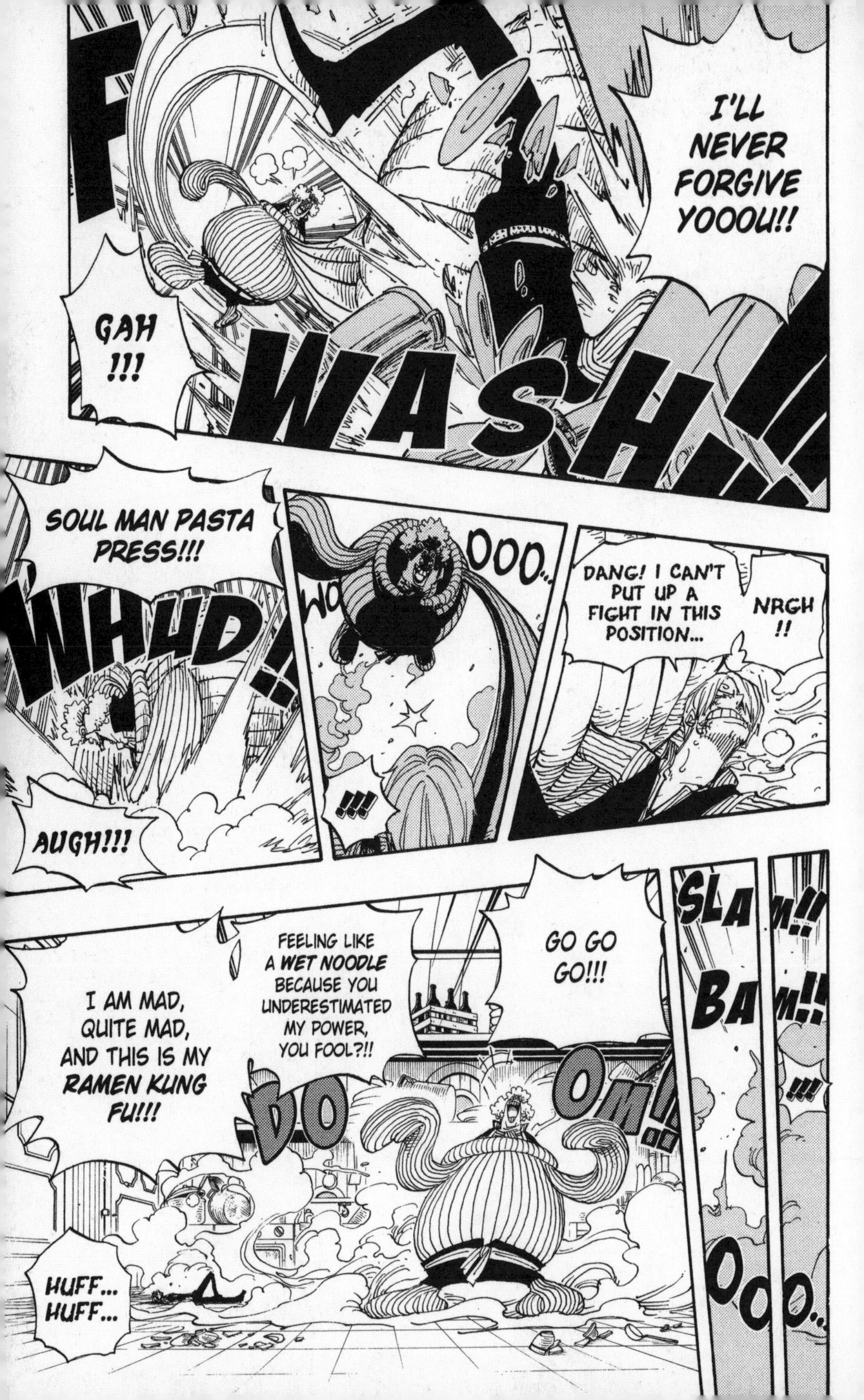
I'LL NEVER FORGIVE YOOOU!!
FWASH!!!
GAH !!!
NRGH !!
DANG! I CAN'T PUT UP A FIGHT IN THIS POSITION...
WOOOO...
!!!
SOUL MAN PASTA PRESS!!!
WHUD!!
AUGH!!!
SLAM!!
BAM!!
!!!
OOOO...
GO GO GO!!!
FEELING LIKE A WET NOODLE BECAUSE YOU UNDERESTIMATED MY POWER, YOU FOOL?!!
I AM MAD, QUITE MAD, AND THIS IS MY RAMEN KUNG FU!!!
DOOM!!
HUFF... HUFF...

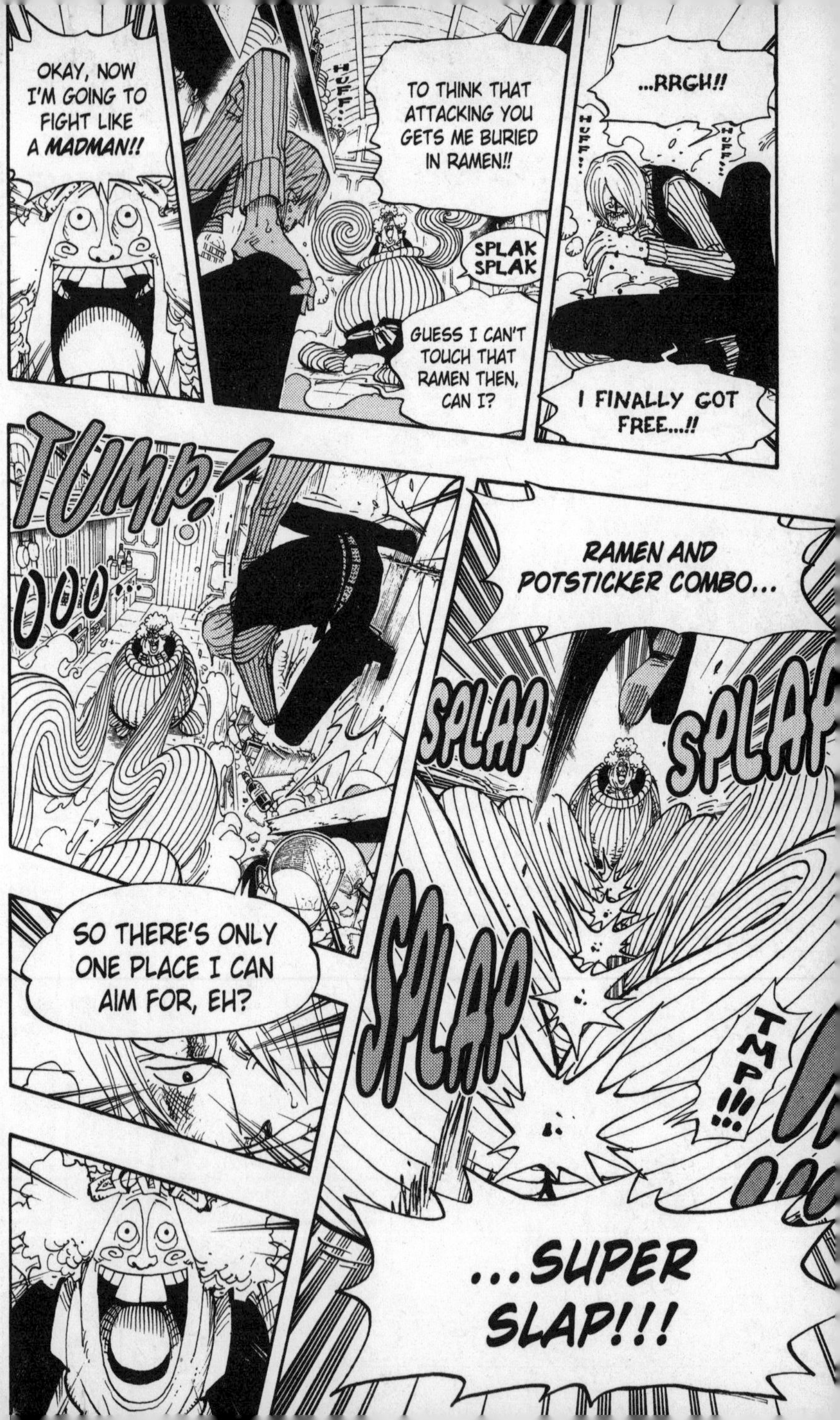
...RRGH!!
HUFF...
HUFF...
I FINALLY GOT FREE...!!
HUFF...
TO THINK THAT ATTACKING YOU GETS ME BURIED IN RAMEN!!
SPLAK SPLAK
GUESS I CAN'T TOUCH THAT RAMEN THEN, CAN I?
OKAY, NOW I'M GOING TO FIGHT LIKE A *MADMAN!!*
RAMEN AND POTSTICKER COMBO...
SPLAP
SPLAP
SPLAP
TMP!!!
...SUPER SLAP!!!
TUMP!
OOO
SO THERE'S ONLY ONE PLACE I CAN AIM FOR, EH?

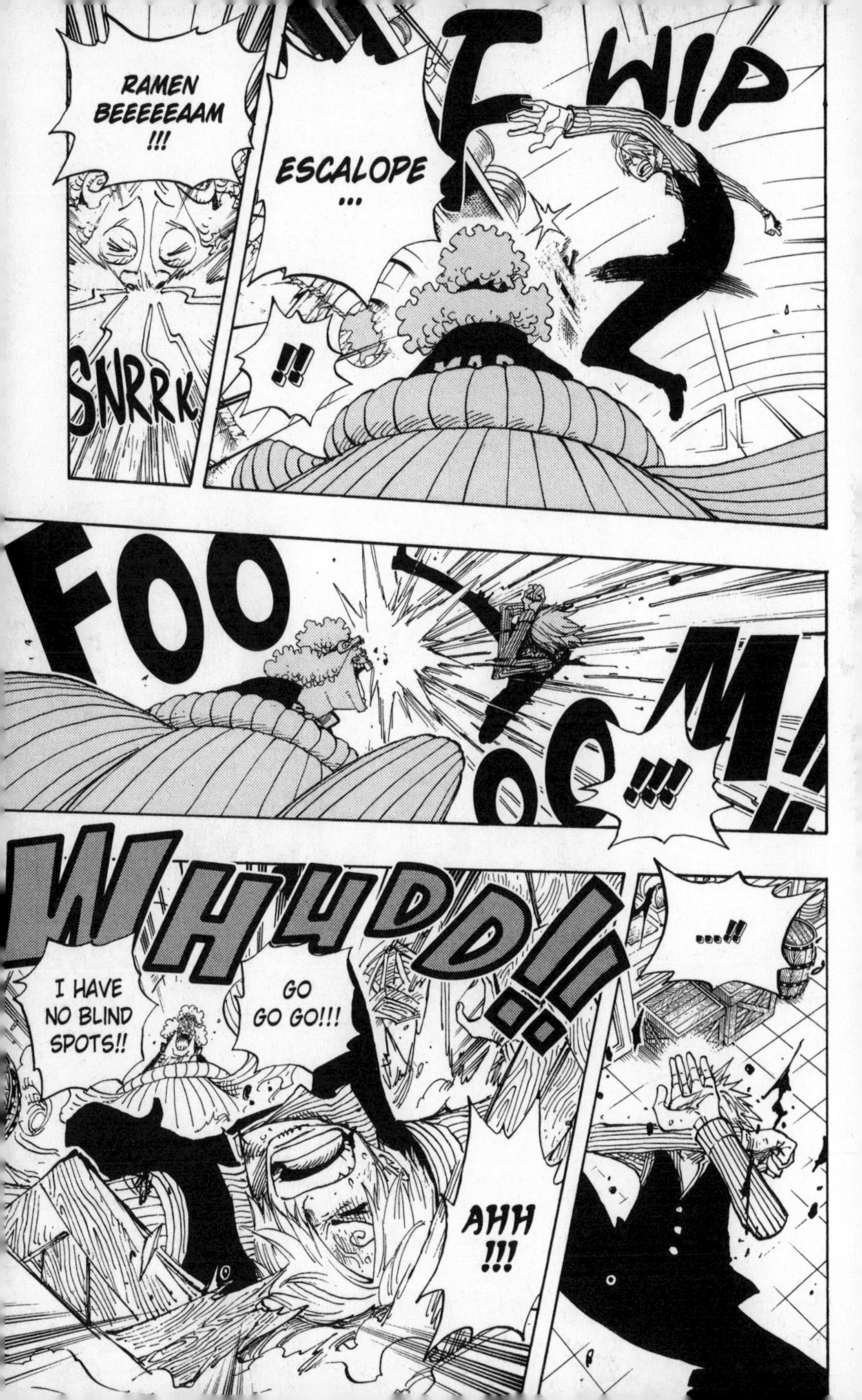
TWIP
ESCALOPE ...
!!
RAMEN BEEEEEEAAM !!!
SNRRK
FOO
M!!
...!!
AHH !!!
WHUDD!!
GO GO GO!!!
I HAVE NO BLIND SPOTS!!

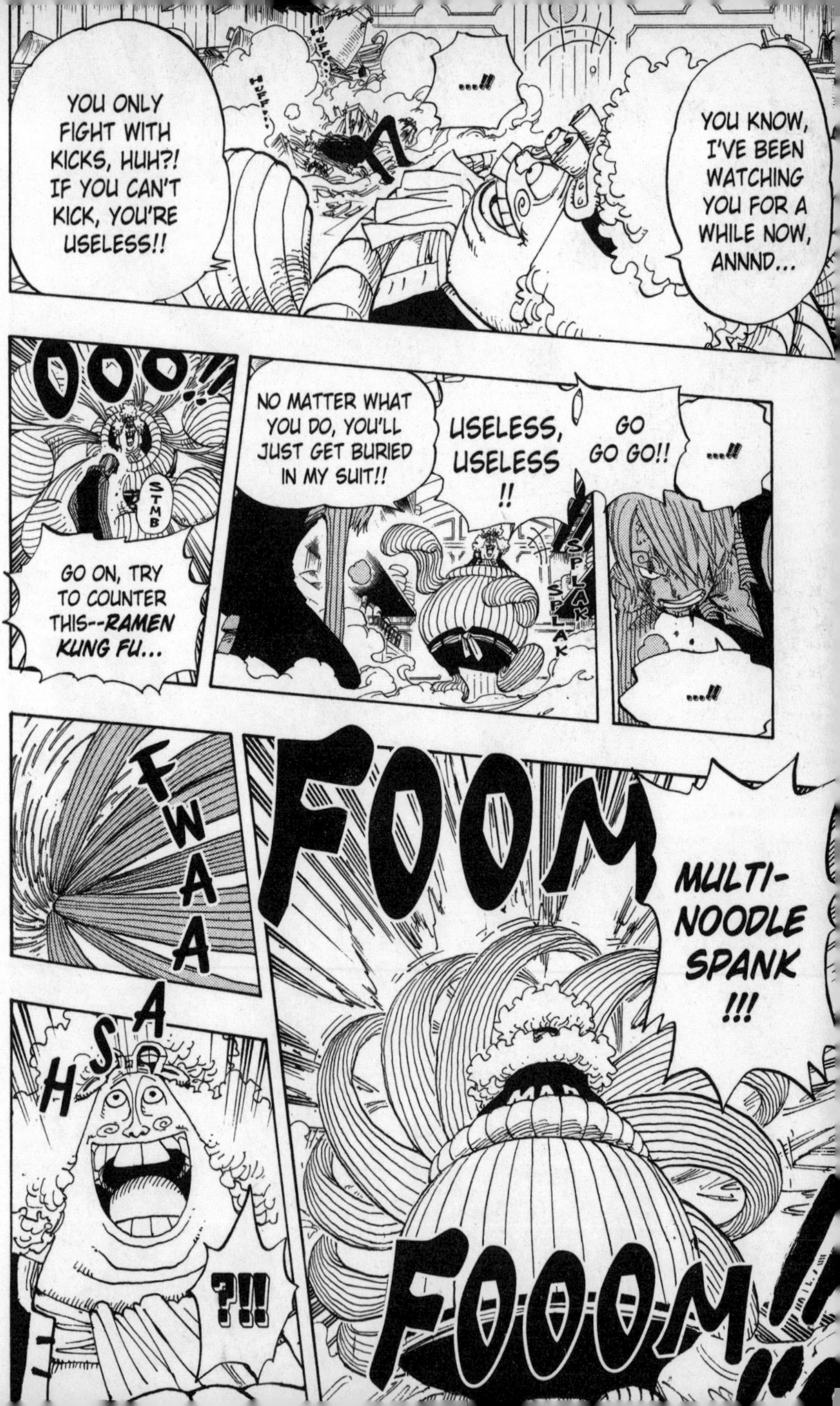
YOU KNOW, I'VE BEEN WATCHING YOU FOR A WHILE NOW, ANNND...
...!!
YOU ONLY FIGHT WITH KICKS, HUH?! IF YOU CAN'T KICK, YOU'RE USELESS!!
...!!
...!!
GO GO GO!!
USELESS, USELESS !!
SPLAK
SPLAK
NO MATTER WHAT YOU DO, YOU'LL JUST GET BURIED IN MY SUIT!!
OOO!!
STMB
GO ON, TRY TO COUNTER THIS--RAMEN KUNG FU...
FOOM
MULTI-NOODLE SPANK !!!
FWAA
?!!
FOOOM!!

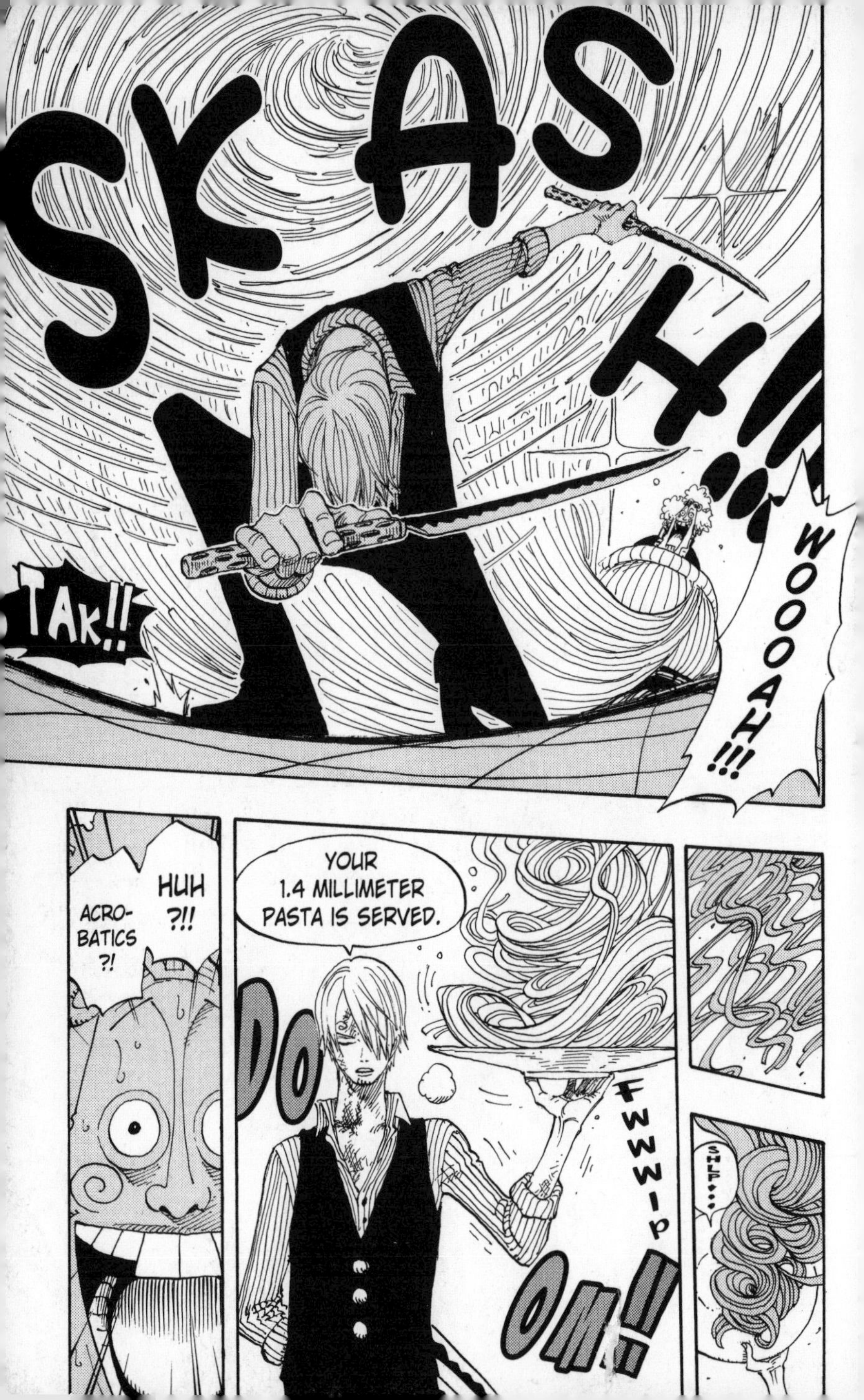
SKASH!!!
WOOOOAH!!!
TAK!!
SHLP...
YOUR 1.4 MILLIMETER PASTA IS SERVED.
FWWWIP
DOOM!!
HUH?!!
ACRO-BATICS?!

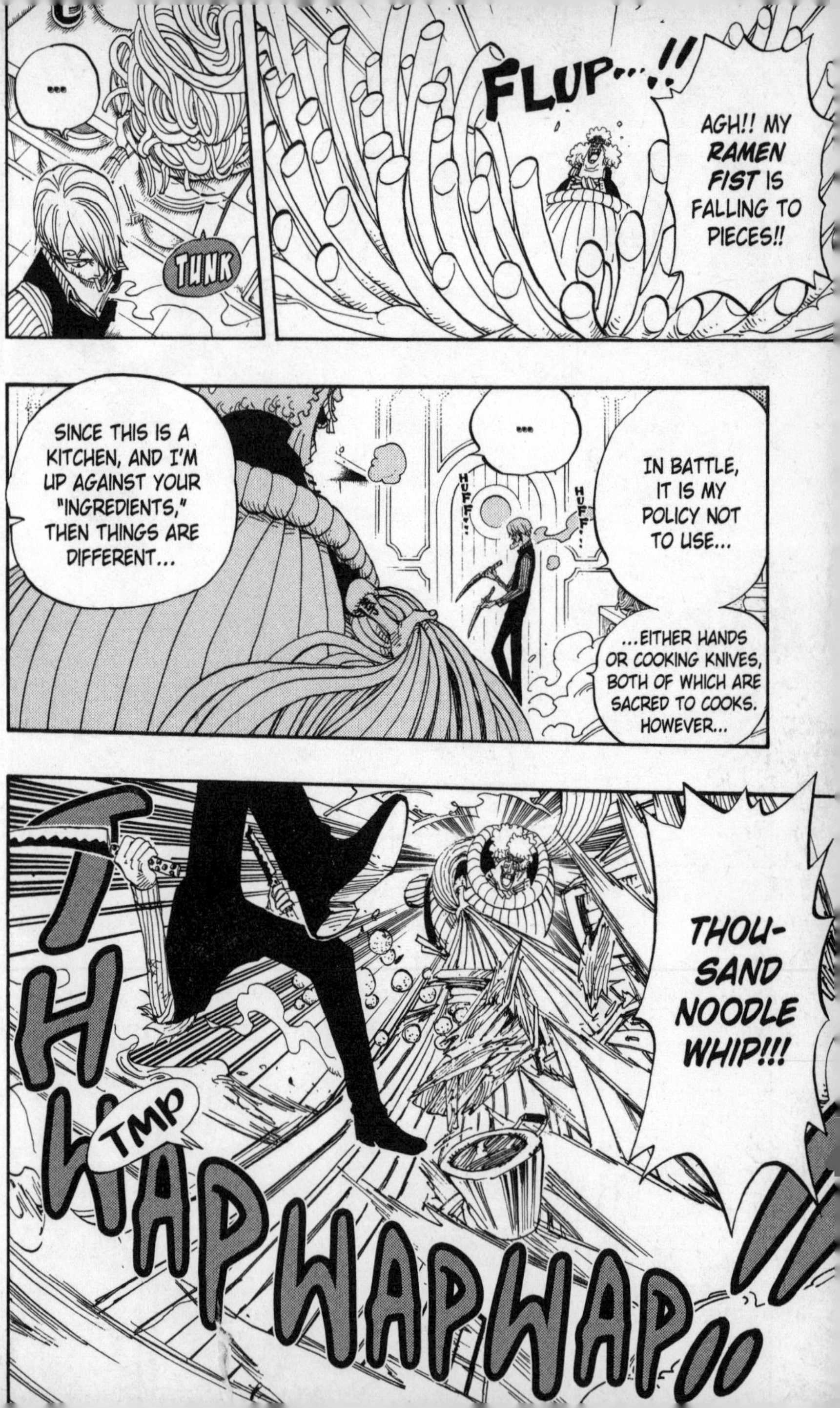
FLUP...!!
AGH!! MY RAMEN FIST IS FALLING TO PIECES!!
...
TUNK
...
IN BATTLE, IT IS MY POLICY NOT TO USE...
...EITHER HANDS OR COOKING KNIVES, BOTH OF WHICH ARE SACRED TO COOKS. HOWEVER...
HUFF...
HUFF...
SINCE THIS IS A KITCHEN, AND I'M UP AGAINST YOUR "INGREDIENTS," THEN THINGS ARE DIFFERENT...
THOU-SAND NOODLE WHIP!!!
WHAP WHAP WHAP WHAP!!
TMP

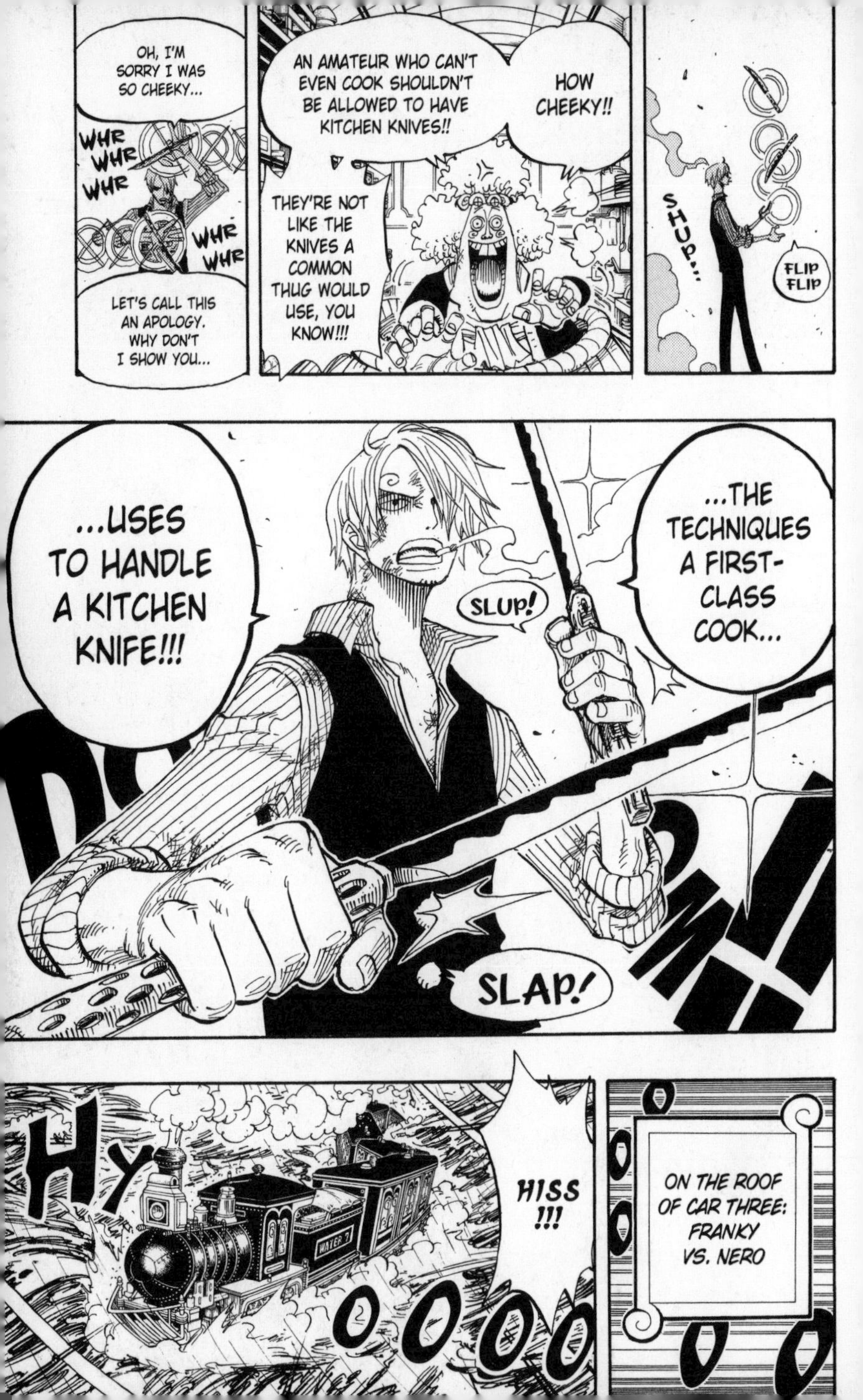
SHUP...!!
FLIP FLIP
HOW CHEEKY!!
AN AMATEUR WHO CAN'T EVEN COOK SHOULDN'T BE ALLOWED TO HAVE KITCHEN KNIVES!!
THEY'RE NOT LIKE THE KNIVES A COMMON THUG WOULD USE, YOU KNOW!!!
OH, I'M SORRY I WAS SO CHEEKY...
WHR WHR WHR
WHR WHR
LET'S CALL THIS AN APOLOGY. WHY DON'T I SHOW YOU...
...THE TECHNIQUES A FIRST-CLASS COOK...
SLUP!
...USES TO HANDLE A KITCHEN KNIFE!!!
SLAP!
ON THE ROOF OF CAR THREE: FRANKY VS. NERO
HISS !!!

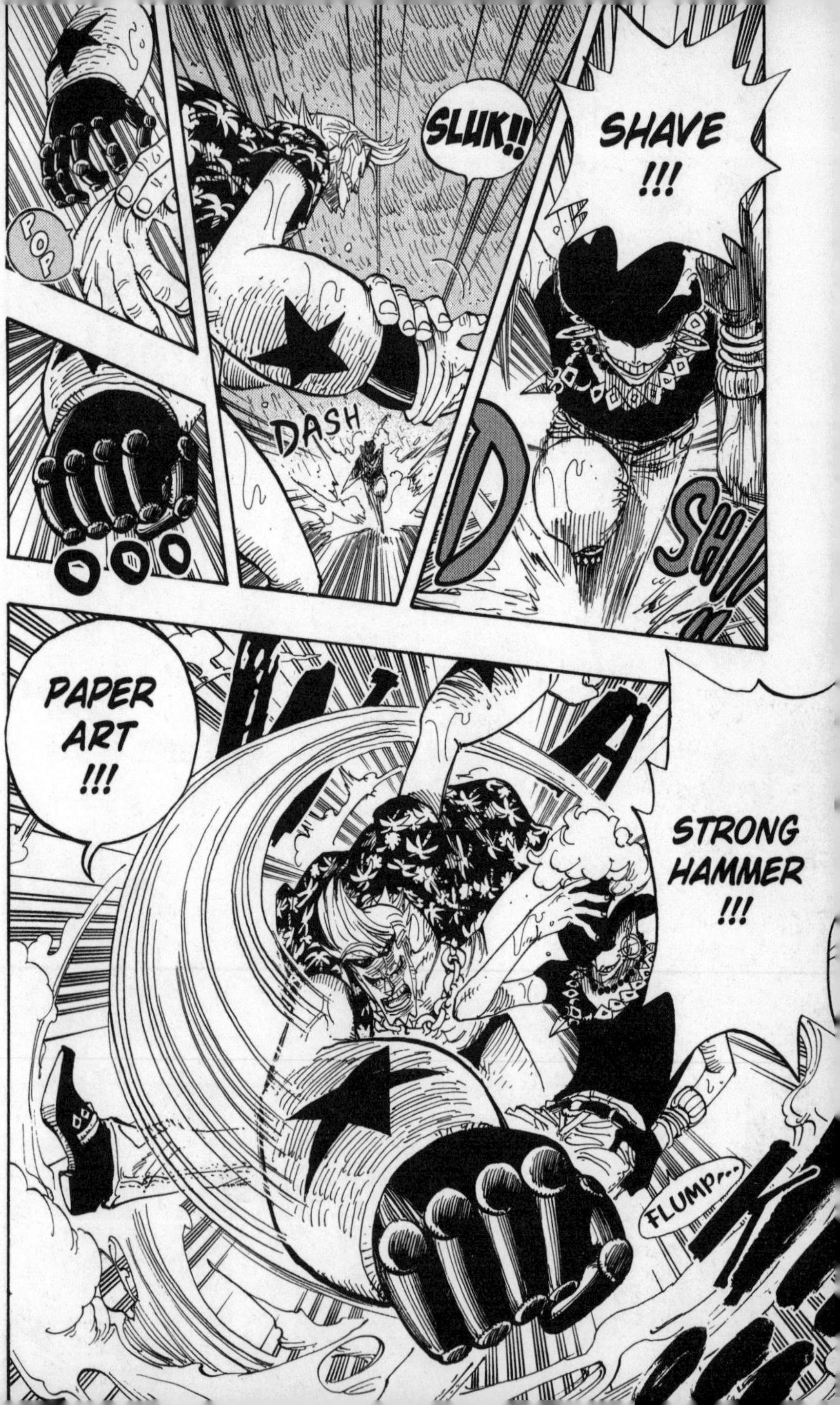

SHAVE !!!
SLUK!!
DASH
POP
STRONG HAMMER !!!
PAPER ART !!!
FLUMP...

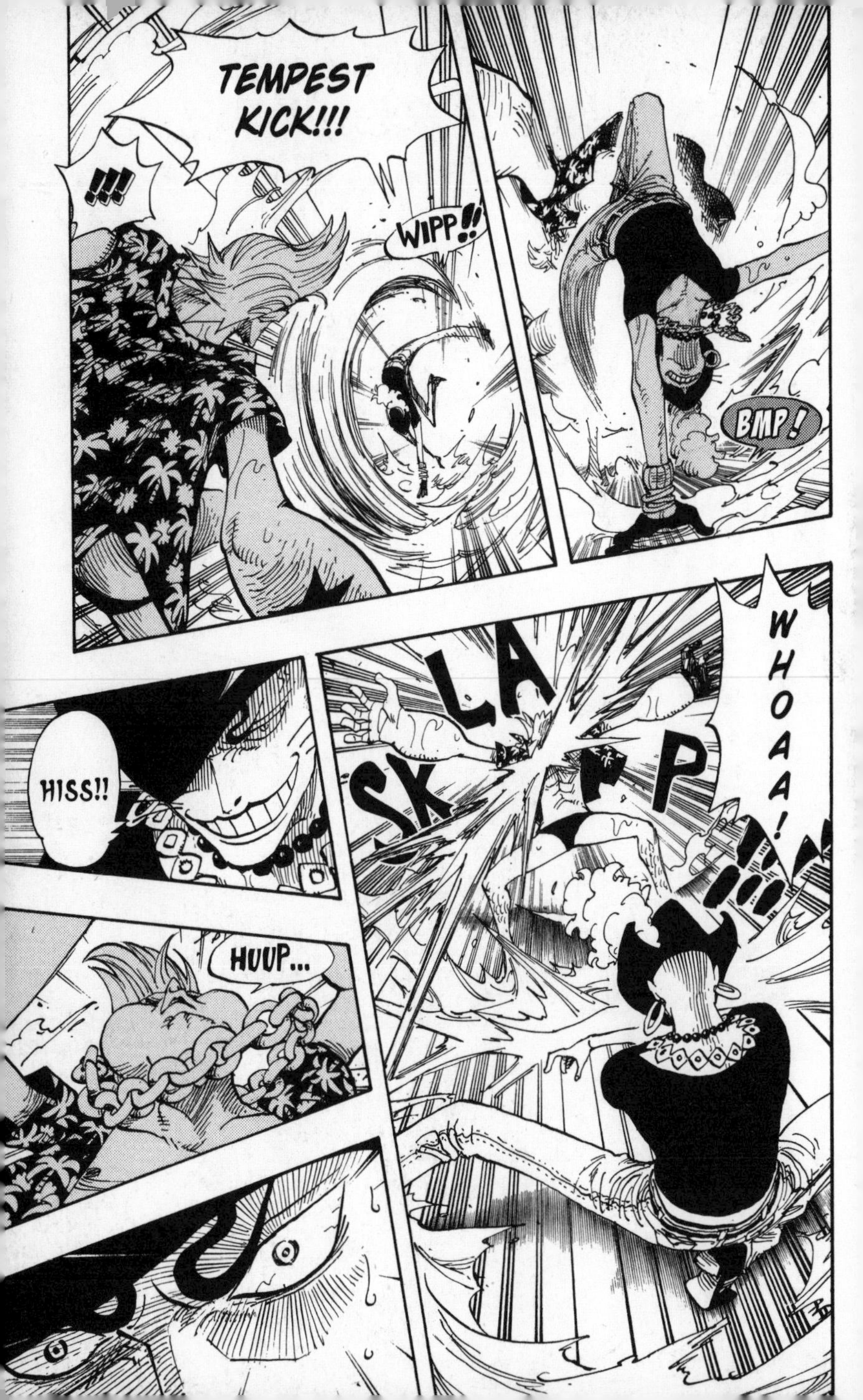
BMP!
TEMPEST KICK!!!
!!!
WIPP!!
WHOAAA!
SKLAP
!!!
HISS!!
HUUP...

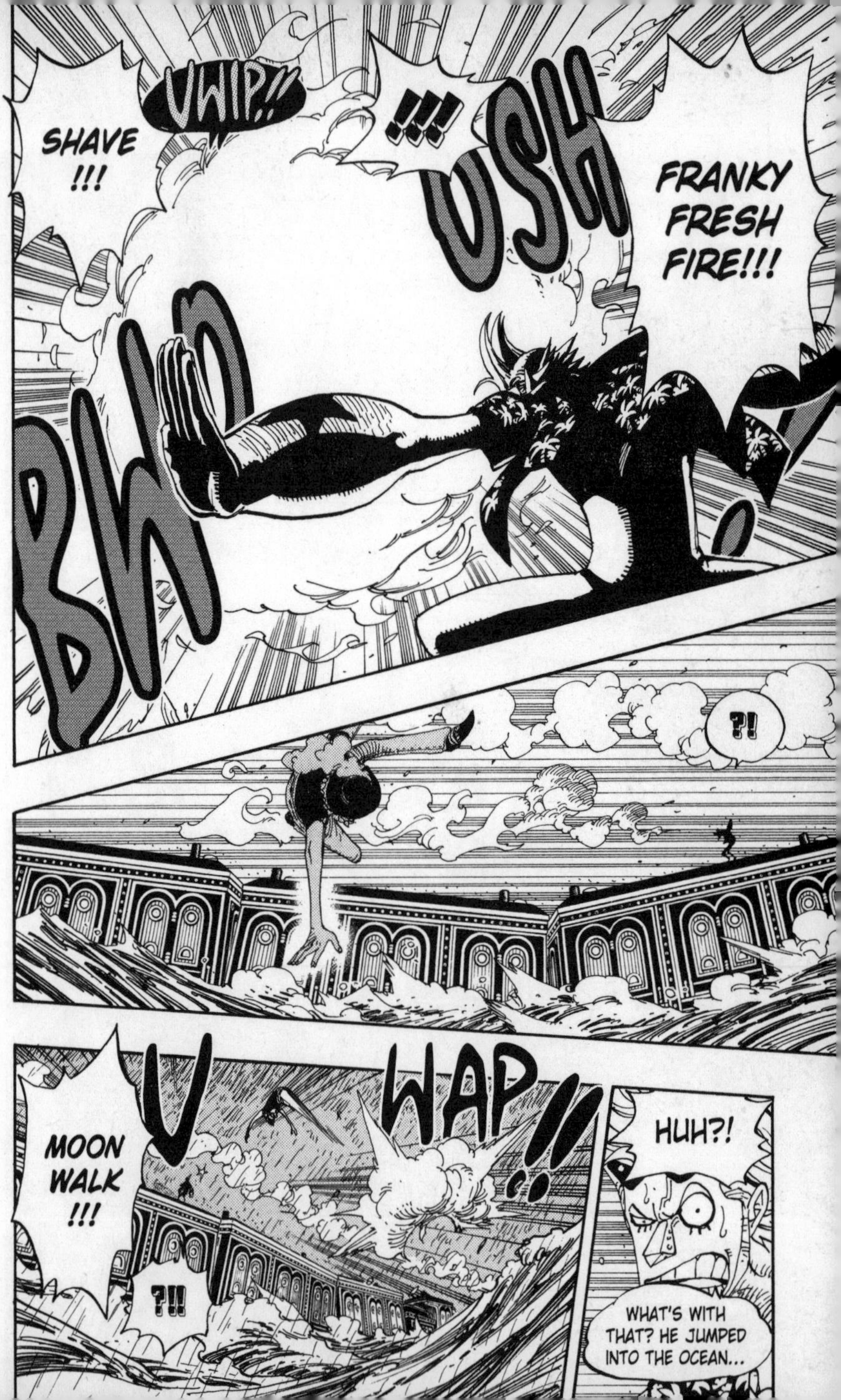
FRANKY FRESH FIRE!!!
USH!!!
UWIP!!
SHAVE !!!
BW
?!
HUH?!
WHAT'S WITH THAT? HE JUMPED INTO THE OCEAN...
U WAP!!
MOON WALK !!!
?!!

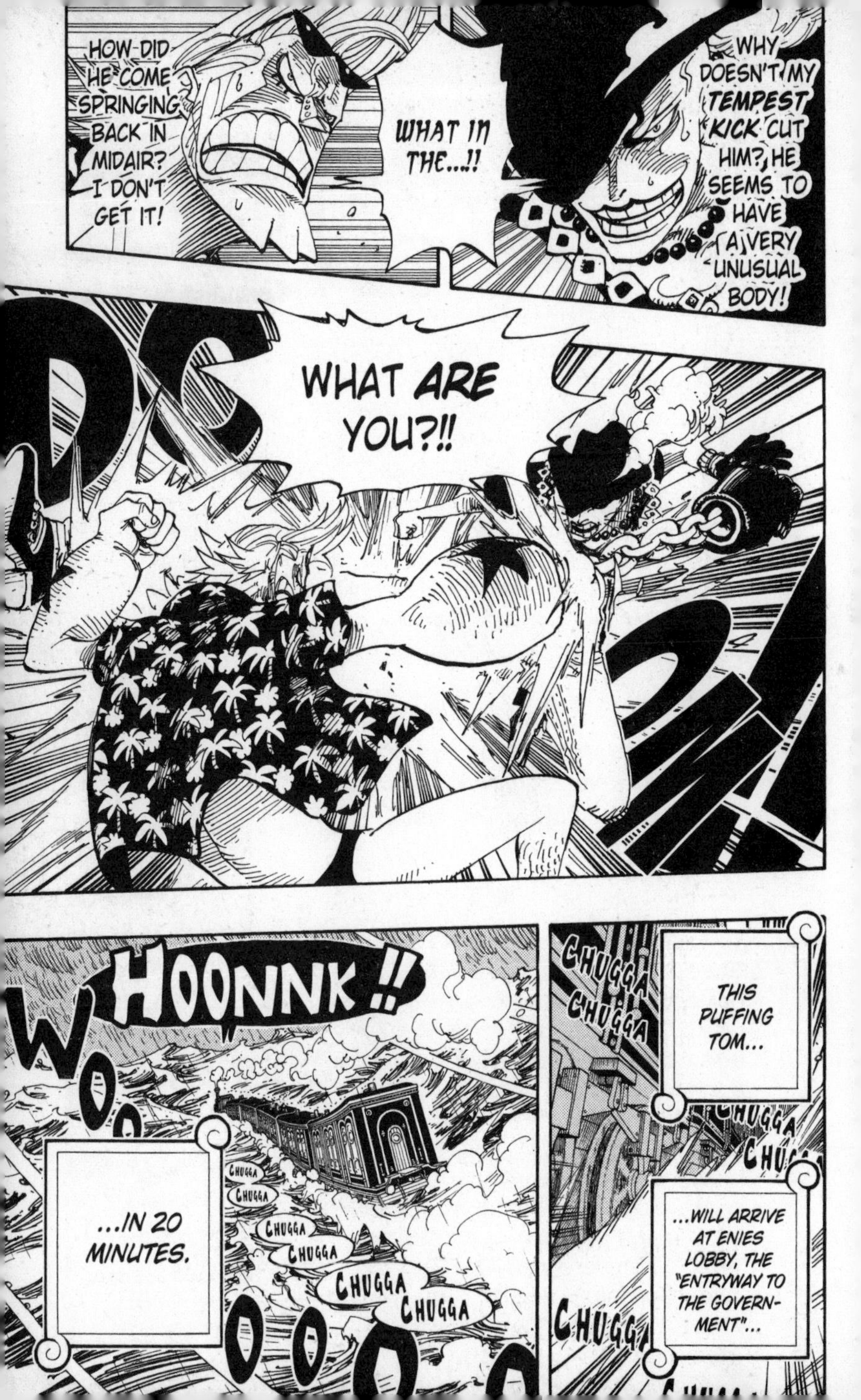
WHY DOESN'T MY TEMPEST KICK CUT HIM? HE SEEMS TO HAVE A VERY UNUSUAL BODY!
WHAT IN THE...!!
HOW DID HE COME SPRINGING BACK IN MIDAIR? I DON'T GET IT!
WHAT ARE YOU?!!
CHUGGA CHUGGA
THIS PUFFING TOM...
CHUGGA CHUGGA
...WILL ARRIVE AT ENIES LOBBY, THE "ENTRYWAY TO THE GOVERNMENT"...
CHUGGA
HOONNK!!
CHUGGA CHUGGA
CHUGGA CHUGGA
CHUGGA CHUGGA
...IN 20 MINUTES.

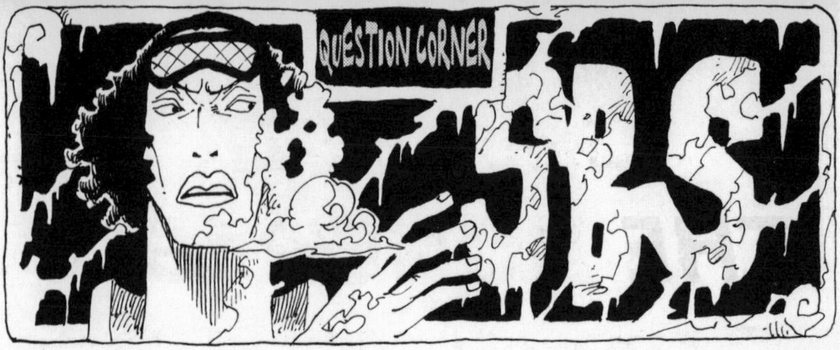
QUESTION CORNER

Reader: Oda Sensei, caaaaatch! TOSS
It's a love-bomb present ♡ !
--I'm a guy, okay?!

Oda: Yaaay, a present, thank y-- KABOOOM!!! THWOMP!! TWEET TWEET "HOOONNK"! (Translation: The impact from the explosion thrust me right into the center of a big cuckoo clock, and there were stars and little chicks flying around my head. Then I popped out of the clock instead of the cuckoo and whistled like a train, with smoke coming out of my mouth.)

Q: Oda Sensei, hello. A while ago I was watching TV and saw some engines called "Puffing Billy" and "Rocket," and it startled me. Is that what you based Puffing Tom and Rocketman on?
--Octopus

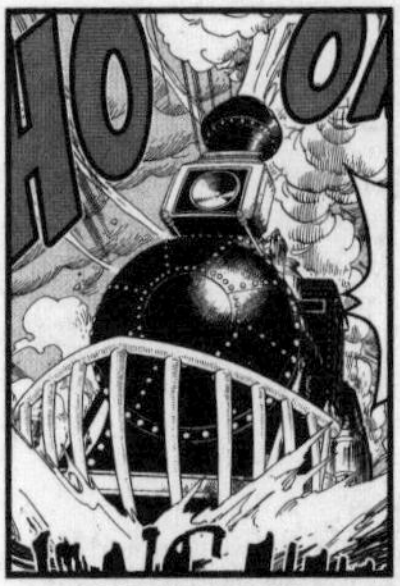
PUFFING TOM

A: Whoa! There was a program like that? That's it exactly. "Puffing Billy" is the name of the oldest engine in the world. "Rocket" is the name of an engine that was famous for its speed a long time ago. Well, they look completely different from the manga engines, but still. By the way, when I was researching how to draw engines, I found out that the name of the guy who designed the world's first steam engine was "Thomas." "I see, so that's where that famous kid's program came from," I thought.

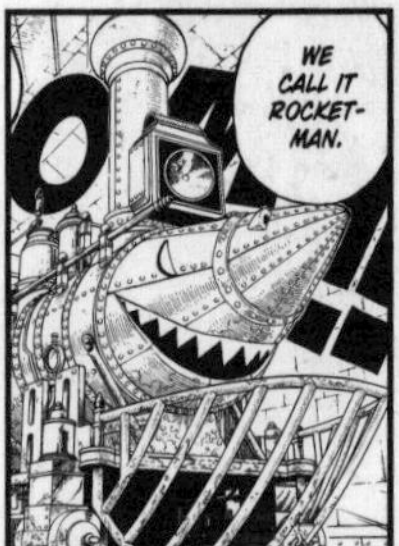
WE CALL IT ROCKET-MAN.
ROCKETMAN

Chapter 371:
THE HONORABLE CAPTAIN T-BONE

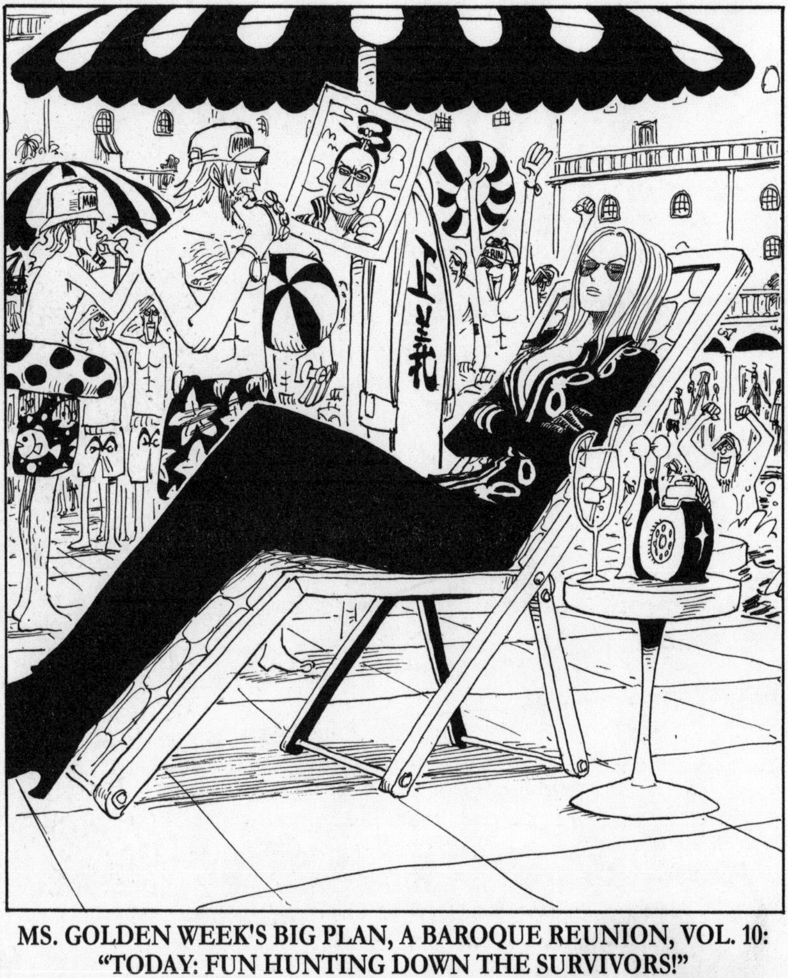

MS. GOLDEN WEEK'S BIG PLAN, A BAROQUE REUNION, VOL. 10:
"TODAY: FUN HUNTING DOWN THE SURVIVORS!"

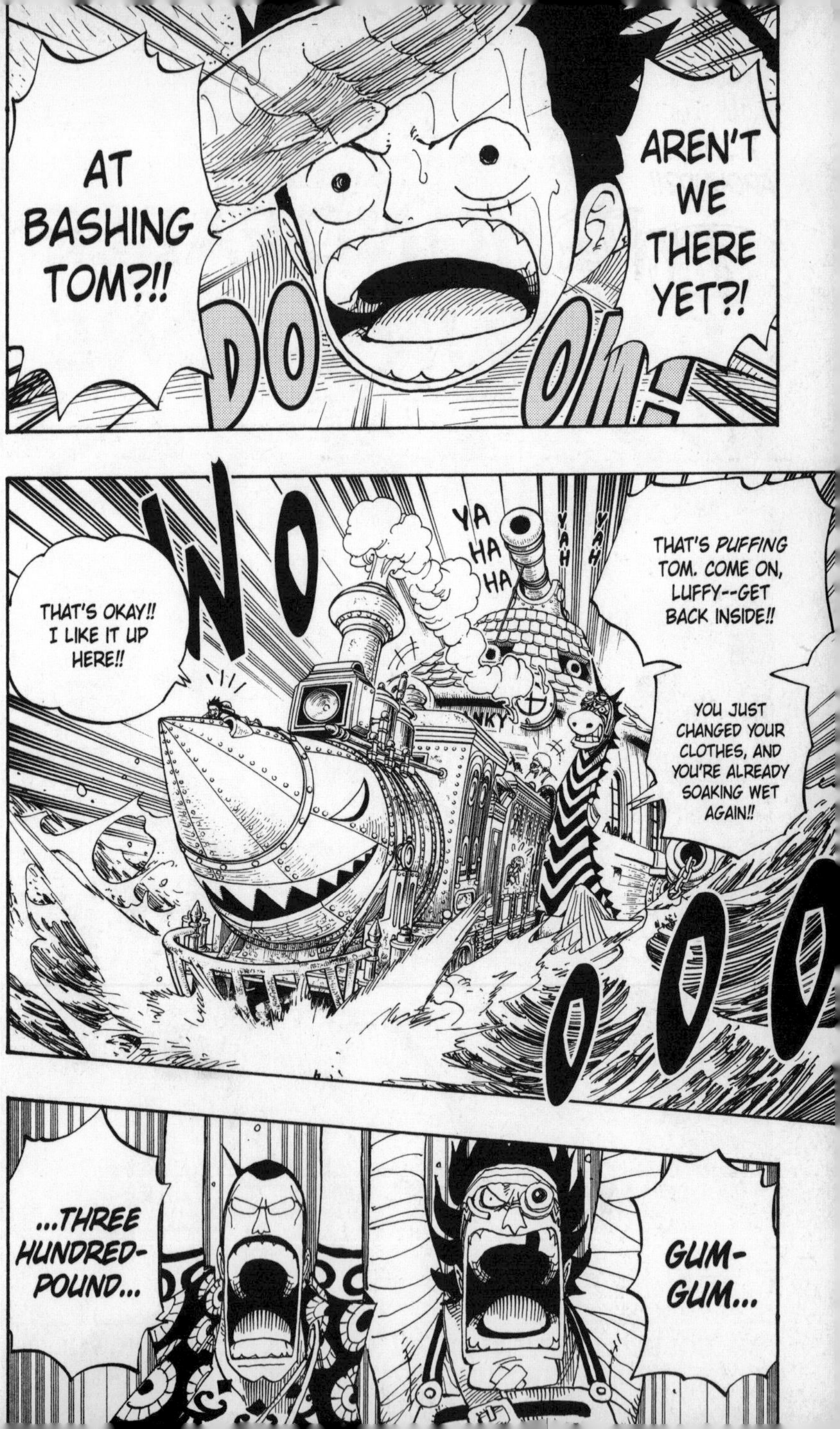
AREN'T WE THERE YET?!
AT BASHING TOM?!!
DO
OM
THAT'S PUFFING TOM. COME ON, LUFFY--GET BACK INSIDE!!
YOU JUST CHANGED YOUR CLOTHES, AND YOU'RE ALREADY SOAKING WET AGAIN!!
YAH YAH
YA HA HA HA
THAT'S OKAY!! I LIKE IT UP HERE!!
WO
OOO
GUM-GUM...
...THREE HUNDRED-POUND...

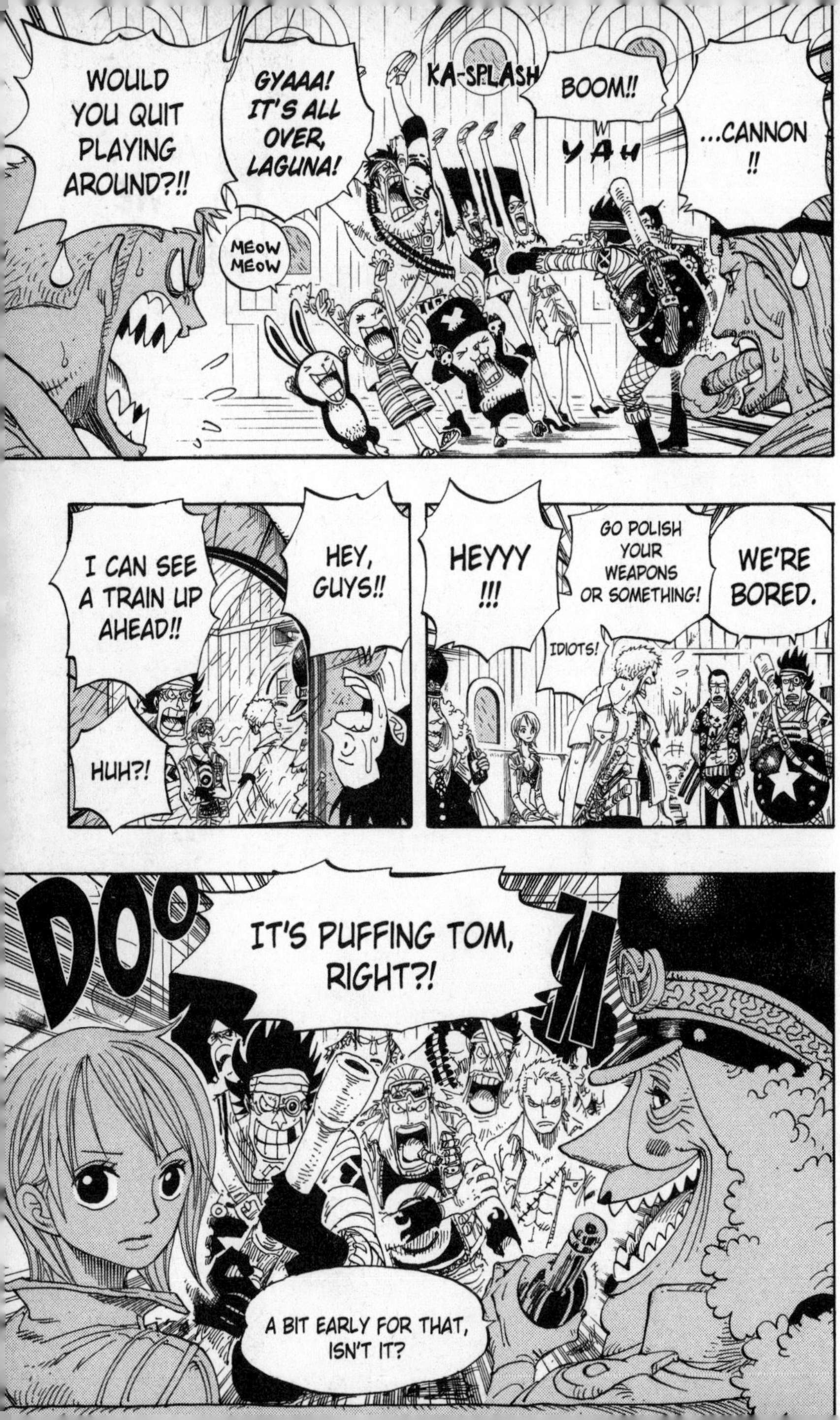
...CANNON !!
YAH
BOOM!!
KA-SPLASH
GYAAA! IT'S ALL OVER, LAGUNA!
MEOW MEOW
WOULD YOU QUIT PLAYING AROUND?!!
WE'RE BORED.
GO POLISH YOUR WEAPONS OR SOMETHING!
IDIOTS!
HEYYY !!!
HEY, GUYS!!
I CAN SEE A TRAIN UP AHEAD!!
HUH?!
DOOM
IT'S PUFFING TOM, RIGHT?!
A BIT EARLY FOR THAT, ISN'T IT?

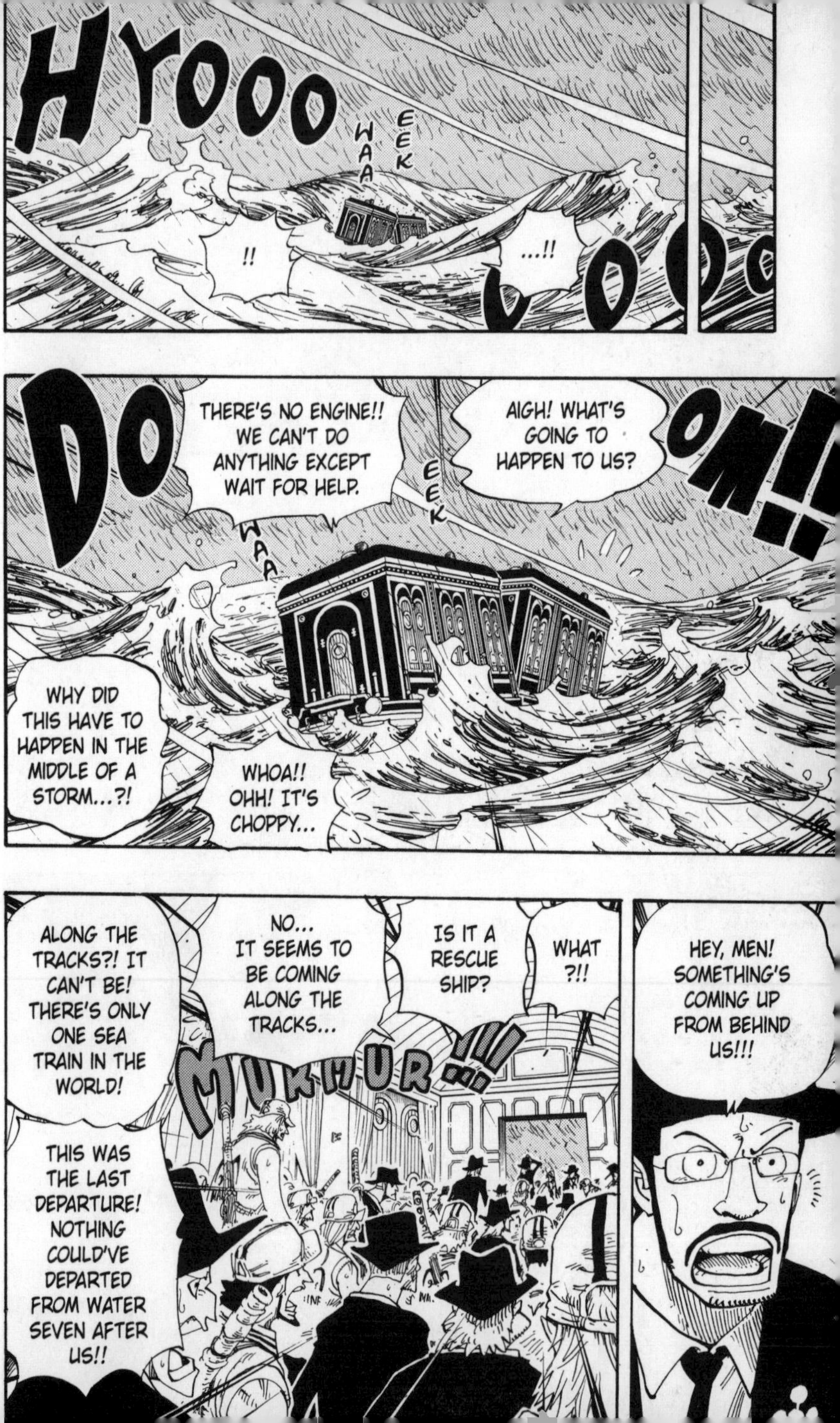
HYOOO
EEK
WAAA
...!!
!!
OOOO
OM!!
AIGH! WHAT'S GOING TO HAPPEN TO US?
EEK
THERE'S NO ENGINE!! WE CAN'T DO ANYTHING EXCEPT WAIT FOR HELP.
WAAA
DO
WHOA!! OHH! IT'S CHOPPY...
WHY DID THIS HAVE TO HAPPEN IN THE MIDDLE OF A STORM...?!
HEY, MEN! SOMETHING'S COMING UP FROM BEHIND US!!!
WHAT ?!!
IS IT A RESCUE SHIP?
NO... IT SEEMS TO BE COMING ALONG THE TRACKS...
ALONG THE TRACKS?! IT CAN'T BE! THERE'S ONLY ONE SEA TRAIN IN THE WORLD!
MURMUR...!!!
THIS WAS THE LAST DEPARTURE! NOTHING COULD'VE DEPARTED FROM WATER SEVEN AFTER US!!

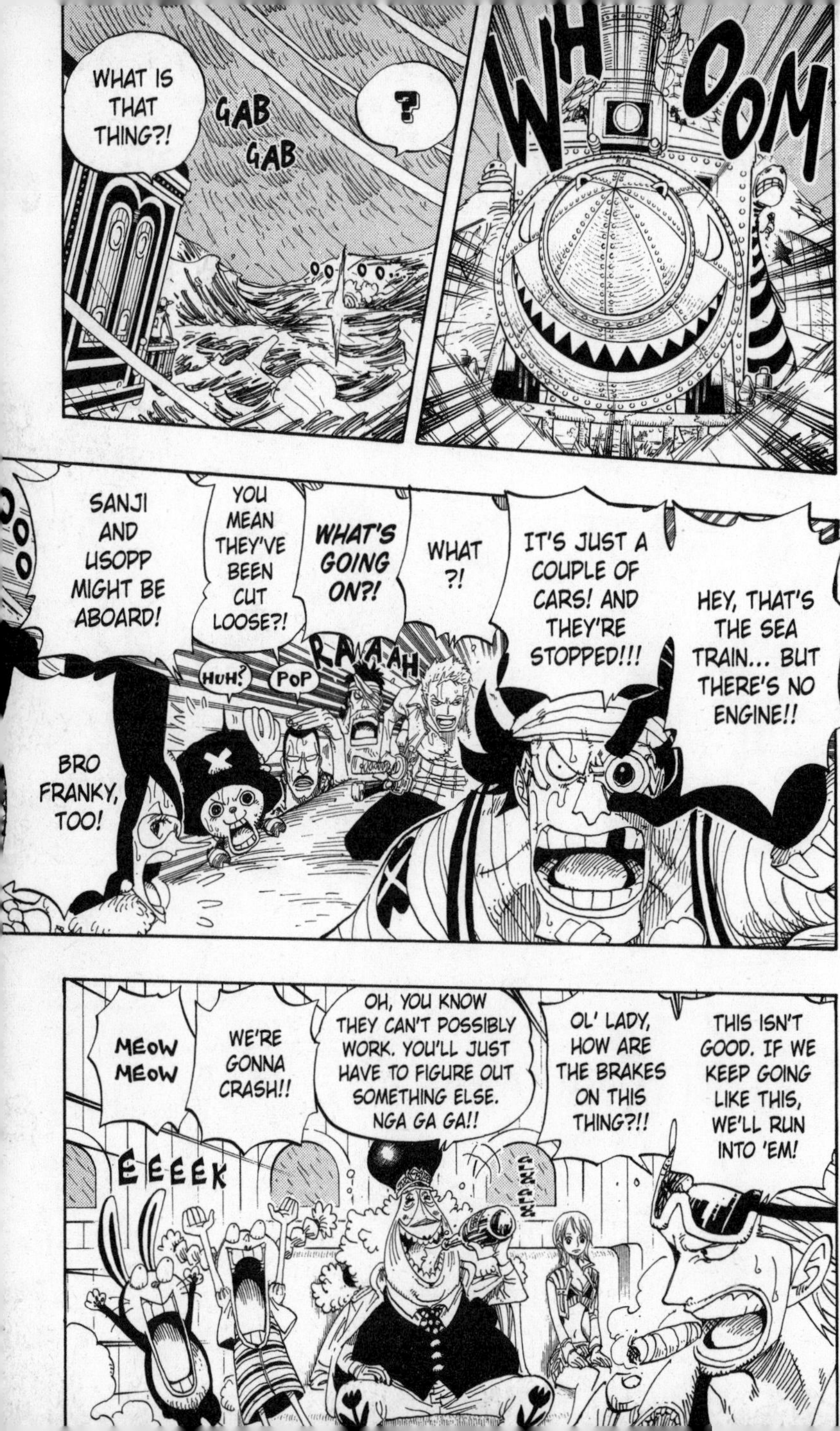
WHOOM
?
GAB GAB
WHAT IS THAT THING?!
HEY, THAT'S THE SEA TRAIN... BUT THERE'S NO ENGINE!!
IT'S JUST A COUPLE OF CARS! AND THEY'RE STOPPED!!!
WHAT ?!
RAAAAH
WHAT'S GOING ON?!
POP
YOU MEAN THEY'VE BEEN CUT LOOSE?!
HUH?
SANJI AND USOPP MIGHT BE ABOARD!
BRO FRANKY, TOO!
THIS ISN'T GOOD. IF WE KEEP GOING LIKE THIS, WE'LL RUN INTO 'EM!
OL' LADY, HOW ARE THE BRAKES ON THIS THING?!!
OH, YOU KNOW THEY CAN'T POSSIBLY WORK. YOU'LL JUST HAVE TO FIGURE OUT SOMETHING ELSE. NGA GA GA!!
WE'RE GONNA CRASH!!
MEOW MEOW
EEEEK

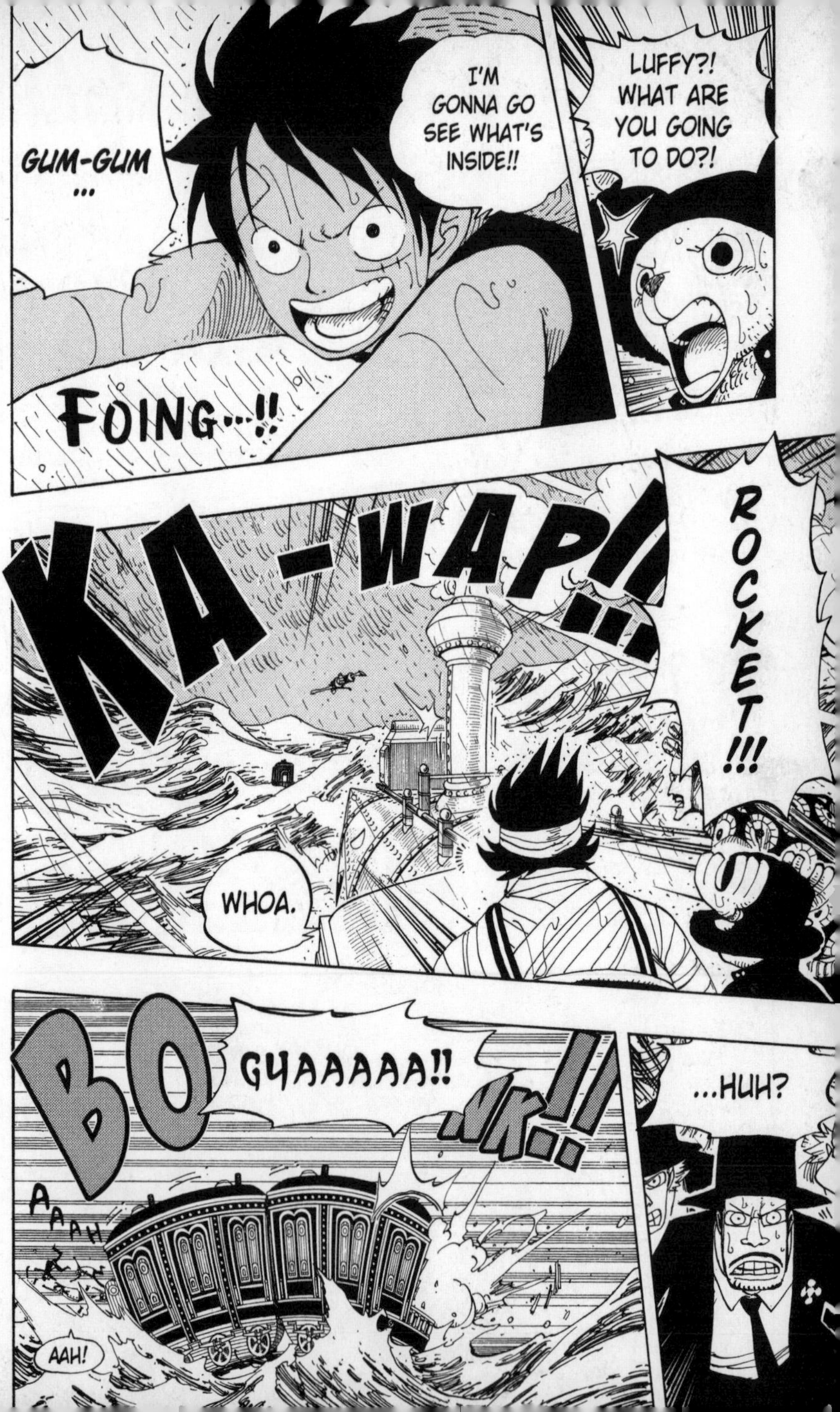

LUFFY?! WHAT ARE YOU GOING TO DO?!
I'M GONNA GO SEE WHAT'S INSIDE!!
GUM-GUM ...
FOING...!!
ROCKET!!!
KA-WAP!!!
WHOA.
...HUH?
BO
GUAAAAA!!
NK!!!
AAAH
AAH!

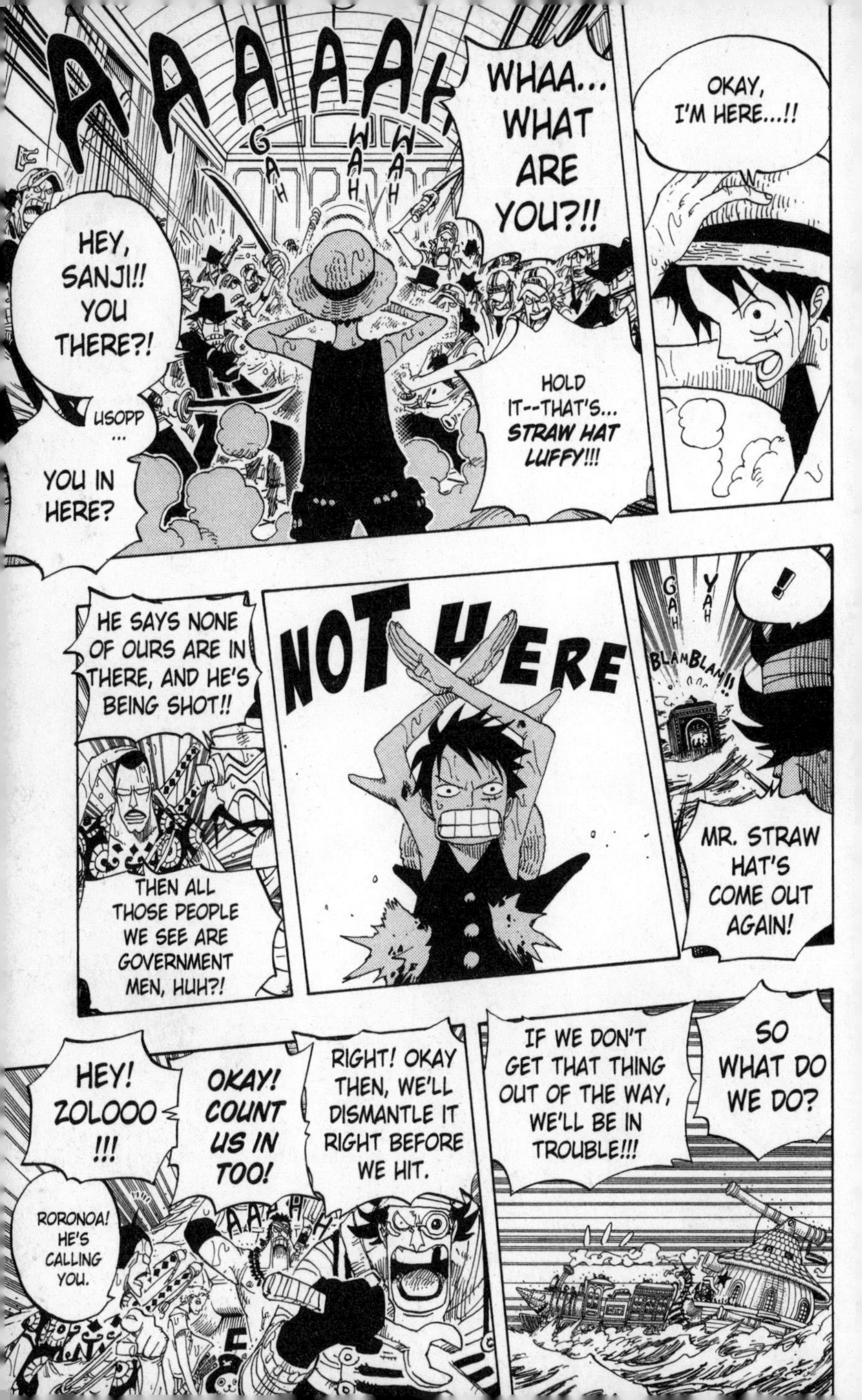
OKAY, I'M HERE...!!
WHAA... WHAT ARE YOU?!!
AAAAAH
GAH
WAH
WAH
HEY, SANJI!! YOU THERE?!
HOLD IT--THAT'S... STRAW HAT LUFFY!!!
USOPP ...
YOU IN HERE?
!
GAH
YAH
BLAMBLAM!!
MR. STRAW HAT'S COME OUT AGAIN!
NOT HERE
HE SAYS NONE OF OURS ARE IN THERE, AND HE'S BEING SHOT!!
THEN ALL THOSE PEOPLE WE SEE ARE GOVERNMENT MEN, HUH?!
SO WHAT DO WE DO?
IF WE DON'T GET THAT THING OUT OF THE WAY, WE'LL BE IN TROUBLE!!!
RIGHT! OKAY THEN, WE'LL DISMANTLE IT RIGHT BEFORE WE HIT.
OKAY! COUNT US IN TOO!
HEY! ZOLOOO!!!
RORONOA! HE'S CALLING YOU.

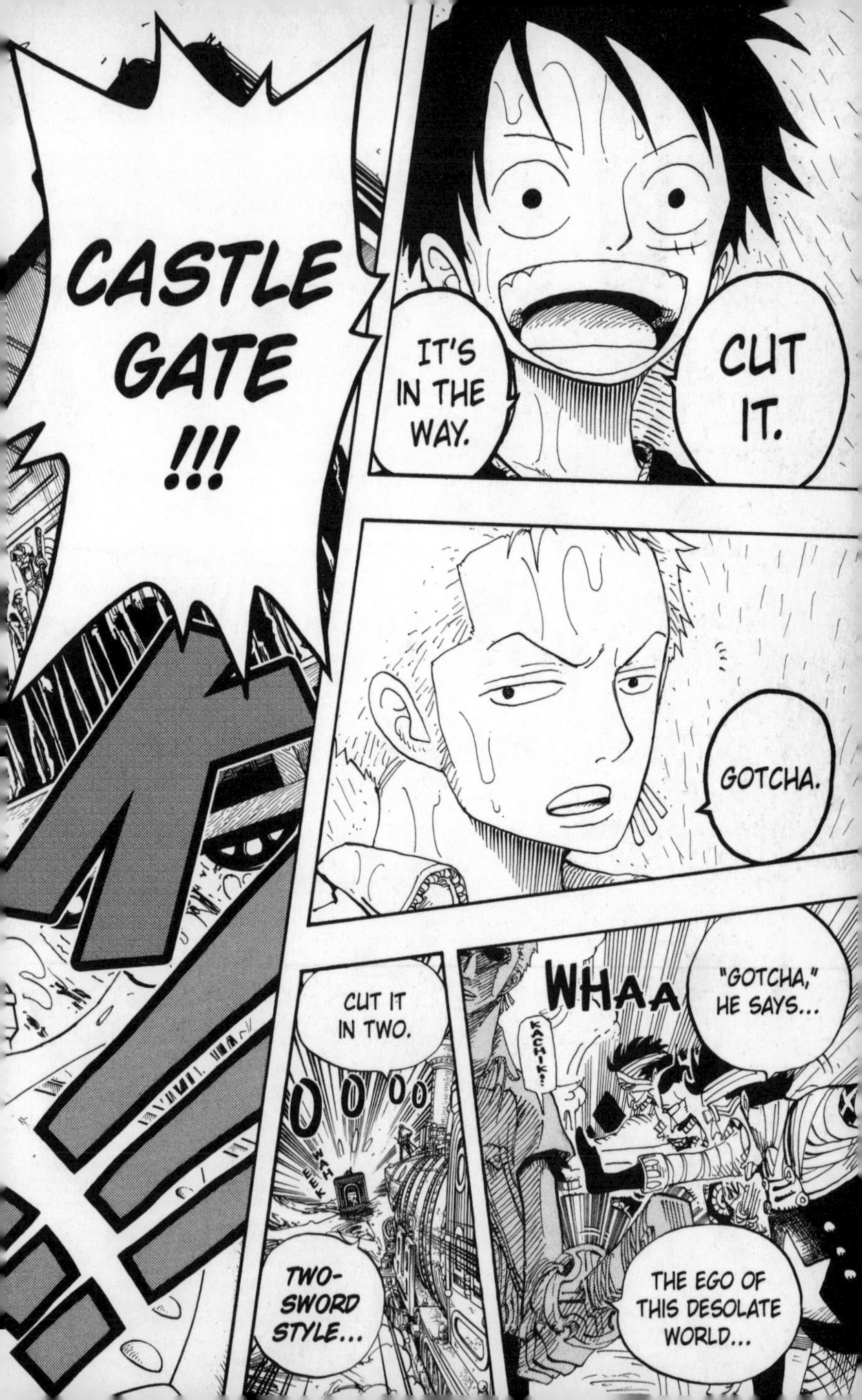
CUT IT.
IT'S IN THE WAY.
GOTCHA.
"GOTCHA," HE SAYS...
WHAA
KACHIK!
THE EGO OF THIS DESOLATE WORLD...
CUT IT IN TWO.
TWO-SWORD STYLE...
CASTLE GATE !!!

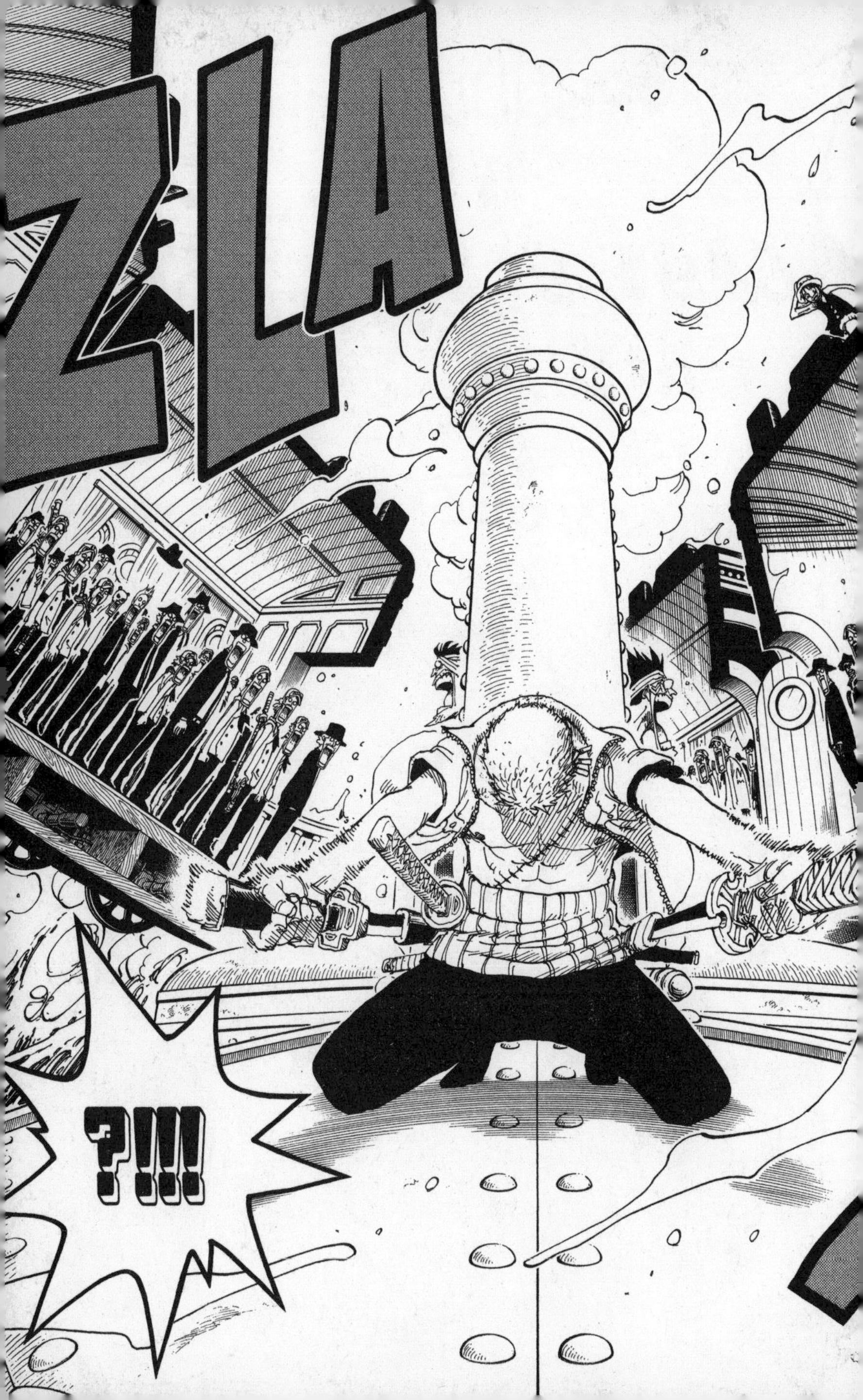

ZLA
?!!!

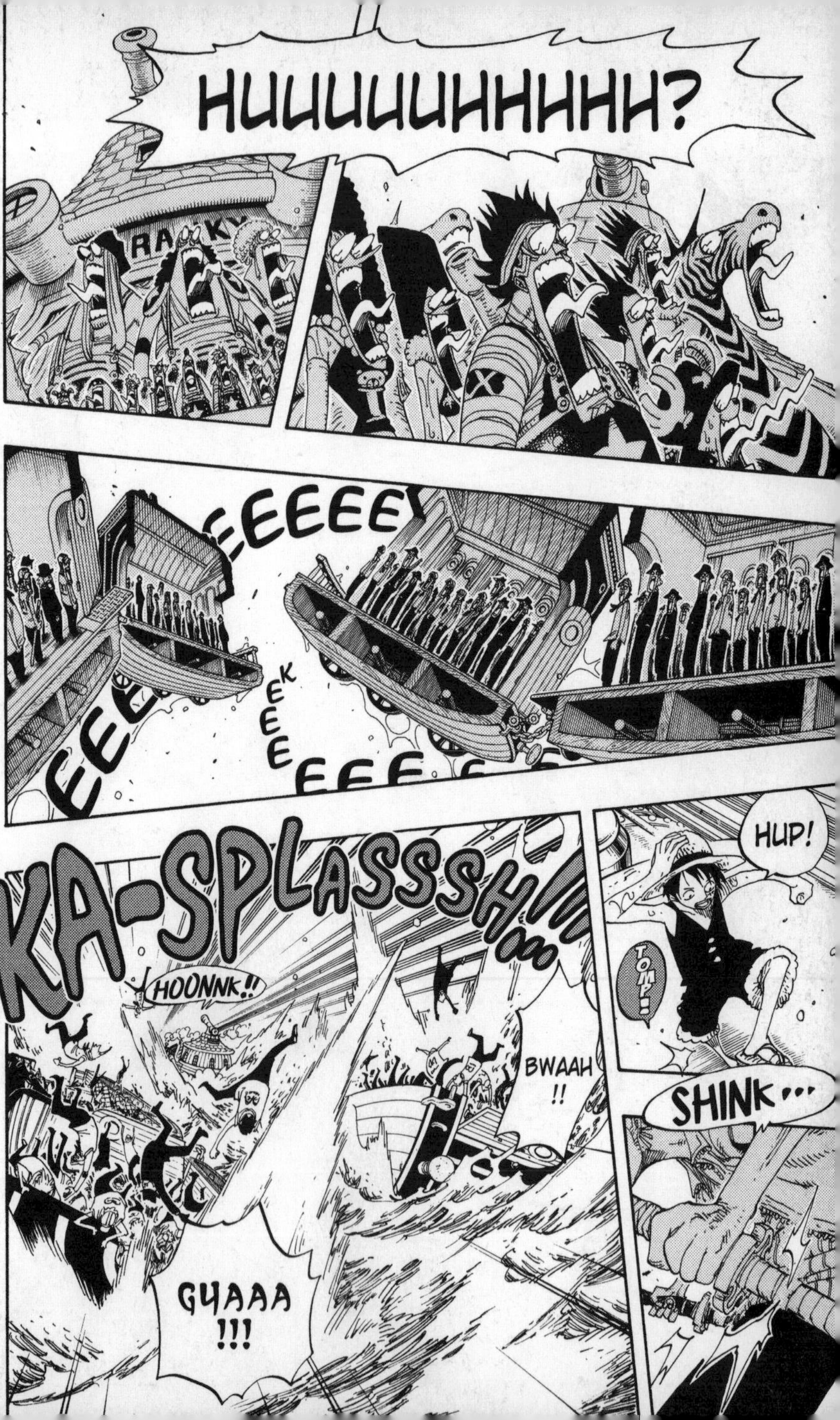
HUUUUUUHHHHH?
EEEEE
EEEK
HUP!
TOMP!
SHINK...
KA-SPLASSSH!!!
HOONNK!!
BWAAH!!
GUAAA!!!

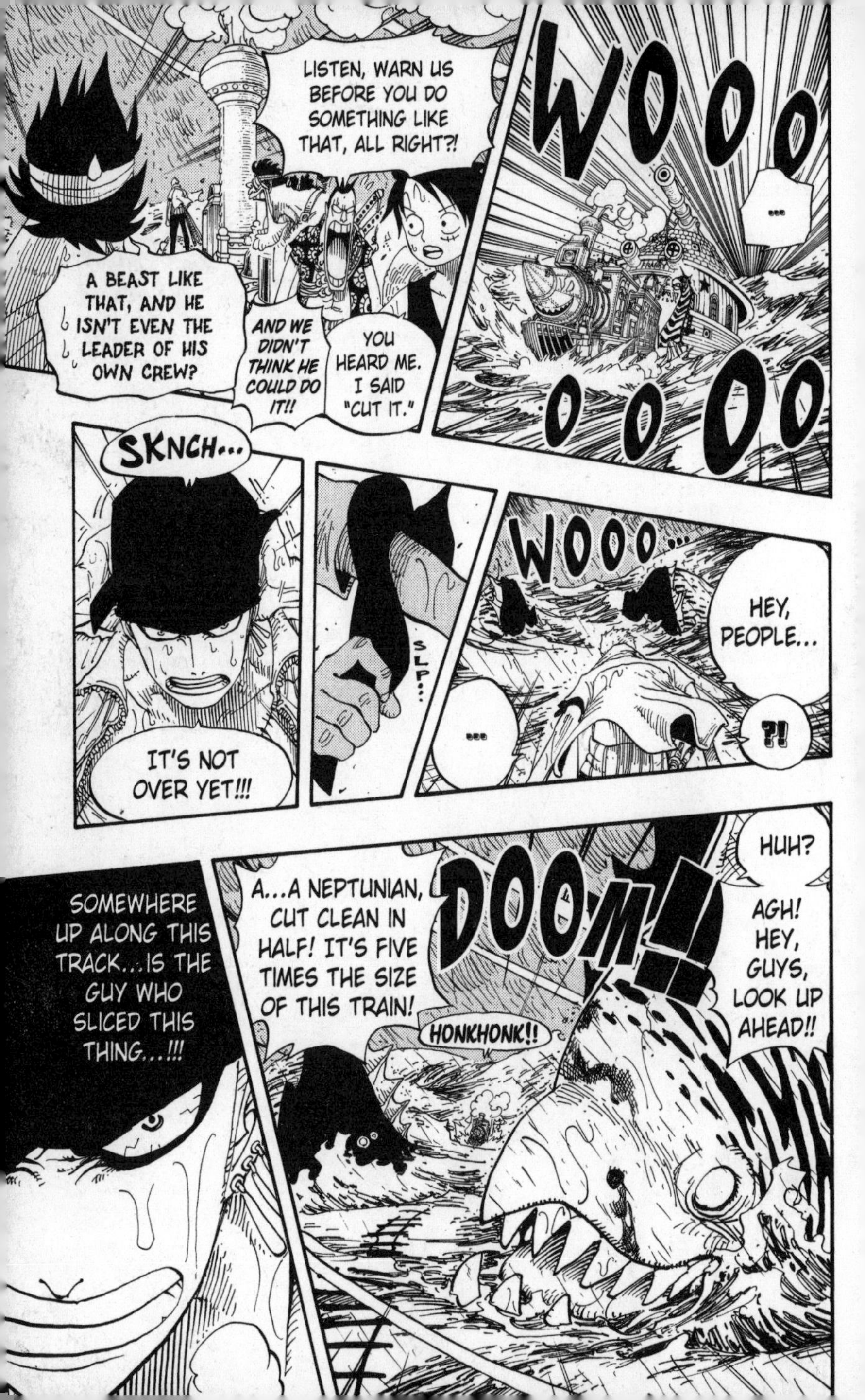
WOOOOOOOO
...
LISTEN, WARN US BEFORE YOU DO SOMETHING LIKE THAT, ALL RIGHT?!
YOU HEARD ME. I SAID "CUT IT."
AND WE DIDN'T THINK HE COULD DO IT!!
A BEAST LIKE THAT, AND HE ISN'T EVEN THE LEADER OF HIS OWN CREW?
WOOO...
HEY, PEOPLE...
?!
...
SLP...
SKNCH...
IT'S NOT OVER YET!!!
HUH?
AGH! HEY, GUYS, LOOK UP AHEAD!!
DOOM!!
A...A NEPTUNIAN, CUT CLEAN IN HALF! IT'S FIVE TIMES THE SIZE OF THIS TRAIN!
HONKHONK!!
SOMEWHERE UP ALONG THIS TRACK...IS THE GUY WHO SLICED THIS THING...!!!

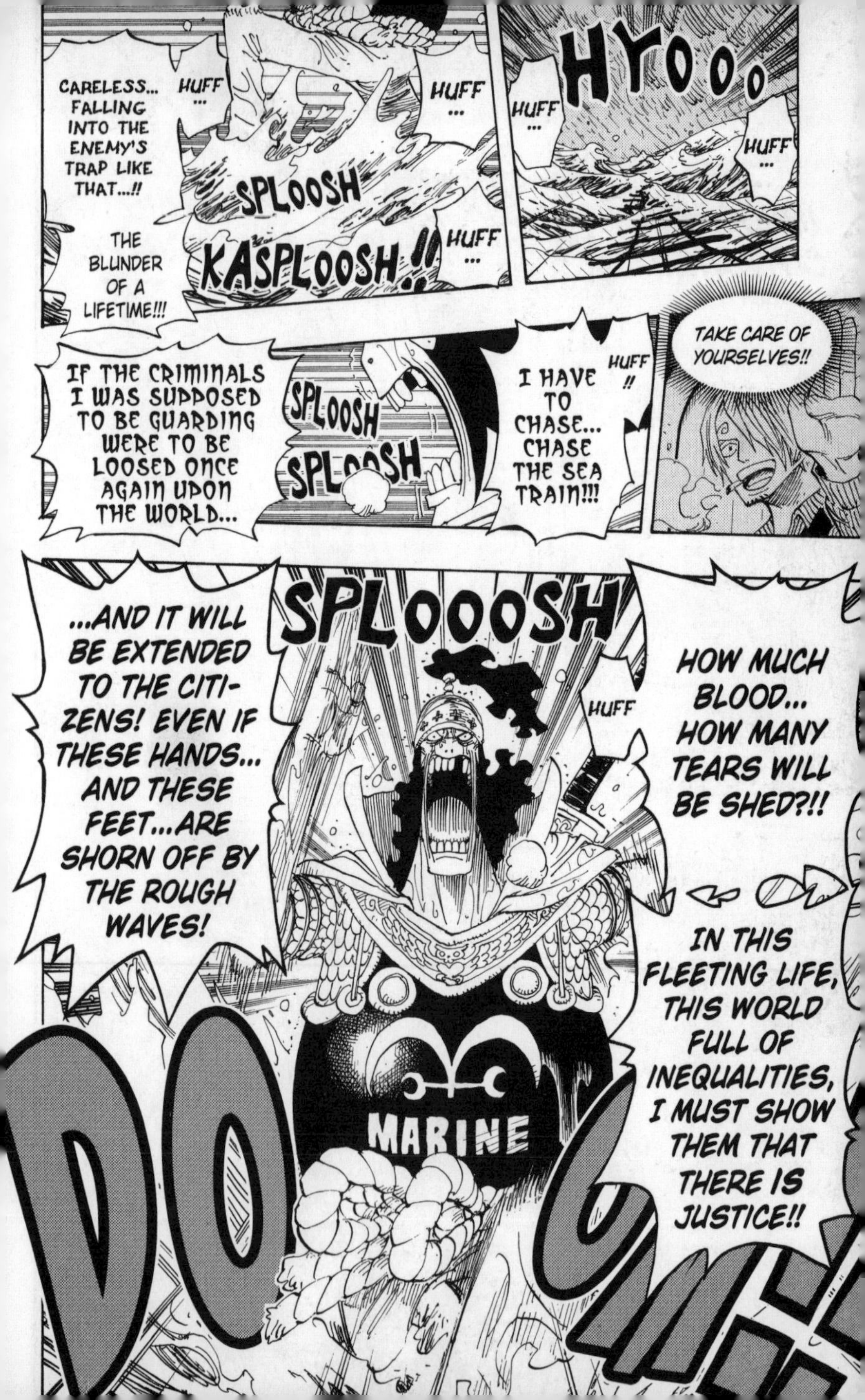
HYOOOO
HUFF...
HUFF...
HUFF...
HUFF...
HUFF...
CARELESS... FALLING INTO THE ENEMY'S TRAP LIKE THAT...!!
SPLOOSH
KASPLOOSH!!
HUFF...
THE BLUNDER OF A LIFETIME!!!
TAKE CARE OF YOURSELVES!!
HUFF!!
I HAVE TO CHASE... CHASE THE SEA TRAIN!!!
SPLOOSH
SPLOOSH
IF THE CRIMINALS I WAS SUPPOSED TO BE GUARDING WERE TO BE LOOSED ONCE AGAIN UPON THE WORLD...
SPLOOOSH
HOW MUCH BLOOD... HOW MANY TEARS WILL BE SHED?!!
HUFF
...AND IT WILL BE EXTENDED TO THE CITI- ZENS! EVEN IF THESE HANDS... AND THESE FEET...ARE SHORN OFF BY THE ROUGH WAVES!
IN THIS FLEETING LIFE, THIS WORLD FULL OF INEQUALITIES, I MUST SHOW THEM THAT THERE IS JUSTICE!!
MARINE
DO

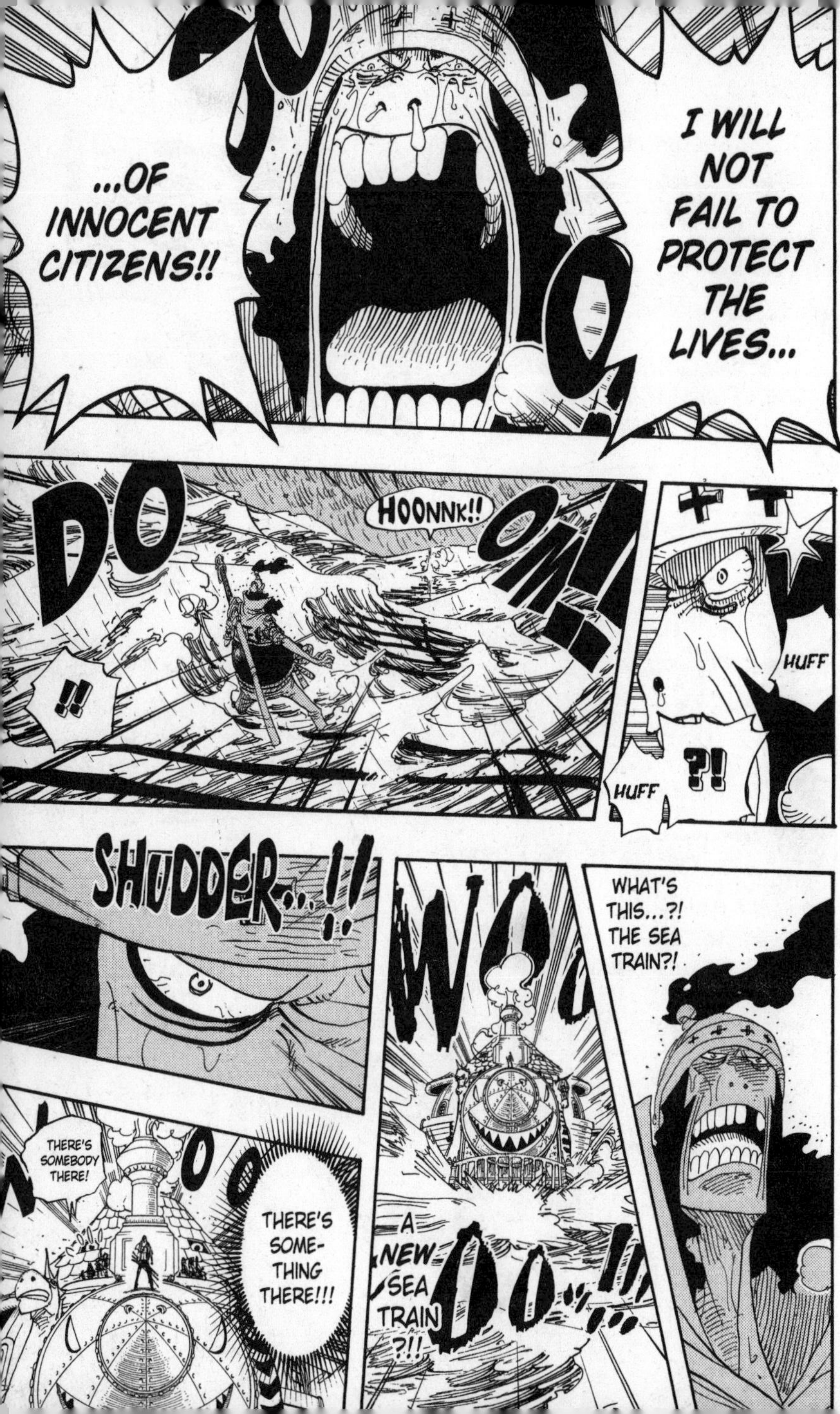
I WILL NOT FAIL TO PROTECT THE LIVES...
...OF INNOCENT CITIZENS!!
HUFF
?!
HUFF
DOON!!
HOONNK!!
!!
WHAT'S THIS...?! THE SEA TRAIN?!
A NEW SEA TRAIN?!!
SHUDDER...!!
THERE'S SOMEBODY THERE!
THERE'S SOME-THING THERE!!!

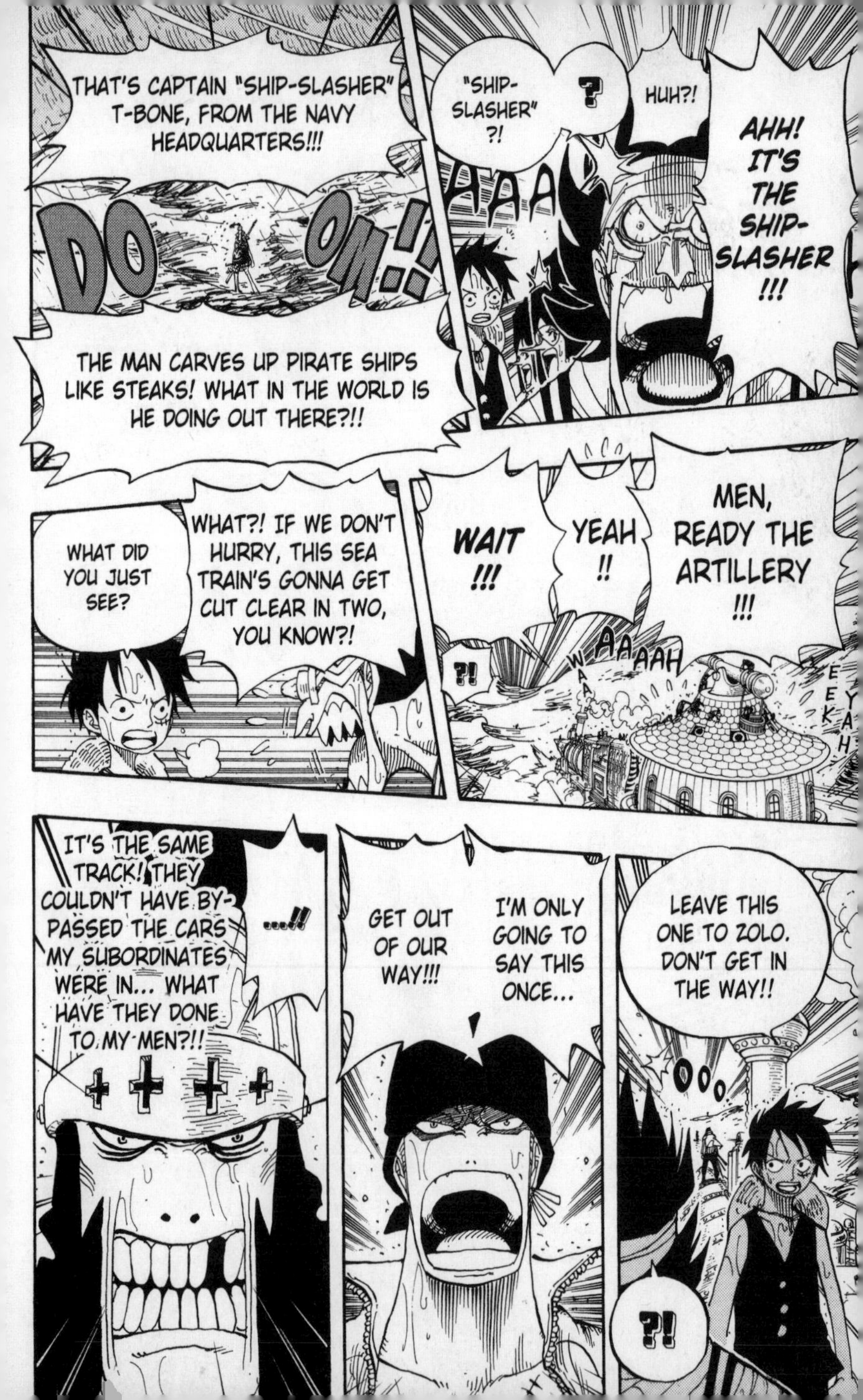
AHH! IT'S THE SHIP-SLASHER !!!
HUH?!
?
"SHIP-SLASHER" ?!
AAA
THAT'S CAPTAIN "SHIP-SLASHER" T-BONE, FROM THE NAVY HEADQUARTERS!!!
DOOM..!!
THE MAN CARVES UP PIRATE SHIPS LIKE STEAKS! WHAT IN THE WORLD IS HE DOING OUT THERE?!!
MEN, READY THE ARTILLERY !!!
YEAH !!
WAIT !!!
WAAAAAAH
EEKYAH
?!
WHAT?! IF WE DON'T HURRY, THIS SEA TRAIN'S GONNA GET CUT CLEAR IN TWO, YOU KNOW?!
WHAT DID YOU JUST SEE?
LEAVE THIS ONE TO ZOLO. DON'T GET IN THE WAY!!
?!
I'M ONLY GOING TO SAY THIS ONCE...
GET OUT OF OUR WAY!!!
...!!
IT'S THE SAME TRACK! THEY COULDN'T HAVE BY-PASSED THE CARS MY SUBORDINATES WERE IN... WHAT HAVE THEY DONE TO MY MEN?!!

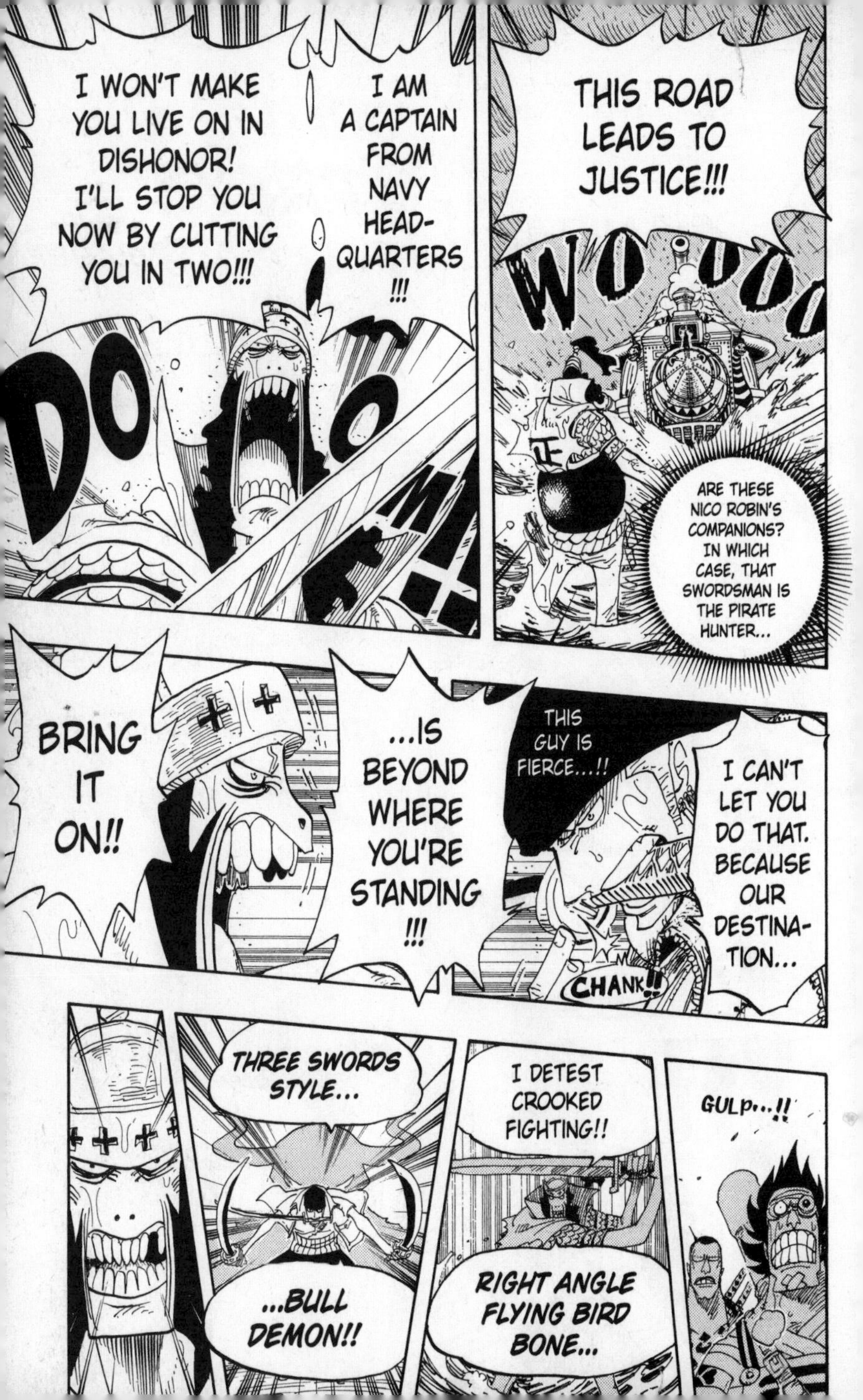
THIS ROAD LEADS TO JUSTICE!!!
WOOOO
ARE THESE NICO ROBIN'S COMPANIONS? IN WHICH CASE, THAT SWORDSMAN IS THE PIRATE HUNTER...
I AM A CAPTAIN FROM NAVY HEAD-QUARTERS!!!
I WON'T MAKE YOU LIVE ON IN DISHONOR! I'LL STOP YOU NOW BY CUTTING YOU IN TWO!!!
DOOM
I CAN'T LET YOU DO THAT. BECAUSE OUR DESTINA-TION...
THIS GUY IS FIERCE...!!
CHANK!!
...IS BEYOND WHERE YOU'RE STANDING!!!
BRING IT ON!!
GULP...!!
I DETEST CROOKED FIGHTING!!
RIGHT ANGLE FLYING BIRD BONE...
THREE SWORDS STYLE...
...BULL DEMON!!

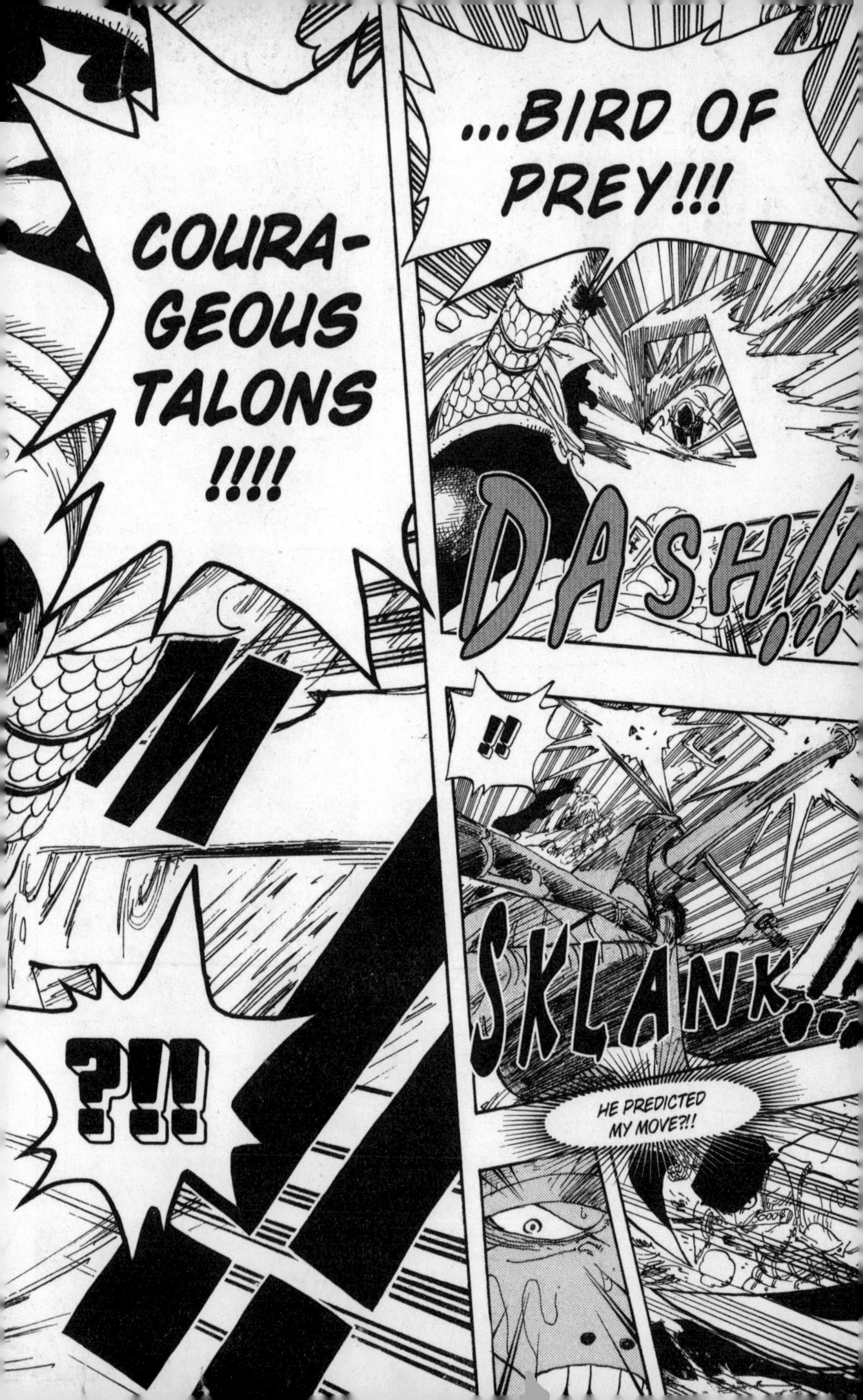

...BIRD OF PREY!!!
DASH!!
!!
SKLANK!!
HE PREDICTED MY MOVE?!!
COURA-GEOUS TALONS !!!!
?!!

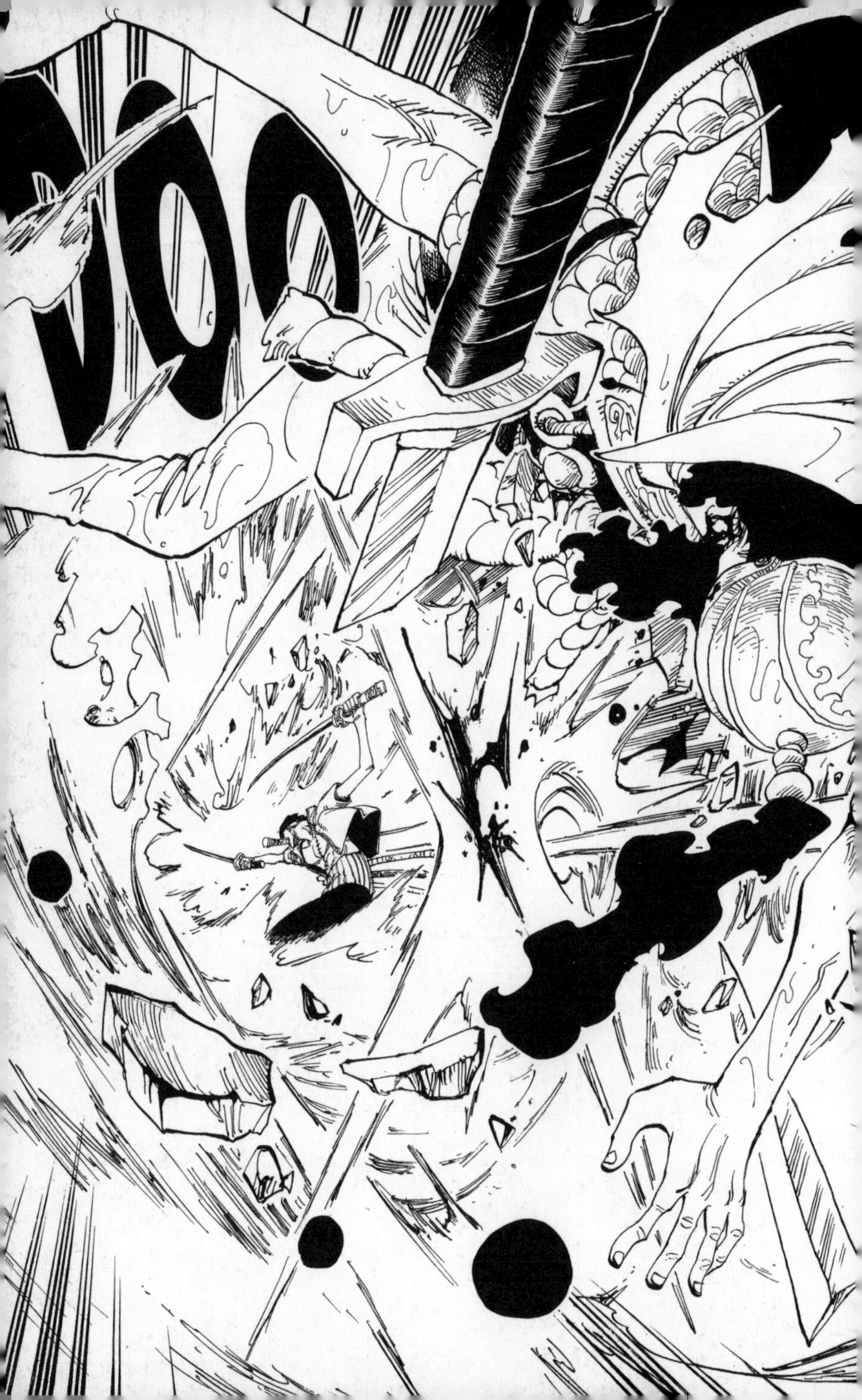

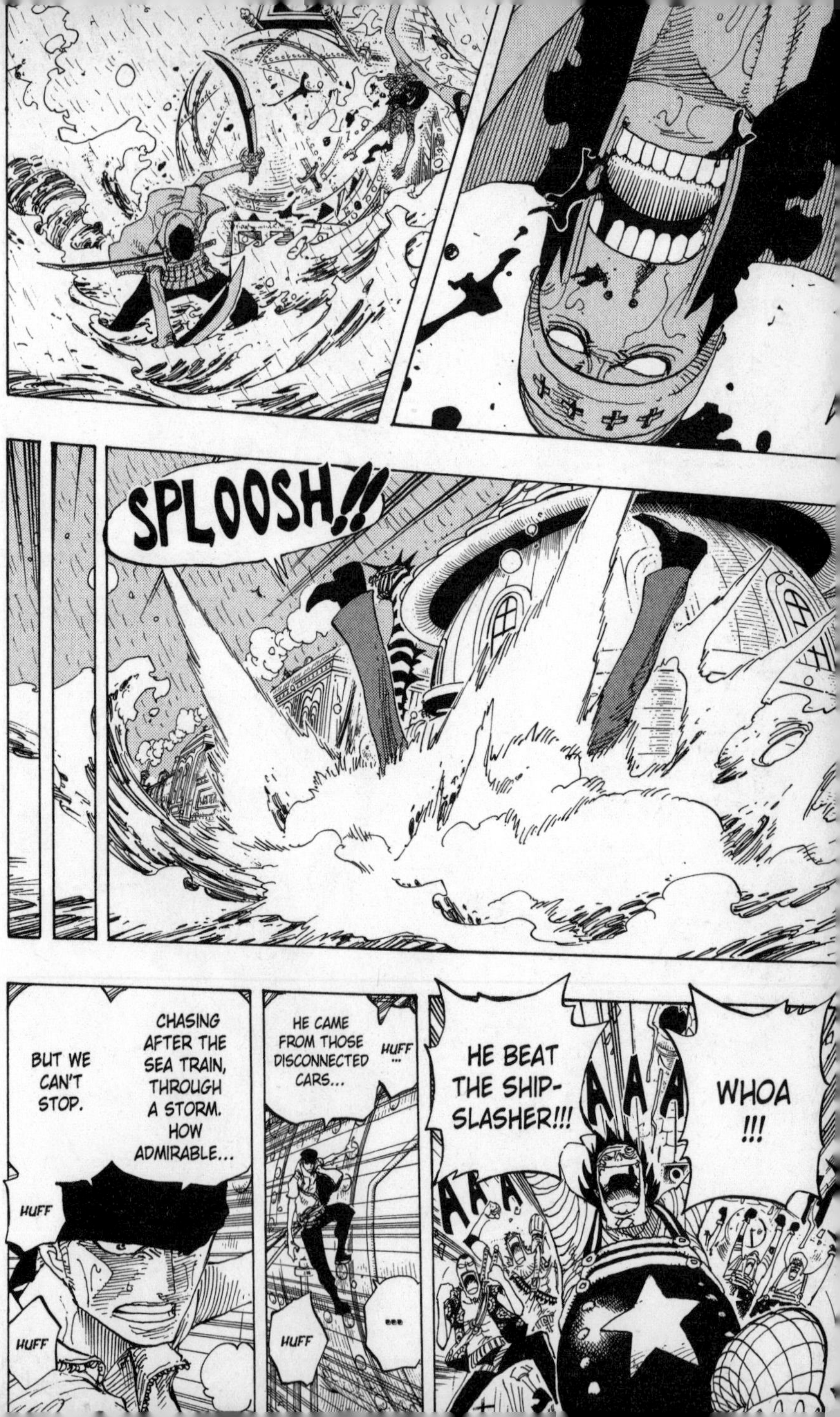
SPLOOSH!!
WHOA !!!
AAA
HE BEAT THE SHIP-SLASHER!!!
AA
HUFF ...
HE CAME FROM THOSE DISCONNECTED CARS...
...
HUFF
CHASING AFTER THE SEA TRAIN, THROUGH A STORM. HOW ADMIRABLE...
BUT WE CAN'T STOP.
HUFF
HUFF

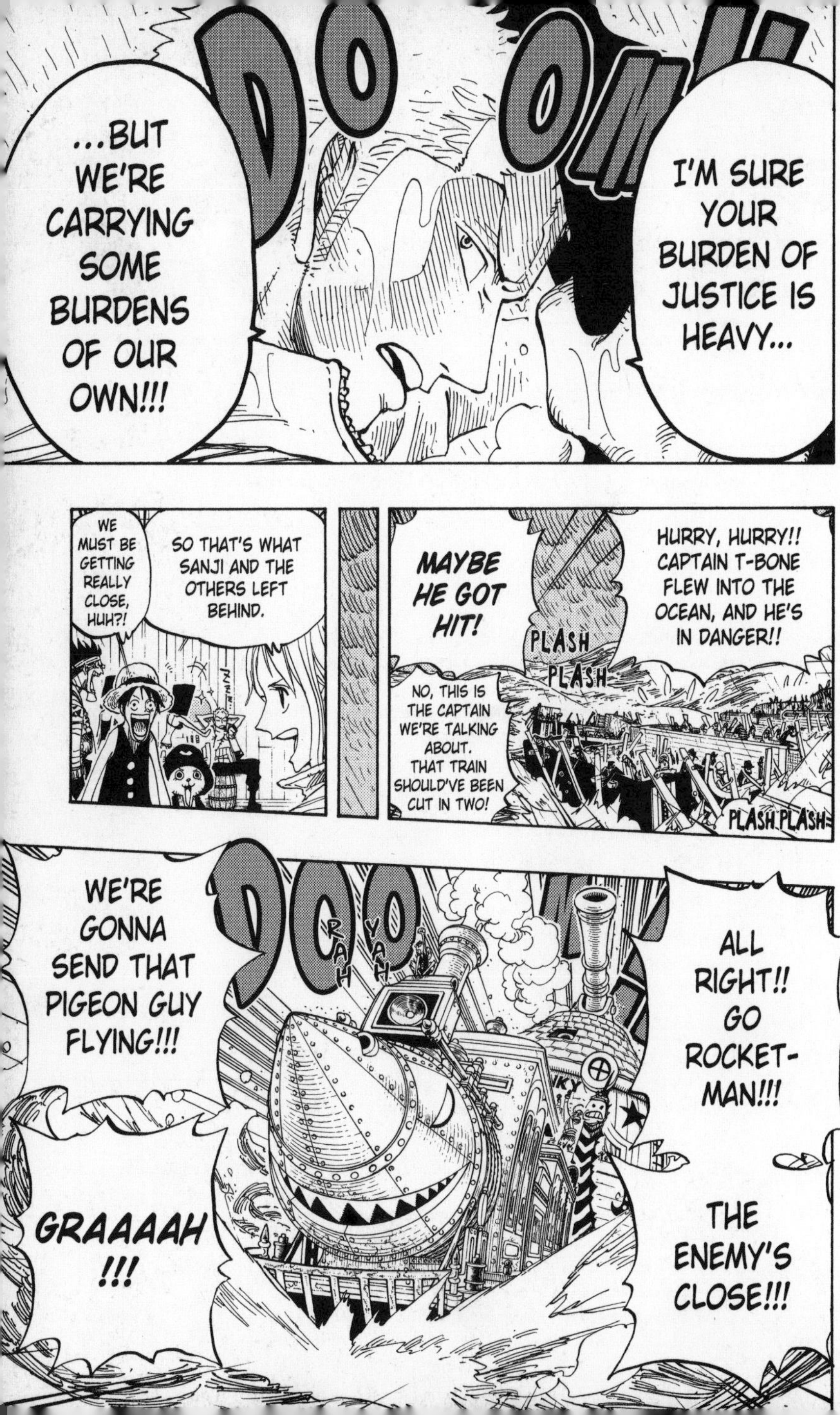
I'M SURE YOUR BURDEN OF JUSTICE IS HEAVY...
DOOM
...BUT WE'RE CARRYING SOME BURDENS OF OUR OWN!!!
HURRY, HURRY!! CAPTAIN T-BONE FLEW INTO THE OCEAN, AND HE'S IN DANGER!!
MAYBE HE GOT HIT!
PLASH
PLASH
NO, THIS IS THE CAPTAIN WE'RE TALKING ABOUT. THAT TRAIN SHOULD'VE BEEN CUT IN TWO!
PLASH PLASH
SO THAT'S WHAT SANJI AND THE OTHERS LEFT BEHIND.
WE MUST BE GETTING REALLY CLOSE, HUH?!
ALL RIGHT!! GO ROCKET-MAN!!!
THE ENEMY'S CLOSE!!!
DOO
YAAH
RAAH
WE'RE GONNA SEND THAT PIGEON GUY FLYING!!!
GRAAAAH!!!

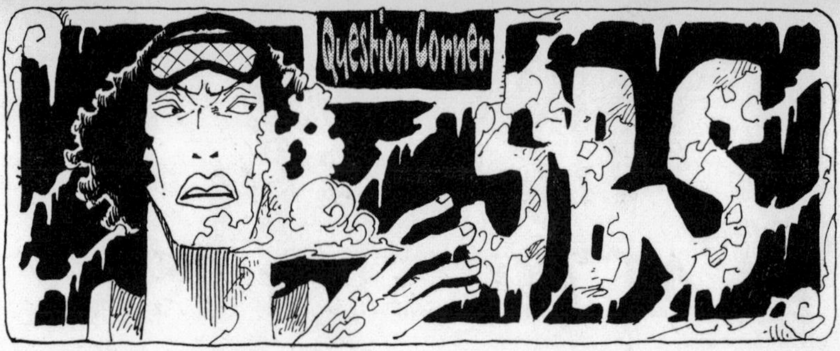
Question Corner

Q: Pass the soy sauce, will you?! --Friend of "Pass the Salt, Will You?!"

A: Oh, sure. Here you go.

Q: Please tell me what Michael and Hoichael from the back alleys look like. It's been bugging me so much I can't get up in the mornings.

--Sanji-boy LOVE

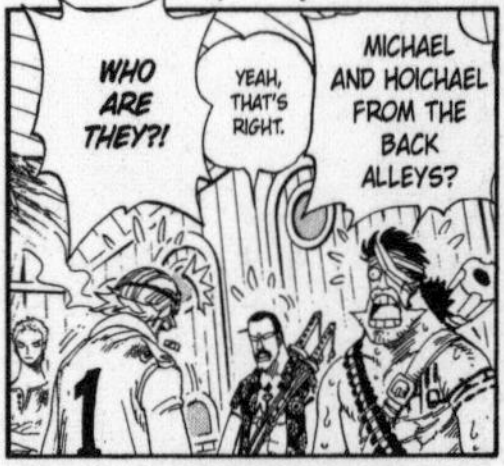
MICHAEL AND HOICHAEL FROM THE BACK ALLEYS?
YEAH, THAT'S RIGHT.
WHO ARE THEY?!

A: So people really did wonder about these guys. I got a lot of questions like this. Well, sure, they're so bad Lulu and Tilestone were convinced they were the assassins who went after Iceberg. Michael and Hoichael: Prepare yourselves, then take a look at these two delinquents, affiliated with a certain gang!!

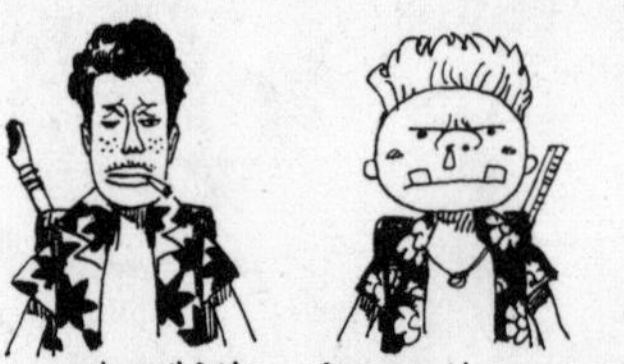

Water Seven Back Alley Elementary School, Sixth Grade, Group 5 (age 12). Left: Michael Right: Hoichael In six years, they've been sent to the counselor 620 times. They've broken a total of 997 school windows. Their Record: Includes reckless bull riding, shoplifting from the supermarket, etc. Their Motto: Mmm, Super!! Their Idol: Franky (they respect Paulie too).

Q: Oda Sensei, hello! I found another item in your bird names series!! It's Mozu, right?!

--Mai

P.S. Twice in a row I meant to write "strange" (変) and twice in a row I ended up writing "love" (恋) instead. Who do you think we can blame for that?

A: First off, you wrote "love" because you haven't practiced your kanji enough! (Being serious here.) And "Mozu" is definitely the name of a bird, but "Kiwi" is also a bird. There's a fruit that looks like the kiwi bird, called a kiwi fruit.

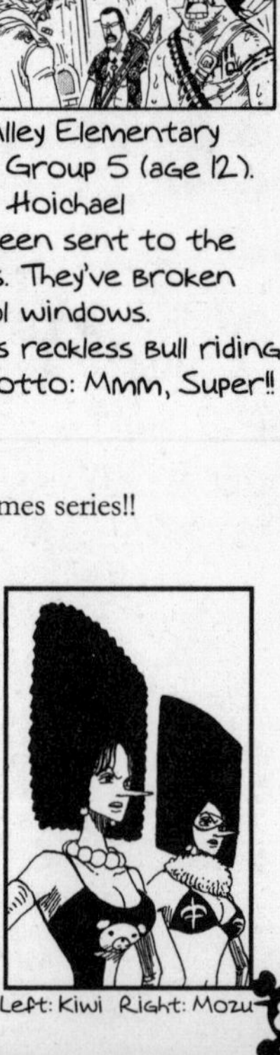

Left: Kiwi Right: Mozu

Chapter 372:
PLASTIC SURGERY

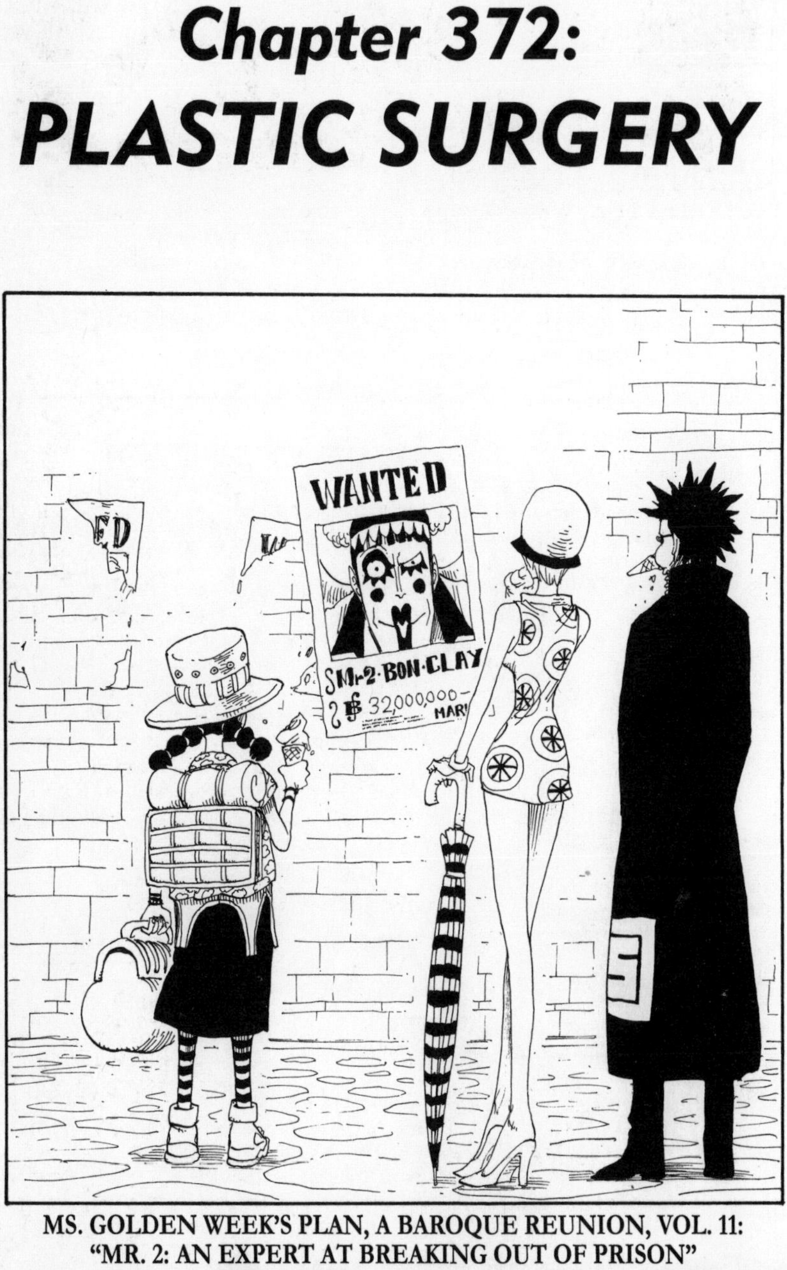
WANTED
Mr.2·BON·CLAY
32,000,000-

MS. GOLDEN WEEK'S PLAN, A BAROQUE REUNION, VOL. 11:
"MR. 2: AN EXPERT AT BREAKING OUT OF PRISON"

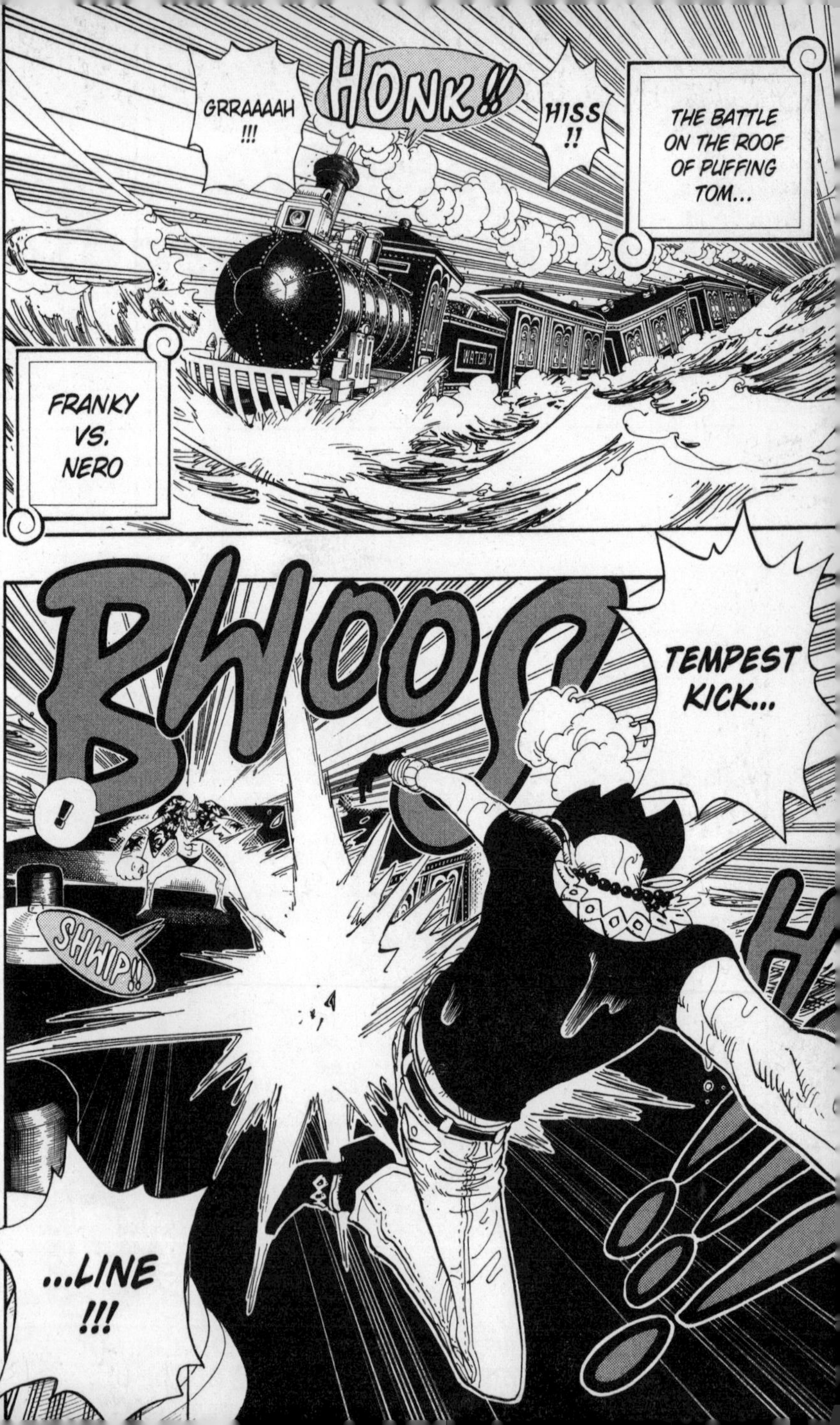
THE BATTLE ON THE ROOF OF PUFFING TOM...
HISS !!
HONK!!
GRRAAAAH !!!
WATER 7
FRANKY VS. NERO
BWOOS
TEMPEST KICK...
H
!
SHWIP!!
...LINE !!!

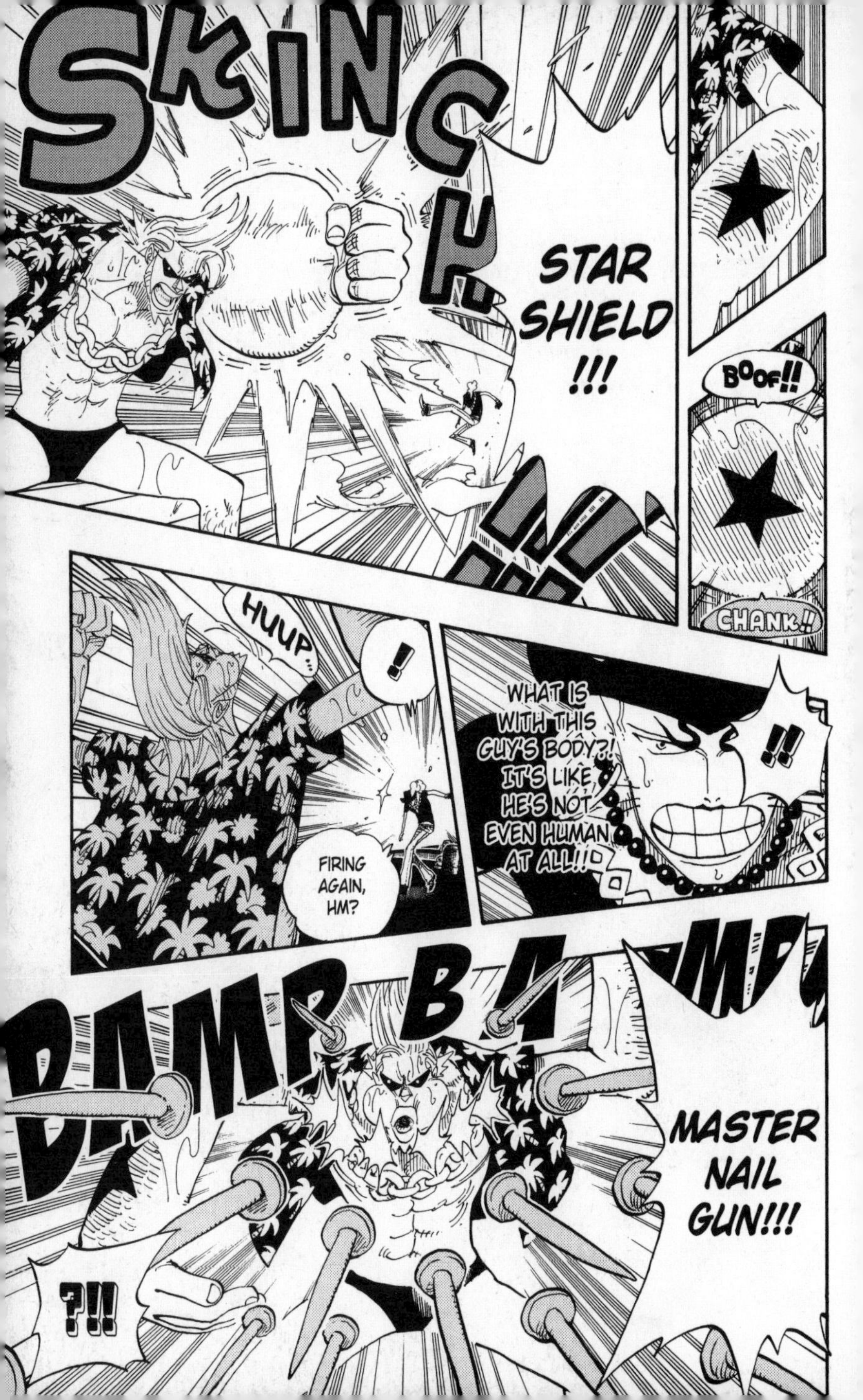
BOOF!!
CHANK!!
SKINCH
STAR SHIELD!!!
HUUP...
!
FIRING AGAIN, HM?
!!
WHAT IS WITH THIS GUY'S BODY?! IT'S LIKE HE'S NOT EVEN HUMAN AT ALL!!
BAMP BA BAMP
MASTER NAIL GUN!!!
?!!

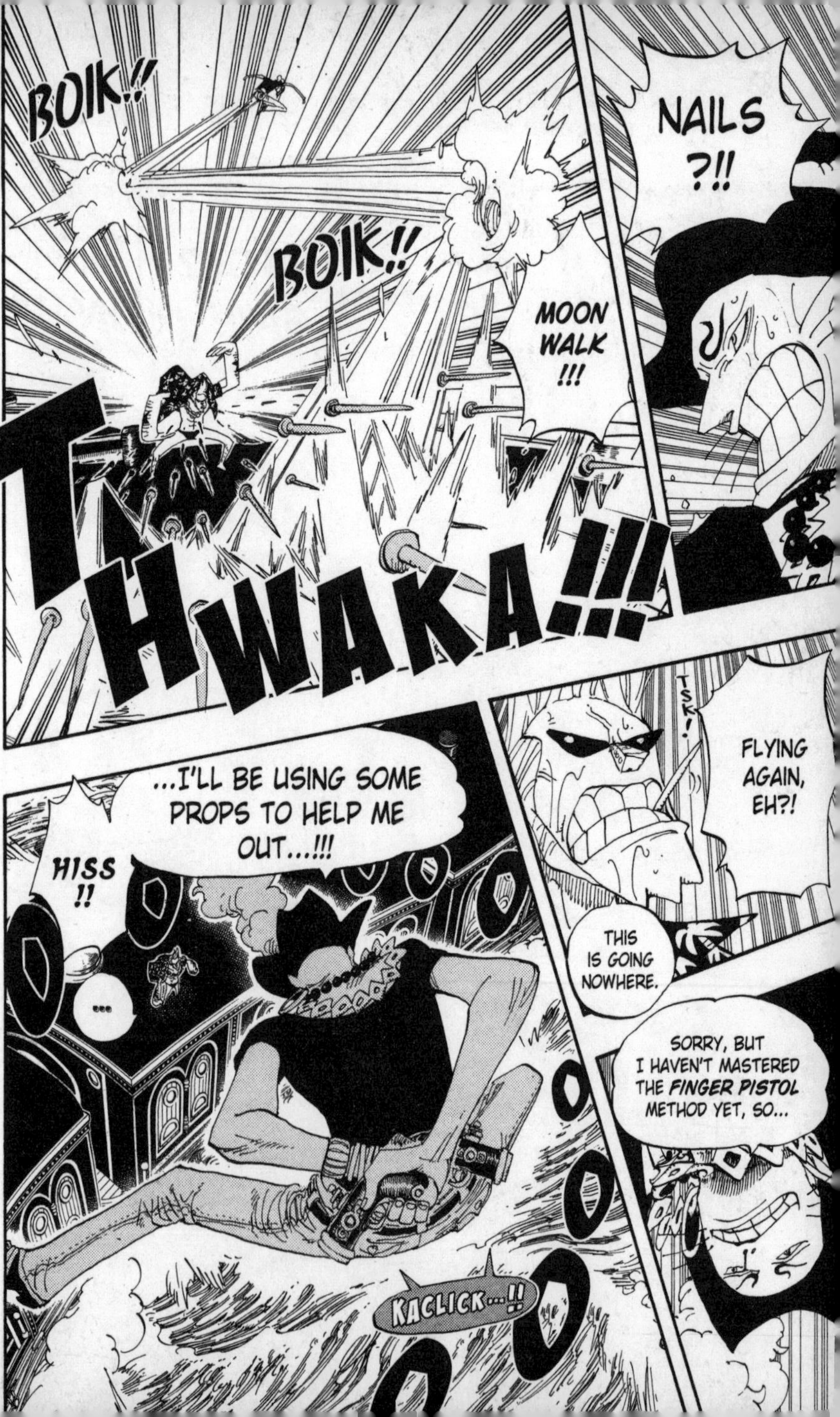
NAILS ?!!
BOIK!!
BOIK!!
MOON WALK !!!
THWAKA!!!
TSK!
FLYING AGAIN, EH?!
THIS IS GOING NOWHERE.
SORRY, BUT I HAVEN'T MASTERED THE *FINGER PISTOL* METHOD YET, SO...
...I'LL BE USING SOME PROPS TO HELP ME OUT...!!!
HISS !!
...
KACLICK...!!

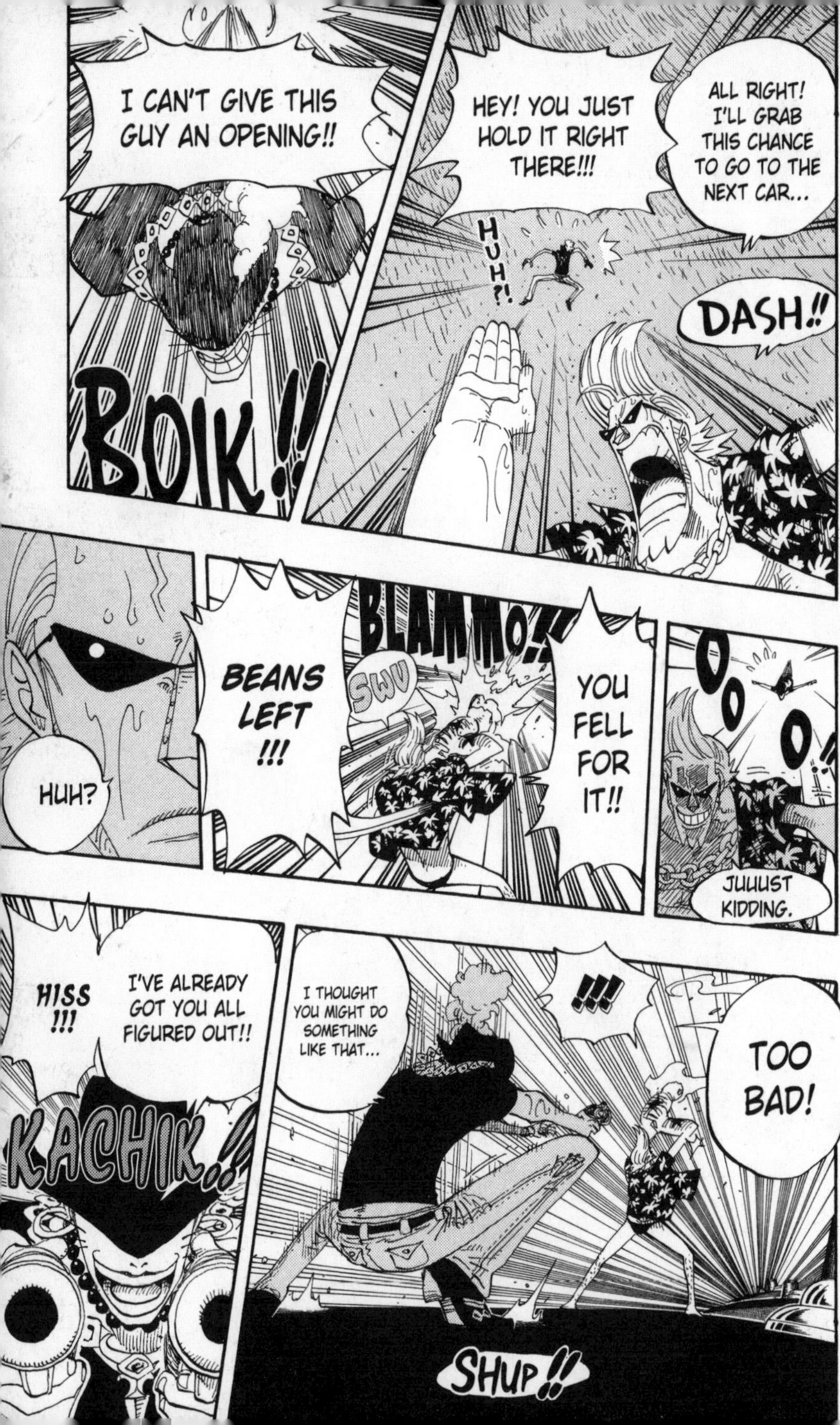
ALL RIGHT! I'LL GRAB THIS CHANCE TO GO TO THE NEXT CAR...
HEY! YOU JUST HOLD IT RIGHT THERE!!!
HUH?!
DASH!!
I CAN'T GIVE THIS GUY AN OPENING!!
BOIK!!
OOO!!
JUUUST KIDDING.
BLAMMO!!
YOU FELL FOR IT!!
SWV
BEANS LEFT!!!
HUH?
TOO BAD!
!!!
I THOUGHT YOU MIGHT DO SOMETHING LIKE THAT...
SHUP!!
I'VE ALREADY GOT YOU ALL FIGURED OUT!!
HISS!!!
KACHIK..!!

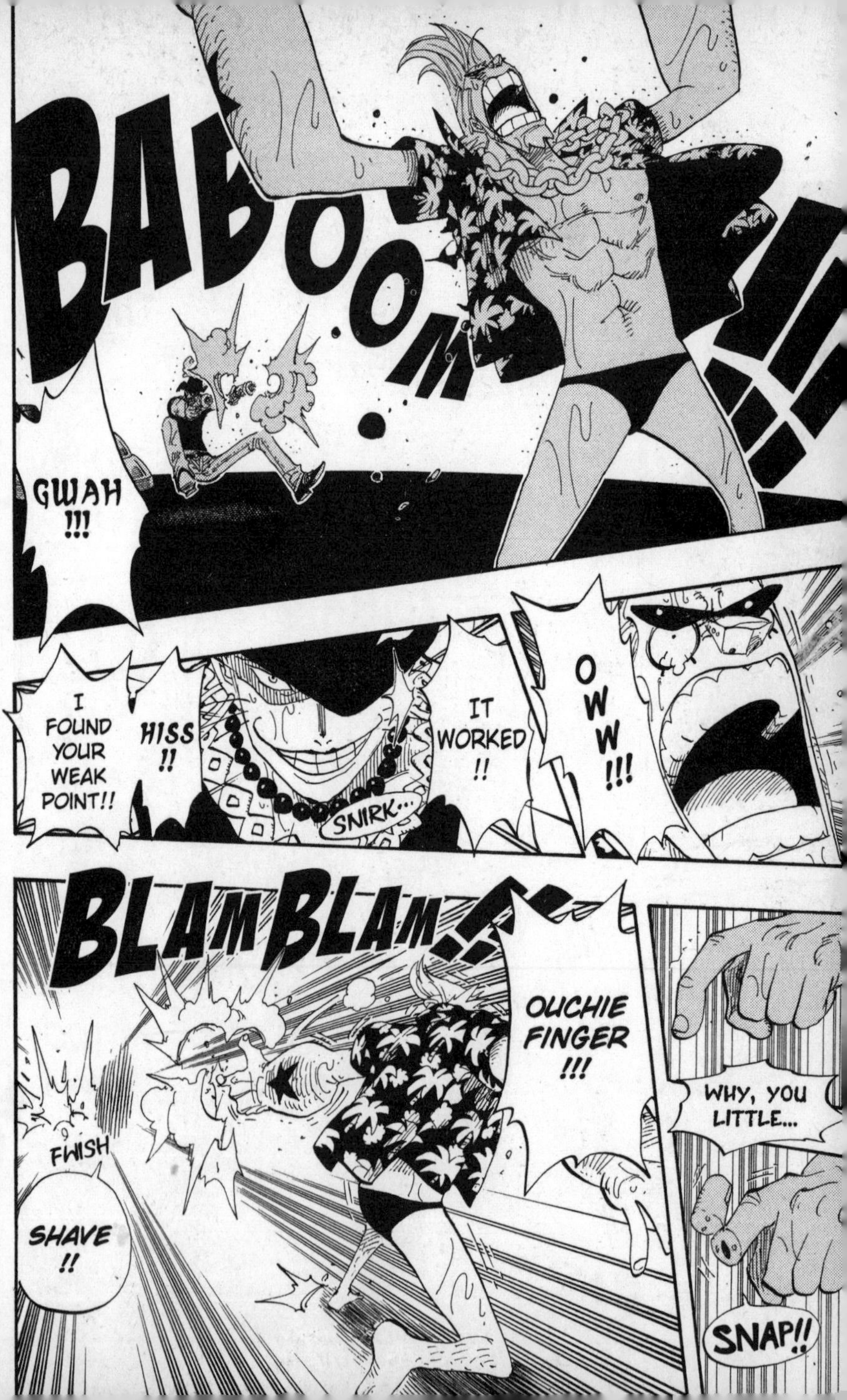
BABOOM!!!
GWAH!!!
OWW!!!
IT WORKED!!
HISS!!
I FOUND YOUR WEAK POINT!!
SNIRK...
WHY, YOU LITTLE...
SNAP!!
BLAM BLAM!!
OUCHIE FINGER!!!
FWISH
SHAVE!!

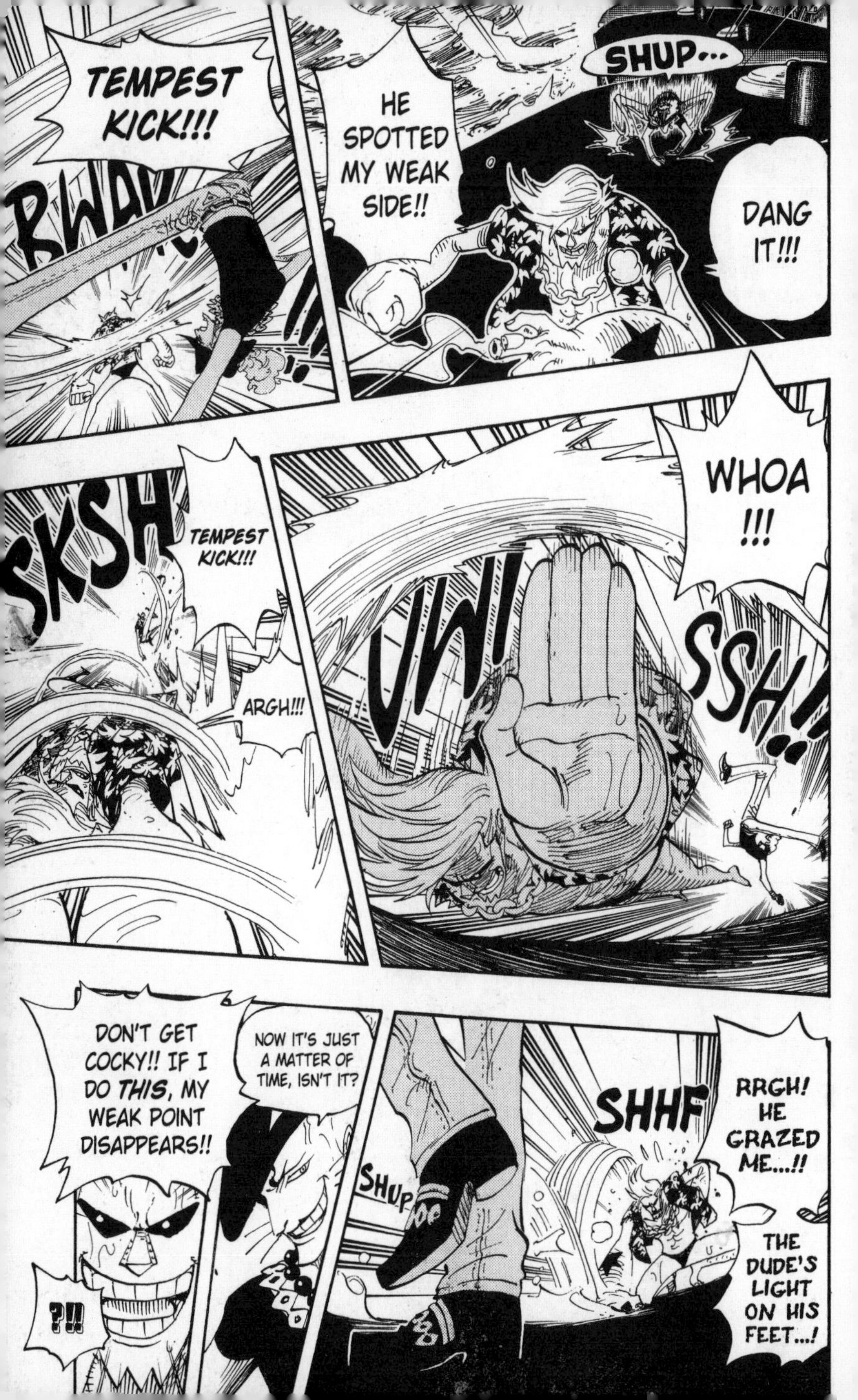
SHUP...
HE SPOTTED MY WEAK SIDE!!
DANG IT!!!
TEMPEST KICK!!!
WHOA !!!
SSH!!
SKSH
TEMPEST KICK!!!
ARGH!!!
RRGH! HE GRAZED ME...!!
SHHF
THE DUDE'S LIGHT ON HIS FEET...!
SHUP
NOW IT'S JUST A MATTER OF TIME, ISN'T IT?
DON'T GET COCKY!! IF I DO *THIS*, MY WEAK POINT DISAPPEARS!!
?!!

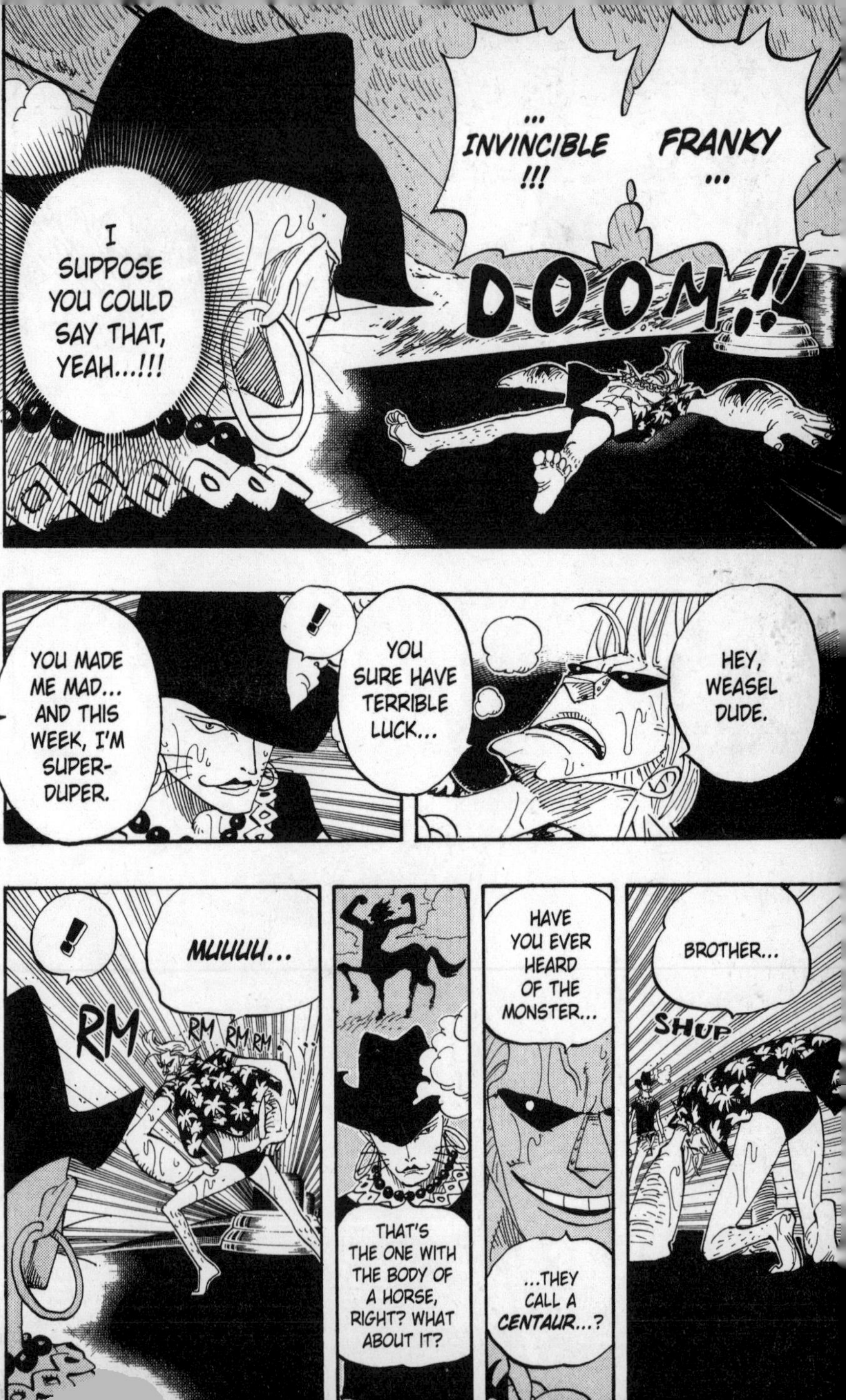
FRANKY ...
... INVINCIBLE !!!
DOOM!!
I SUPPOSE YOU COULD SAY THAT, YEAH...!!!
HEY, WEASEL DUDE.
YOU SURE HAVE TERRIBLE LUCK...
!
YOU MADE ME MAD... AND THIS WEEK, I'M SUPER-DUPER.
BROTHER...
SHUP
HAVE YOU EVER HEARD OF THE MONSTER...
...THEY CALL A CENTAUR...?
THAT'S THE ONE WITH THE BODY OF A HORSE, RIGHT? WHAT ABOUT IT?
MUUUU...
!
RM RM RM RM

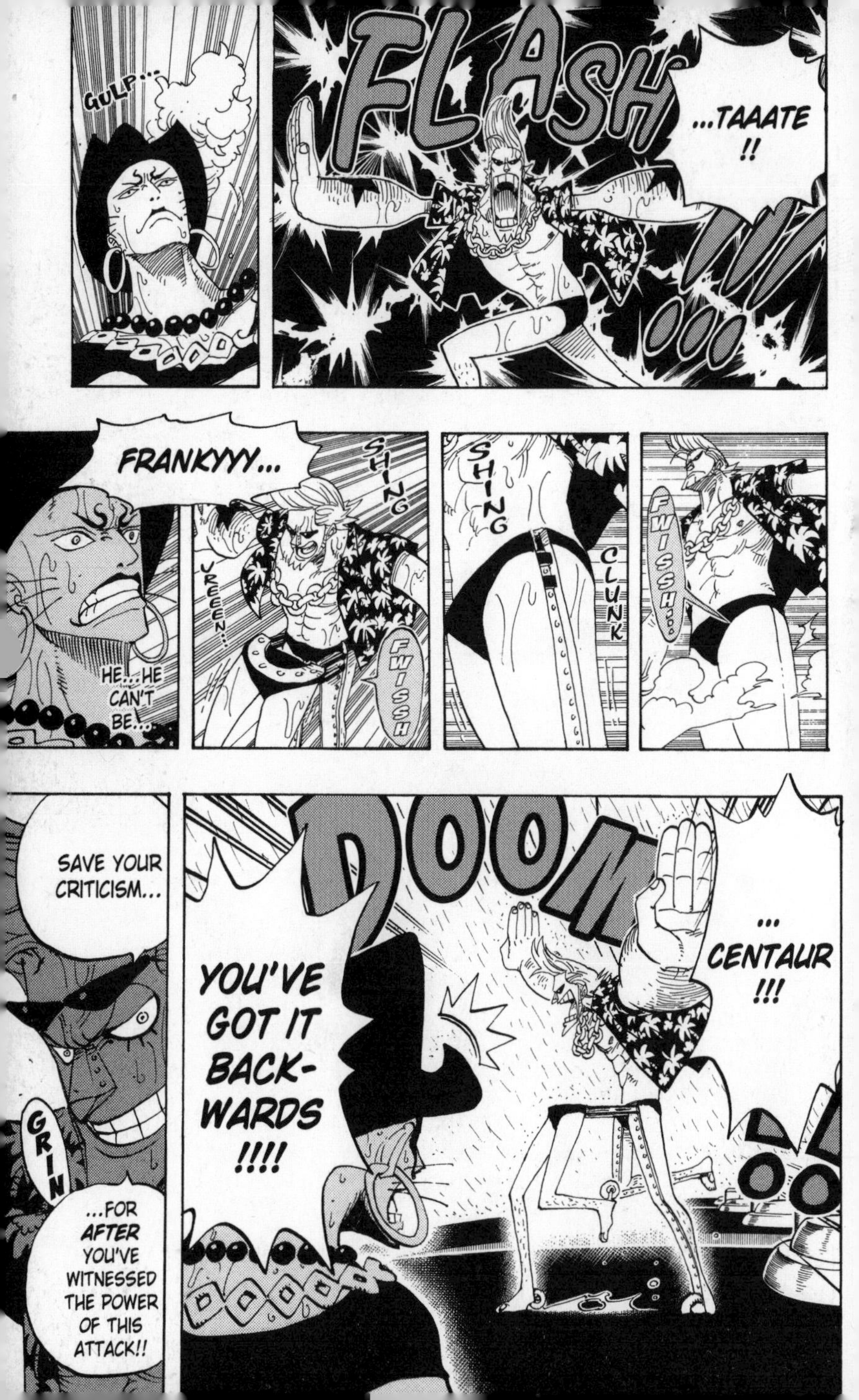
FLASH
...TAAATE !!
GULP...
FWISSH...
SHING
CLUNK
SHING
URREEEN...
FWISSH
FRANKYYY...
HE... HE CAN'T BE...
DOOM
... CENTAUR !!!
YOU'VE GOT IT BACKWARDS !!!!
SAVE YOUR CRITICISM...
GRIN
...FOR AFTER YOU'VE WITNESSED THE POWER OF THIS ATTACK!!

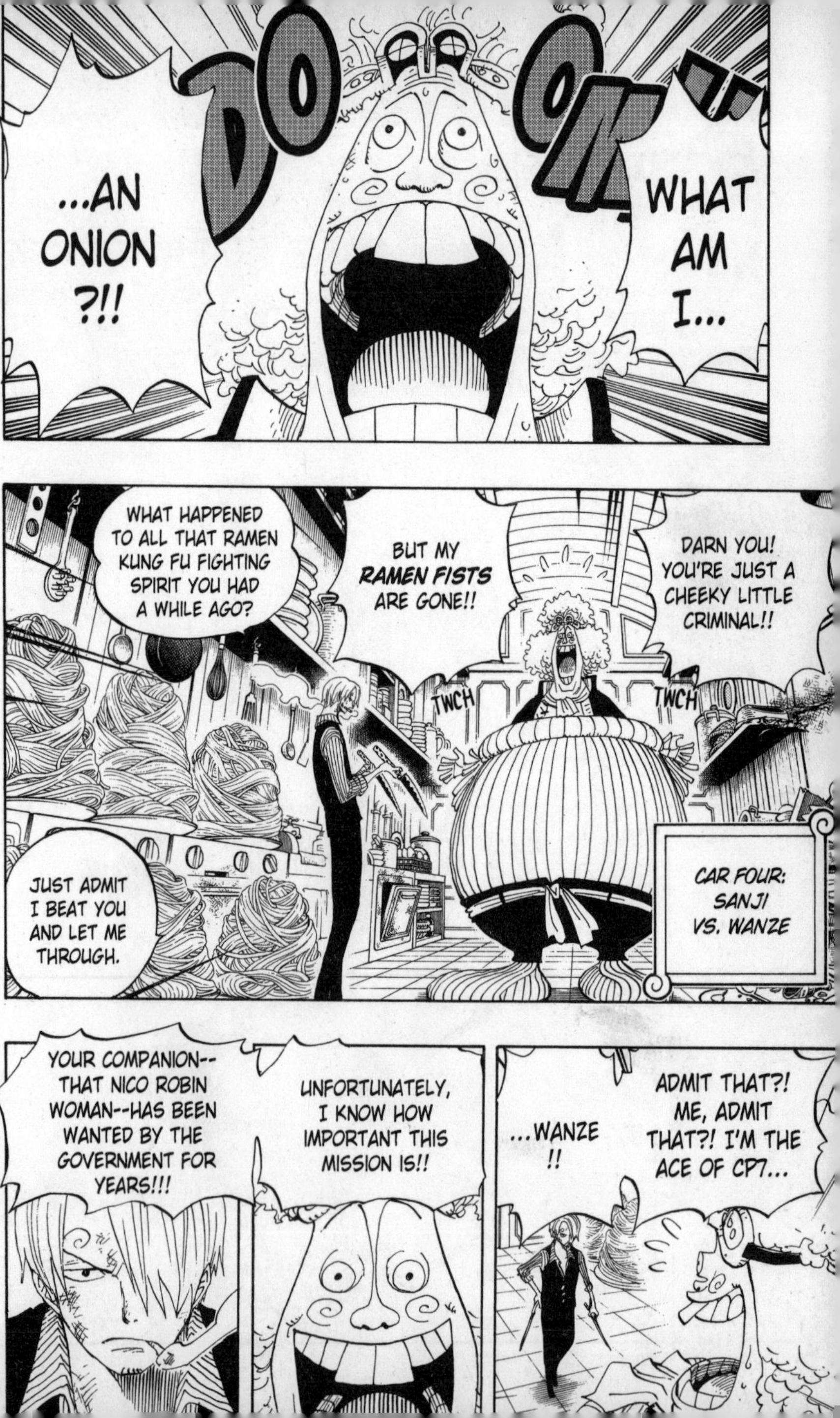
DOON
WHAT AM I...
...AN ONION ?!!
DARN YOU! YOU'RE JUST A CHEEKY LITTLE CRIMINAL!!
BUT MY *RAMEN FISTS* ARE GONE!!
WHAT HAPPENED TO ALL THAT RAMEN KUNG FU FIGHTING SPIRIT YOU HAD A WHILE AGO?
TWCH
TWCH
CAR FOUR: SANJI VS. WANZE
JUST ADMIT I BEAT YOU AND LET ME THROUGH.
ADMIT THAT?! ME, ADMIT THAT?! I'M THE ACE OF CP7...
...WANZE !!
UNFORTUNATELY, I KNOW HOW IMPORTANT THIS MISSION IS!!
YOUR COMPANION--THAT NICO ROBIN WOMAN--HAS BEEN WANTED BY THE GOVERNMENT FOR YEARS!!!

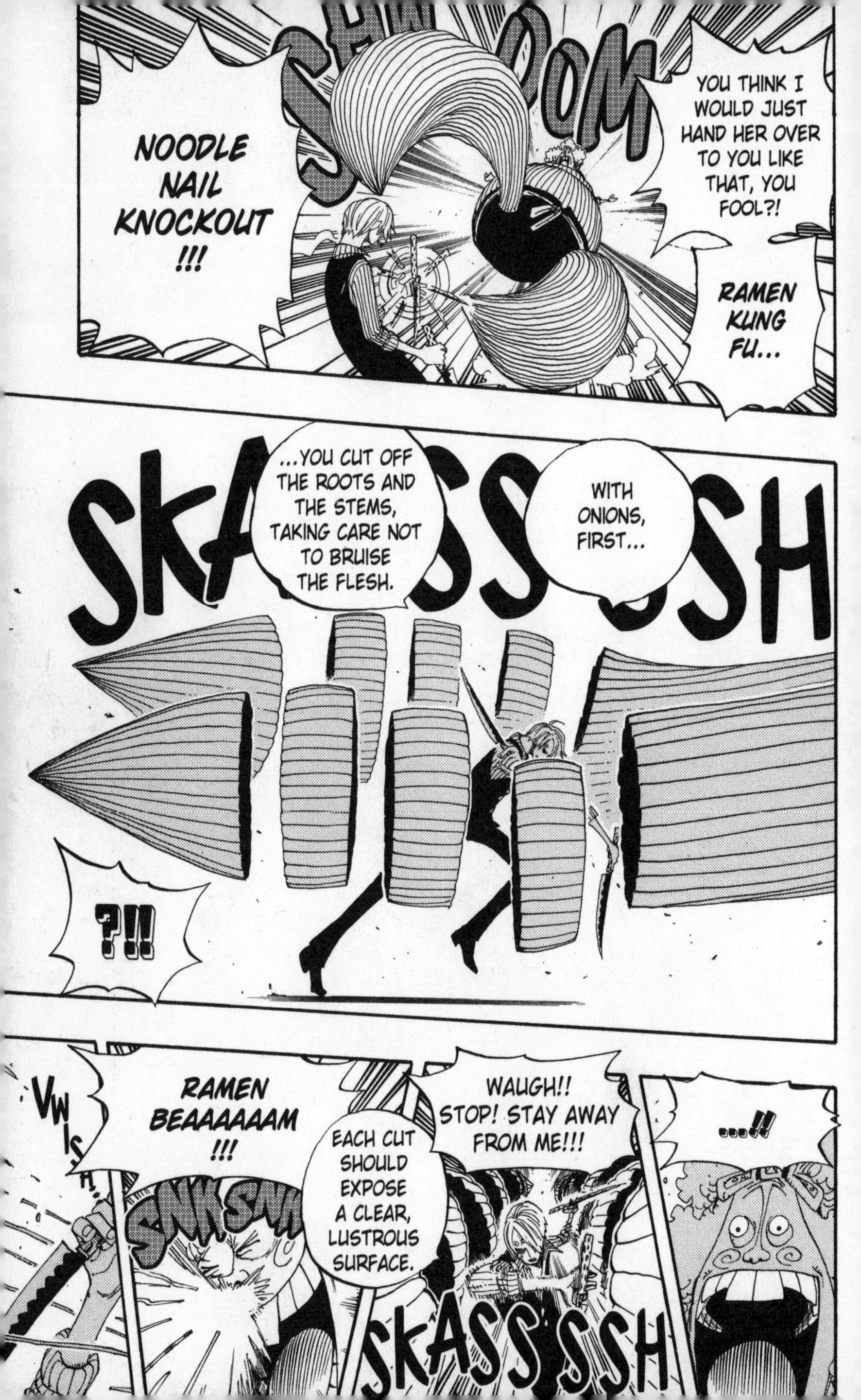
YOU THINK I WOULD JUST HAND HER OVER TO YOU LIKE THAT, YOU FOOL?!
RAMEN KUNG FU...
NOODLE NAIL KNOCKOUT !!!
WITH ONIONS, FIRST...
...YOU CUT OFF THE ROOTS AND THE STEMS, TAKING CARE NOT TO BRUISE THE FLESH.
?!!
...!!
WAUGH!! STOP! STAY AWAY FROM ME!!!
EACH CUT SHOULD EXPOSE A CLEAR, LUSTROUS SURFACE.
SKASS SSH
RAMEN BEAAAAAAM !!!
VWISH

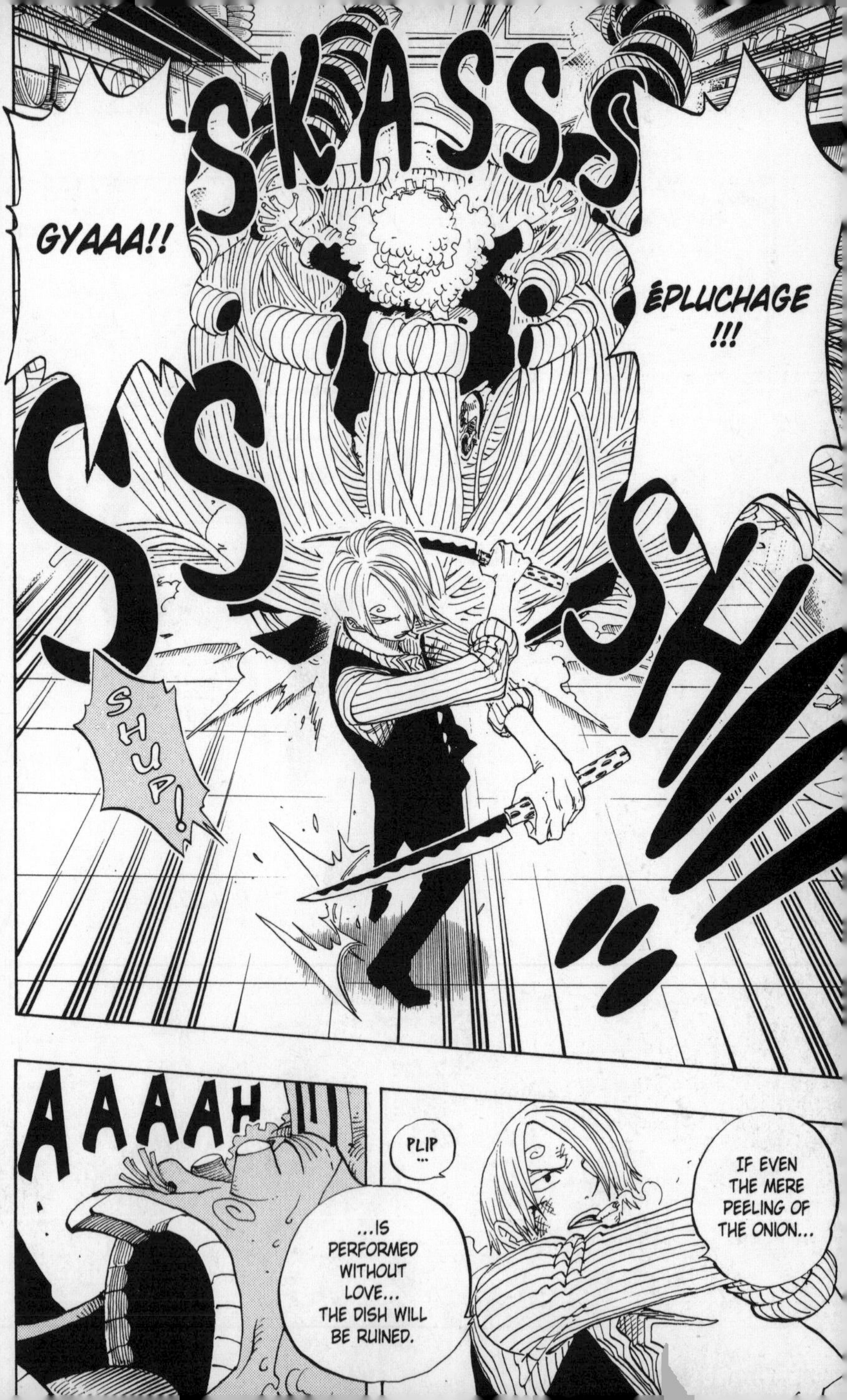
ÉPLUCHAGE !!!
SKASSS
GYAAA!!
SSSH!!!
SHUP!
IF EVEN THE MERE PEELING OF THE ONION...
...IS PERFORMED WITHOUT LOVE... THE DISH WILL BE RUINED.
PLIP...
AAAAH

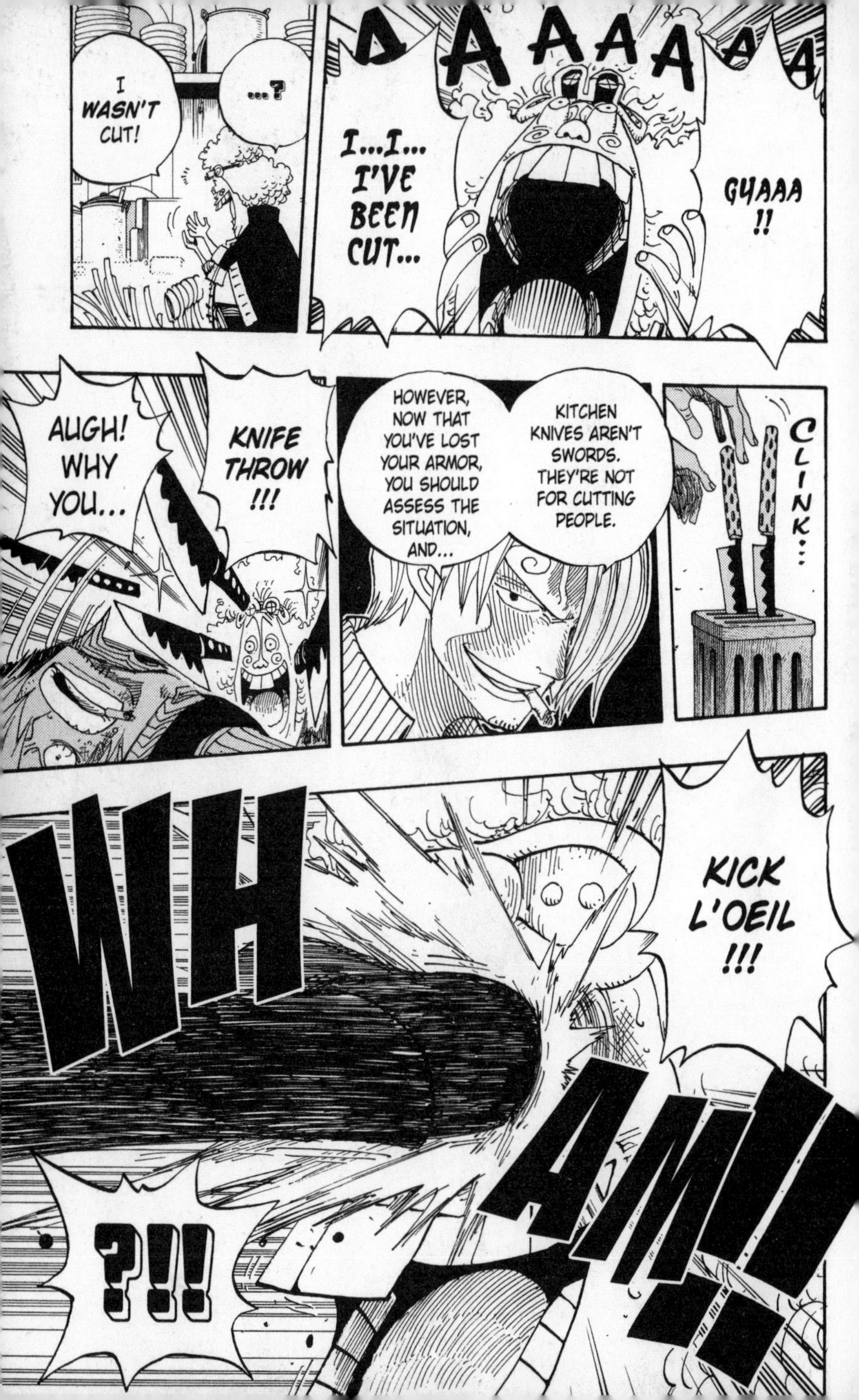
AAAAAA
GYAAA !!
I...I... I'VE BEEN CUT...
...?
I WASN'T CUT!
CLINK...
KITCHEN KNIVES AREN'T SWORDS. THEY'RE NOT FOR CUTTING PEOPLE.
HOWEVER, NOW THAT YOU'VE LOST YOUR ARMOR, YOU SHOULD ASSESS THE SITUATION, AND...
KNIFE THROW !!!
AUGH! WHY YOU...
KICK L'OEIL !!!
WHAM!!
?!!

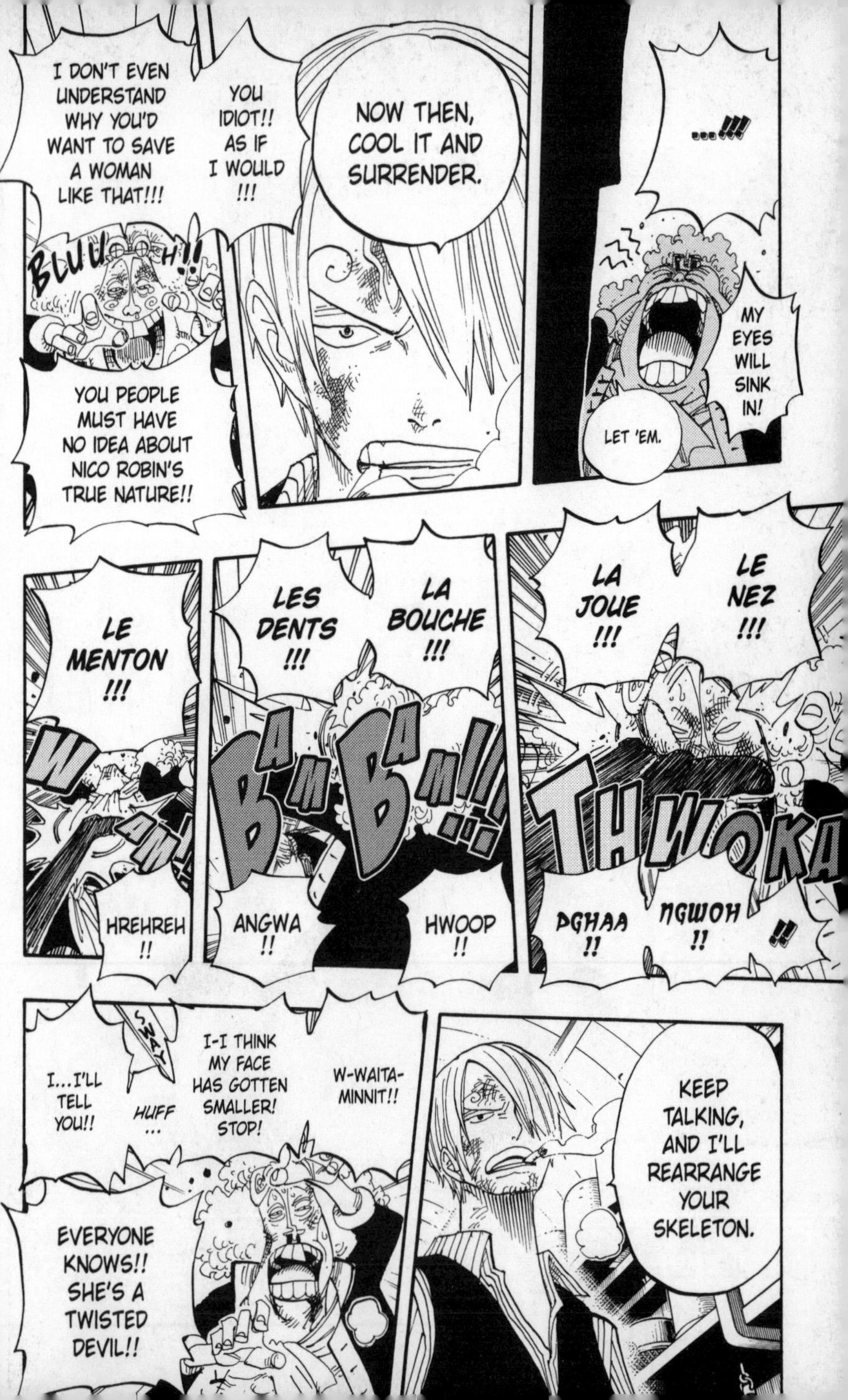
...!!!
MY EYES WILL SINK IN!
LET 'EM.
NOW THEN, COOL IT AND SURRENDER.
YOU IDIOT!! AS IF I WOULD !!!
I DON'T EVEN UNDERSTAND WHY YOU'D WANT TO SAVE A WOMAN LIKE THAT!!!
YOU PEOPLE MUST HAVE NO IDEA ABOUT NICO ROBIN'S TRUE NATURE!!
LE NEZ !!!
LA JOUE !!!
THWOKA
NGWOH !!
PGHAA !!
LA BOUCHE !!!
LES DENTS !!!
BAM BAM!!
HWOOP !!
ANGWA !!
LE MENTON !!!
HREHREH !!
KEEP TALKING, AND I'LL REARRANGE YOUR SKELETON.
W-WAITA-MINNIT!!
I-I THINK MY FACE HAS GOTTEN SMALLER! STOP!
SWAY
HUFF ...
I...I'LL TELL YOU!!
EVERYONE KNOWS!! SHE'S A TWISTED DEVIL!!

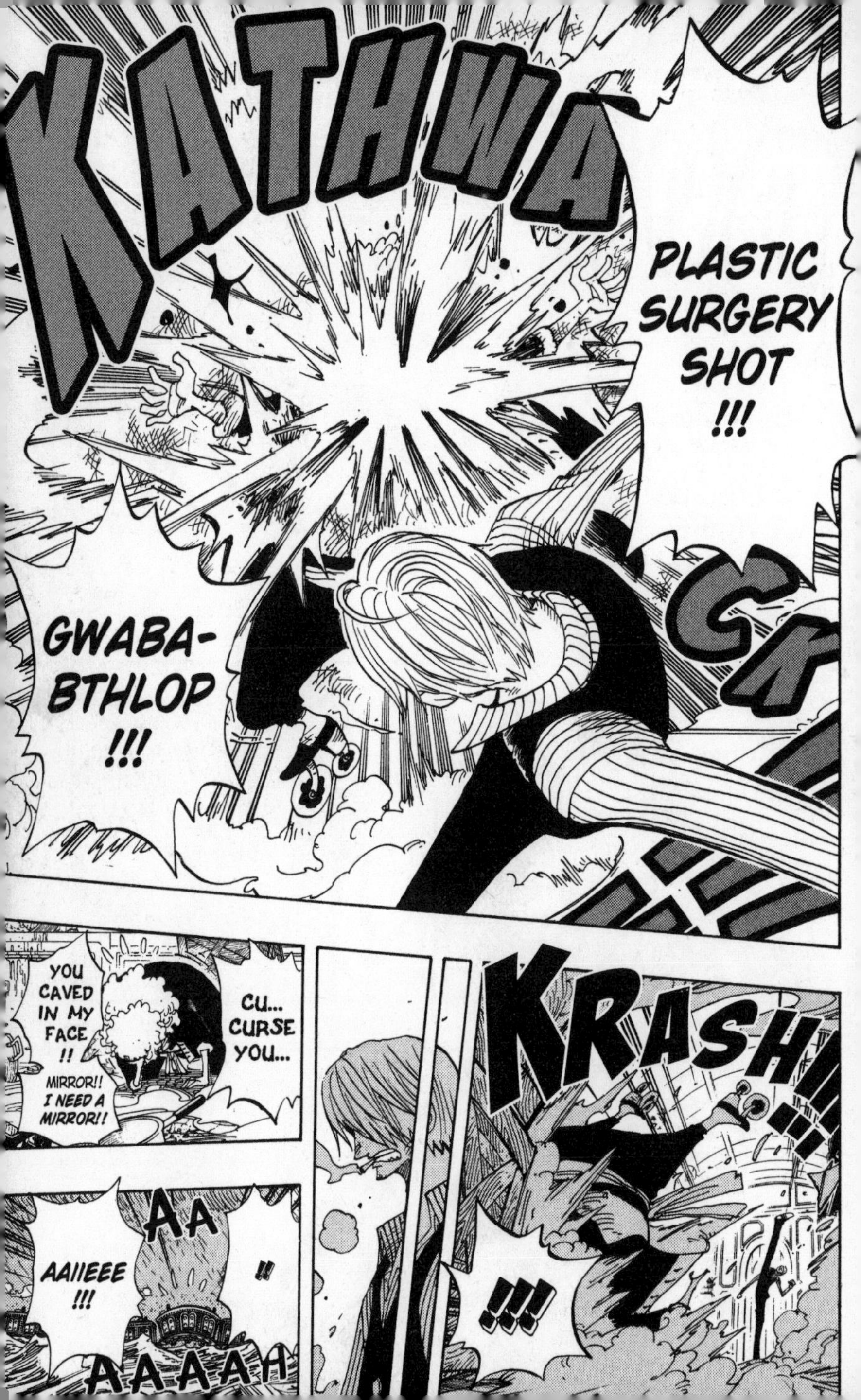
KATHWA
PLASTIC SURGERY SHOT !!!
CK
GWABA-BTHLOP !!!
KRASH!!
!!!
CU... CURSE YOU...
YOU CAVED IN MY FACE !!
MIRROR!! I NEED A MIRROR!!
AA !!
AAIIEEE !!!
AAAAH

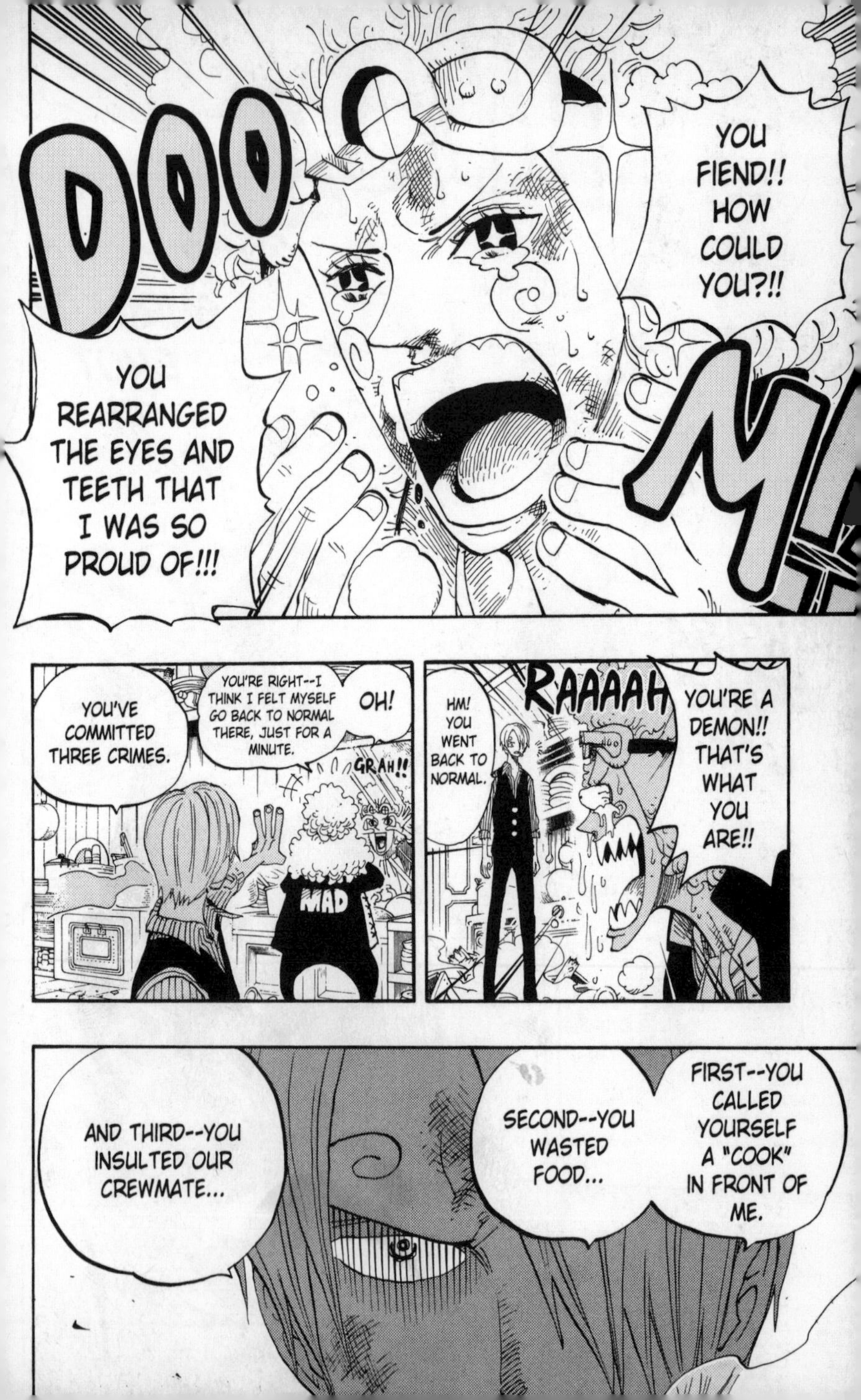
YOU FIEND!! HOW COULD YOU?!!
DOO
YOU REARRANGED THE EYES AND TEETH THAT I WAS SO PROUD OF!!!
YOU'RE A DEMON!! THAT'S WHAT YOU ARE!!
RAAAAH
HM! YOU WENT BACK TO NORMAL.
OH!
GRAH!!
YOU'RE RIGHT--I THINK I FELT MYSELF GO BACK TO NORMAL THERE, JUST FOR A MINUTE.
YOU'VE COMMITTED THREE CRIMES.
MAD
FIRST--YOU CALLED YOURSELF A "COOK" IN FRONT OF ME.
SECOND--YOU WASTED FOOD...
AND THIRD--YOU INSULTED OUR CREWMATE...

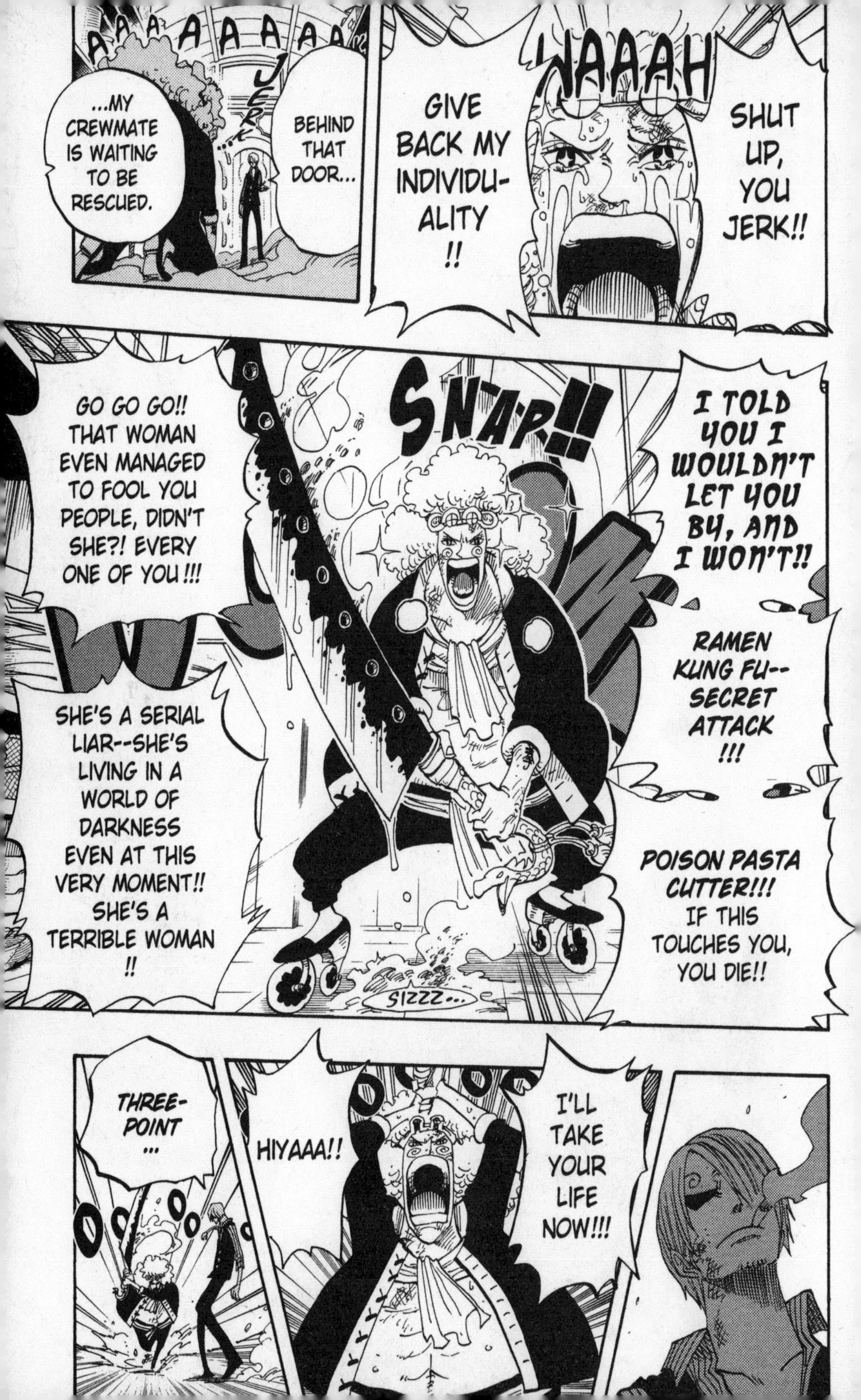
WAAAAH
SHUT UP, YOU JERK!!
GIVE BACK MY INDIVIDU-ALITY !!
AAAAAAAA
JERK
BEHIND THAT DOOR...
...MY CREWMATE IS WAITING TO BE RESCUED.
I TOLD YOU I WOULDN'T LET YOU BY, AND I WON'T!!
SNAP!!
GO GO GO!! THAT WOMAN EVEN MANAGED TO FOOL YOU PEOPLE, DIDN'T SHE?! EVERY ONE OF YOU!!!
RAMEN KUNG FU-- SECRET ATTACK !!!
POISON PASTA CUTTER!!! IF THIS TOUCHES YOU, YOU DIE!!
SHE'S A SERIAL LIAR--SHE'S LIVING IN A WORLD OF DARKNESS EVEN AT THIS VERY MOMENT!! SHE'S A TERRIBLE WOMAN !!
SIZZZ...
I'LL TAKE YOUR LIFE NOW!!!
HIYAAA!!
THREE-POINT ...

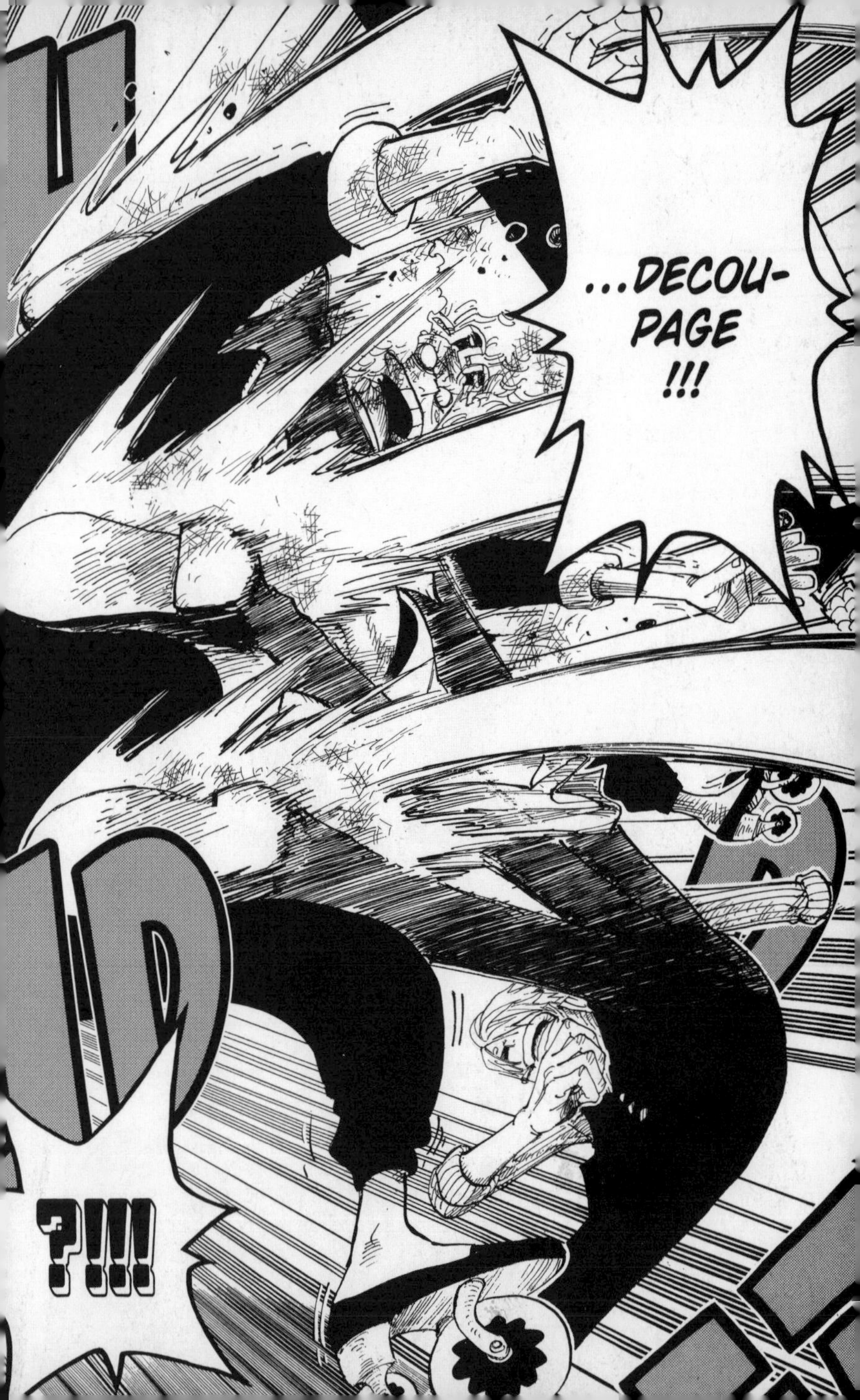
...DECOU-
PAGE
!!!
?!!!

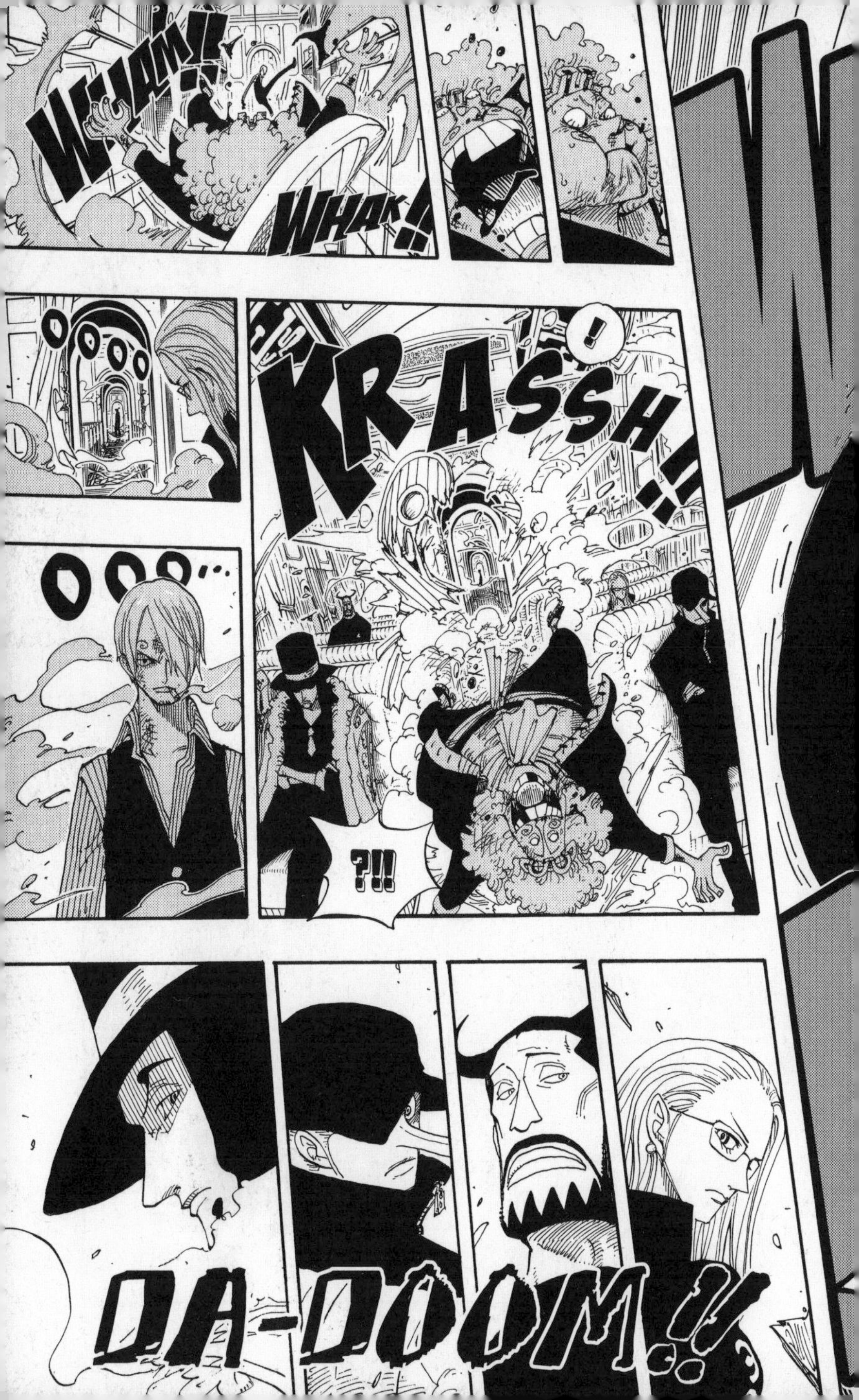

WHAM!!
WHAK!!
!
KRASSH!!
?!!
DA-DOOM!!

Chapter 373: NECESSARY EVIL

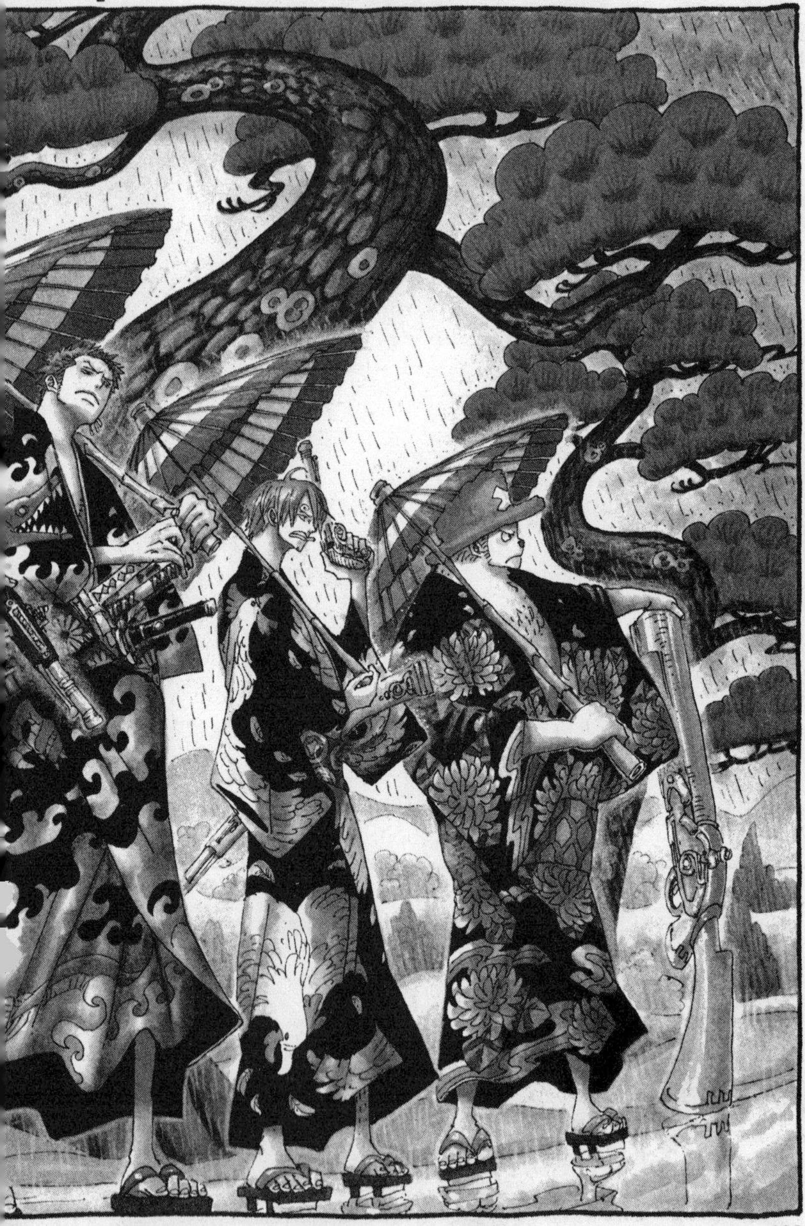

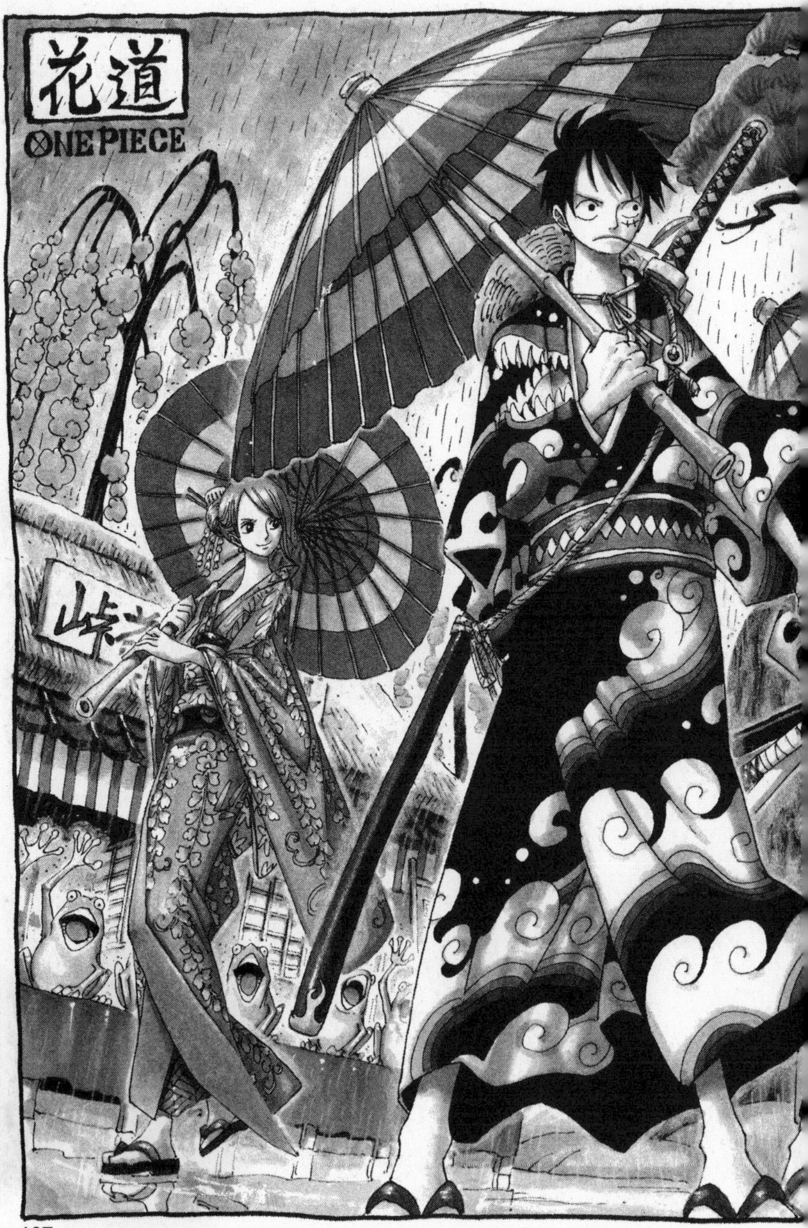
花道
ONE PIECE

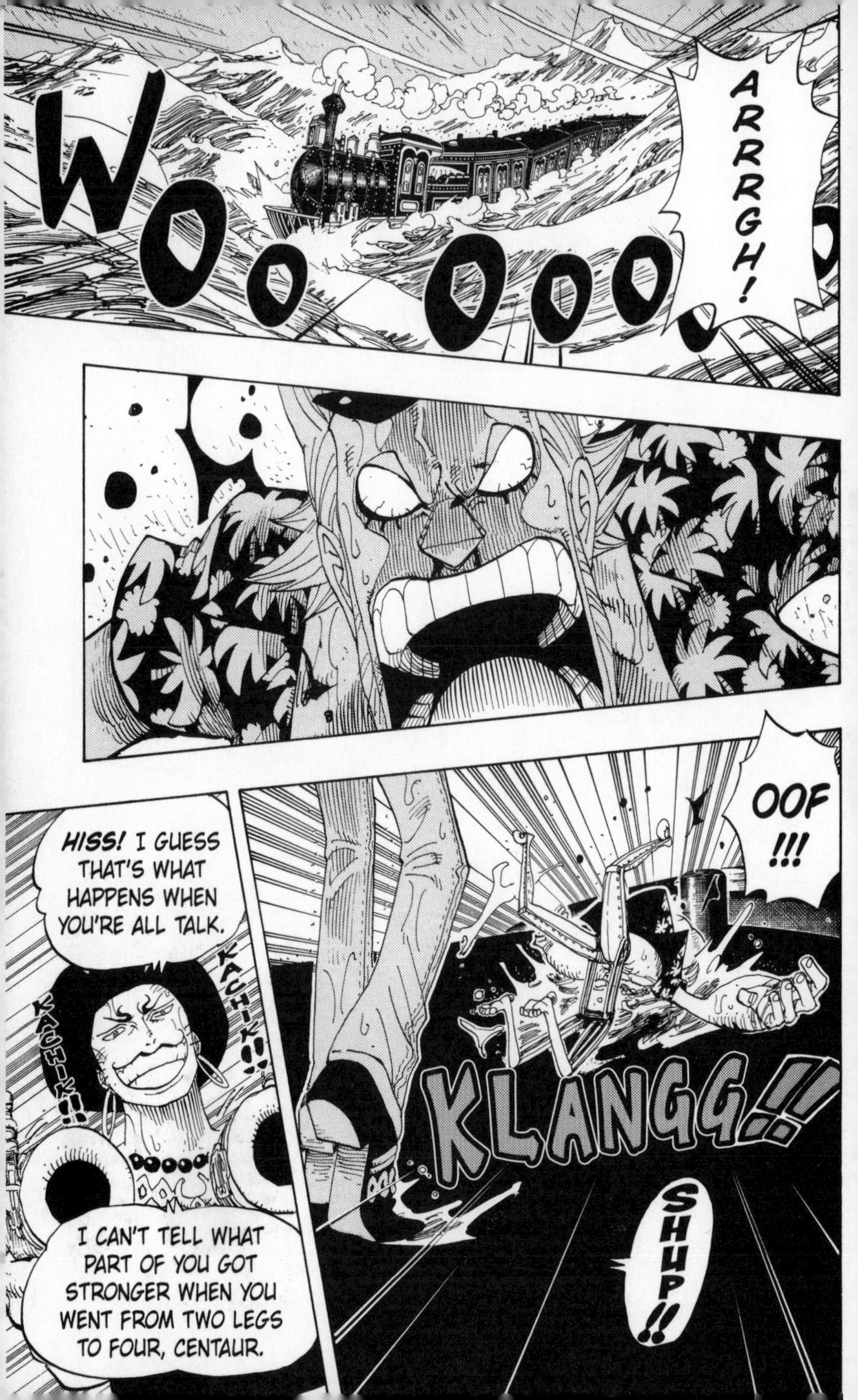
ARRRGH!
WOOOOOO
OOF!!!
KLANGG!!
SHUP!!
HISS! I GUESS THAT'S WHAT HAPPENS WHEN YOU'RE ALL TALK.
KACHIK!!
KACHIK!!
I CAN'T TELL WHAT PART OF YOU GOT STRONGER WHEN YOU WENT FROM TWO LEGS TO FOUR, CENTAUR.

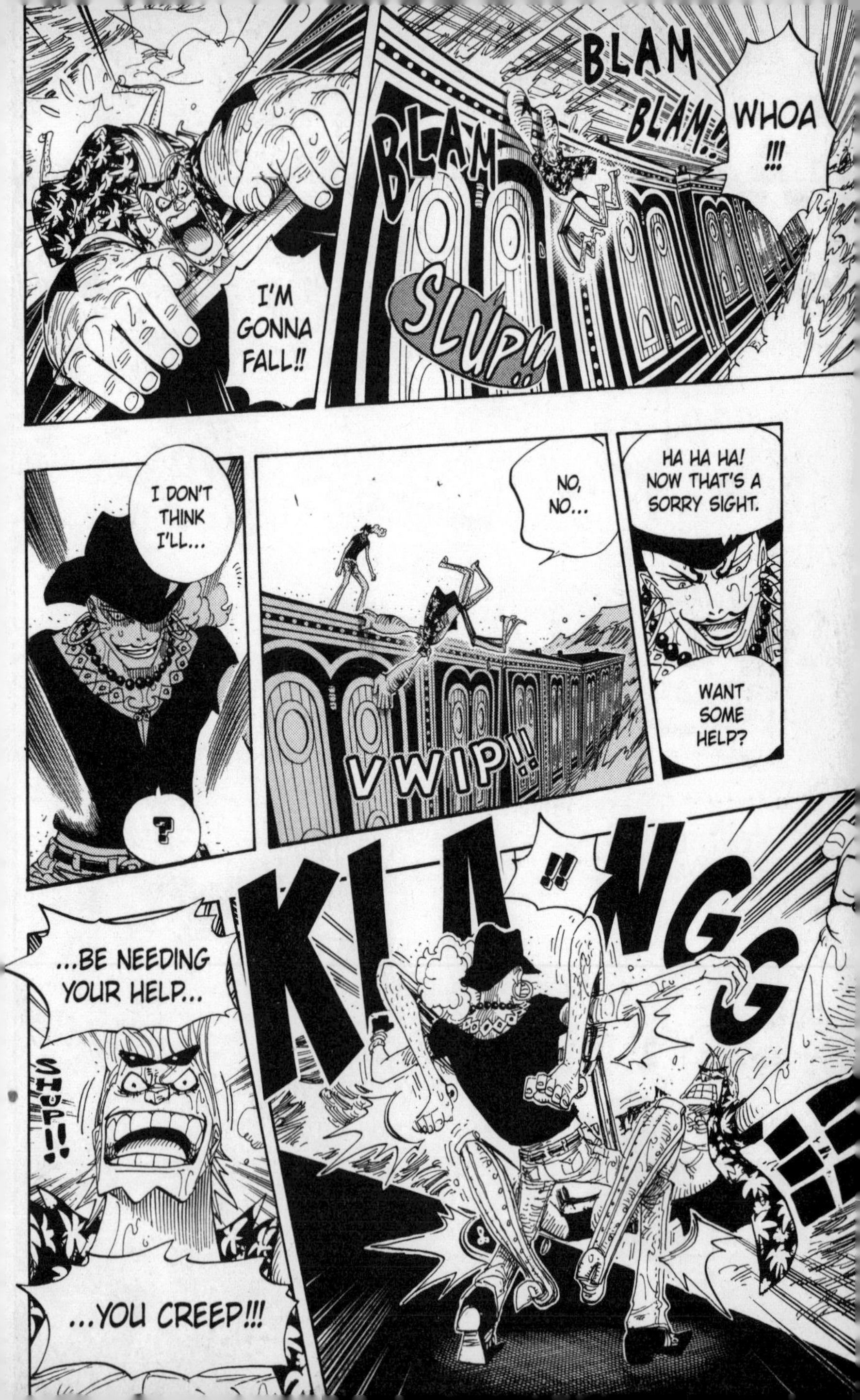
BLAM
BLAM!!
WHOA !!!
BLAM
SLUP!!
I'M GONNA FALL!!
HA HA HA! NOW THAT'S A SORRY SIGHT.
WANT SOME HELP?
NO, NO...
VWIP!!
I DON'T THINK I'LL...
?
KLANG
!!
...BE NEEDING YOUR HELP...
SHUP!!
...YOU CREEP!!!

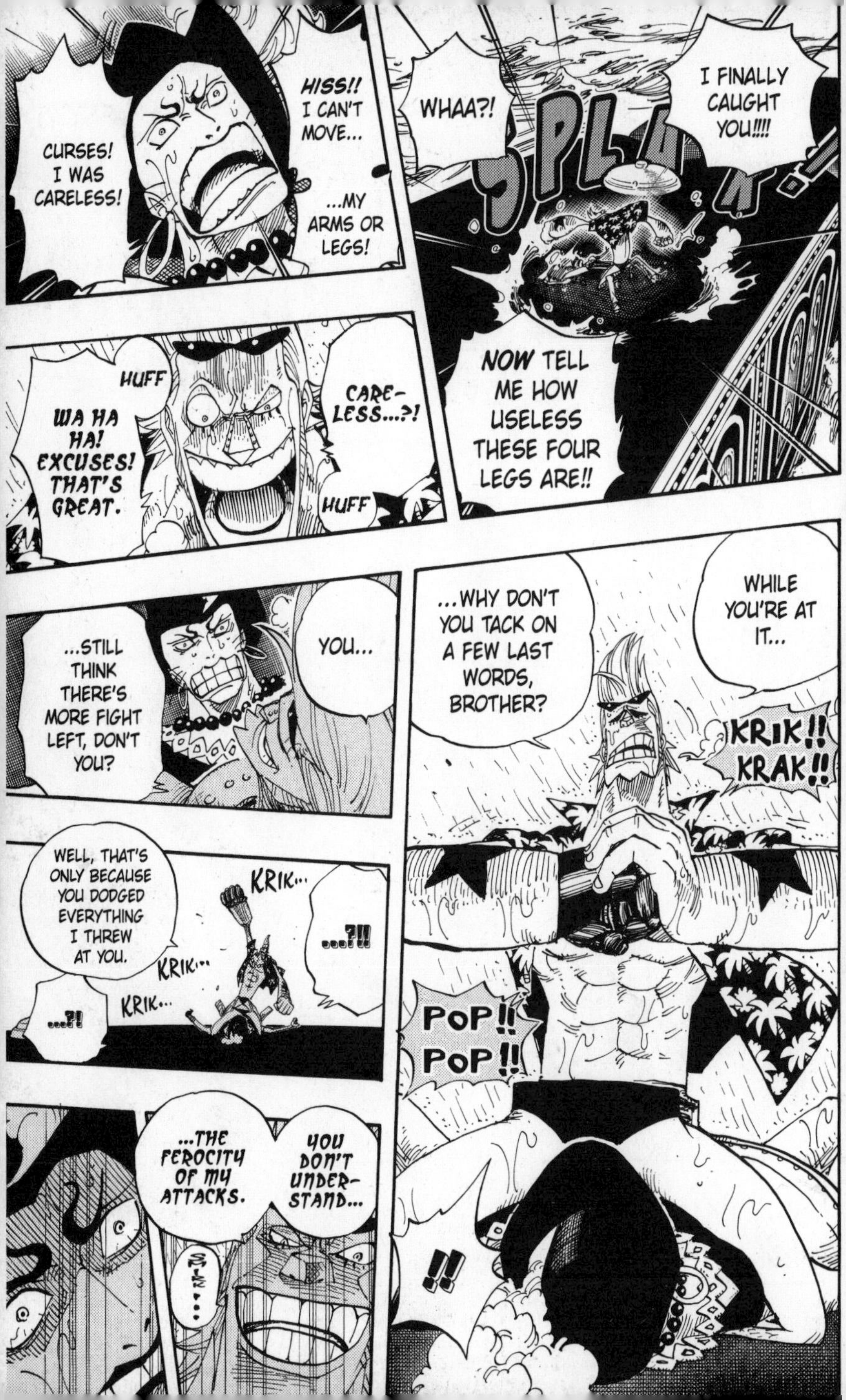
I FINALLY CAUGHT YOU!!!!
WHAA?!
NOW TELL ME HOW USELESS THESE FOUR LEGS ARE!!
HISS!! I CAN'T MOVE...
...MY ARMS OR LEGS!
CURSES! I WAS CARELESS!
CARE-LESS...?!
HUFF
WA HA HA! EXCUSES! THAT'S GREAT.
HUFF
WHILE YOU'RE AT IT...
...WHY DON'T YOU TACK ON A FEW LAST WORDS, BROTHER?
KRIK!! KRAK!!
POP!! POP!!
!!
YOU...
...STILL THINK THERE'S MORE FIGHT LEFT, DON'T YOU?
...?!!
KRIK...
WELL, THAT'S ONLY BECAUSE YOU DODGED EVERYTHING I THREW AT YOU.
KRIK...
KRIK...
...?!
YOU DON'T UNDERSTAND...
...THE FEROCITY OF MY ATTACKS.

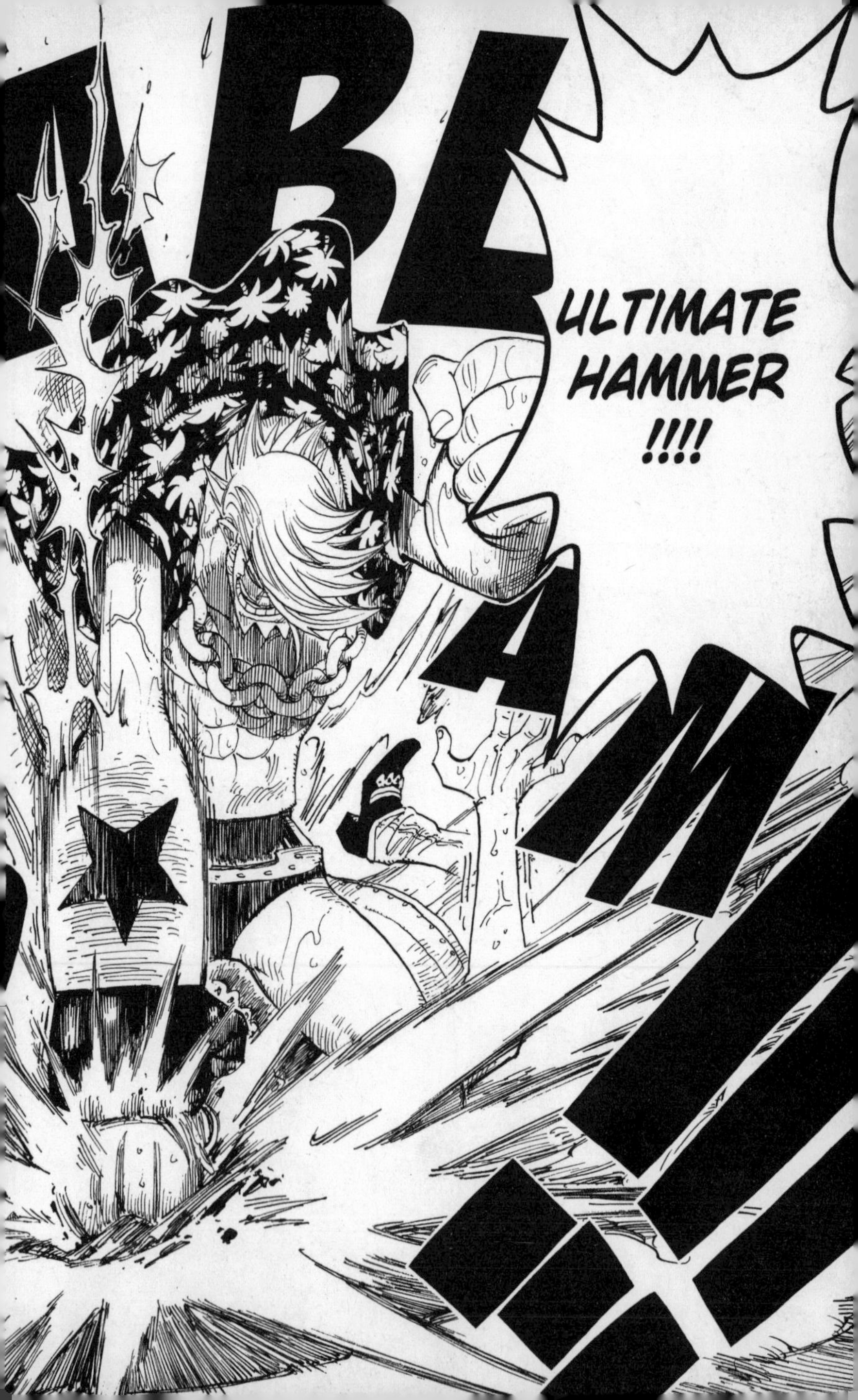
ULTIMATE HAMMER !!!!

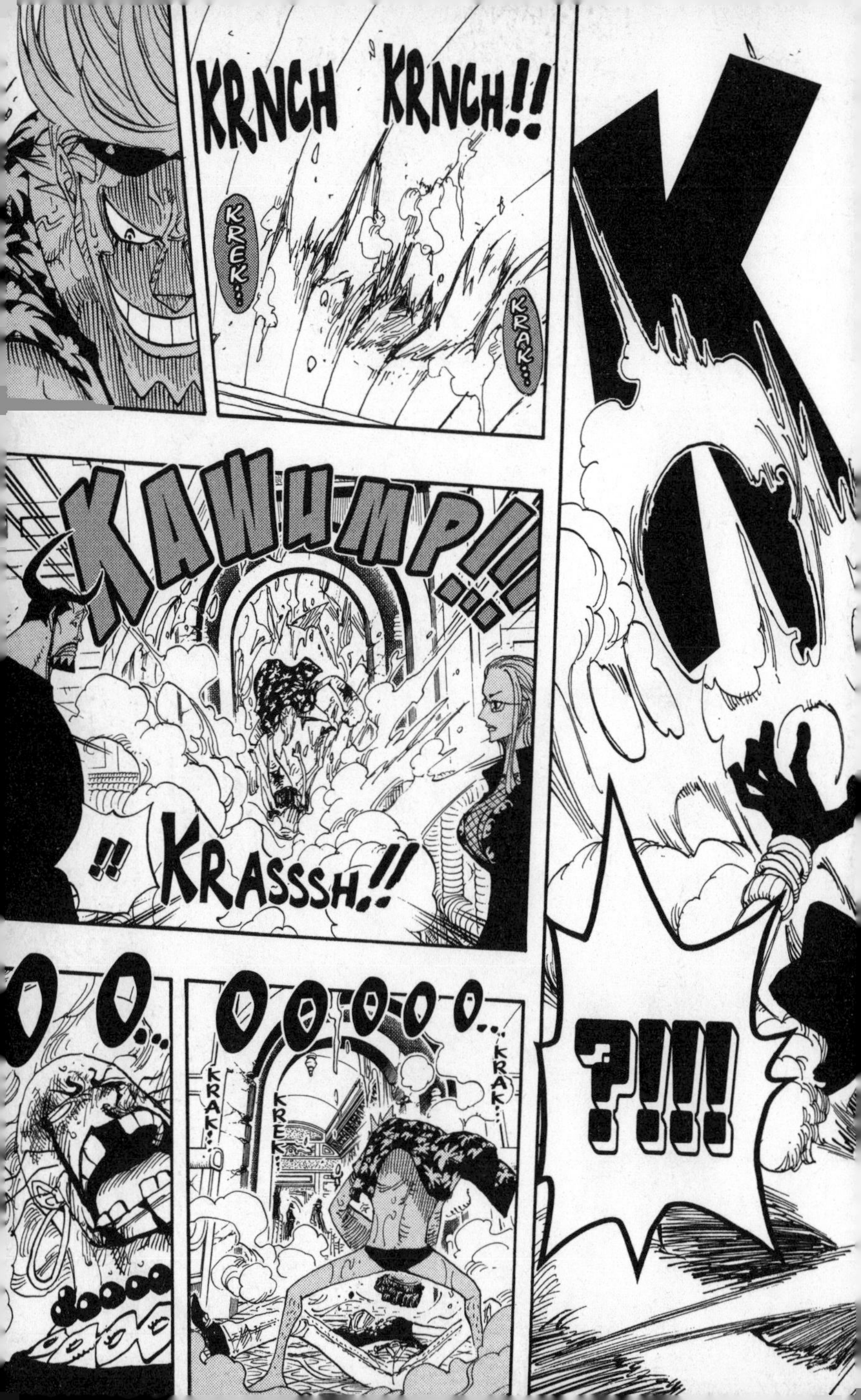

?!!!
KRNCH KRNCH!!
KREK...
KRAK...
KAWUMP!!!
!!
KRASSSH!!
O O O O O O...
KRAK...
KREK...
KRAK...
O O...

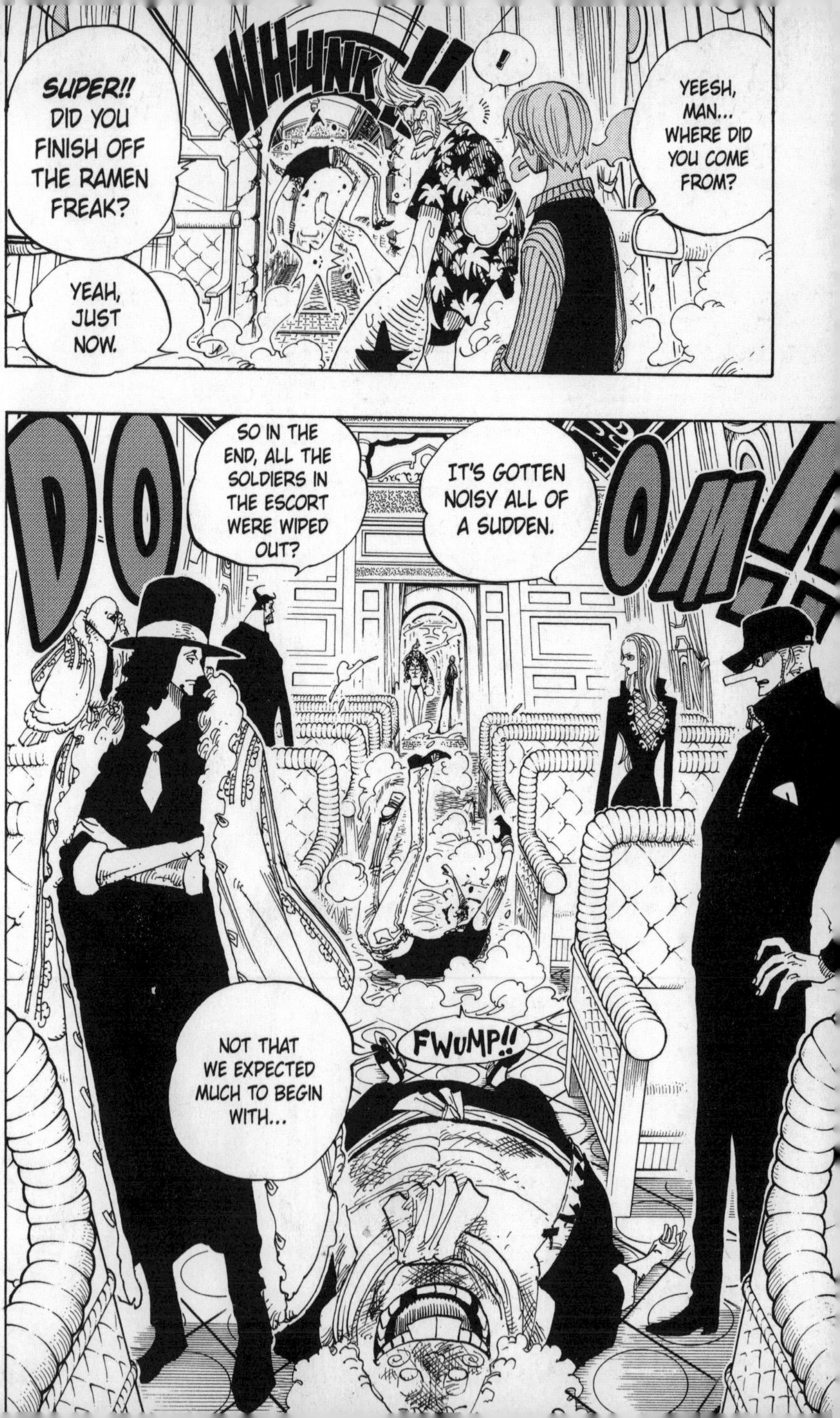
YEESH, MAN... WHERE DID YOU COME FROM?
!
WHUNK!!
SUPER!! DID YOU FINISH OFF THE RAMEN FREAK?
YEAH, JUST NOW.
DOOM!!
IT'S GOTTEN NOISY ALL OF A SUDDEN.
SO IN THE END, ALL THE SOLDIERS IN THE ESCORT WERE WIPED OUT?
FWUMP!!
NOT THAT WE EXPECTED MUCH TO BEGIN WITH...

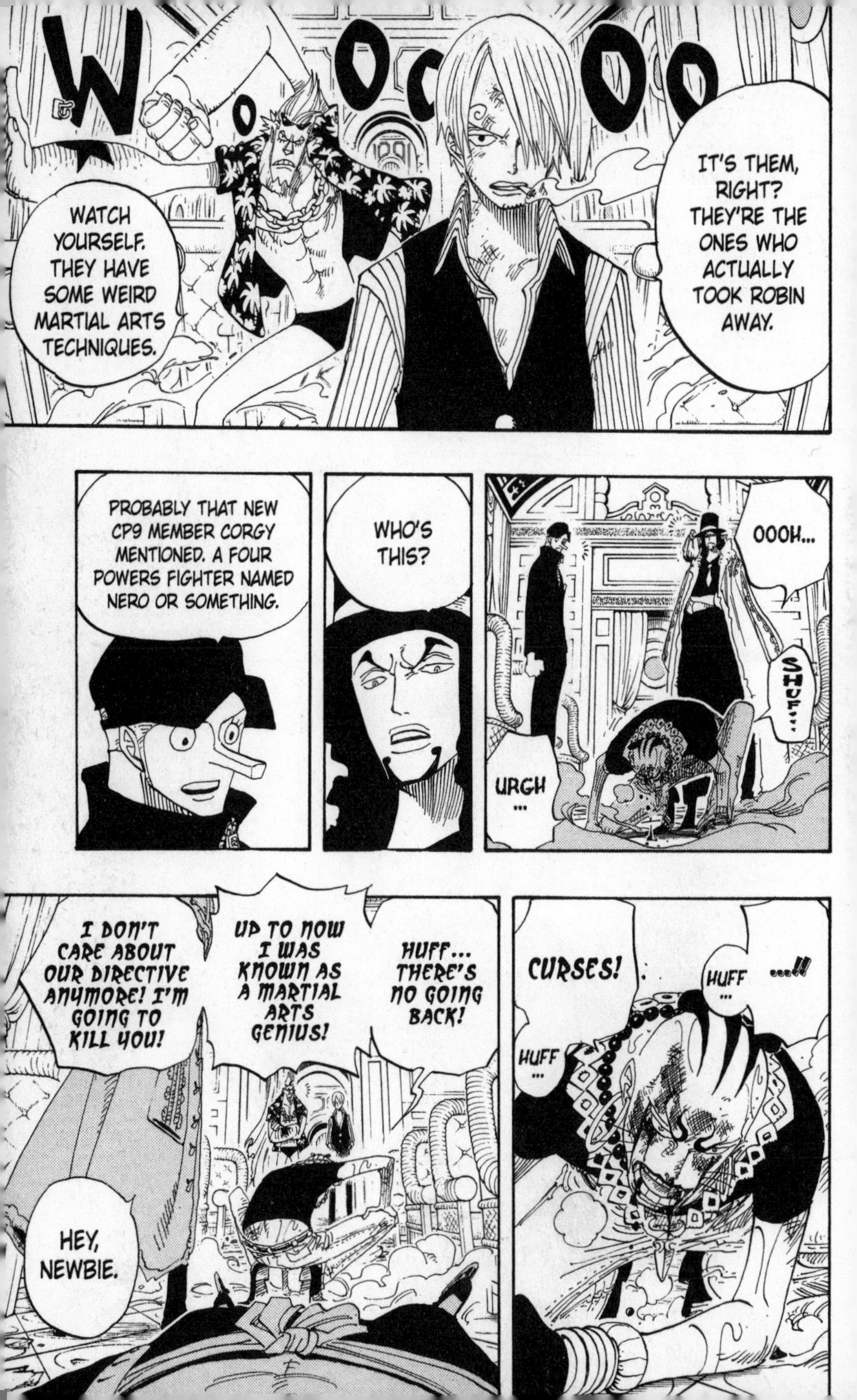
WOOOOO
IT'S THEM, RIGHT? THEY'RE THE ONES WHO ACTUALLY TOOK ROBIN AWAY.
WATCH YOURSELF. THEY HAVE SOME WEIRD MARTIAL ARTS TECHNIQUES.
OOOH...
SHUF...
URGH ...
WHO'S THIS?
PROBABLY THAT NEW CP9 MEMBER CORGY MENTIONED. A FOUR POWERS FIGHTER NAMED NERO OR SOMETHING.
...!!
HUFF ...
CURSES!
HUFF ...
HUFF... THERE'S NO GOING BACK!
UP TO NOW I WAS KNOWN AS A MARTIAL ARTS GENIUS!
I DON'T CARE ABOUT OUR DIRECTIVE ANYMORE! I'M GOING TO KILL YOU!
HEY, NEWBIE.

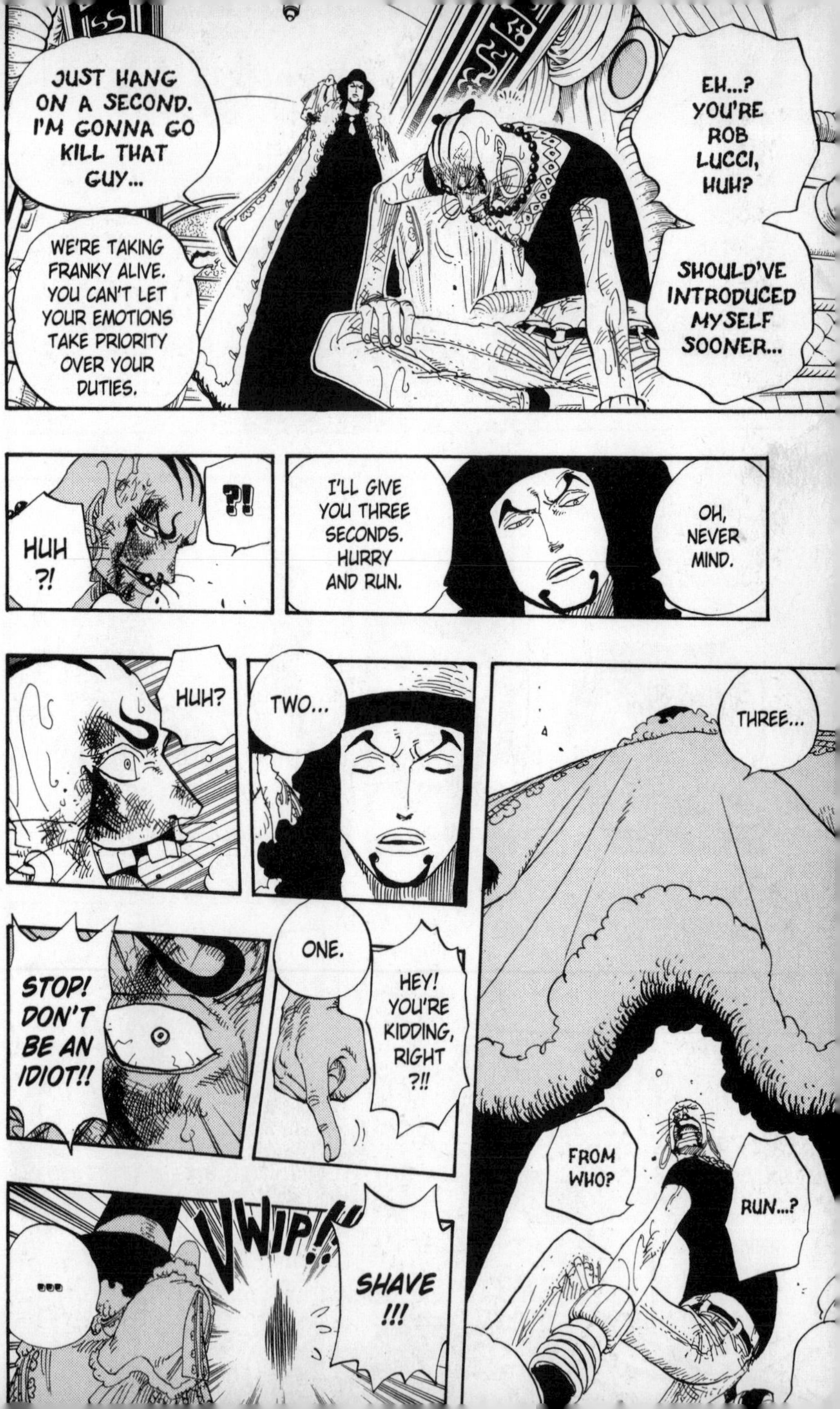
EH...? YOU'RE ROB LUCCI, HUH?
SHOULD'VE INTRODUCED MYSELF SOONER...
JUST HANG ON A SECOND. I'M GONNA GO KILL THAT GUY...
WE'RE TAKING FRANKY ALIVE. YOU CAN'T LET YOUR EMOTIONS TAKE PRIORITY OVER YOUR DUTIES.
OH, NEVER MIND.
I'LL GIVE YOU THREE SECONDS. HURRY AND RUN.
?!
HUH ?!
THREE...
RUN...?
FROM WHO?
TWO...
HUH?
ONE.
HEY! YOU'RE KIDDING, RIGHT ?!!
STOP! DON'T BE AN IDIOT!!
VWIP!!
SHAVE !!!
...

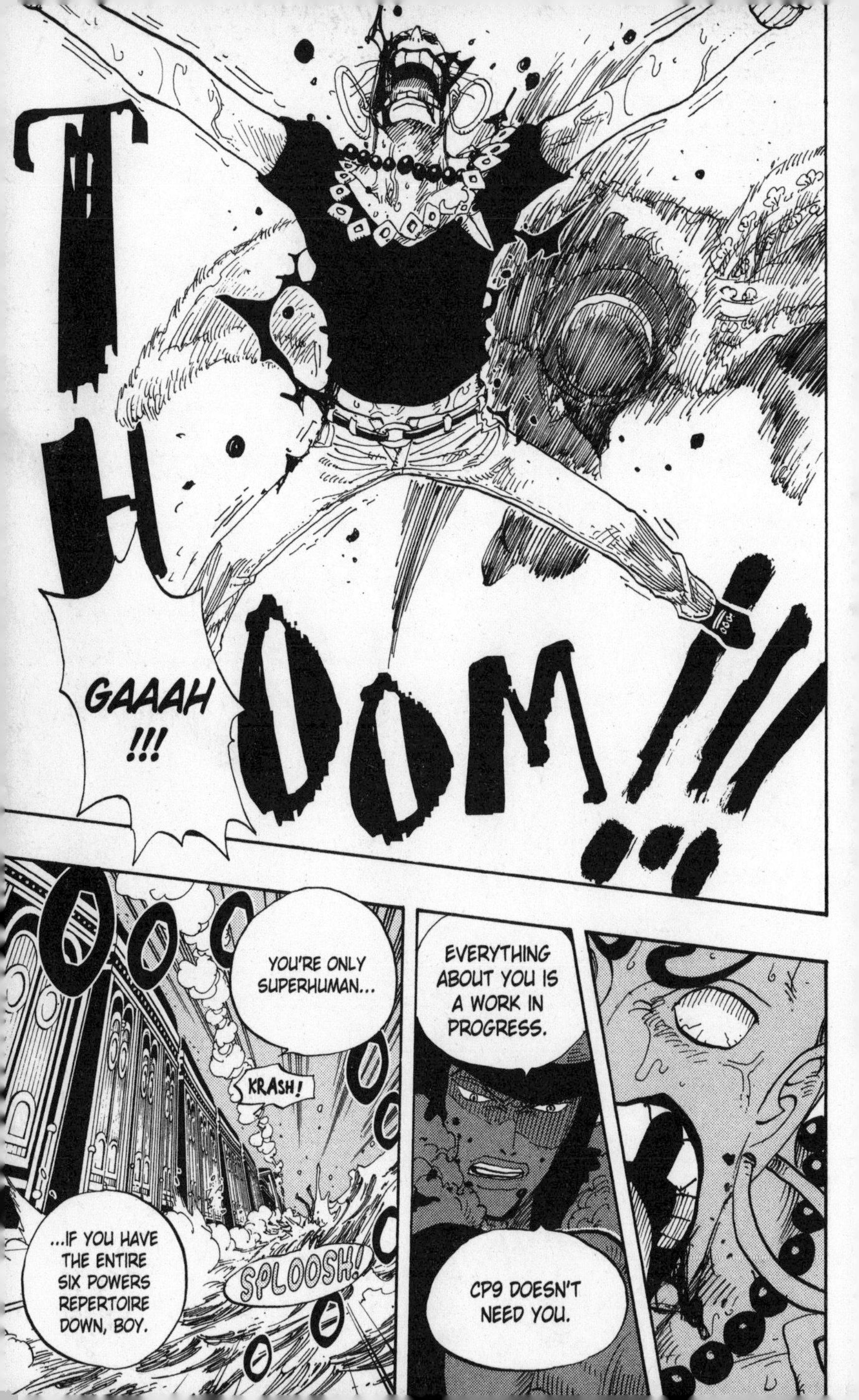
THOOM!!
GAAAH!!!
EVERYTHING ABOUT YOU IS A WORK IN PROGRESS.
CP9 DOESN'T NEED YOU.
YOU'RE ONLY SUPERHUMAN...
KRASH!
SPLOOSH!
...IF YOU HAVE THE ENTIRE SIX POWERS REPERTOIRE DOWN, BOY.

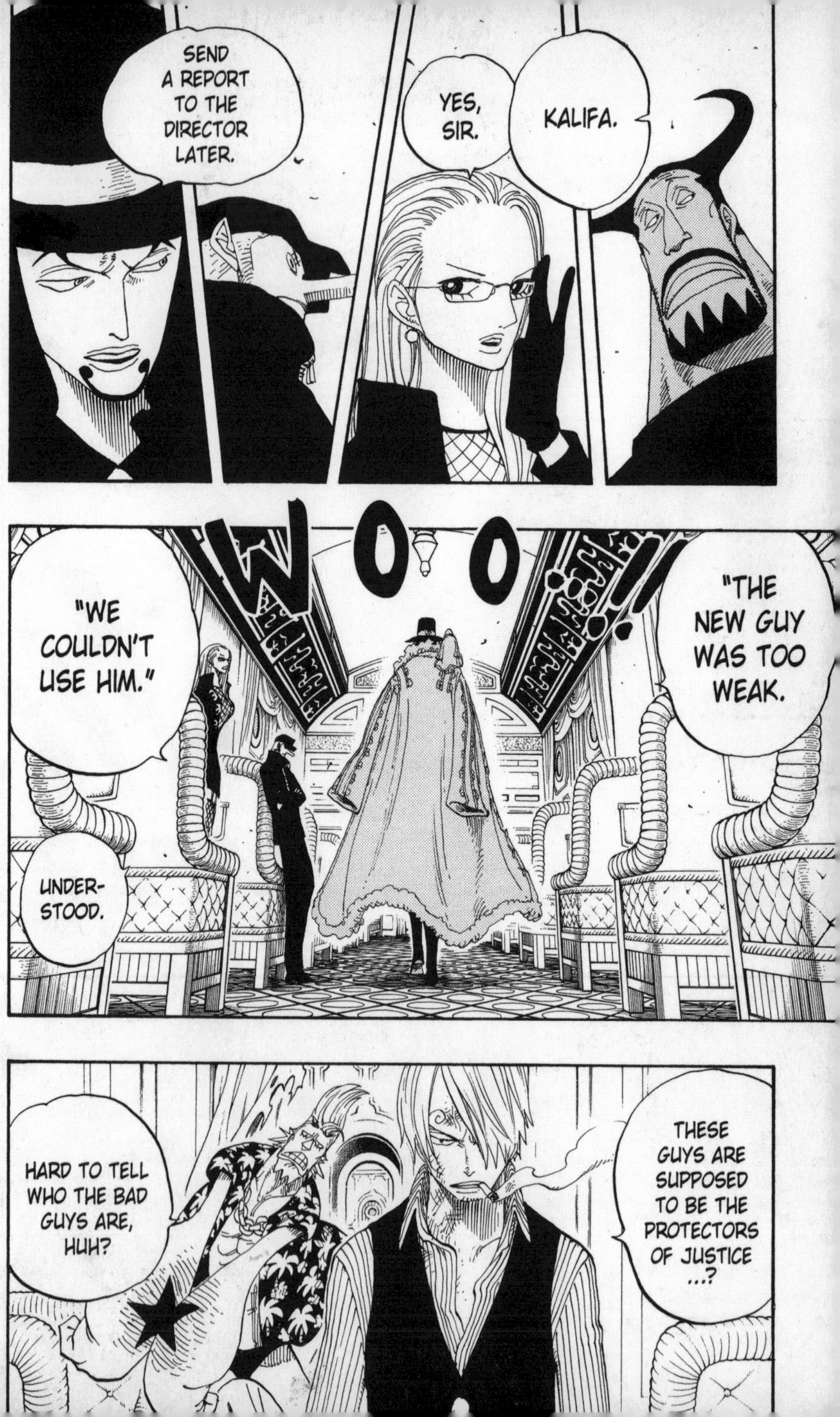
KALIFA.
YES, SIR.
SEND A REPORT TO THE DIRECTOR LATER.
WOOO
"THE NEW GUY WAS TOO WEAK.
"WE COULDN'T USE HIM."
UNDER-STOOD.
THESE GUYS ARE SUPPOSED TO BE THE PROTECTORS OF JUSTICE ...?
HARD TO TELL WHO THE BAD GUYS ARE, HUH?

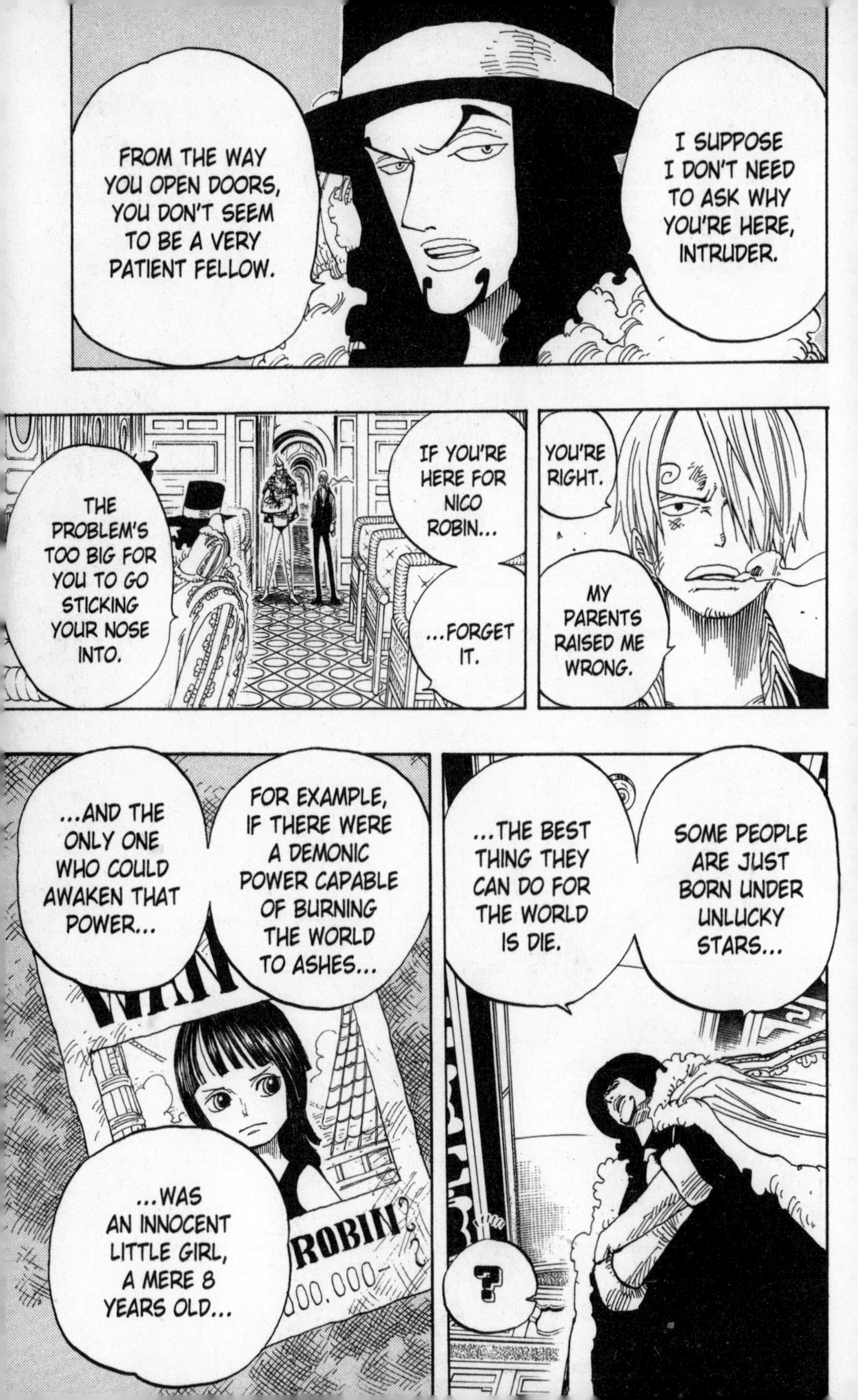
I SUPPOSE I DON'T NEED TO ASK WHY YOU'RE HERE, INTRUDER.
FROM THE WAY YOU OPEN DOORS, YOU DON'T SEEM TO BE A VERY PATIENT FELLOW.
YOU'RE RIGHT.
MY PARENTS RAISED ME WRONG.
IF YOU'RE HERE FOR NICO ROBIN...
...FORGET IT.
THE PROBLEM'S TOO BIG FOR YOU TO GO STICKING YOUR NOSE INTO.
SOME PEOPLE ARE JUST BORN UNDER UNLUCKY STARS...
...THE BEST THING THEY CAN DO FOR THE WORLD IS DIE.
?
FOR EXAMPLE, IF THERE WERE A DEMONIC POWER CAPABLE OF BURNING THE WORLD TO ASHES...
...AND THE ONLY ONE WHO COULD AWAKEN THAT POWER...
ROBIN
...WAS AN INNOCENT LITTLE GIRL, A MERE 8 YEARS OLD...

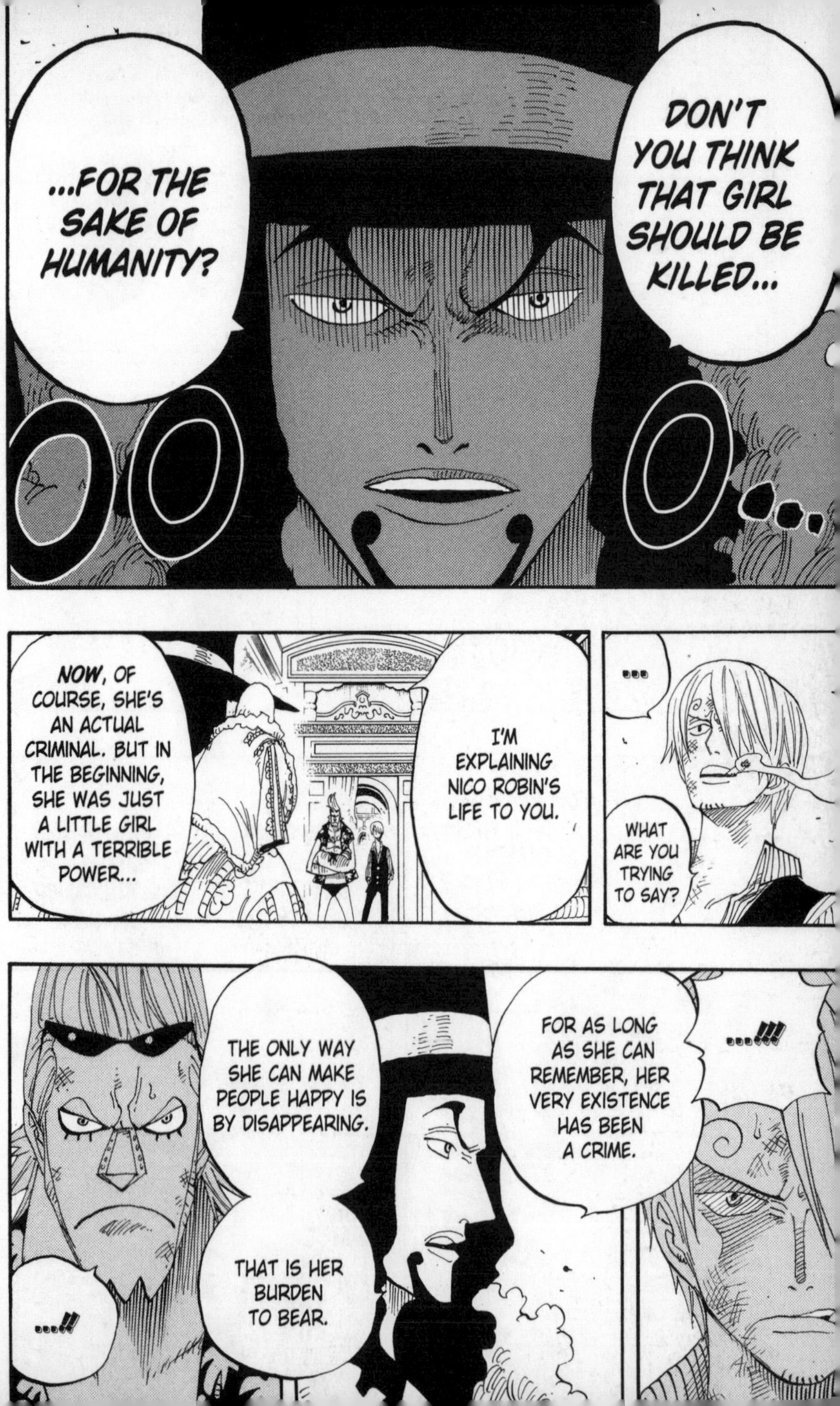
DON'T YOU THINK THAT GIRL SHOULD BE KILLED...
...FOR THE SAKE OF HUMANITY?
...
WHAT ARE YOU TRYING TO SAY?
I'M EXPLAINING NICO ROBIN'S LIFE TO YOU.
NOW, OF COURSE, SHE'S AN ACTUAL CRIMINAL. BUT IN THE BEGINNING, SHE WAS JUST A LITTLE GIRL WITH A TERRIBLE POWER...
...!!!
FOR AS LONG AS SHE CAN REMEMBER, HER VERY EXISTENCE HAS BEEN A CRIME.
THE ONLY WAY SHE CAN MAKE PEOPLE HAPPY IS BY DISAPPEARING.
THAT IS HER BURDEN TO BEAR.
...!!

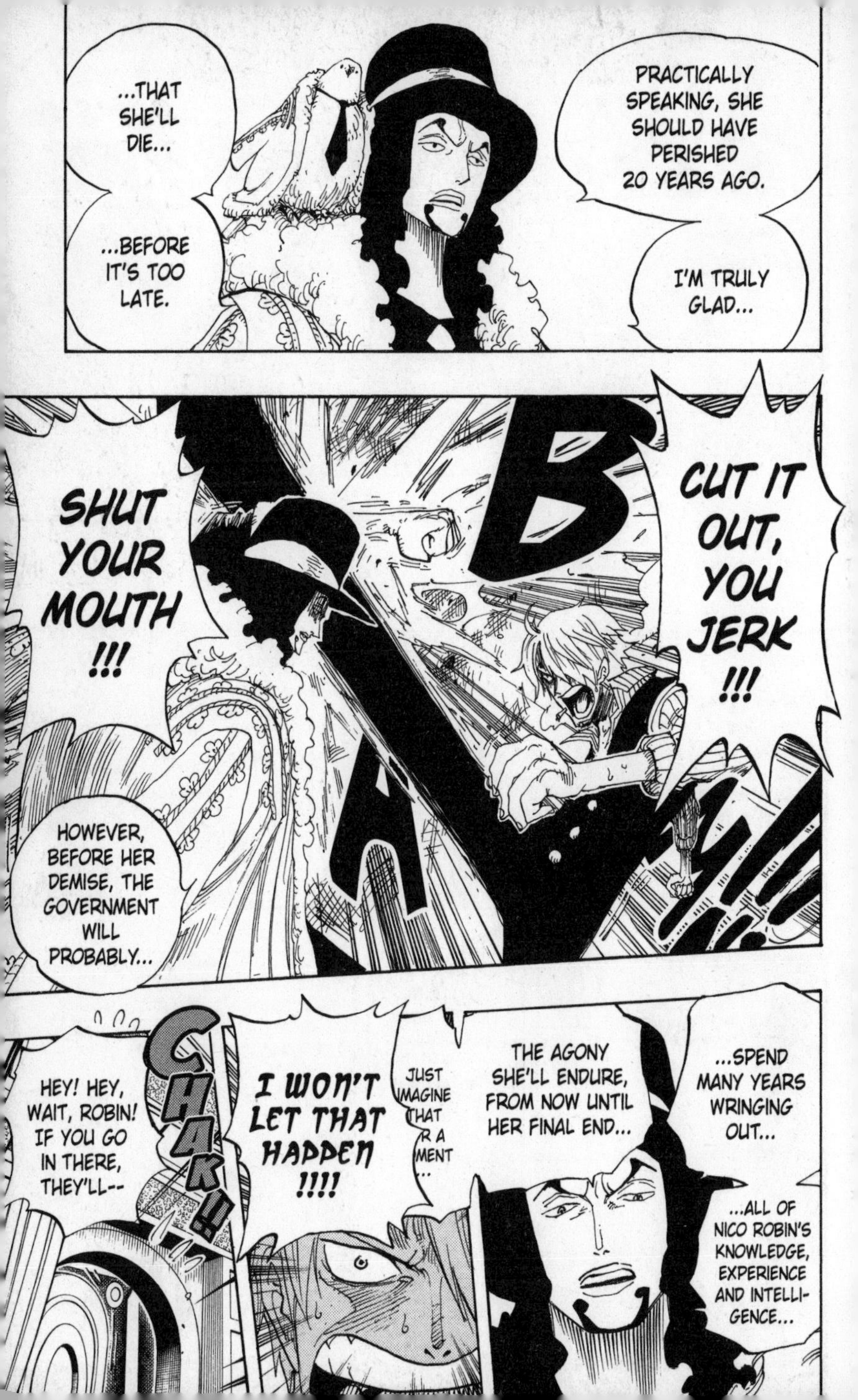
PRACTICALLY SPEAKING, SHE SHOULD HAVE PERISHED 20 YEARS AGO.
I'M TRULY GLAD...
...THAT SHE'LL DIE...
...BEFORE IT'S TOO LATE.
CUT IT OUT, YOU JERK!!!
SHUT YOUR MOUTH!!!
HOWEVER, BEFORE HER DEMISE, THE GOVERNMENT WILL PROBABLY...
...SPEND MANY YEARS WRINGING OUT...
...ALL OF NICO ROBIN'S KNOWLEDGE, EXPERIENCE AND INTELLIGENCE...
THE AGONY SHE'LL ENDURE, FROM NOW UNTIL HER FINAL END...
JUST IMAGINE THAT
I WON'T LET THAT HAPPEN!!!!
CHAK!!
HEY! HEY, WAIT, ROBIN! IF YOU GO IN THERE, THEY'LL--

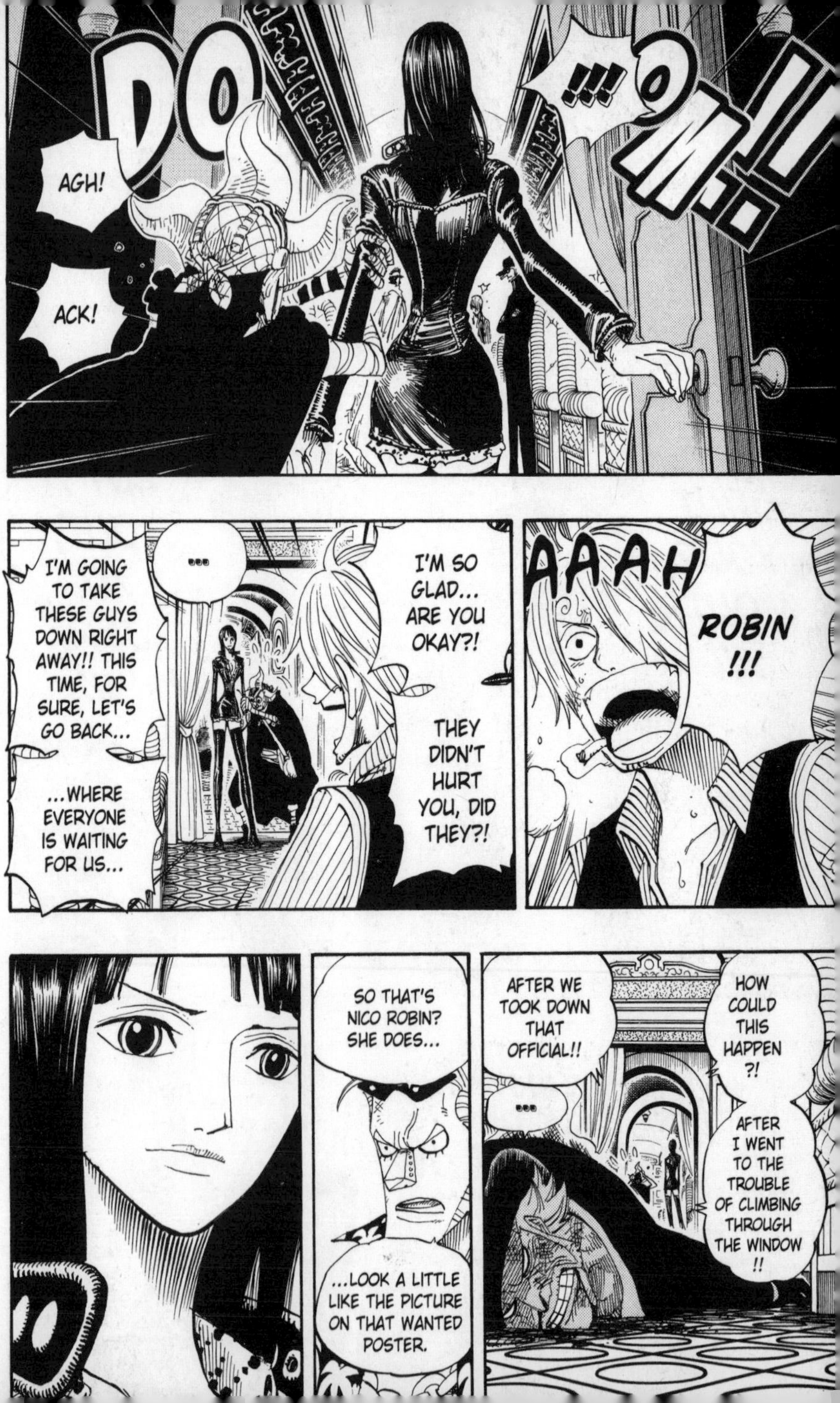
DO
OM!!
AGH!
ACK!
AAAH
ROBIN!!!
I'M SO GLAD... ARE YOU OKAY?!
THEY DIDN'T HURT YOU, DID THEY?!
...
I'M GOING TO TAKE THESE GUYS DOWN RIGHT AWAY!! THIS TIME, FOR SURE, LET'S GO BACK...
...WHERE EVERYONE IS WAITING FOR US...
HOW COULD THIS HAPPEN?!
AFTER I WENT TO THE TROUBLE OF CLIMBING THROUGH THE WINDOW!!
AFTER WE TOOK DOWN THAT OFFICIAL!!
...
SO THAT'S NICO ROBIN? SHE DOES...
...LOOK A LITTLE LIKE THE PICTURE ON THAT WANTED POSTER.

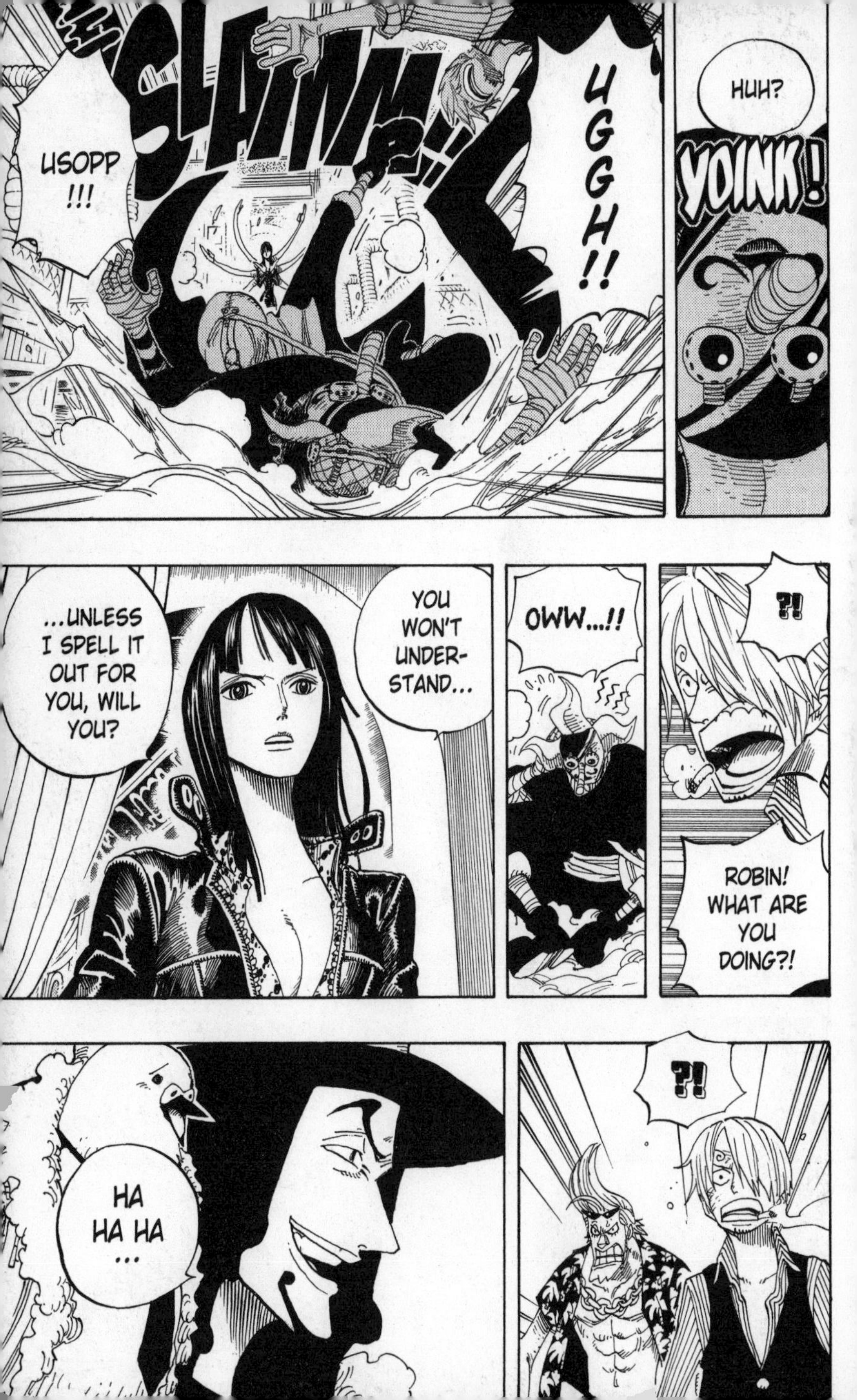
HUH?
YOINK!
SLAMM!!
UGGH!!
USOPP !!!
?!
ROBIN! WHAT ARE YOU DOING?!
OWW...!!
YOU WON'T UNDER-STAND...
...UNLESS I SPELL IT OUT FOR YOU, WILL YOU?
?!
HA HA HA ...

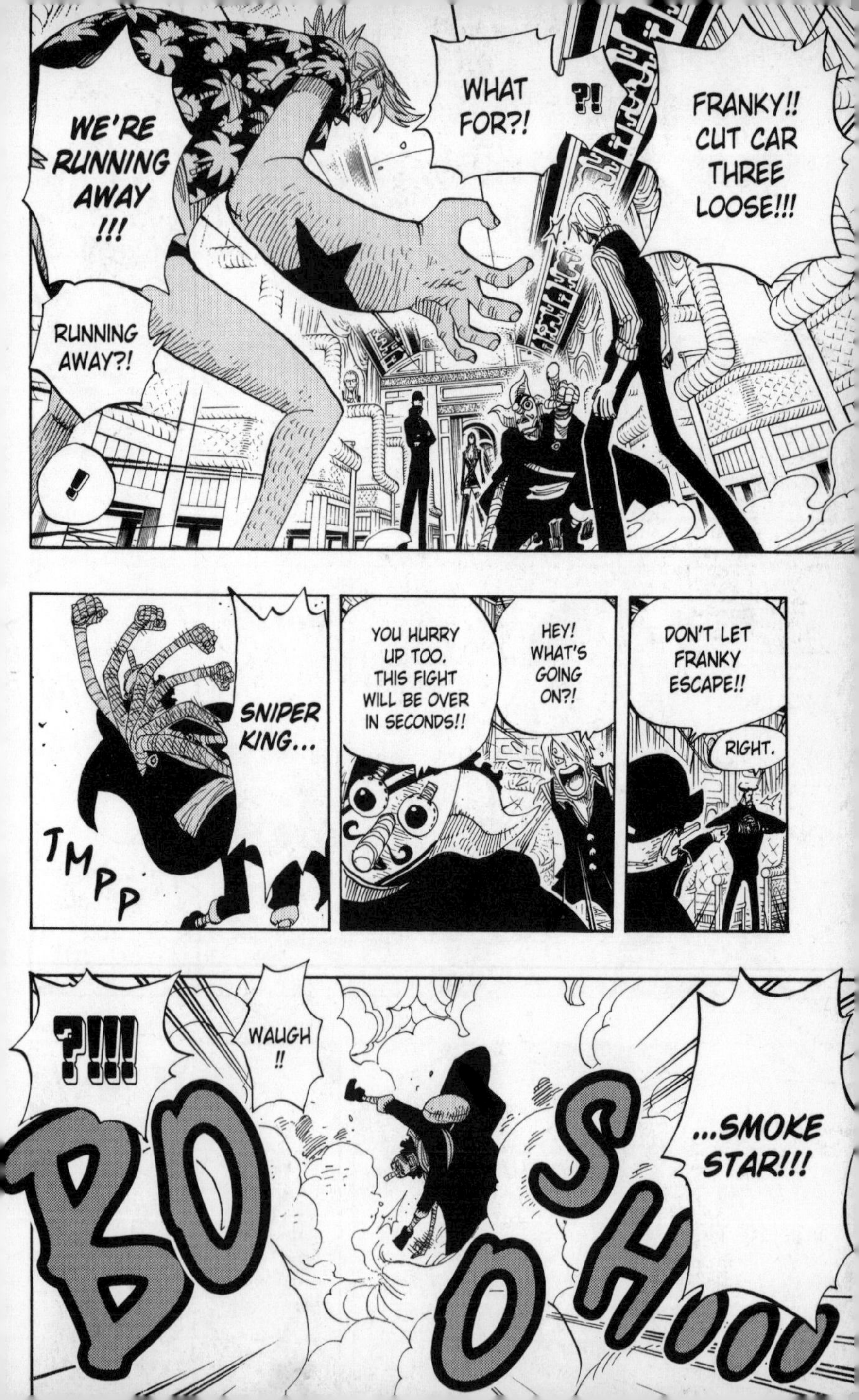
FRANKY!! CUT CAR THREE LOOSE!!!
?!
WHAT FOR?!
WE'RE RUNNING AWAY!!!
RUNNING AWAY?!
!
DON'T LET FRANKY ESCAPE!!
RIGHT.
HEY! WHAT'S GOING ON?!
YOU HURRY UP TOO. THIS FIGHT WILL BE OVER IN SECONDS!!
SNIPER KING...
TMPP
...SMOKE STAR!!!
WAUGH !!
?!!!
BOSHOOO

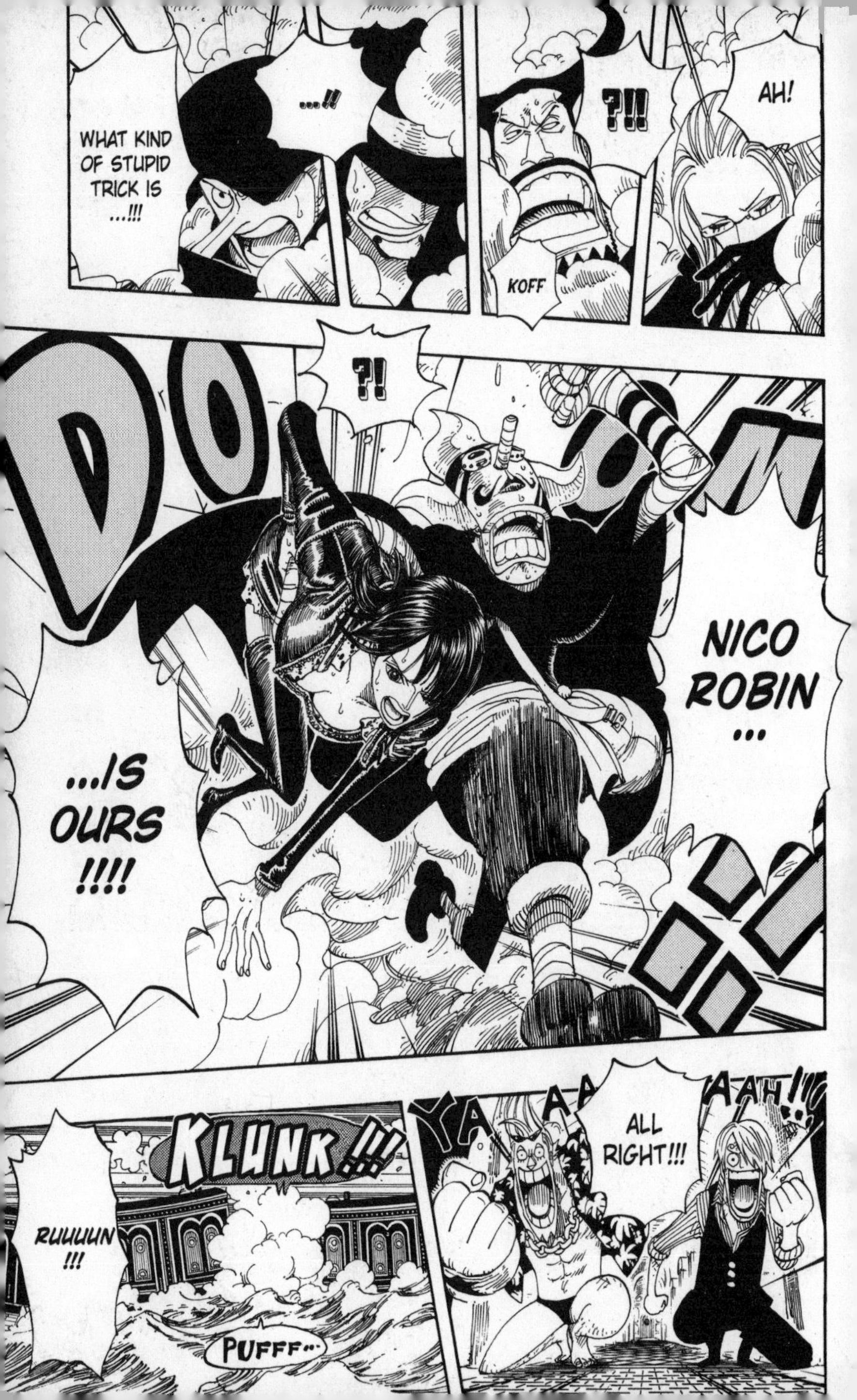
AH!
?!!
KOFF
...!!
WHAT KIND OF STUPID TRICK IS ...!!!
?!
NICO ROBIN ...
...IS OURS !!!!
YAAAAH!!!
ALL RIGHT!!!
KLUNK!!!
RUUUUN !!!
PUFFF...

THE FIRST ONE PIECE FAN FAVORITE MOVES CONTEST RESULTS!

GUM-GUM GATLING

FIRST PLACE
(3785 VOTES)

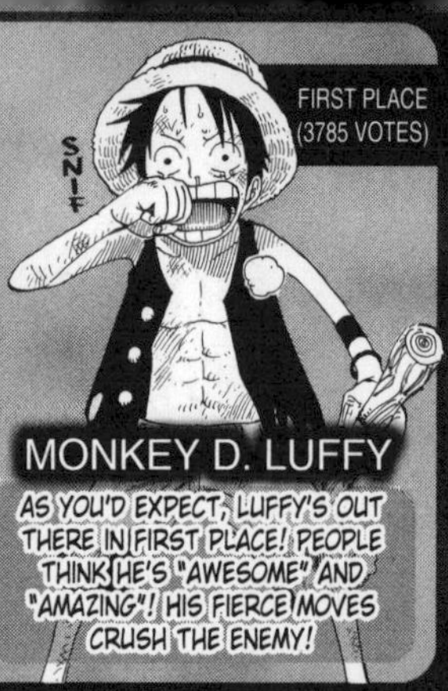
S
N
I
F

MONKEY D. LUFFY

AS YOU'D EXPECT, LUFFY'S OUT THERE IN FIRST PLACE! PEOPLE THINK HE'S "AWESOME" AND "AMAZING"! HIS FIERCE MOVES CRUSH THE ENEMY!

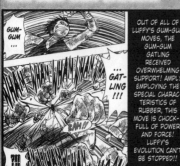

OUT OF ALL OF LUFFY'S GUM-GUM MOVES, THE GUM-GUM GATLING RECEIVED OVERWHELMING SUPPORT! AMPLY EMPLOYING THE SPECIAL CHARACTERISTICS OF RUBBER, THIS MOVE IS CHOCK-FULL OF POWER AND FORCE! LUFFY'S EVOLUTION CAN'T BE STOPPED!!

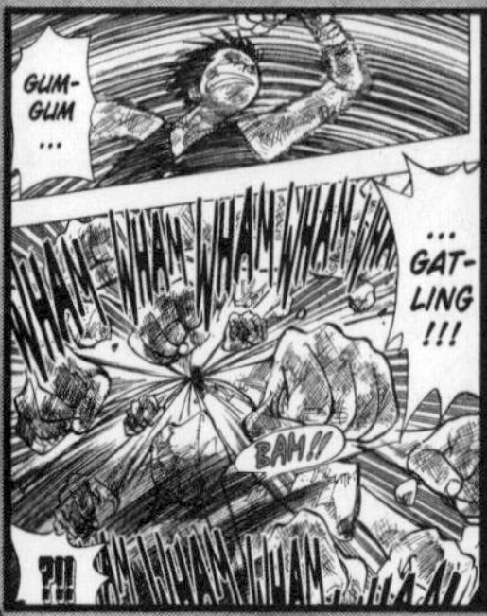
GUM-GUM ...
... GAT-LING !!!
BAM!!
?!!

THREE THOUSAND WORLDS

SECOND PLACE
(3625 VOTES)

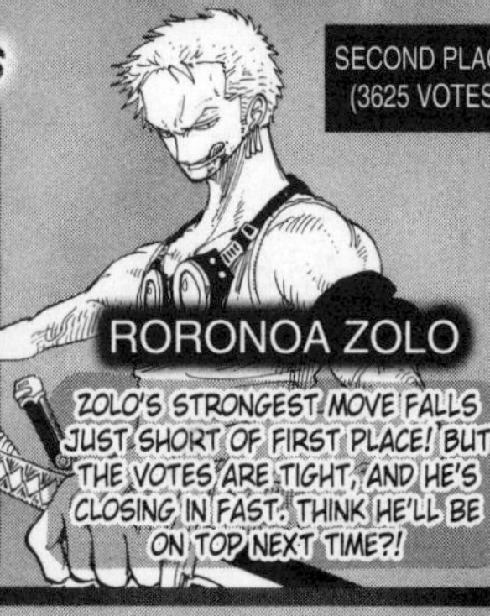

RORONOA ZOLO

ZOLO'S STRONGEST MOVE FALLS JUST SHORT OF FIRST PLACE! BUT THE VOTES ARE TIGHT, AND HE'S CLOSING IN FAST. THINK HE'LL BE ON TOP NEXT TIME?!

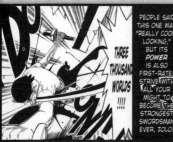

PEOPLE SAID THIS ONE WAS "REALLY COOL-LOOKING," BUT ITS ***POWER*** IS ALSO FIRST-RATE! STRIVE WITH ALL YOUR MIGHT TO BECOME THE STRONGEST SWORDSMAN EVER, ZOLO!

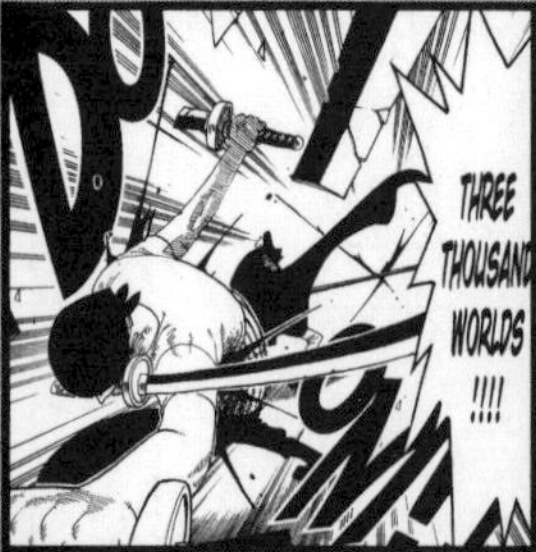
THREE THOUSAND WORLDS !!!!

MOUTON MALLET

THIRD PLACE
(1445 VOTES)

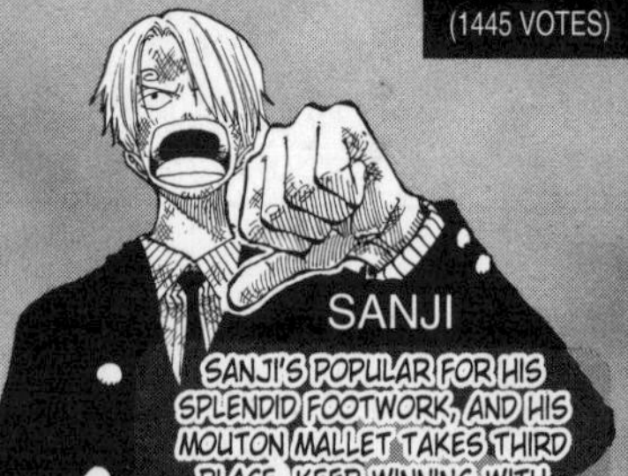

SANJI

SANJI'S POPULAR FOR HIS SPLENDID FOOTWORK, AND HIS MOUTON MALLET TAKES THIRD PLACE. KEEP WINNING WITH STYLE, SANJI!

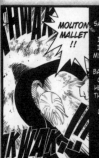

SANJI'S MAXIM IS "SINCE I'M A COOK, I DON'T USE MY HANDS FOR FIGHTING." BASED ON THIS CONVICTION, HE'S POUNDED THE BAD GUYS TO PIECES USING ONLY KICKS! EXCELLENT FINISH, EXCELLENT POWER!!

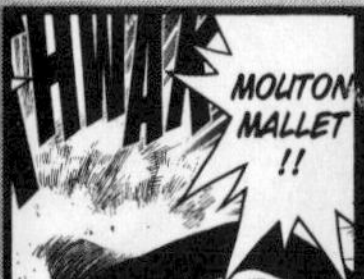
MOUTON MALLET !!
KWAK...!!

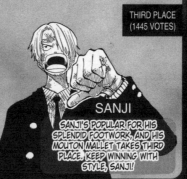

NAMI CALLED THEM ALL!

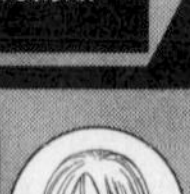

JUST AS I EXPECTED, LUFFY TOOK FIRST PLACE, BUT SINCE ZOLO AND SANJI HAVE MOVES WE HAVEN'T SEEN YET, IT'S BOUND TO BE A FREE-FOR-ALL! AND BY THE WAY, WHAT ABOUT *MY* MOVES?!

WE'LL RUN THE FOURTH PLACE AND UNDER RESULTS IN THE NEXT VOLUME! WHICH MOVE DID YOU VOTE FOR?! AND HOW ABOUT THAT POWERHOUSE MOVE OF LUFFY'S?! THE RESULTS ARE ALREADY IN! HANG ON UNTIL VOLUME 40!!!

Chapter 374: SCRAMBLE

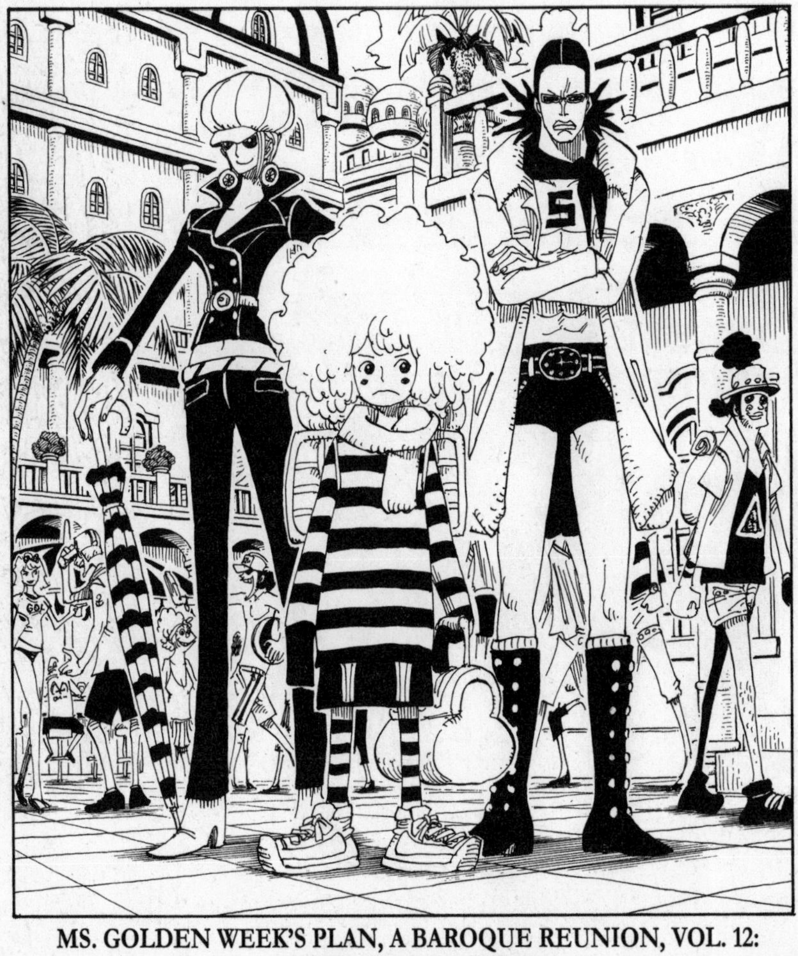

MS. GOLDEN WEEK'S PLAN, A BAROQUE REUNION, VOL. 12:
"WE TRIED DISGUISES"

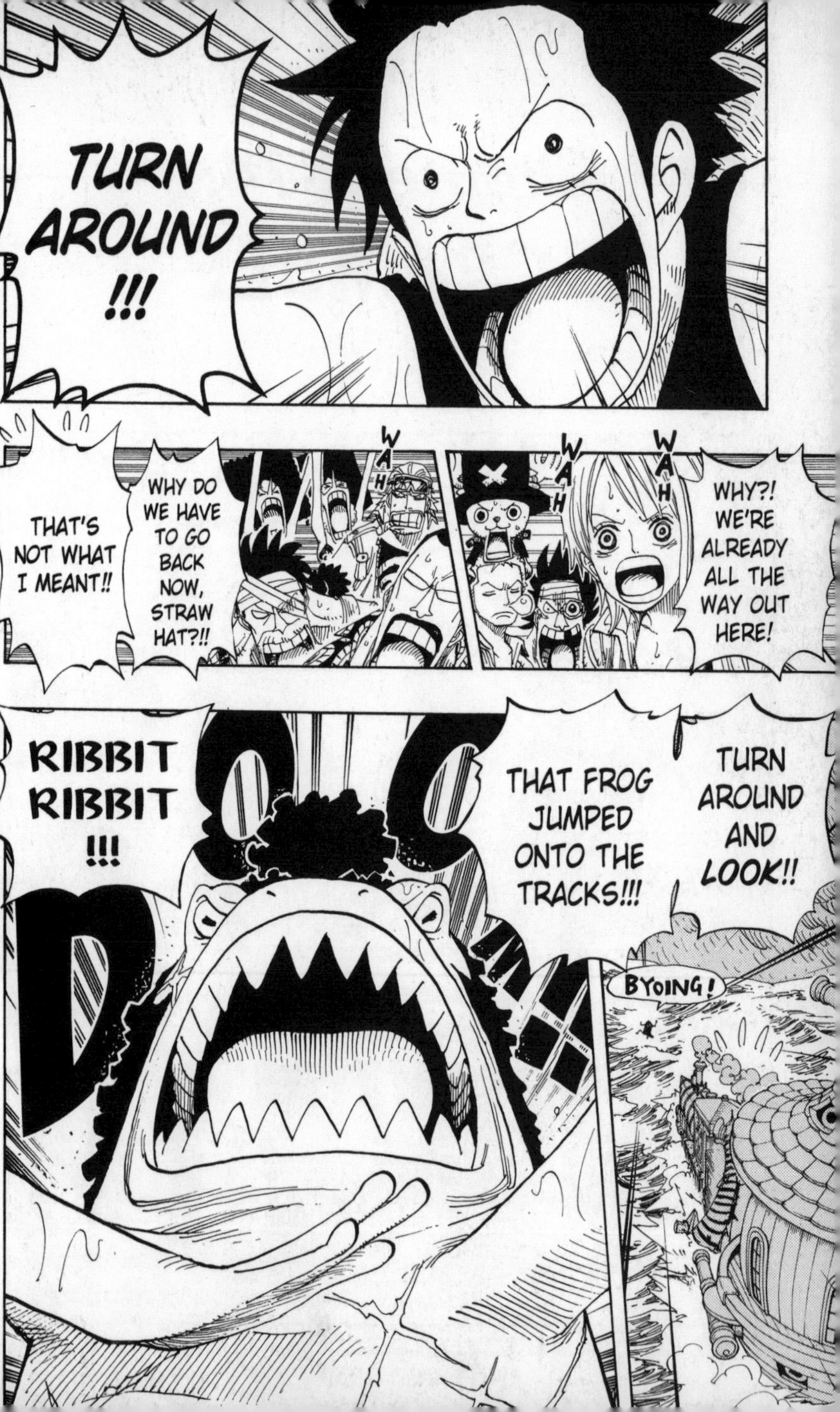
TURN AROUND!!!
WAH
WAH
WHY?! WE'RE ALREADY ALL THE WAY OUT HERE!
WAH
WHY DO WE HAVE TO GO BACK NOW, STRAW HAT?!!
THAT'S NOT WHAT I MEANT!!
TURN AROUND AND LOOK!!
THAT FROG JUMPED ONTO THE TRACKS!!!
BYOING!
RIBBIT RIBBIT!!!

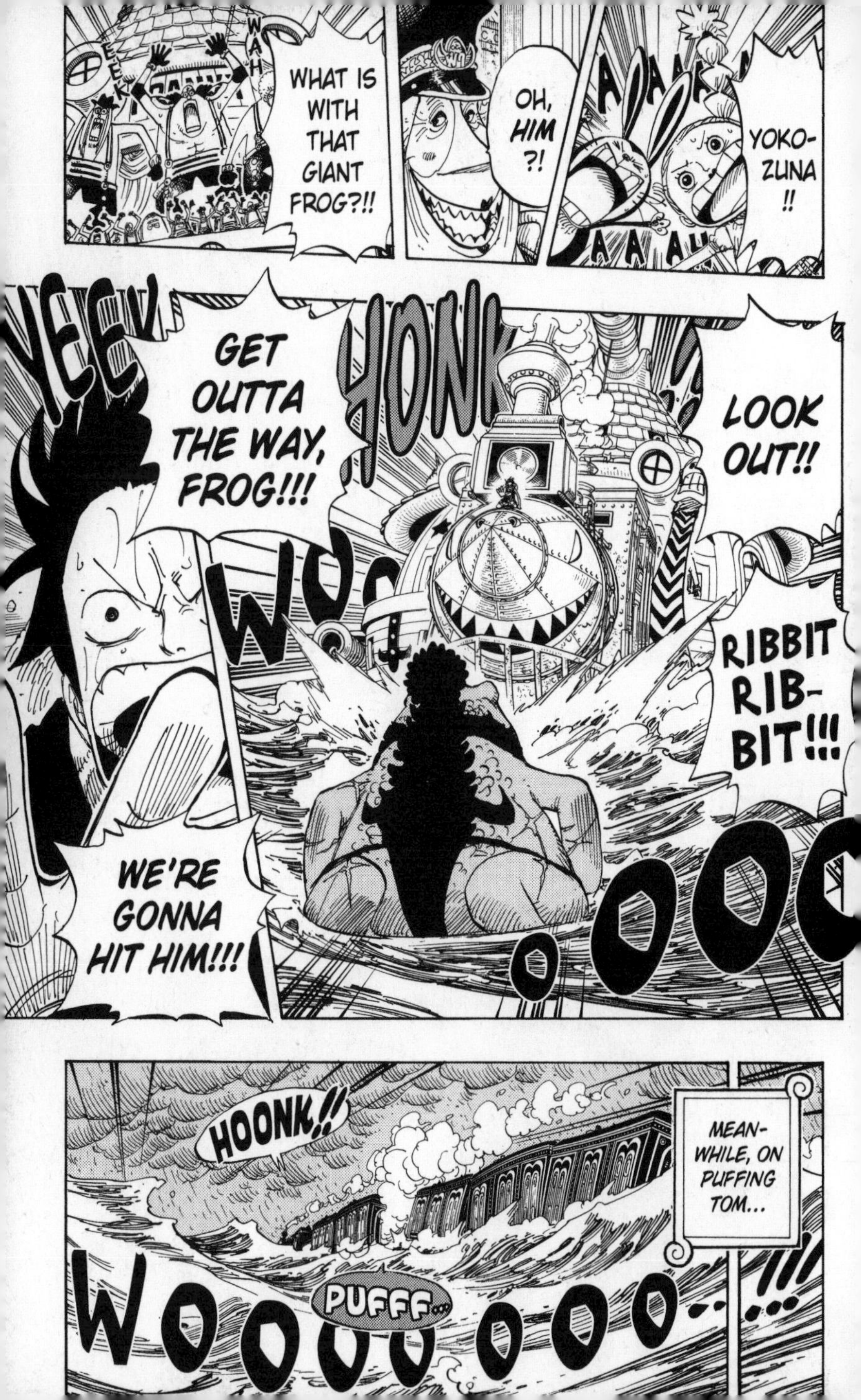
AAAA
YOKO-ZUNA!!
AAAAU
OH, HIM?!
WHAT IS WITH THAT GIANT FROG?!!
WAH
EEEK
LOOK OUT!!
HONK
GET OUTTA THE WAY, FROG!!!
RIBBIT RIB-BIT!!!
WO
WE'RE GONNA HIT HIM!!!
MEAN-WHILE, ON PUFFING TOM...
HOONK!!
WOOOOO-OOO-...!!!
PUFFF...

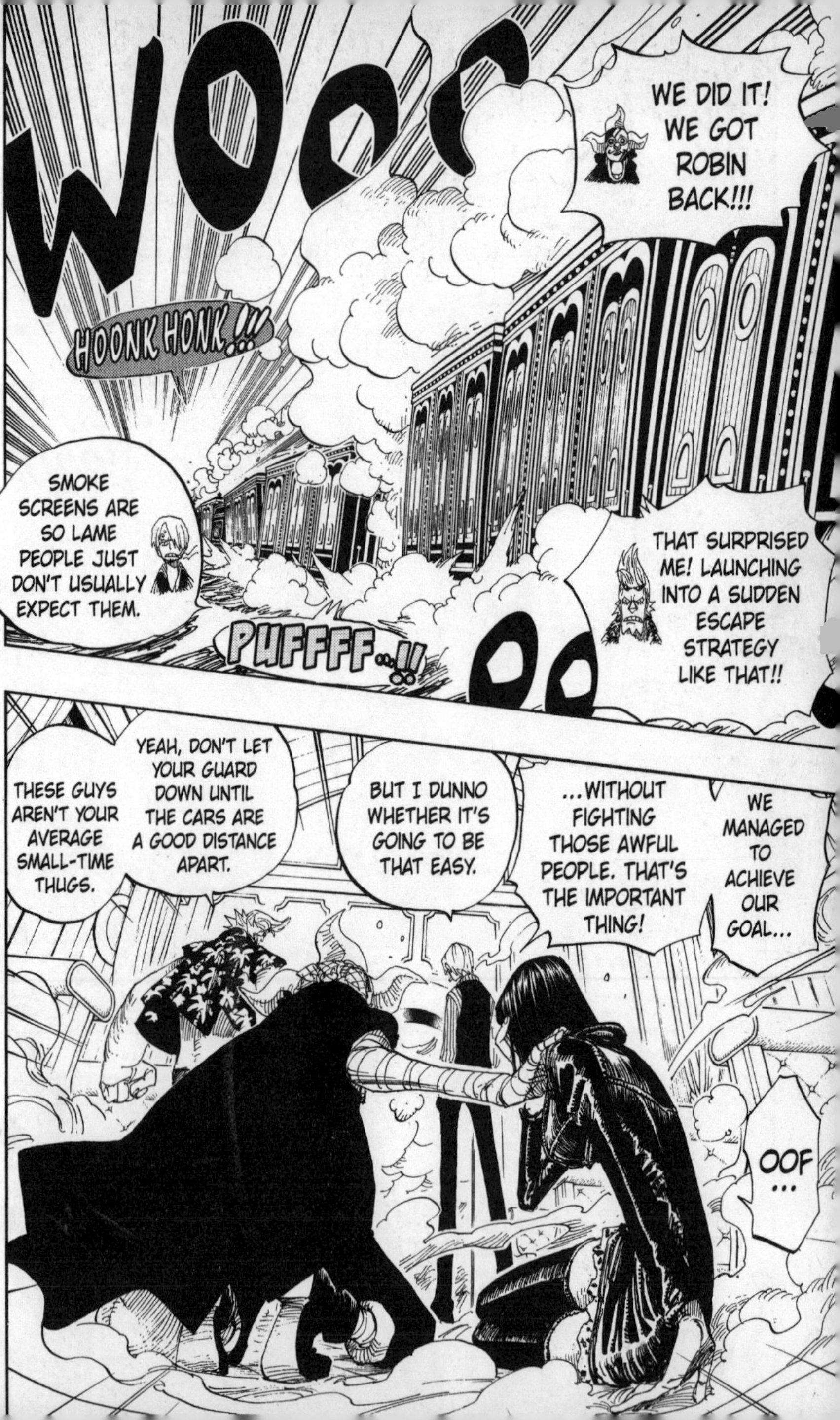
WE DID IT! WE GOT ROBIN BACK!!!
HOONK HONK...!!!
THAT SURPRISED ME! LAUNCHING INTO A SUDDEN ESCAPE STRATEGY LIKE THAT!!
SMOKE SCREENS ARE SO LAME PEOPLE JUST DON'T USUALLY EXPECT THEM.
PUFFFF...!!
WE MANAGED TO ACHIEVE OUR GOAL...
...WITHOUT FIGHTING THOSE AWFUL PEOPLE. THAT'S THE IMPORTANT THING!
BUT I DUNNO WHETHER IT'S GOING TO BE THAT EASY.
YEAH, DON'T LET YOUR GUARD DOWN UNTIL THE CARS ARE A GOOD DISTANCE APART.
THESE GUYS AREN'T YOUR AVERAGE SMALL-TIME THUGS.
OOF...

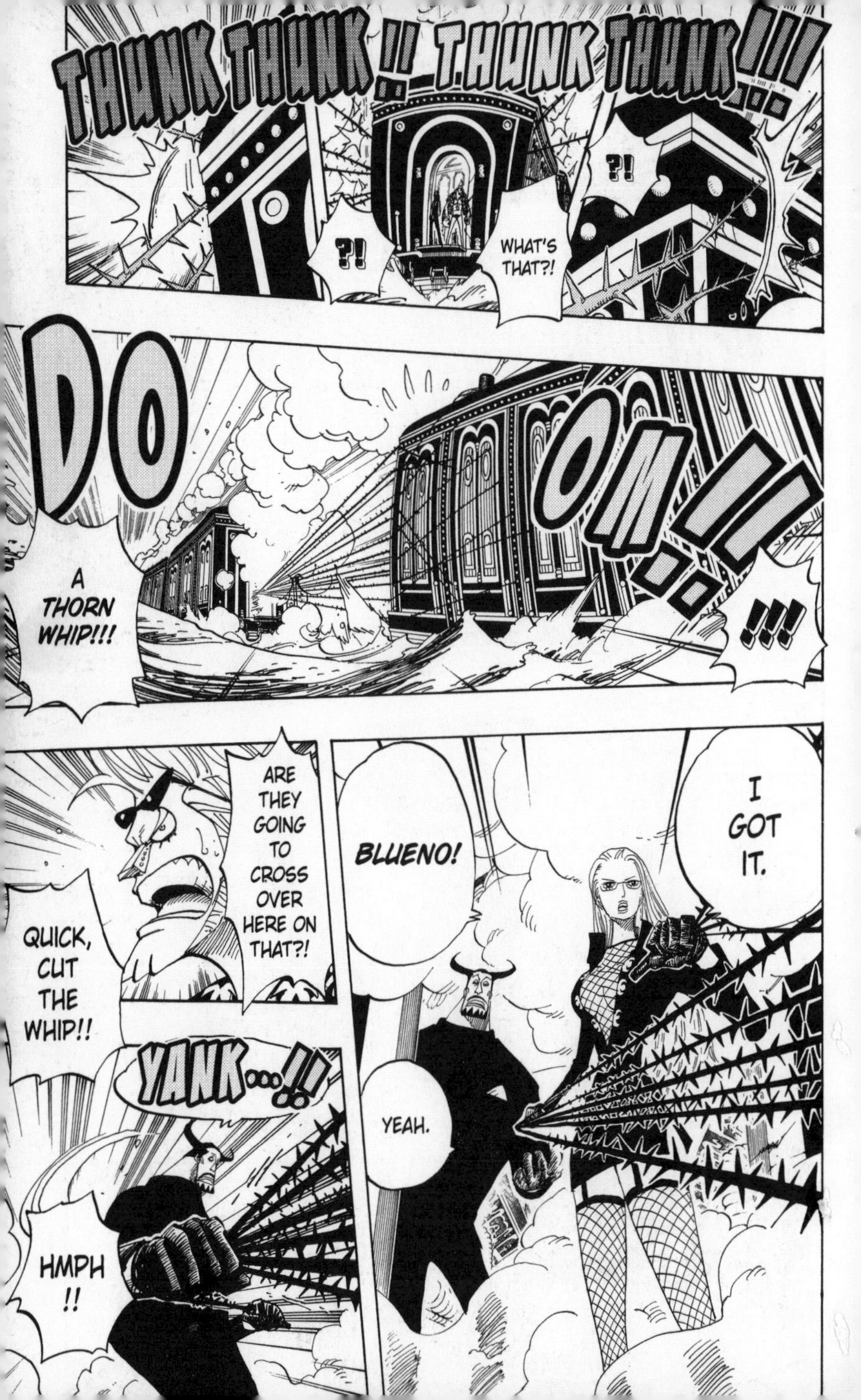
THUNK THUNK!! THUNK THUNK!!!
?!
WHAT'S THAT?!
?!
DOOM!!
!!!
A THORN WHIP!!!
I GOT IT.
BLUENO!
YEAH.
ARE THEY GOING TO CROSS OVER HERE ON THAT?!
QUICK, CUT THE WHIP!!
YANK...!!
HMPH!!

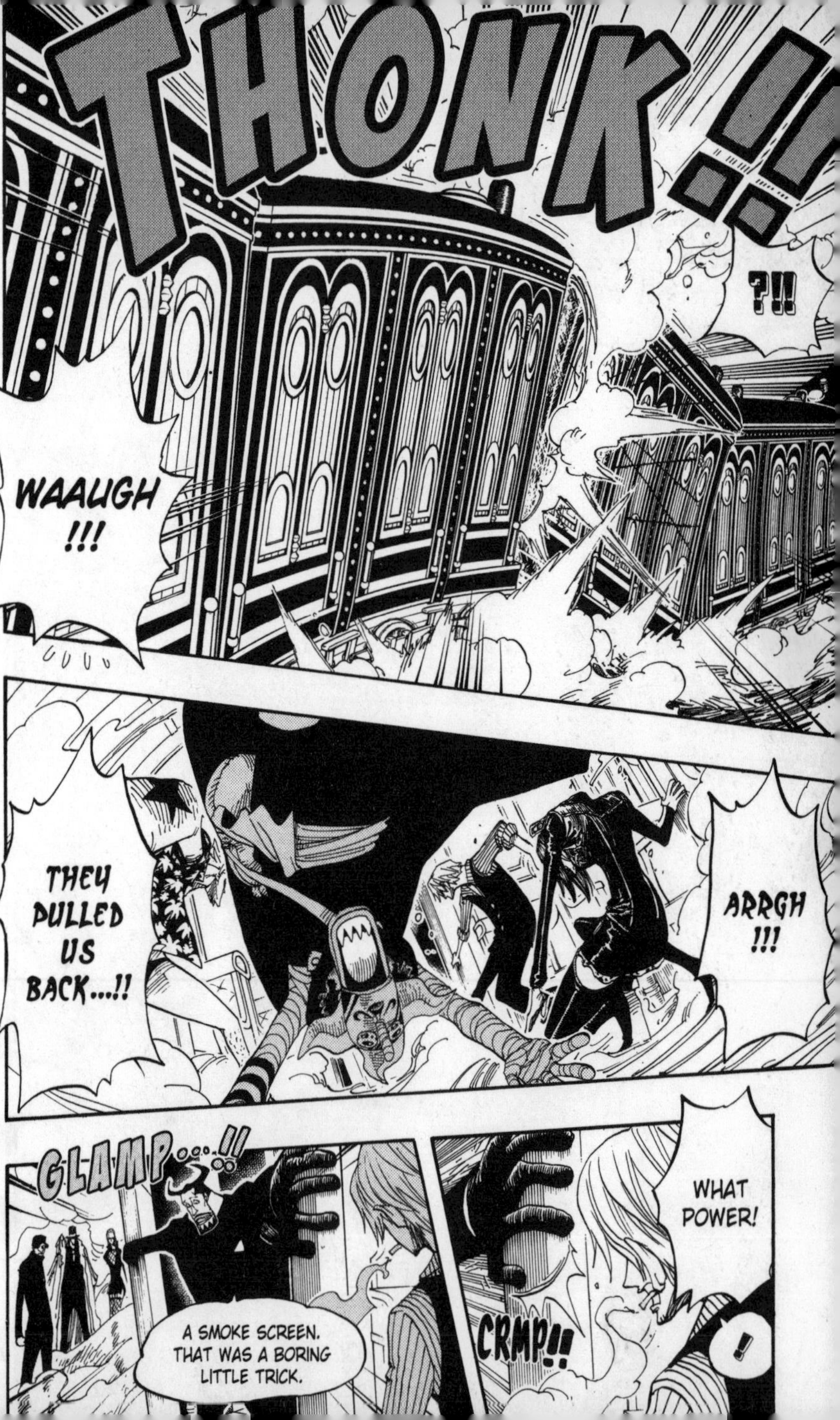
THONK!!
?!!
WAAUGH!!!
ARRGH!!!
THEY PULLED US BACK...!!
WHAT POWER!
!
CRMP!!
GLAMP...!!
A SMOKE SCREEN. THAT WAS A BORING LITTLE TRICK.

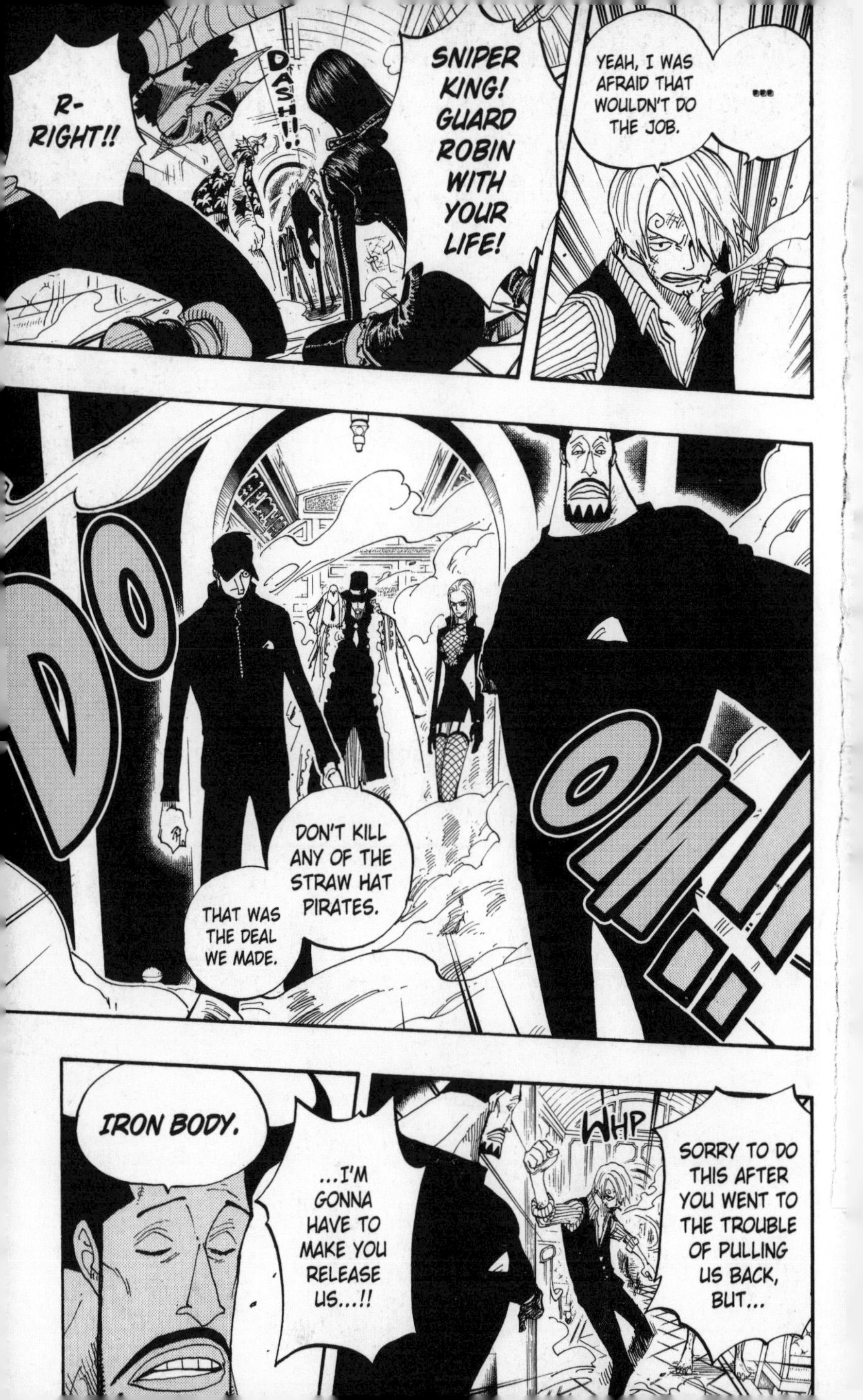
YEAH, I WAS AFRAID THAT WOULDN'T DO THE JOB.
...
SNIPER KING! GUARD ROBIN WITH YOUR LIFE!
DASH!!
R-RIGHT!!
DON'T KILL ANY OF THE STRAW HAT PIRATES.
THAT WAS THE DEAL WE MADE.
SORRY TO DO THIS AFTER YOU WENT TO THE TROUBLE OF PULLING US BACK, BUT...
WHP
...I'M GONNA HAVE TO MAKE YOU RELEASE US...!!
IRON BODY.

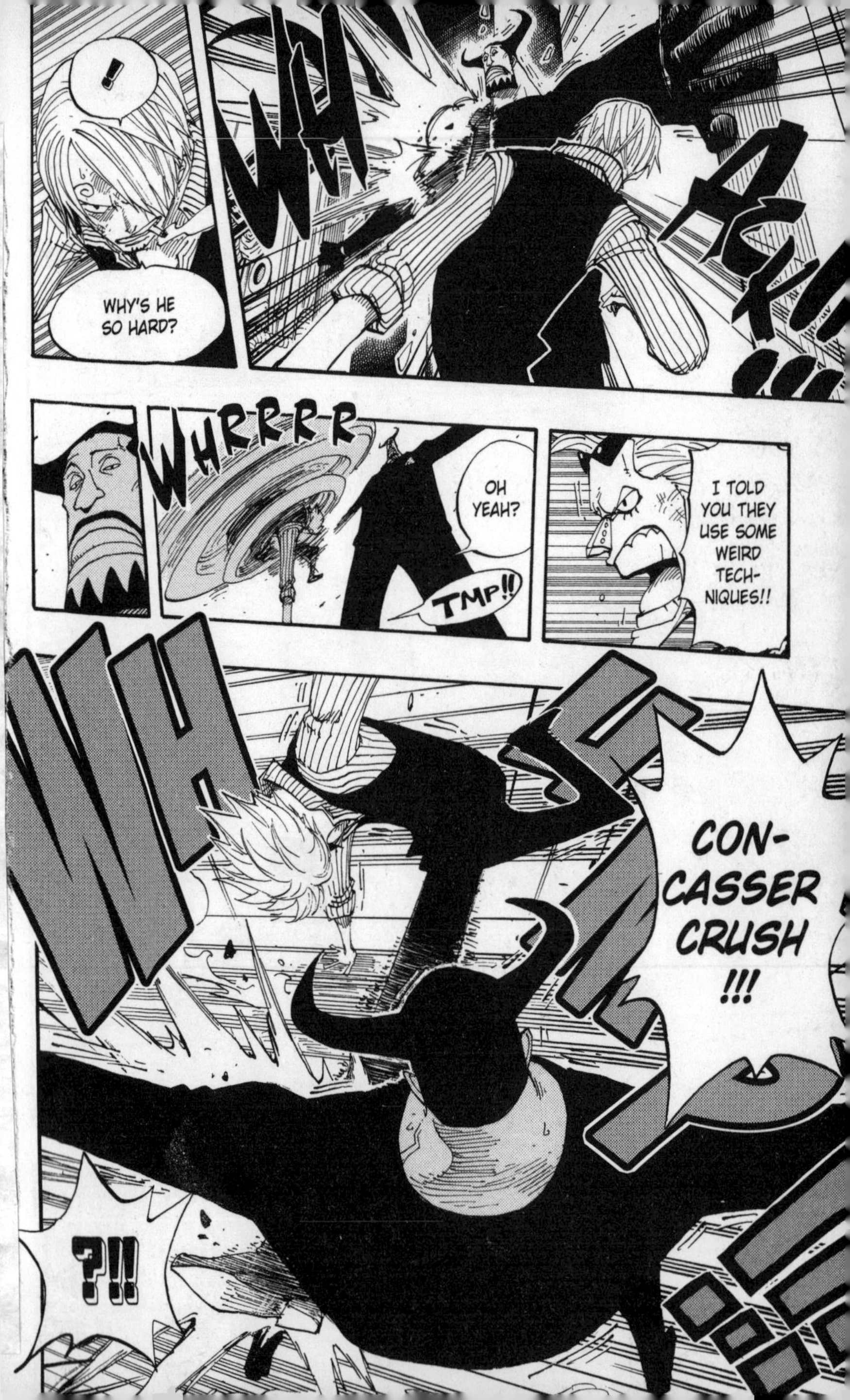
WHACK!!
!
WHY'S HE SO HARD?
I TOLD YOU THEY USE SOME WEIRD TECH-NIQUES!!
OH YEAH?
TMP!!
WHRRRR
CON-CASSER CRUSH !!!
?!!

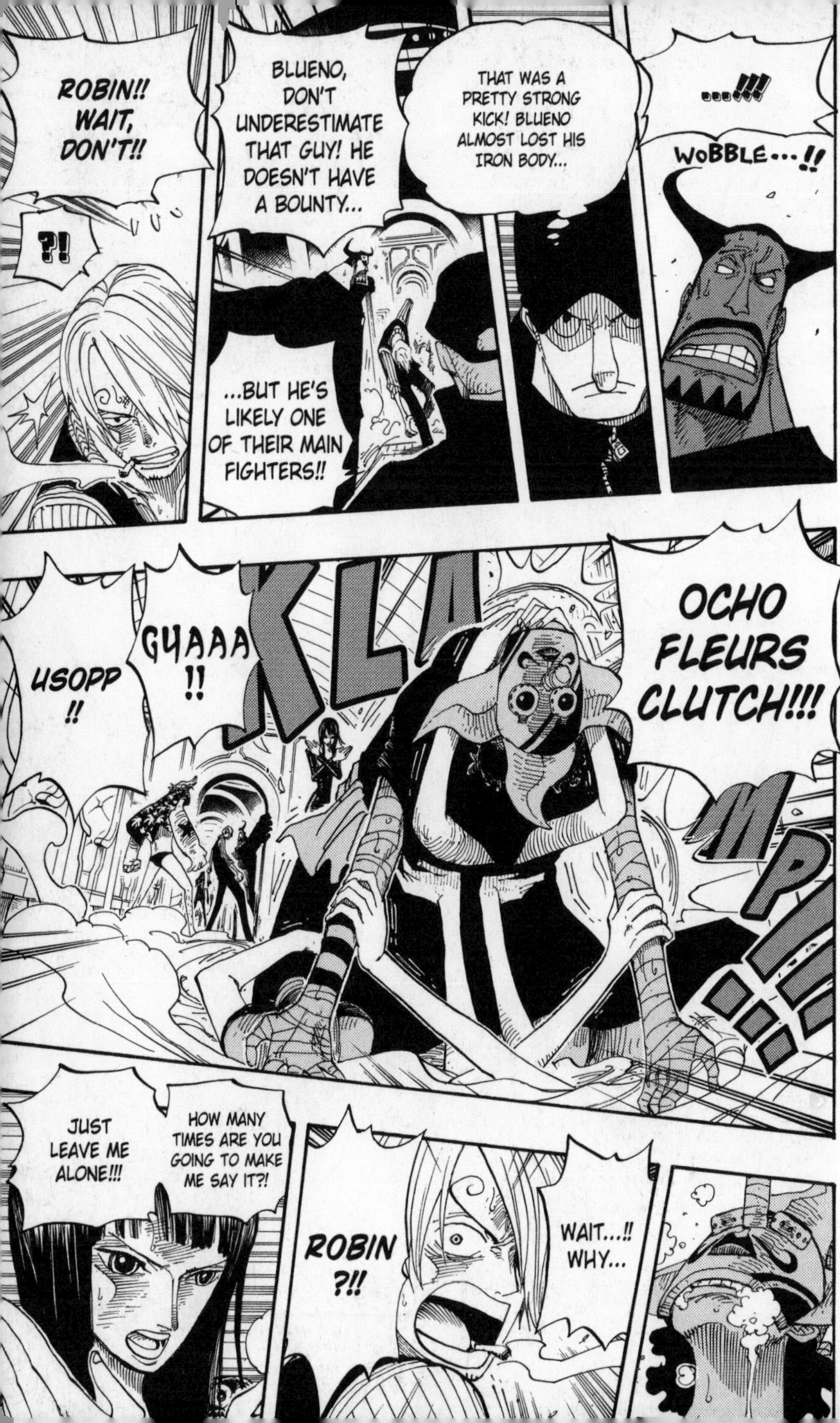
...!!!
WOBBLE...!!
THAT WAS A PRETTY STRONG KICK! BLUENO ALMOST LOST HIS IRON BODY...
BLUENO, DON'T UNDERESTIMATE THAT GUY! HE DOESN'T HAVE A BOUNTY...
...BUT HE'S LIKELY ONE OF THEIR MAIN FIGHTERS!!
ROBIN!! WAIT, DON'T!!
?!
OCHO FLEURS CLUTCH!!!
GUAAA !!
USOPP !!
WAIT...!! WHY...
ROBIN ?!!
HOW MANY TIMES ARE YOU GOING TO MAKE ME SAY IT?!
JUST LEAVE ME ALONE!!!

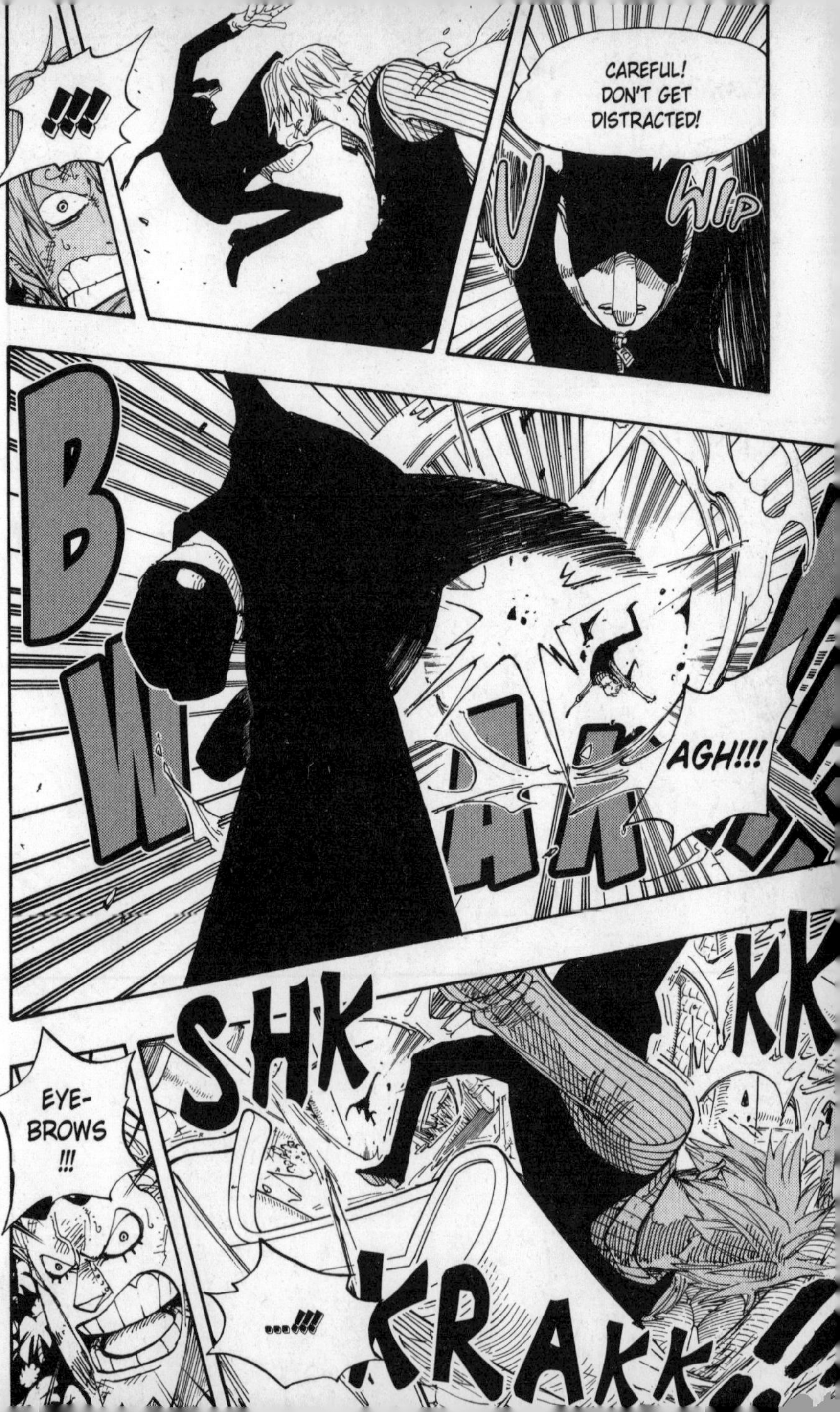

CAREFUL! DON'T GET DISTRACTED!
WIP
!!!
AGH!!!
SHK
KRAKK!!!
...!!!
EYE-BROWS !!!

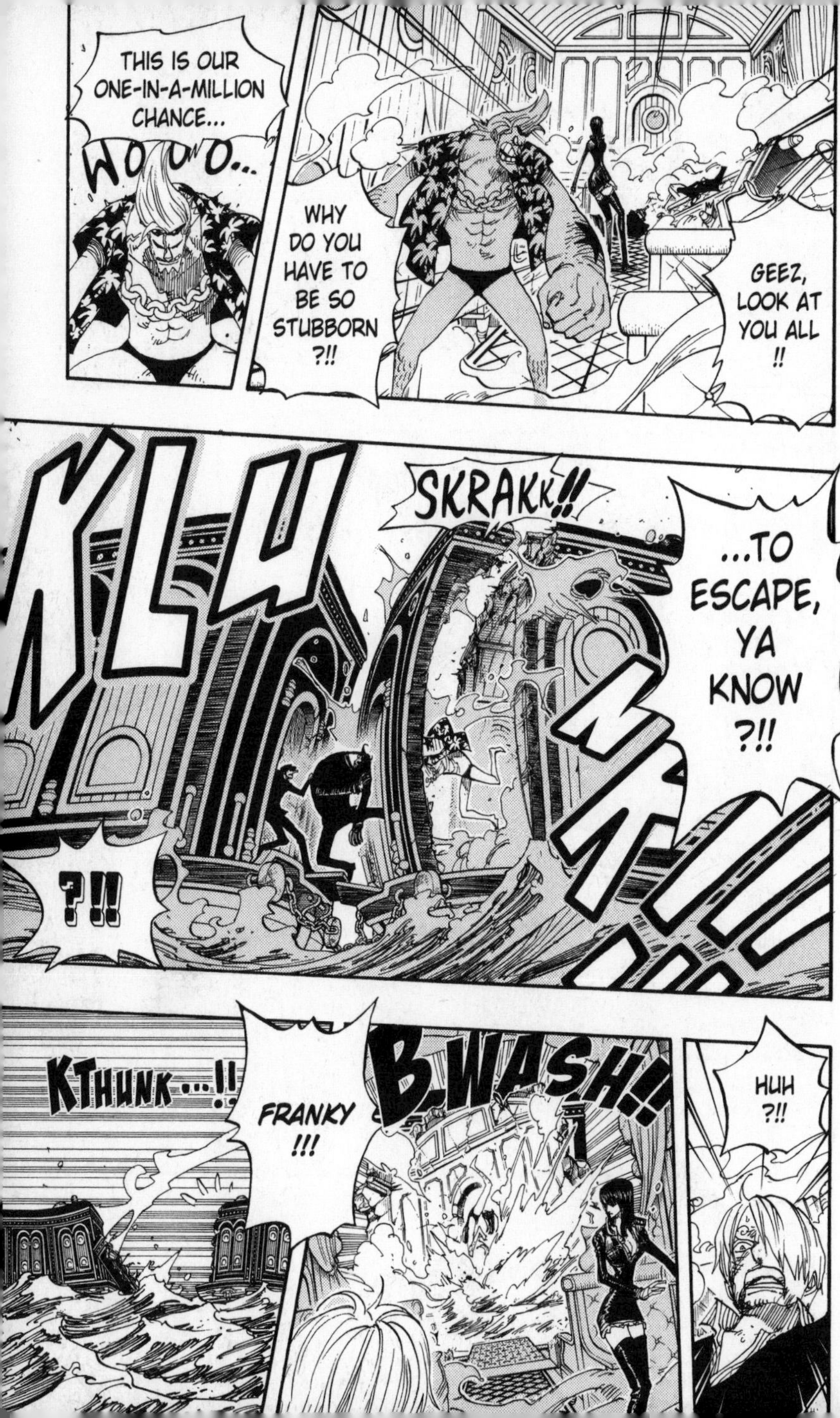
GEEZ, LOOK AT YOU ALL !!
WHY DO YOU HAVE TO BE SO STUBBORN ?!!
THIS IS OUR ONE-IN-A-MILLION CHANCE...
WOOO...
...TO ESCAPE, YA KNOW ?!!
SKRAKK!!
?!!
HUH ?!!
BWASH!!
FRANKY !!!
KTHUNK...!!

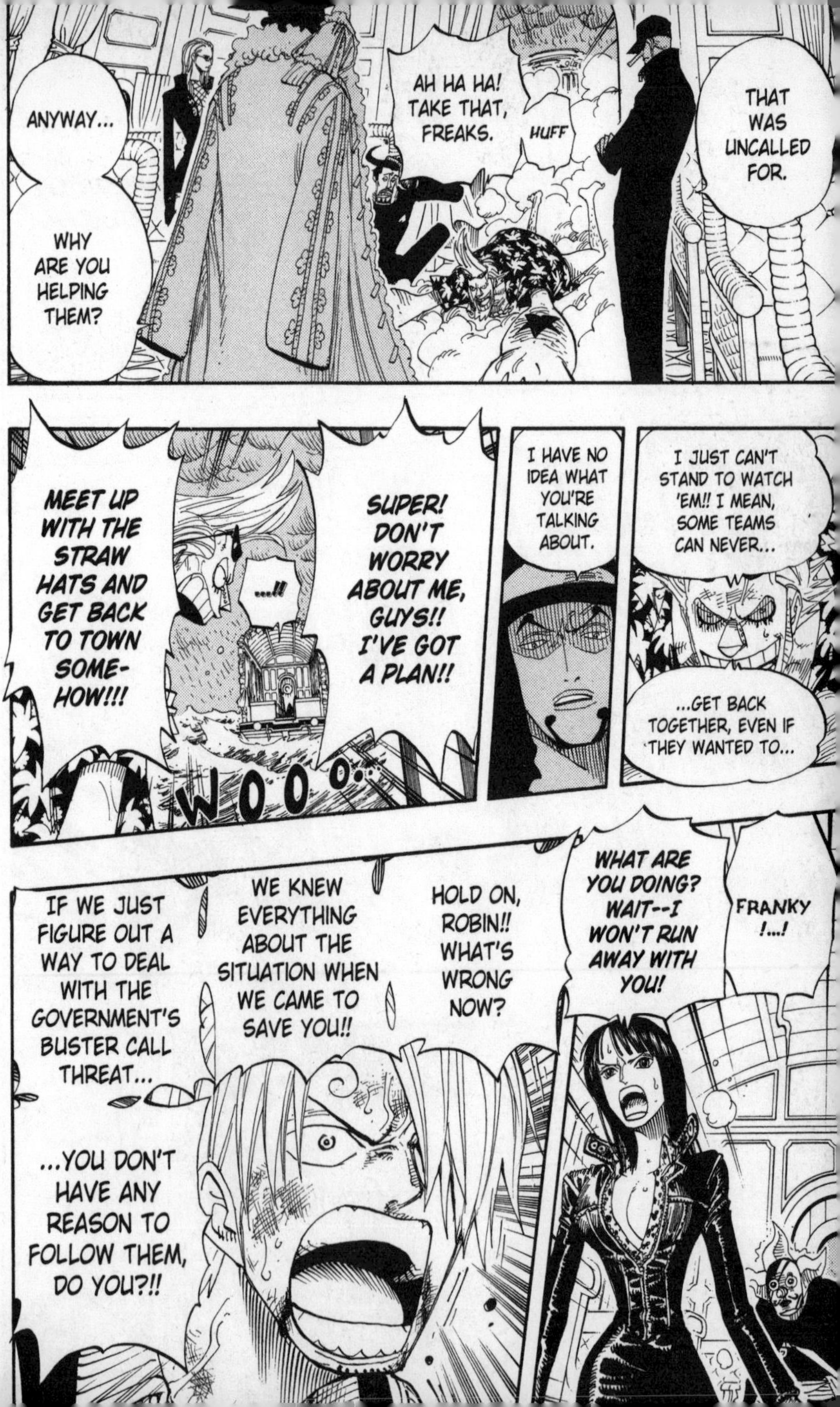
THAT WAS UNCALLED FOR.
AH HA HA! TAKE THAT, FREAKS.
HUFF
ANYWAY...
WHY ARE YOU HELPING THEM?
I JUST CAN'T STAND TO WATCH 'EM!! I MEAN, SOME TEAMS CAN NEVER...
...GET BACK TOGETHER, EVEN IF THEY WANTED TO...
I HAVE NO IDEA WHAT YOU'RE TALKING ABOUT.
SUPER! DON'T WORRY ABOUT ME, GUYS!! I'VE GOT A PLAN!!
...!!
MEET UP WITH THE STRAW HATS AND GET BACK TO TOWN SOME-HOW!!!
WOOO
FRANKY !...!
WHAT ARE YOU DOING? WAIT--I WON'T RUN AWAY WITH YOU!
HOLD ON, ROBIN!! WHAT'S WRONG NOW?
WE KNEW EVERYTHING ABOUT THE SITUATION WHEN WE CAME TO SAVE YOU!!
IF WE JUST FIGURE OUT A WAY TO DEAL WITH THE GOVERNMENT'S BUSTER CALL THREAT...
...YOU DON'T HAVE ANY REASON TO FOLLOW THEM, DO YOU?!!

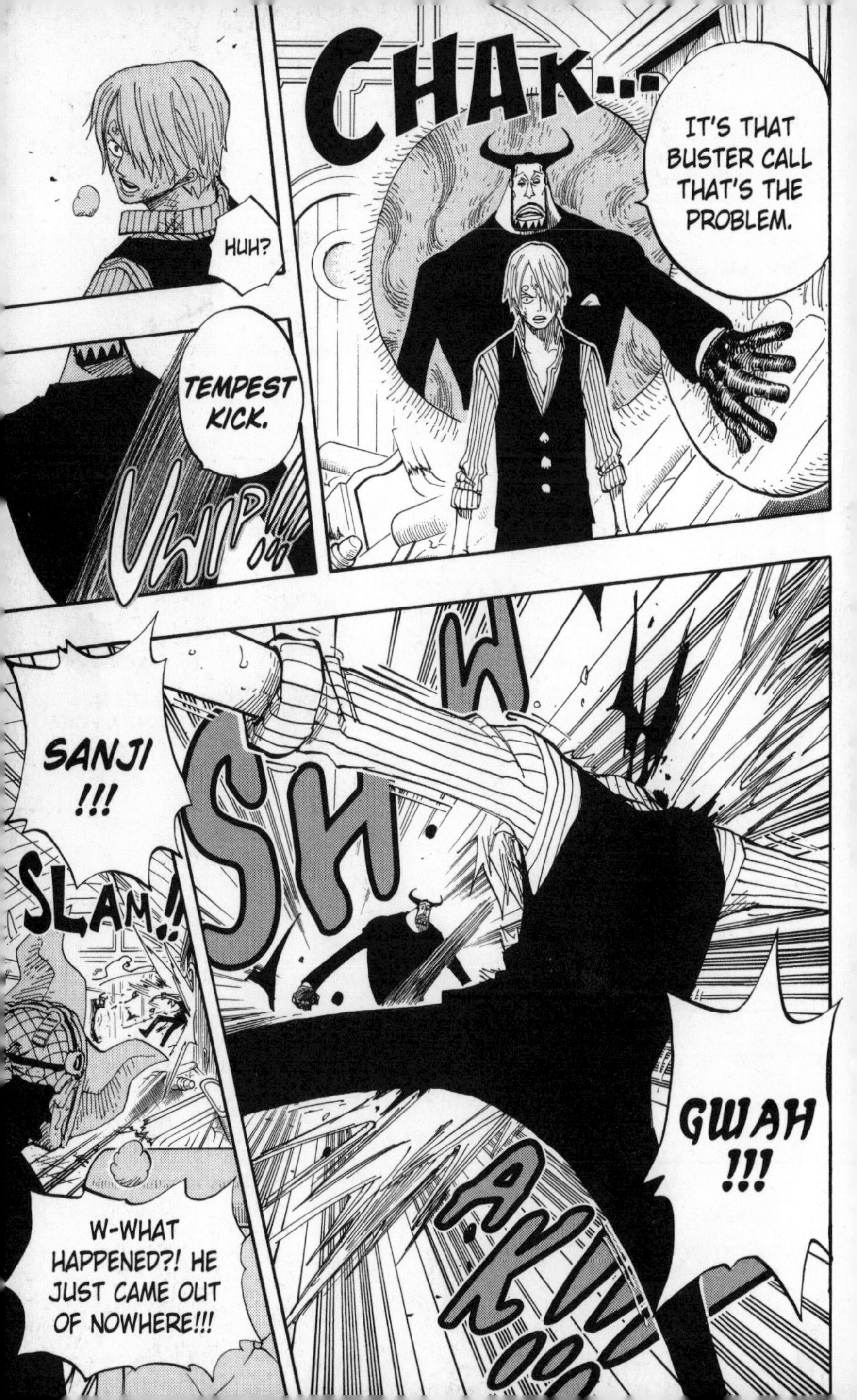
CHAK...
IT'S THAT BUSTER CALL THAT'S THE PROBLEM.
HUH?
TEMPEST KICK.
WHIP...
GWAH!!!
SANJI!!!
SLAM!!
W-WHAT HAPPENED?! HE JUST CAME OUT OF NOWHERE!!!

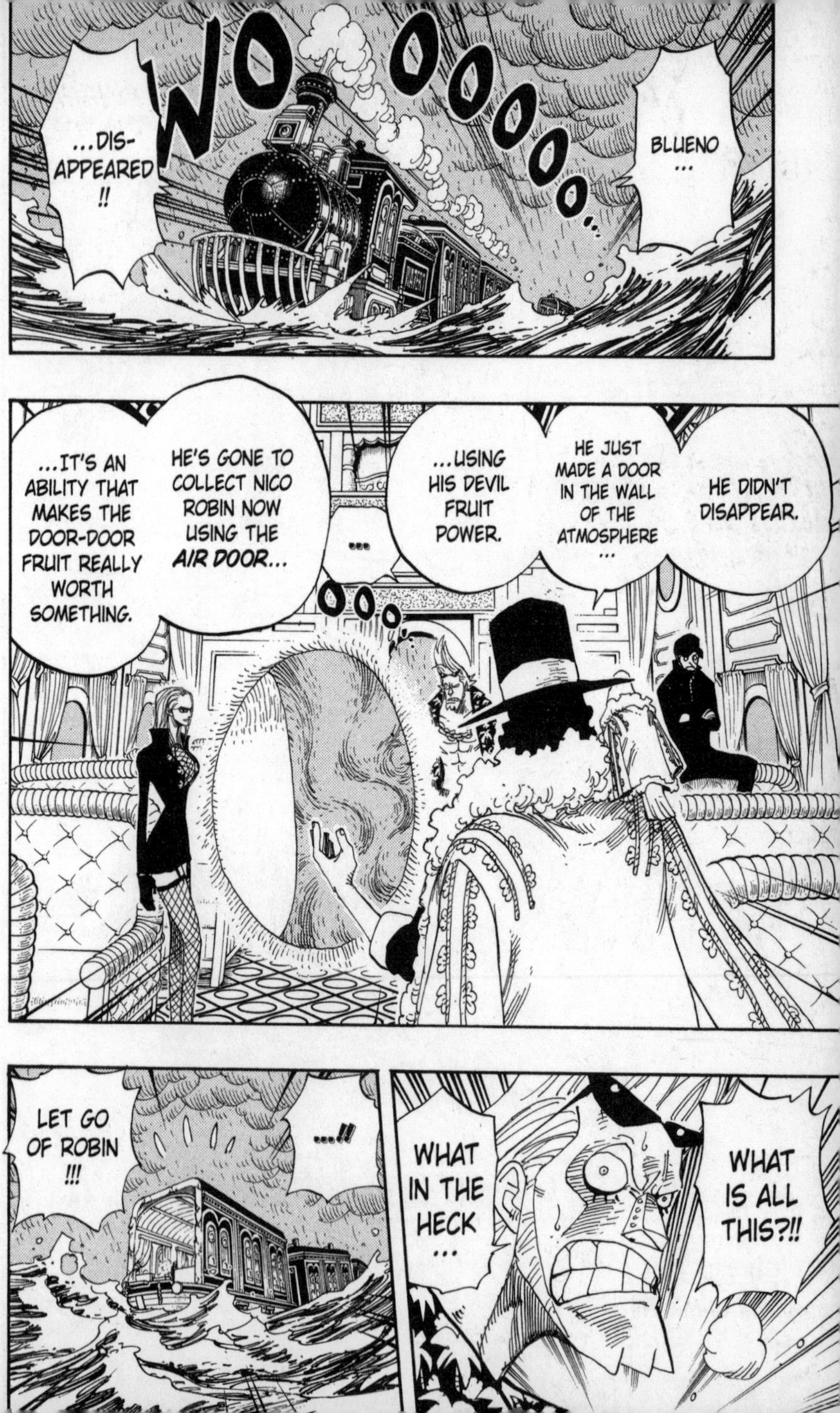
BLUENO ...
WOOOOOO...
...DIS-APPEARED !!
HE DIDN'T DISAPPEAR.
HE JUST MADE A DOOR IN THE WALL OF THE ATMOSPHERE ...
...USING HIS DEVIL FRUIT POWER.
...
HE'S GONE TO COLLECT NICO ROBIN NOW USING THE *AIR DOOR*...
...IT'S AN ABILITY THAT MAKES THE DOOR-DOOR FRUIT REALLY WORTH SOMETHING.
WHAT IS ALL THIS?!!
WHAT IN THE HECK ...
...!!
LET GO OF ROBIN !!!

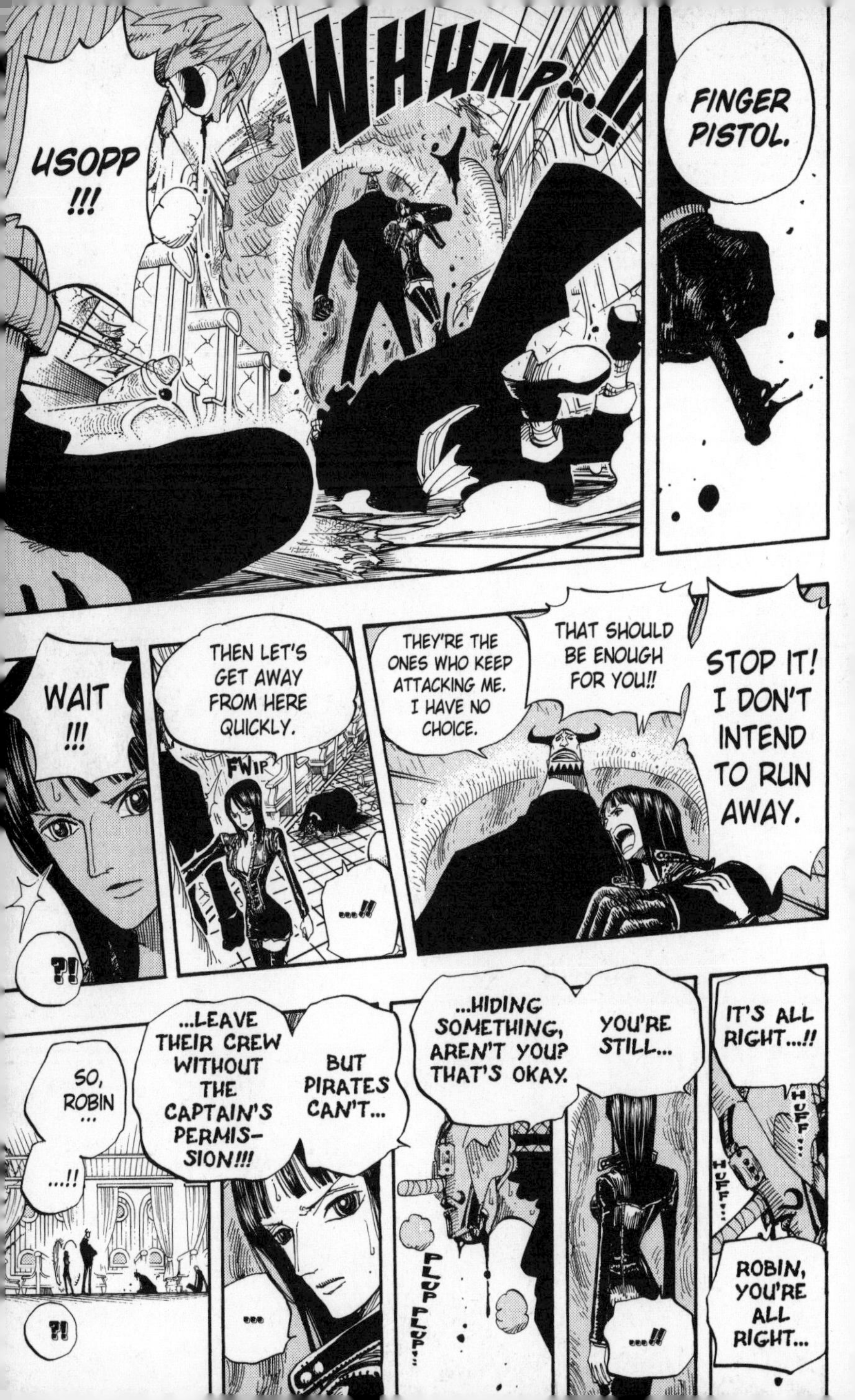
FINGER PISTOL.
WHUMP...!!
USOPP!!!
STOP IT! I DON'T INTEND TO RUN AWAY.
THAT SHOULD BE ENOUGH FOR YOU!!
THEY'RE THE ONES WHO KEEP ATTACKING ME. I HAVE NO CHOICE.
THEN LET'S GET AWAY FROM HERE QUICKLY.
FWIP
...!!
WAIT!!!
?!
IT'S ALL RIGHT...!!
HUFF...
HUFF...
ROBIN, YOU'RE ALL RIGHT...
YOU'RE STILL...
...HIDING SOMETHING, AREN'T YOU? THAT'S OKAY.
...!!
PLUP PLUP...
BUT PIRATES CAN'T...
...LEAVE THEIR CREW WITHOUT THE CAPTAIN'S PERMIS-SION!!!
...
SO, ROBIN...
...!!
?!

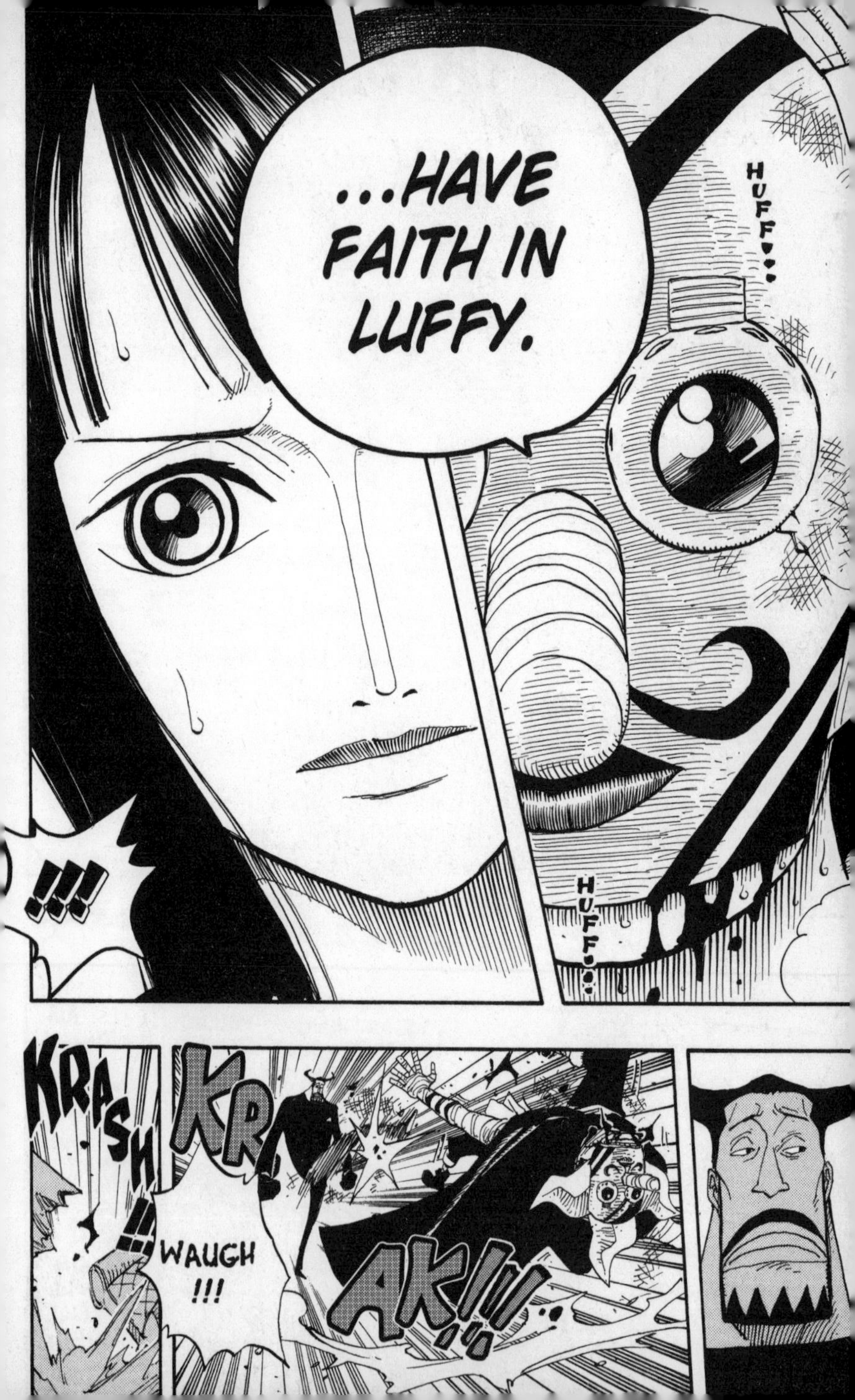
...HAVE FAITH IN LUFFY.
HUFF...
!!!
HUFF...
KR
AK!!!
KRASH!!
WAUGH !!!

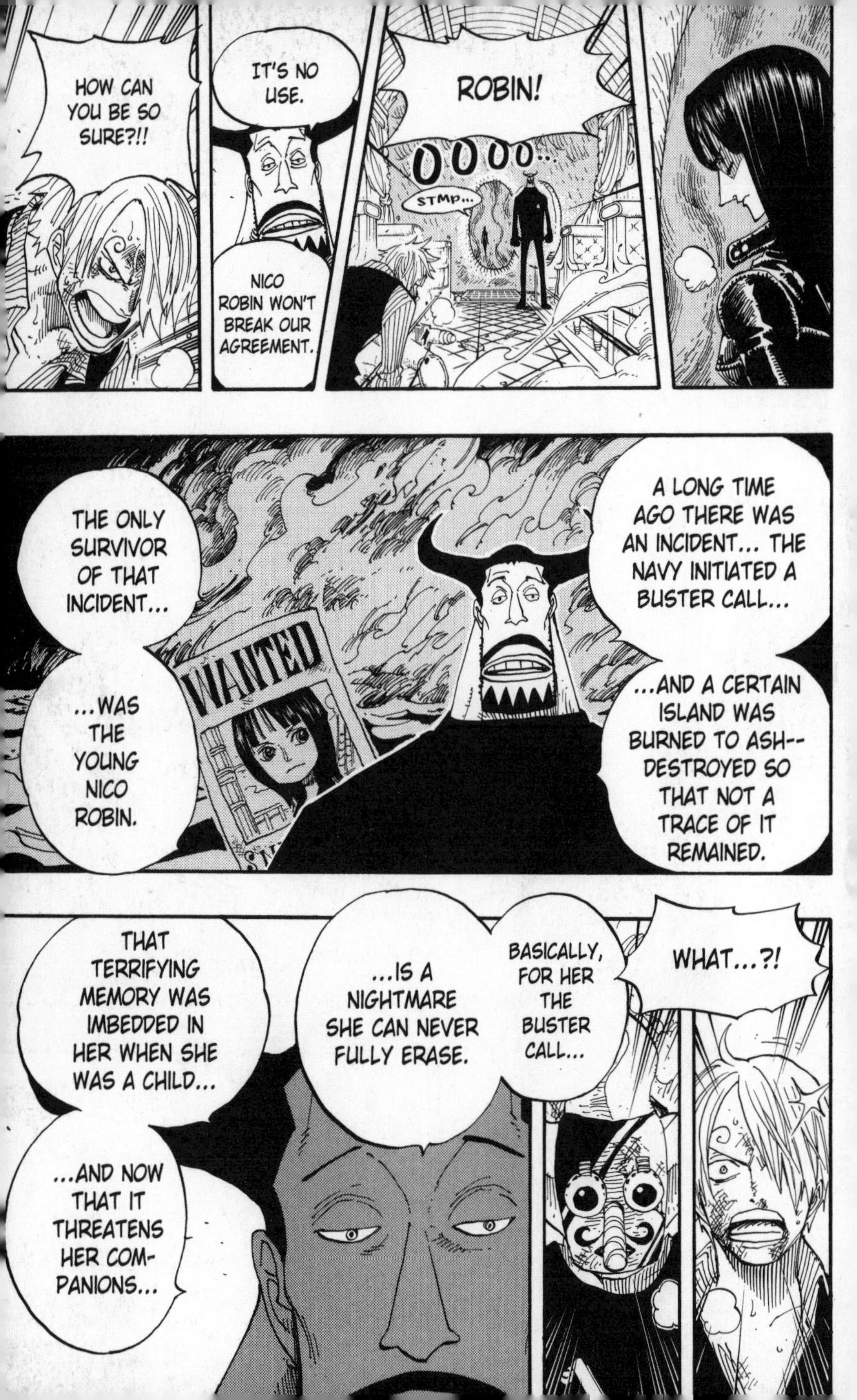
ROBIN!
OOOO...
STMP...
IT'S NO USE.
NICO ROBIN WON'T BREAK OUR AGREEMENT.
HOW CAN YOU BE SO SURE?!!
A LONG TIME AGO THERE WAS AN INCIDENT... THE NAVY INITIATED A BUSTER CALL...
...AND A CERTAIN ISLAND WAS BURNED TO ASH-- DESTROYED SO THAT NOT A TRACE OF IT REMAINED.
THE ONLY SURVIVOR OF THAT INCIDENT...
...WAS THE YOUNG NICO ROBIN.
WANTED
WHAT...?!
BASICALLY, FOR HER THE BUSTER CALL...
...IS A NIGHTMARE SHE CAN NEVER FULLY ERASE.
THAT TERRIFYING MEMORY WAS IMBEDDED IN HER WHEN SHE WAS A CHILD...
...AND NOW THAT IT THREATENS HER COM-PANIONS...

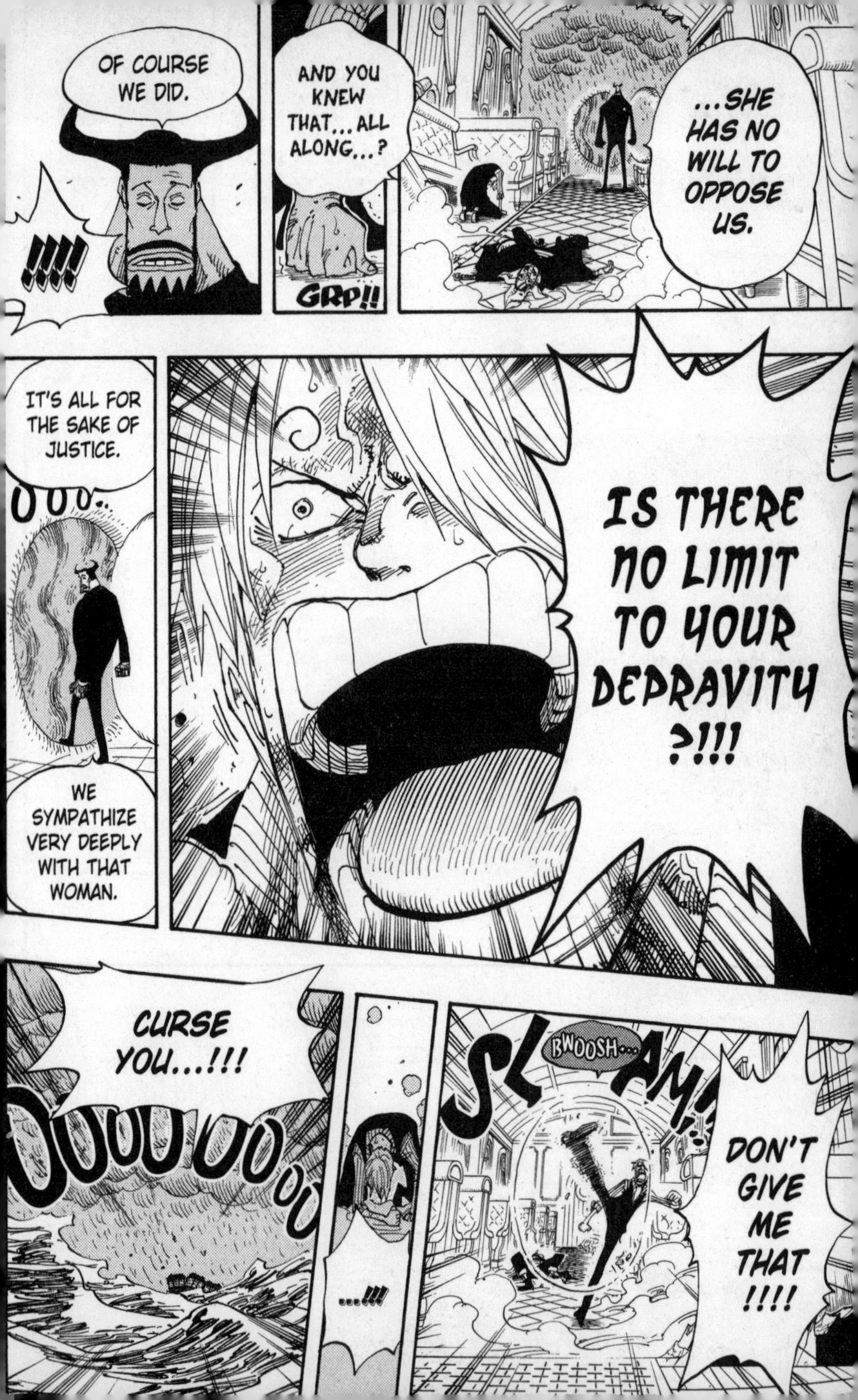
...SHE HAS NO WILL TO OPPOSE US.
AND YOU KNEW THAT... ALL ALONG...?
GRP!!
OF COURSE WE DID.
!!!!
IS THERE NO LIMIT TO YOUR DEPRAVITY?!!!
IT'S ALL FOR THE SAKE OF JUSTICE.
WE SYMPATHIZE VERY DEEPLY WITH THAT WOMAN.
SLAM!!
BWOOSH...
DON'T GIVE ME THAT!!!!
...!!!
CURSE YOU...!!!

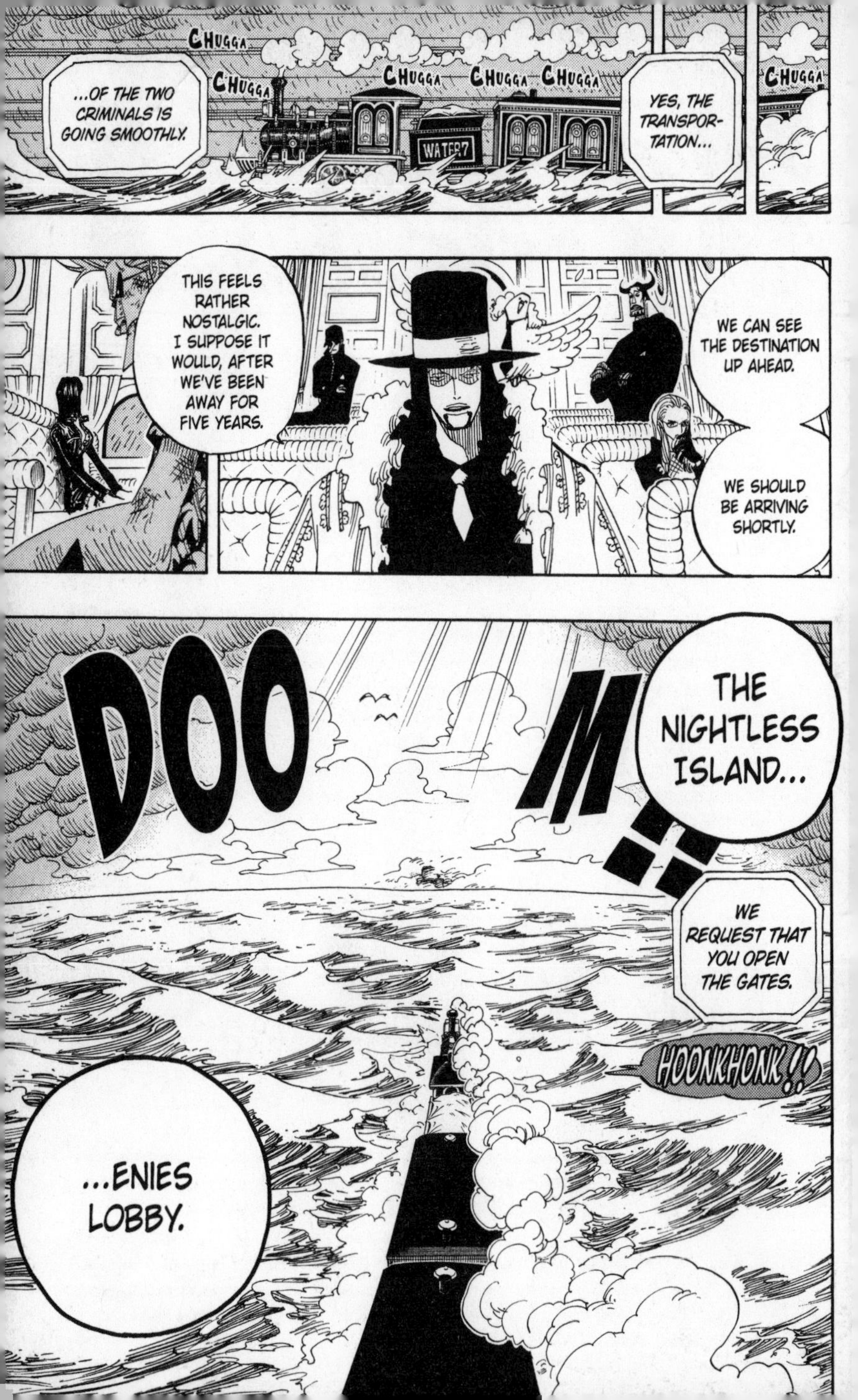
CHUGGA
YES, THE TRANSPORTATION...
CHUGGA CHUGGA CHUGGA
CHUGGA
CHUGGA
...OF THE TWO CRIMINALS IS GOING SMOOTHLY.
WE CAN SEE THE DESTINATION UP AHEAD.
WE SHOULD BE ARRIVING SHORTLY.
THIS FEELS RATHER NOSTALGIC. I SUPPOSE IT WOULD, AFTER WE'VE BEEN AWAY FOR FIVE YEARS.
THE NIGHTLESS ISLAND...
DOOOM!!
WE REQUEST THAT YOU OPEN THE GATES.
HOONKHONK!!
...ENIES LOBBY.

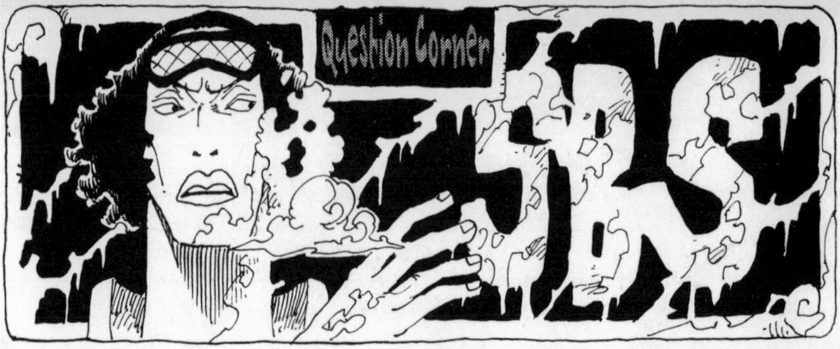
Question Corner

Q: Oda, good day, poop. I had a question for you; it's about the fourth panel on page 180 of volume 34. Isn't that a burglar right there in the money exchange, plain as day?! What is he up to? Poop.

--Ji

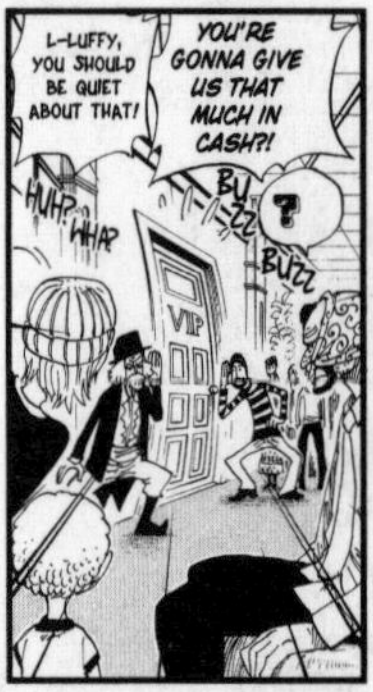
YOU'RE GONNA GIVE US THAT MUCH IN CASH?!
L-LUFFY, YOU SHOULD BE QUIET ABOUT THAT!
BUZZ
?
HUH? WHA?
VIP

A: "Poop, poop"! Man, you're gross! If you like poop so much, you should become poop when you grow up. (← Now there's an ambition.) Now then, sometimes people will tell you not to judge people by appearances and things to that effect, but yeah, that's a burglar no matter how you look at him. Of course I think he's someone who was trying for Luffy and company's money, but he ran out of luck when he decided to go after pooo-werful (← not "poop") pirates. Apparently he overheard that they had bounties on their heads, and then he couldn't do anything.

Q: Oda! If you don't want to be squeezed into a container jam-packed with sea urchins, please answer this question! On page 65 of chapter 360, in volume 38, Zolo's stuck in a smokestack, but if his "foot slipped," you'd think he'd have fallen forward or gone in feet-first. So how did he end up stuck like a sea anemone?

--Mahito

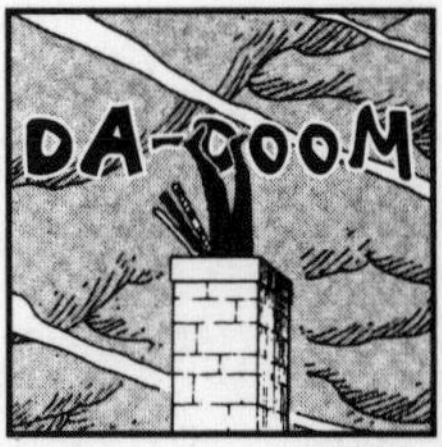
DA-GOOM

A: First of all, Lucci sent Zolo flying from the Galley-La mansion, and he then fell into the ocean. He managed to get out of the ocean, soaking wet, and then... what on earth happened to him? Zolo: "Dangit, I got thrown quite a ways, didn't I?" "Where am I?" "Okay, I'll try looking around from up on that smokestack." "Up we go." "Whoops, that was close--I almost fell down into the smokestack." "But, hey, that's a pretty deep hole." "I think I'll try looking down into it." STARE! SLIP! JAM!

Chapter 375:
THE SUPERMEN OF ENIES LOBBY

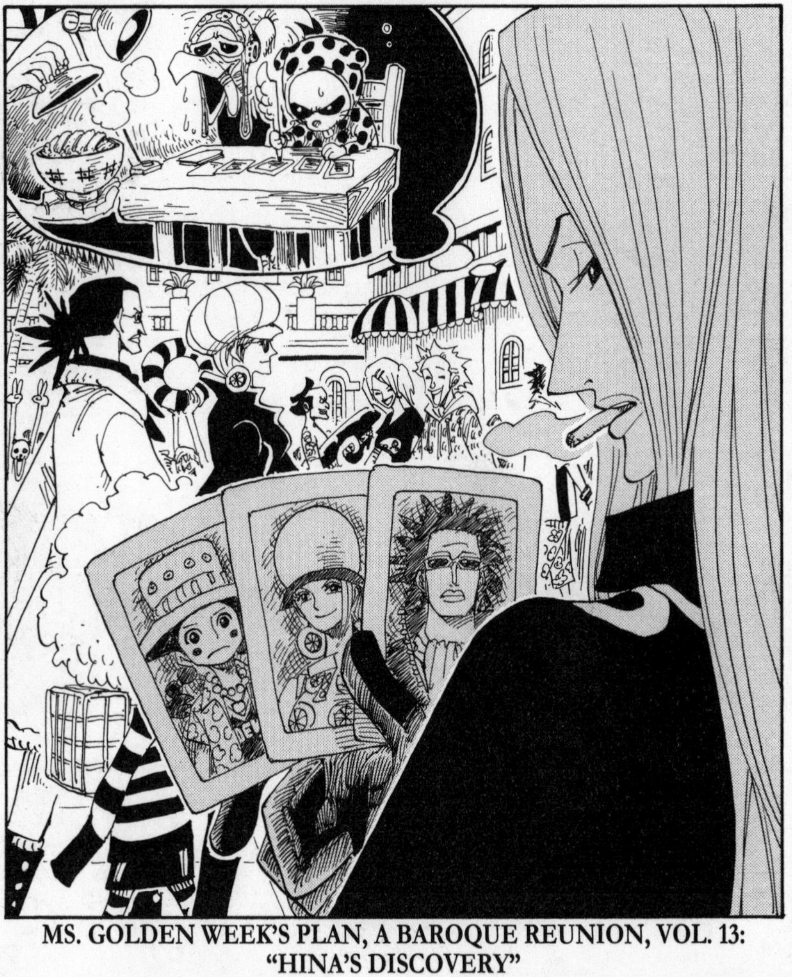

MS. GOLDEN WEEK'S PLAN, A BAROQUE REUNION, VOL. 13:
"HINA'S DISCOVERY"

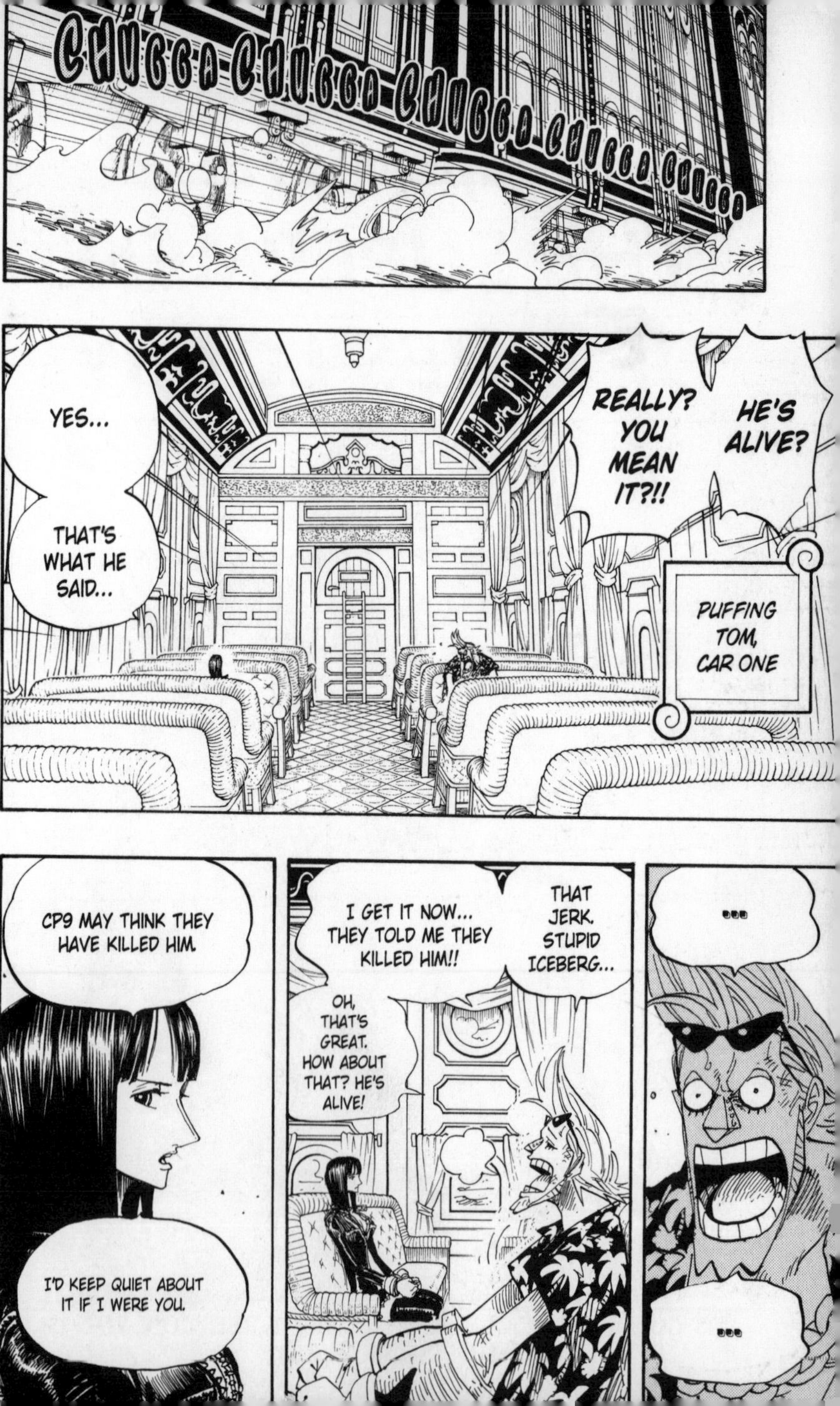
CHUGGA CHUGGA CHUGGA CHUGGA CHUGGA
PUFFING TOM, CAR ONE
HE'S ALIVE?
REALLY? YOU MEAN IT?!!
YES...
THAT'S WHAT HE SAID...
...
...
THAT JERK. STUPID ICEBERG...
I GET IT NOW... THEY TOLD ME THEY KILLED HIM!!
OH, THAT'S GREAT. HOW ABOUT THAT? HE'S ALIVE!
CP9 MAY THINK THEY HAVE KILLED HIM.
I'D KEEP QUIET ABOUT IT IF I WERE YOU.

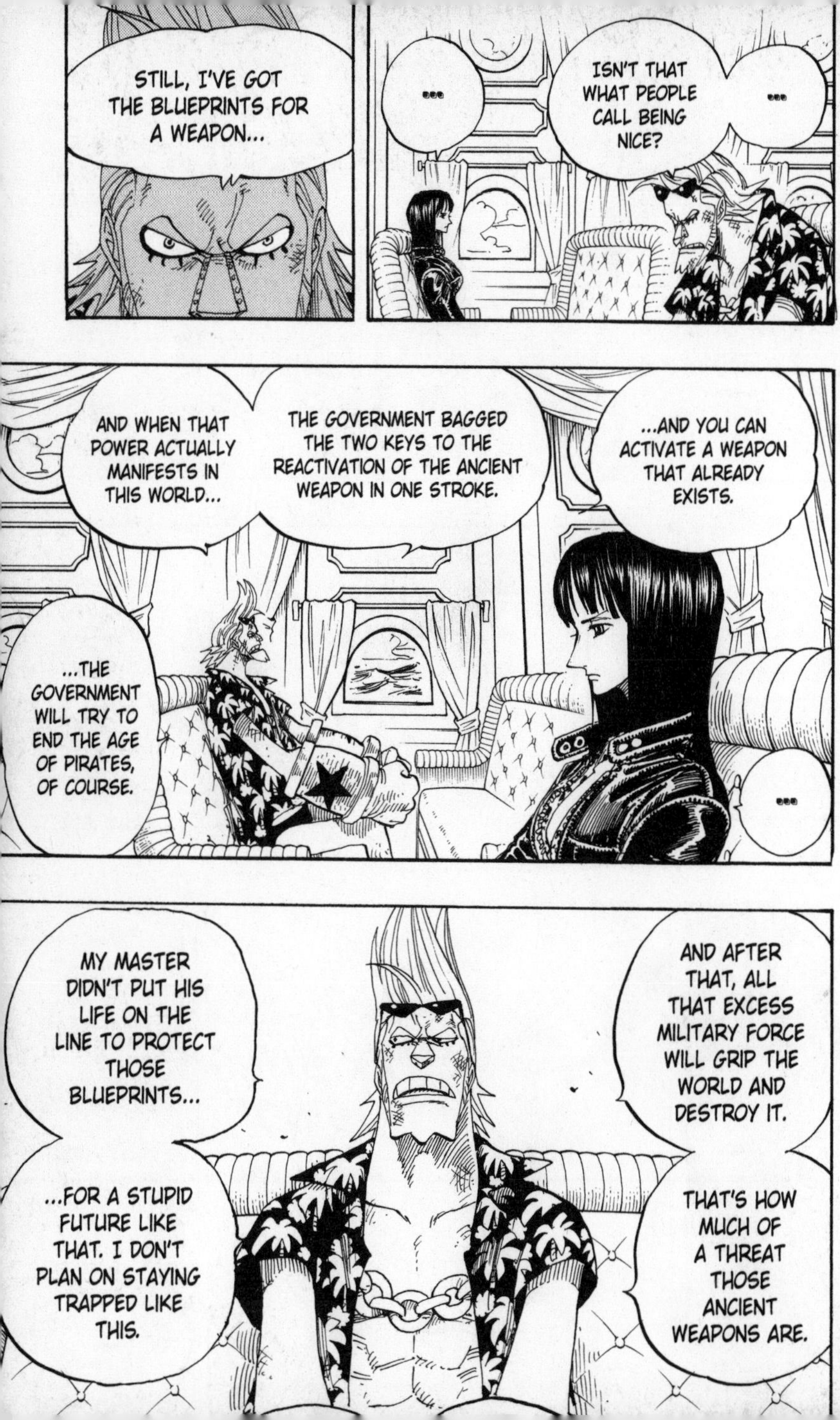
...
ISN'T THAT WHAT PEOPLE CALL BEING NICE?
...
STILL, I'VE GOT THE BLUEPRINTS FOR A WEAPON...
THE GOVERNMENT BAGGED THE TWO KEYS TO THE REACTIVATION OF THE ANCIENT WEAPON IN ONE STROKE.
...AND YOU CAN ACTIVATE A WEAPON THAT ALREADY EXISTS.
AND WHEN THAT POWER ACTUALLY MANIFESTS IN THIS WORLD...
...THE GOVERNMENT WILL TRY TO END THE AGE OF PIRATES, OF COURSE.
...
AND AFTER THAT, ALL THAT EXCESS MILITARY FORCE WILL GRIP THE WORLD AND DESTROY IT.
THAT'S HOW MUCH OF A THREAT THOSE ANCIENT WEAPONS ARE.
MY MASTER DIDN'T PUT HIS LIFE ON THE LINE TO PROTECT THOSE BLUEPRINTS...
...FOR A STUPID FUTURE LIKE THAT. I DON'T PLAN ON STAYING TRAPPED LIKE THIS.

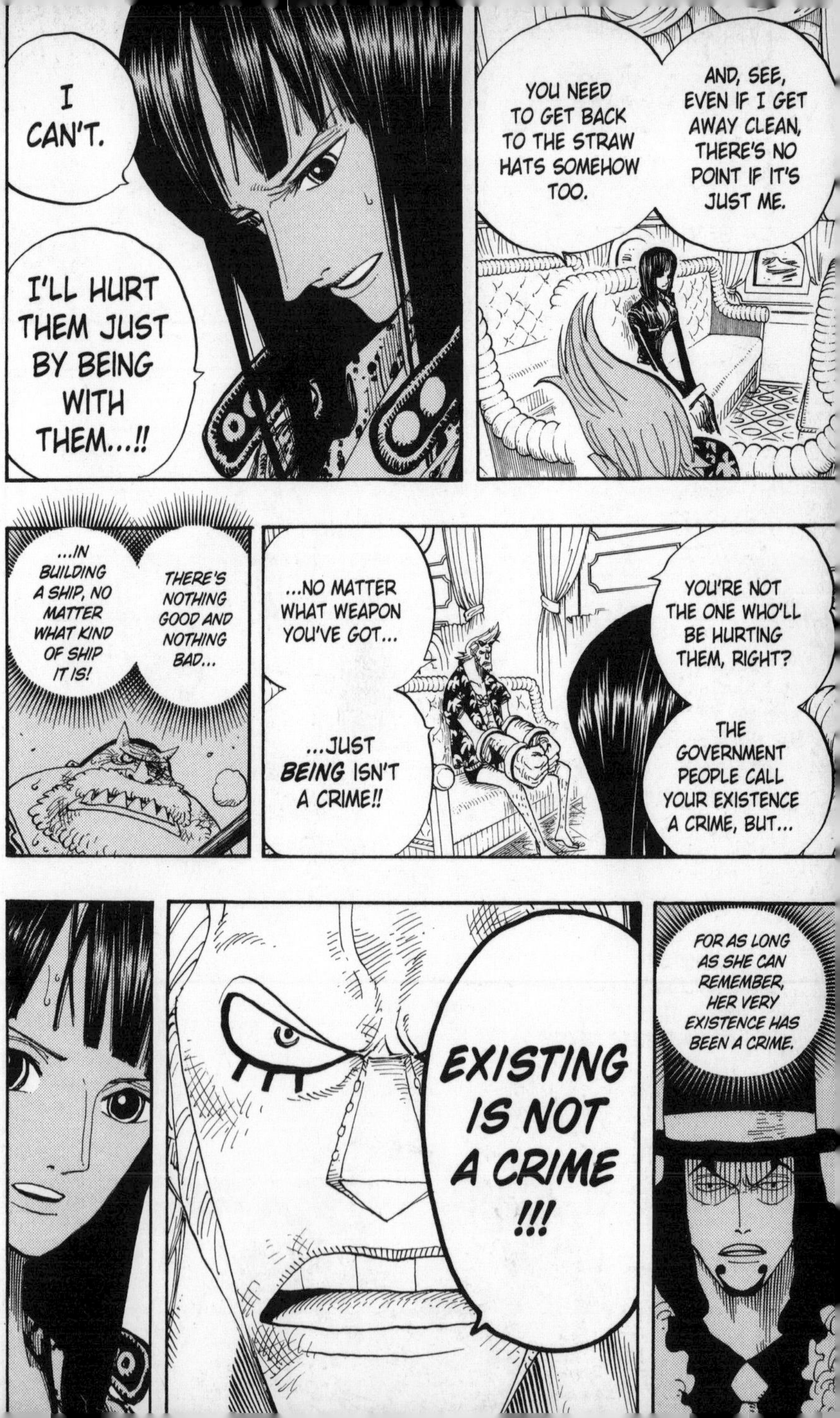
AND, SEE, EVEN IF I GET AWAY CLEAN, THERE'S NO POINT IF IT'S JUST ME.
YOU NEED TO GET BACK TO THE STRAW HATS SOMEHOW TOO.
I CAN'T.
I'LL HURT THEM JUST BY BEING WITH THEM...!!
YOU'RE NOT THE ONE WHO'LL BE HURTING THEM, RIGHT?
THE GOVERNMENT PEOPLE CALL YOUR EXISTENCE A CRIME, BUT...
...NO MATTER WHAT WEAPON YOU'VE GOT...
...JUST BEING ISN'T A CRIME!!
THERE'S NOTHING GOOD AND NOTHING BAD...
...IN BUILDING A SHIP, NO MATTER WHAT KIND OF SHIP IT IS!
FOR AS LONG AS SHE CAN REMEMBER, HER VERY EXISTENCE HAS BEEN A CRIME.
EXISTING IS NOT A CRIME !!!

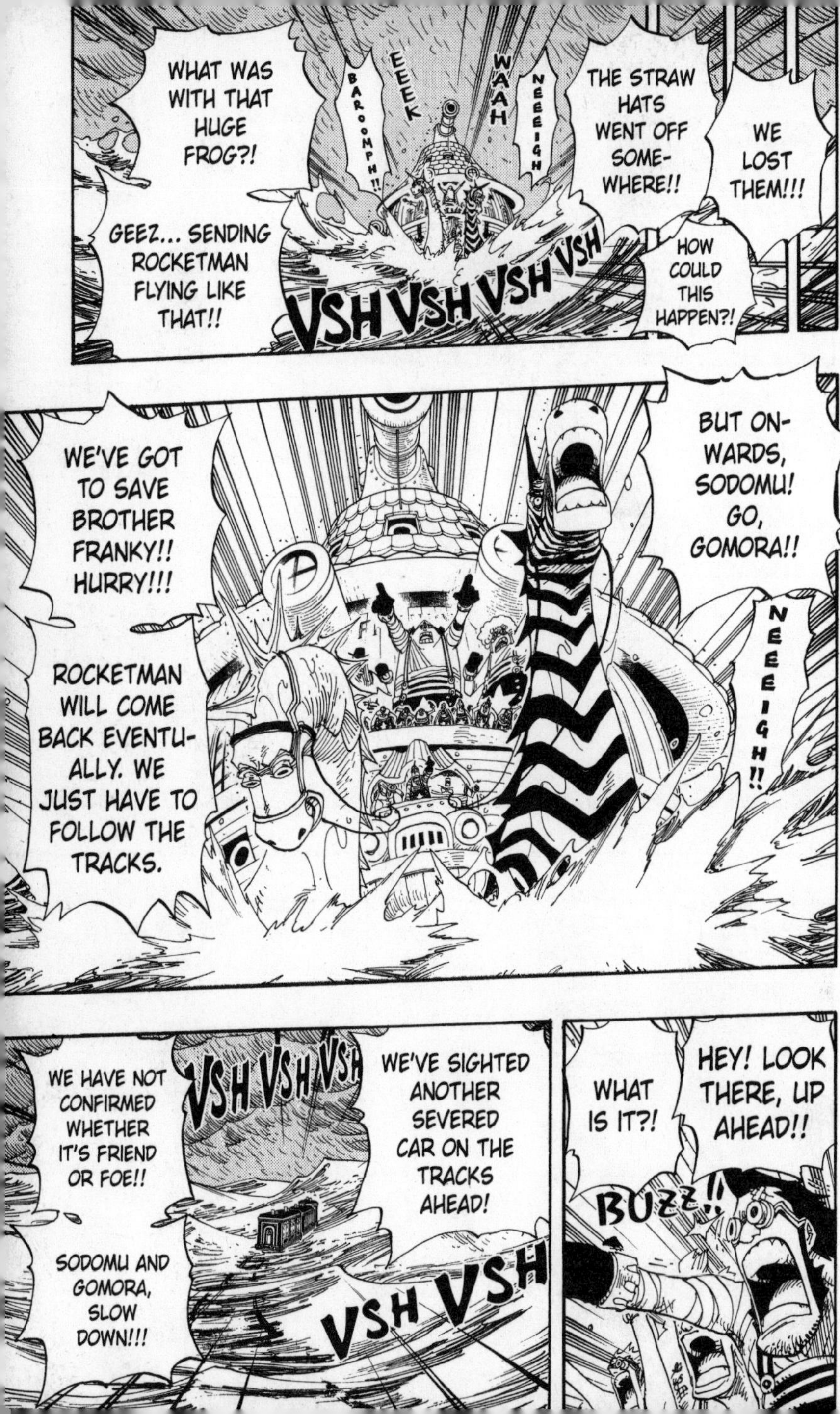
WE LOST THEM!!!
HOW COULD THIS HAPPEN?!
THE STRAW HATS WENT OFF SOME-WHERE!!
NEEEIGH
WAAH
EEEK
BAROOOMPH!!
WHAT WAS WITH THAT HUGE FROG?!
GEEZ... SENDING ROCKETMAN FLYING LIKE THAT!!
VSH VSH VSH VSH
BUT ON-WARDS, SODOMU! GO, GOMORA!!
NEEEIGH!!
WE'VE GOT TO SAVE BROTHER FRANKY!! HURRY!!!
ROCKETMAN WILL COME BACK EVENTU-ALLY. WE JUST HAVE TO FOLLOW THE TRACKS.
HEY! LOOK THERE, UP AHEAD!!
WHAT IS IT?!
BUZZ!!
WE'VE SIGHTED ANOTHER SEVERED CAR ON THE TRACKS AHEAD!
VSH VSH VSH
WE HAVE NOT CONFIRMED WHETHER IT'S FRIEND OR FOE!!
SODOMU AND GOMORA, SLOW DOWN!!!
VSH VSH

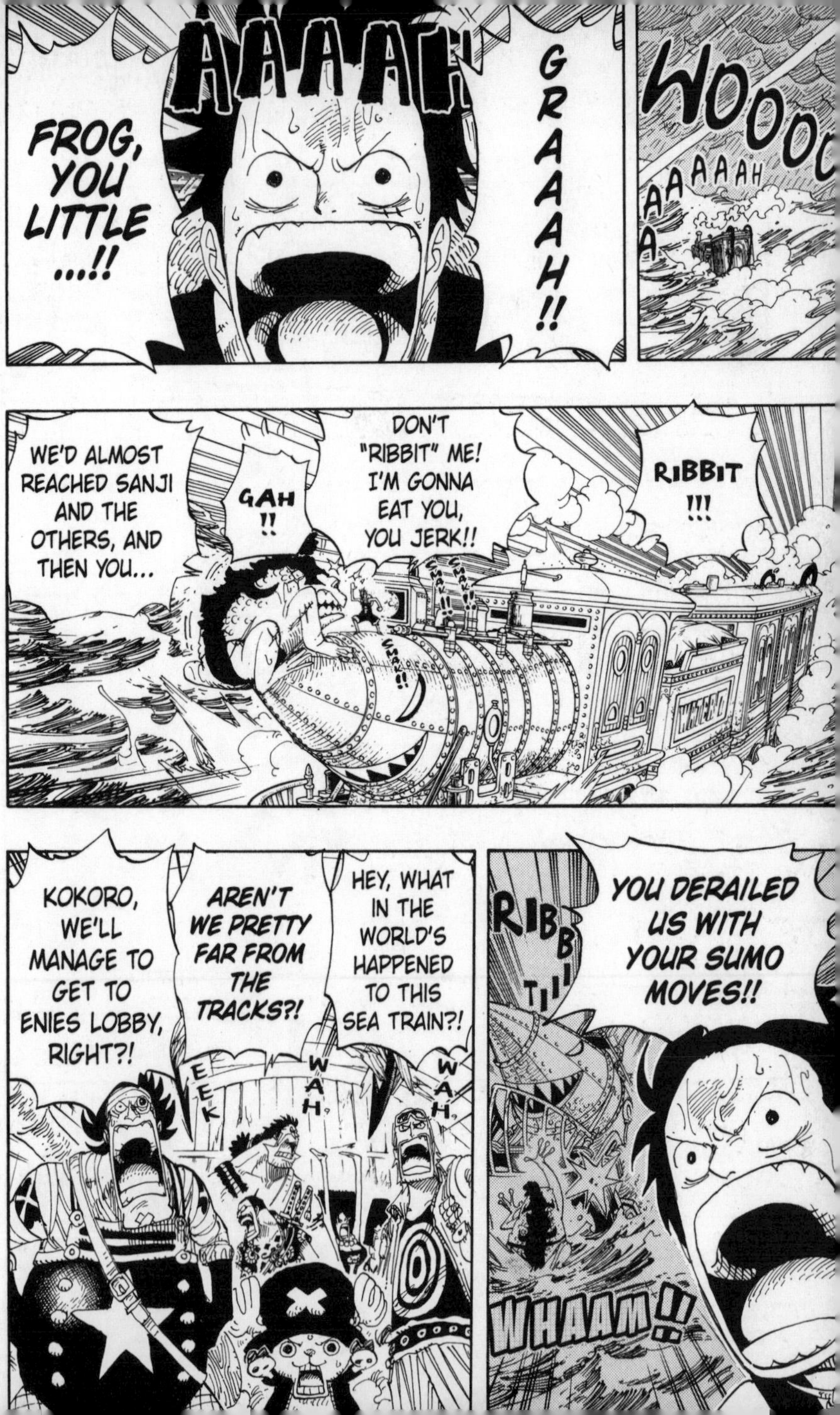
WOOOO
AAAAAAH
GRAAAAAH!!
AAAAAH
FROG, YOU LITTLE...!!
RIBBIT!!!
DON'T "RIBBIT" ME! I'M GONNA EAT YOU, YOU JERK!!
GAH!!
SMAK!!
SMAK!!
SMAK!!
WE'D ALMOST REACHED SANJI AND THE OTHERS, AND THEN YOU...
YOU DERAILED US WITH YOUR SUMO MOVES!!
RIBBIT!!
WHAAM!!
HEY, WHAT IN THE WORLD'S HAPPENED TO THIS SEA TRAIN?!
WAH
AREN'T WE PRETTY FAR FROM THE TRACKS?!
WAH
KOKORO, WE'LL MANAGE TO GET TO ENIES LOBBY, RIGHT?!
EEK

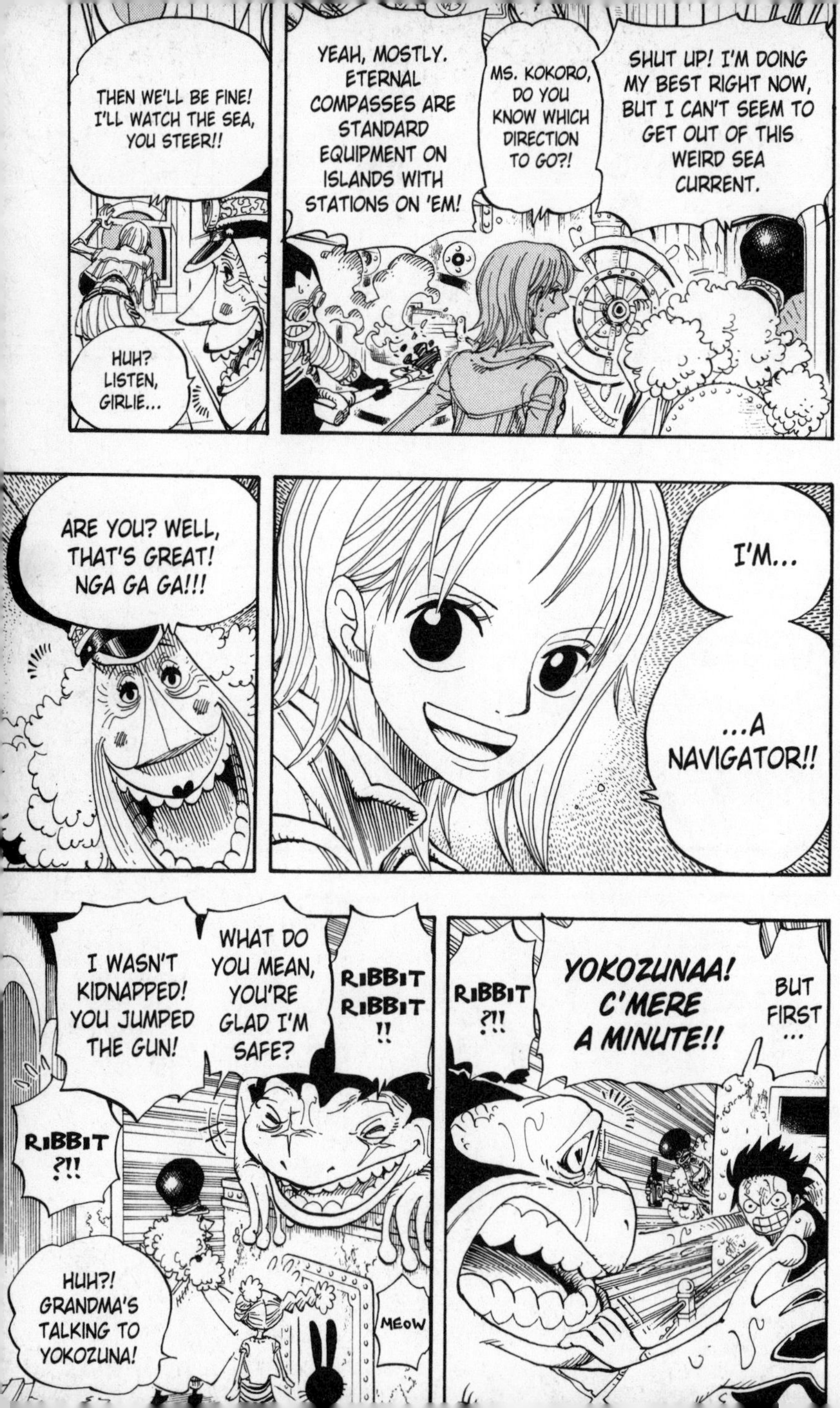
SHUT UP! I'M DOING MY BEST RIGHT NOW, BUT I CAN'T SEEM TO GET OUT OF THIS WEIRD SEA CURRENT.
MS. KOKORO, DO YOU KNOW WHICH DIRECTION TO GO?!
YEAH, MOSTLY. ETERNAL COMPASSES ARE STANDARD EQUIPMENT ON ISLANDS WITH STATIONS ON 'EM!
THEN WE'LL BE FINE! I'LL WATCH THE SEA, YOU STEER!!
HUH? LISTEN, GIRLIE...
I'M...
...A NAVIGATOR!!
ARE YOU? WELL, THAT'S GREAT! NGA GA GA!!!
BUT FIRST...
YOKOZUNAA! C'MERE A MINUTE!!
RIBBIT ?!!
RIBBIT RIBBIT !!
WHAT DO YOU MEAN, YOU'RE GLAD I'M SAFE?
I WASN'T KIDNAPPED! YOU JUMPED THE GUN!
RIBBIT ?!!
HUH?! GRANDMA'S TALKING TO YOKOZUNA!
MEOW

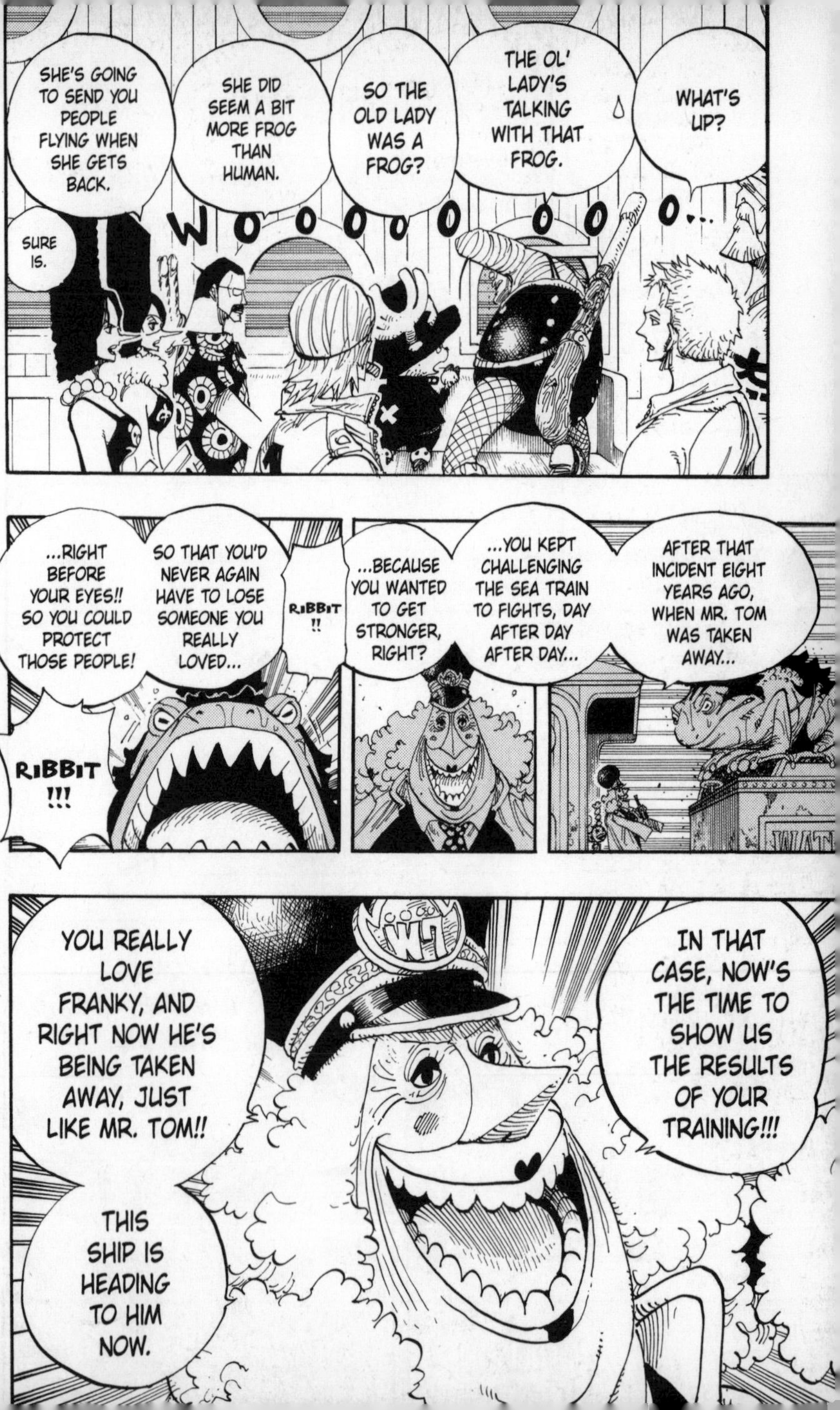
WHAT'S UP?
THE OL' LADY'S TALKING WITH THAT FROG.
SO THE OLD LADY WAS A FROG?
SHE DID SEEM A BIT MORE FROG THAN HUMAN.
SHE'S GOING TO SEND YOU PEOPLE FLYING WHEN SHE GETS BACK.
WOOOOOOO...
SURE IS.
AFTER THAT INCIDENT EIGHT YEARS AGO, WHEN MR. TOM WAS TAKEN AWAY...
...YOU KEPT CHALLENGING THE SEA TRAIN TO FIGHTS, DAY AFTER DAY AFTER DAY...
...BECAUSE YOU WANTED TO GET STRONGER, RIGHT?
RIBBIT!!
SO THAT YOU'D NEVER AGAIN HAVE TO LOSE SOMEONE YOU REALLY LOVED...
...RIGHT BEFORE YOUR EYES!! SO YOU COULD PROTECT THOSE PEOPLE!
RIBBIT!!!
YOU REALLY LOVE FRANKY, AND RIGHT NOW HE'S BEING TAKEN AWAY, JUST LIKE MR. TOM!!
THIS SHIP IS HEADING TO HIM NOW.
IN THAT CASE, NOW'S THE TIME TO SHOW US THE RESULTS OF YOUR TRAINING!!!

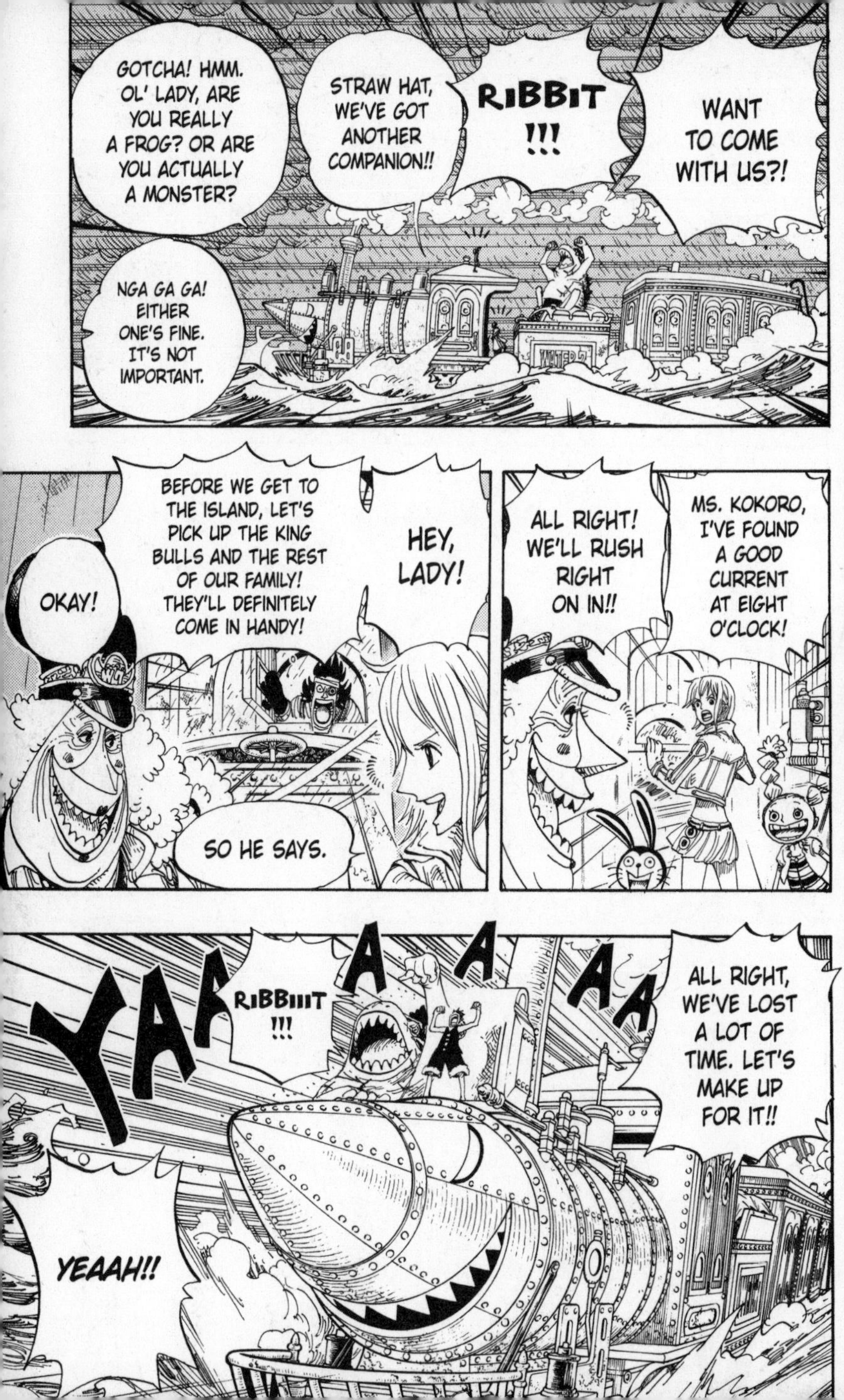
WANT TO COME WITH US?!
RIBBIT!!!
STRAW HAT, WE'VE GOT ANOTHER COMPANION!!
GOTCHA! HMM. OL' LADY, ARE YOU REALLY A FROG? OR ARE YOU ACTUALLY A MONSTER?
NGA GA GA! EITHER ONE'S FINE. IT'S NOT IMPORTANT.
MS. KOKORO, I'VE FOUND A GOOD CURRENT AT EIGHT O'CLOCK!
ALL RIGHT! WE'LL RUSH RIGHT ON IN!!
HEY, LADY!
BEFORE WE GET TO THE ISLAND, LET'S PICK UP THE KING BULLS AND THE REST OF OUR FAMILY! THEY'LL DEFINITELY COME IN HANDY!
OKAY!
SO HE SAYS.
ALL RIGHT, WE'VE LOST A LOT OF TIME. LET'S MAKE UP FOR IT!!
RIBBIIIT!!!
YAAAAAA
YEAAH!!

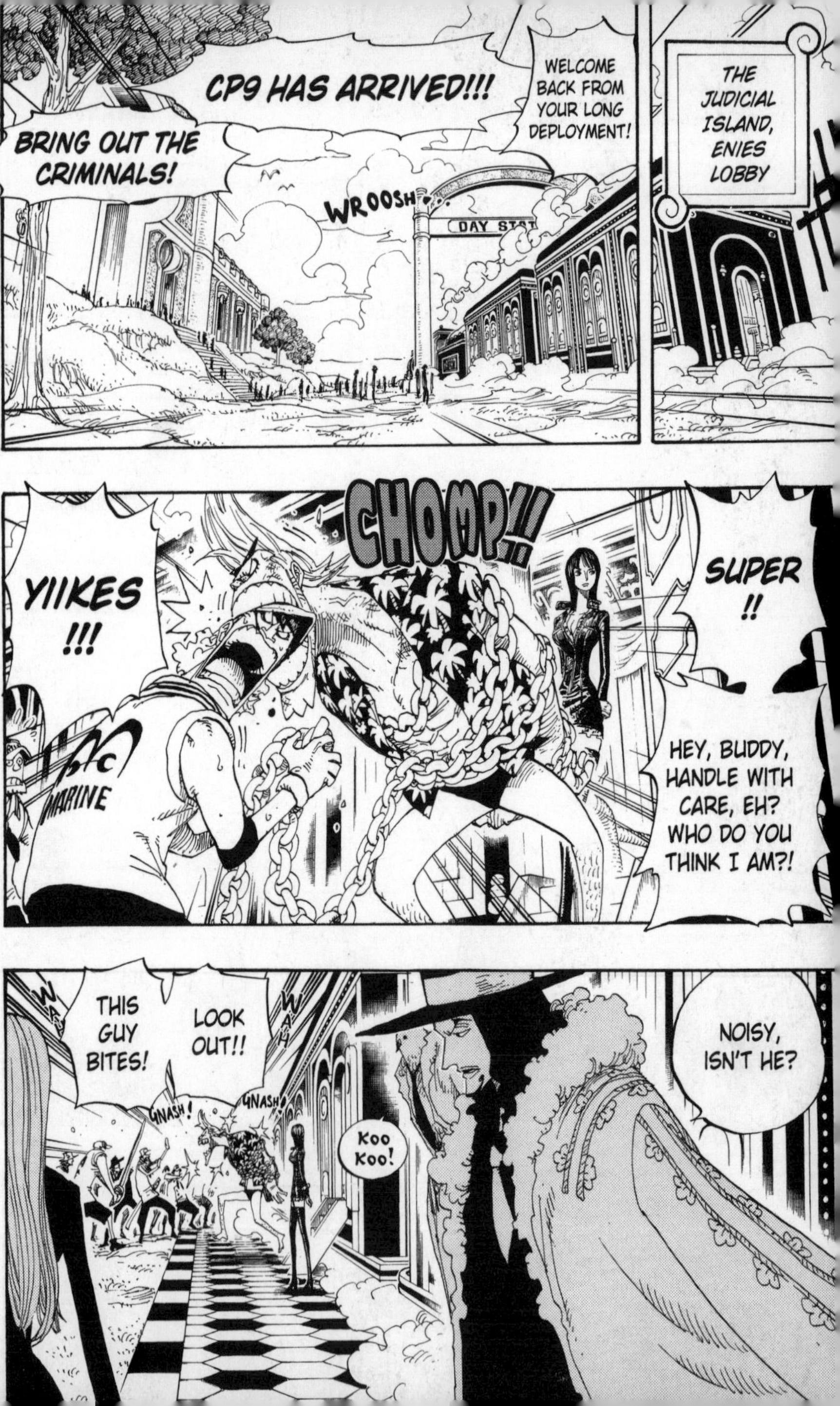
THE JUDICIAL ISLAND, ENIES LOBBY
WELCOME BACK FROM YOUR LONG DEPLOYMENT!
CP9 HAS ARRIVED!!!
BRING OUT THE CRIMINALS!
WROOSH
SUPER !!
CHOMP!!
YIIKES !!!
HEY, BUDDY, HANDLE WITH CARE, EH? WHO DO YOU THINK I AM?!
MARINE
NOISY, ISN'T HE?
WAH
LOOK OUT!!
THIS GUY BITES!
WAH
GNASH!
GNASH!
KOO KOO!

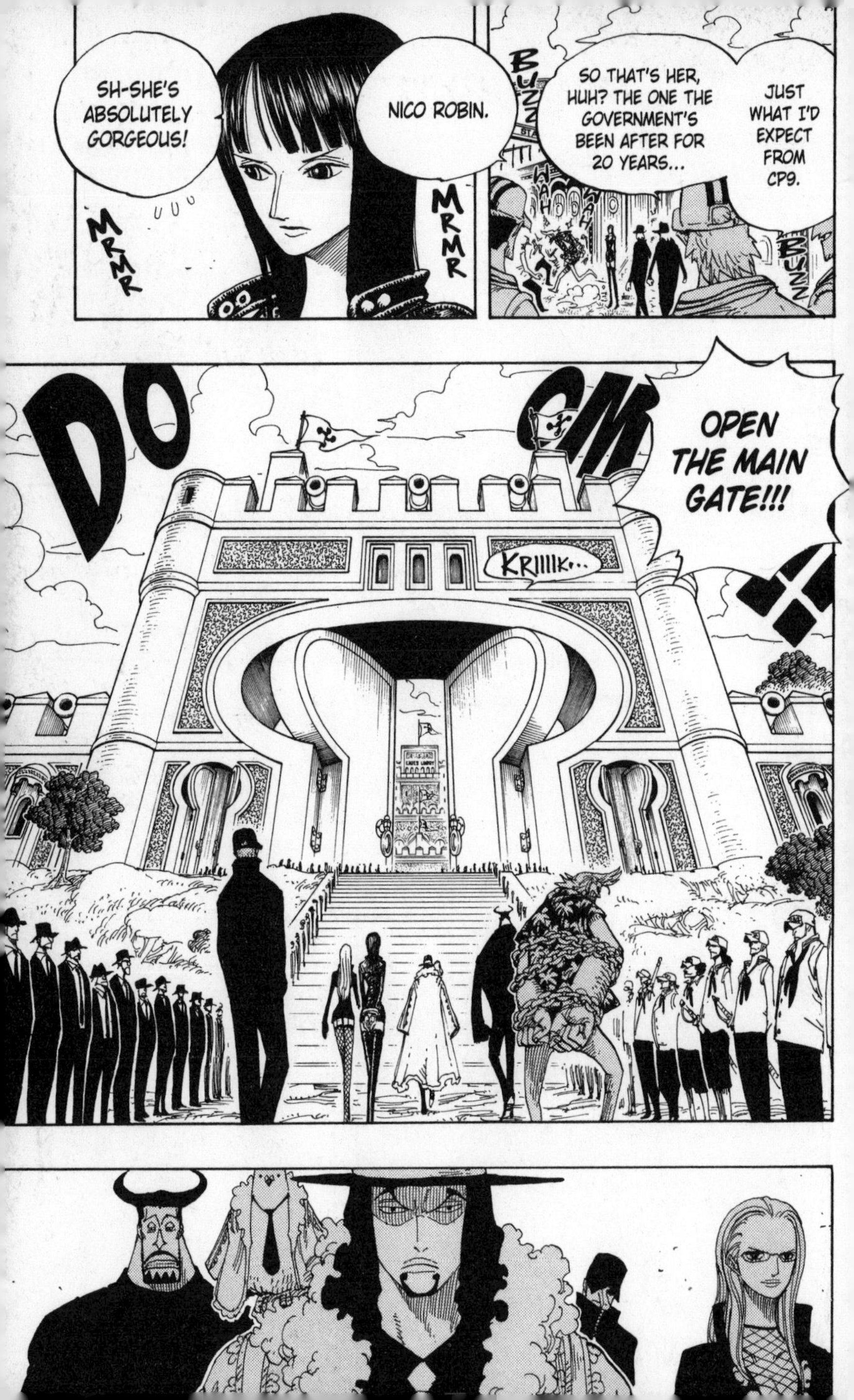

BUZZ
JUST WHAT I'D EXPECT FROM CP9.
SO THAT'S HER, HUH? THE ONE THE GOVERNMENT'S BEEN AFTER FOR 20 YEARS...
BUZZ
NICO ROBIN.
MRMR
SH-SHE'S ABSOLUTELY GORGEOUS!
MRMR
OPEN THE MAIN GATE!!!
KRIIIIK...

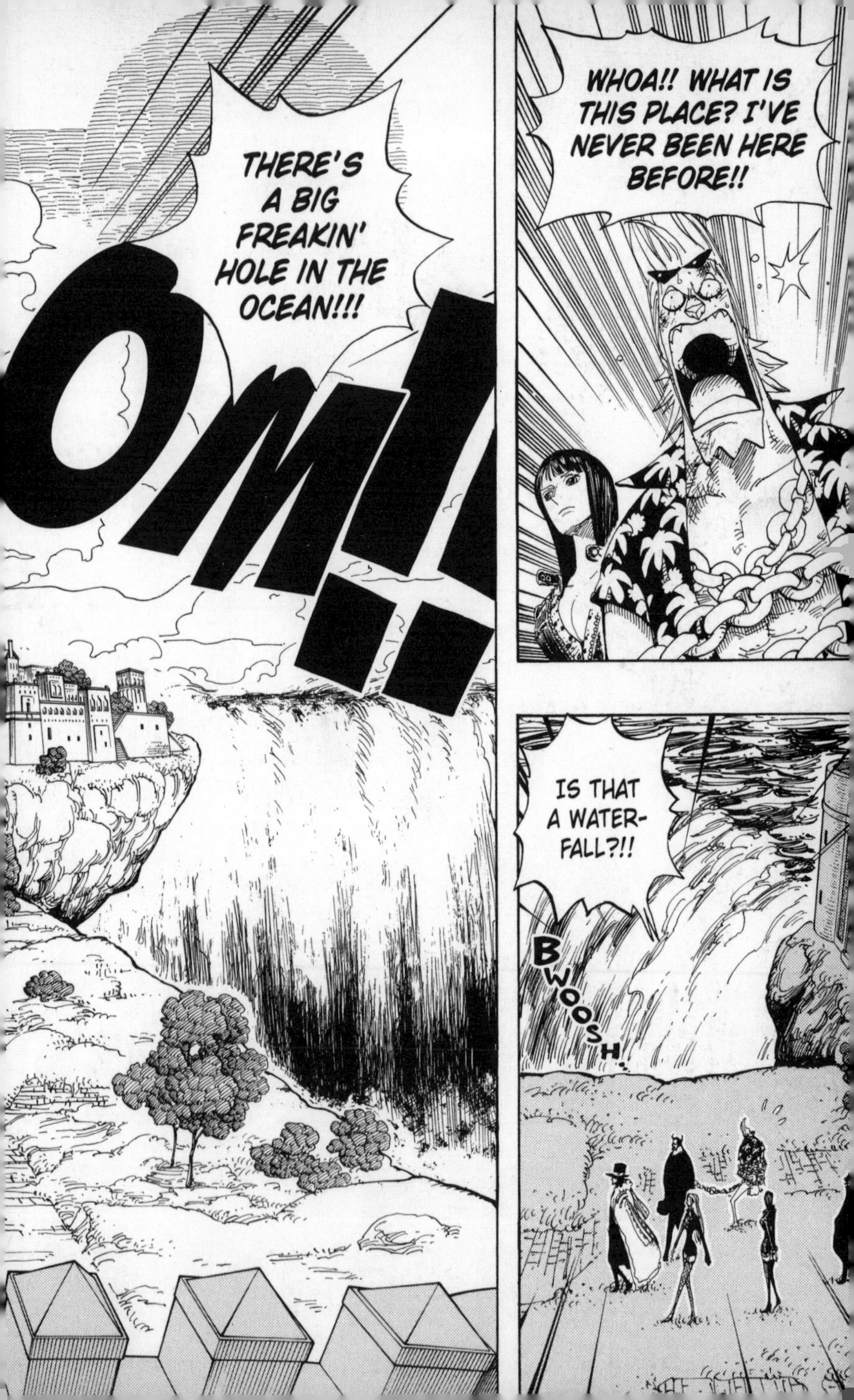
WHOA!! WHAT IS THIS PLACE? I'VE NEVER BEEN HERE BEFORE!!
IS THAT A WATER-FALL?!!
BWOOSH
THERE'S A BIG FREAKIN' HOLE IN THE OCEAN!!!
OM!!

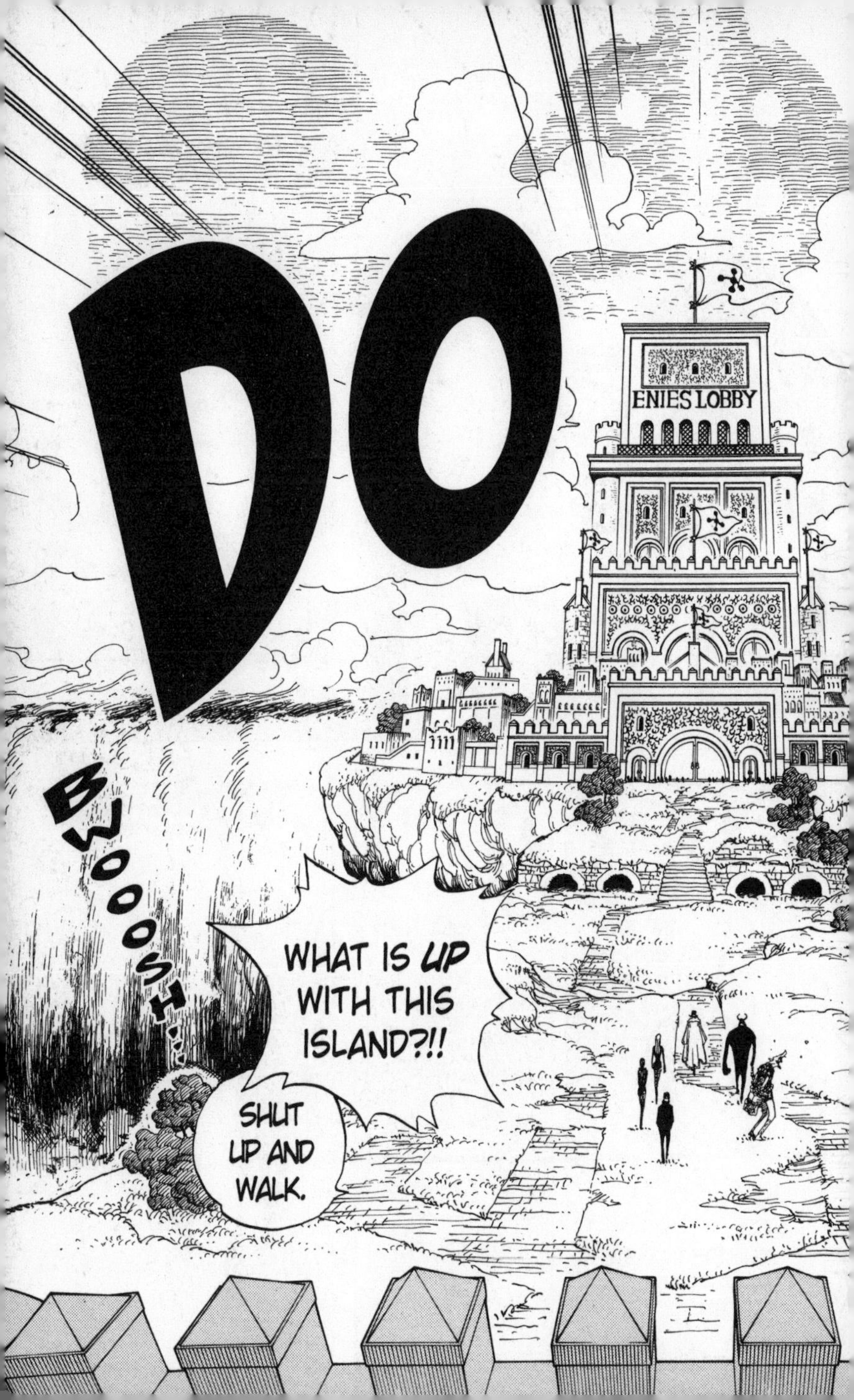
ENIES LOBBY
DO
BWOOOSH!!
WHAT IS UP WITH THIS ISLAND?!!
SHUT UP AND WALK.

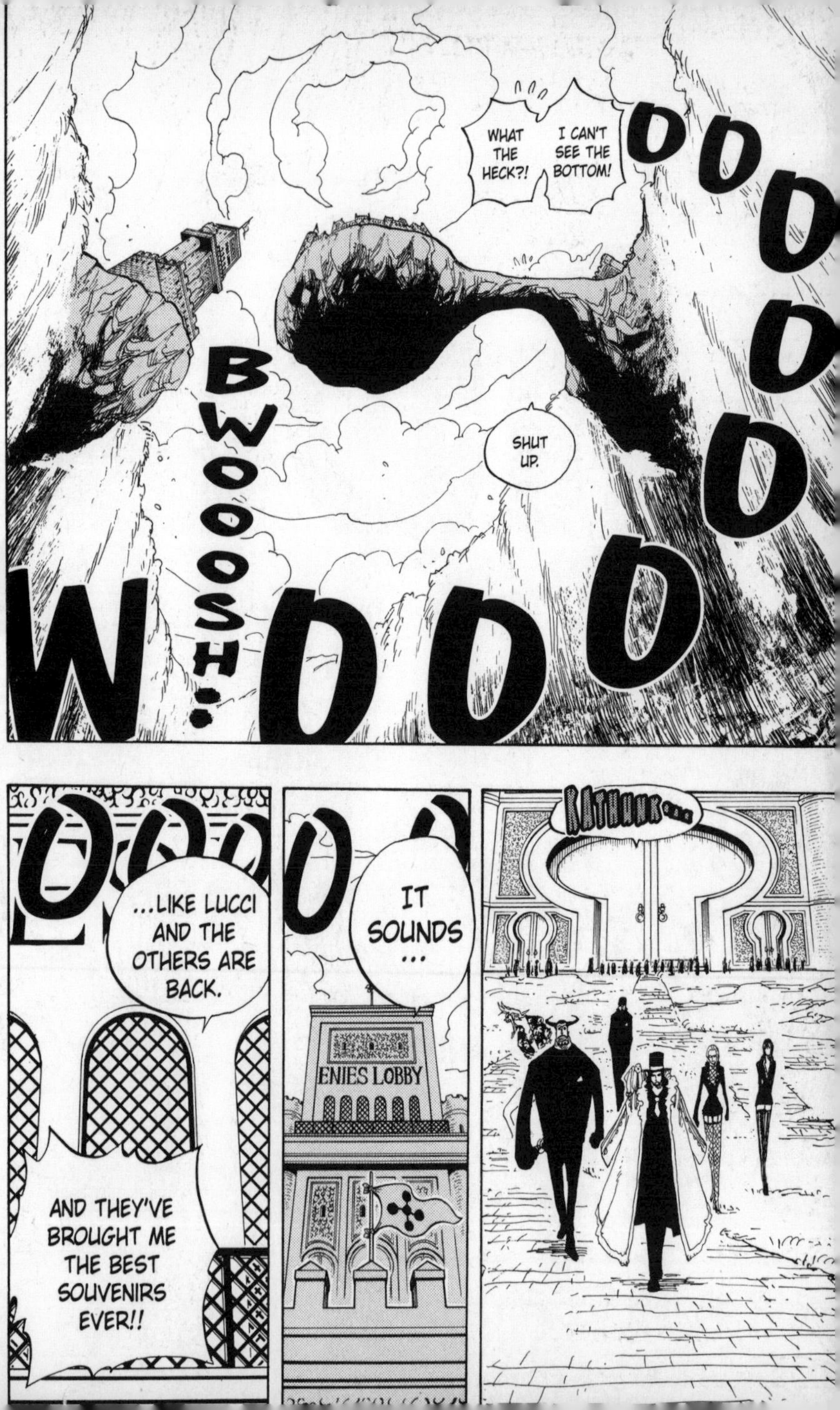
I CAN'T SEE THE BOTTOM!
WHAT THE HECK?!
SHUT UP.
WDDDDDDDDD
BWOOOSH!!
KATHUNK...
IT SOUNDS...
ENIES LOBBY
...LIKE LUCCI AND THE OTHERS ARE BACK.
AND THEY'VE BROUGHT ME THE BEST SOUVENIRS EVER!!

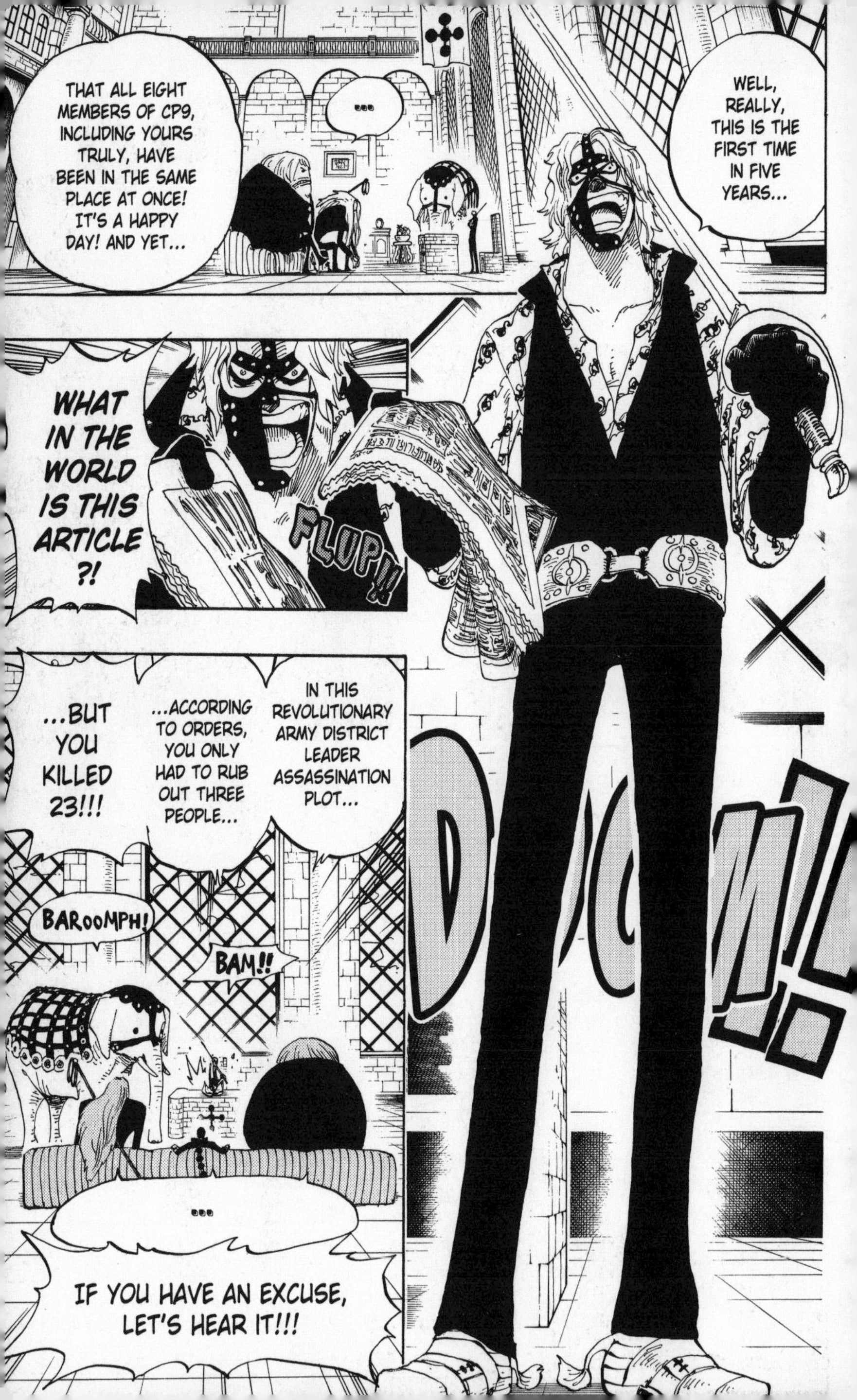
WELL, REALLY, THIS IS THE FIRST TIME IN FIVE YEARS...
DOOM!!
THAT ALL EIGHT MEMBERS OF CP9, INCLUDING YOURS TRULY, HAVE BEEN IN THE SAME PLACE AT ONCE! IT'S A HAPPY DAY! AND YET...
...
WHAT IN THE WORLD IS THIS ARTICLE ?!
FLUP!!
IN THIS REVOLUTIONARY ARMY DISTRICT LEADER ASSASSINATION PLOT...
...ACCORDING TO ORDERS, YOU ONLY HAD TO RUB OUT THREE PEOPLE...
...BUT YOU KILLED 23!!!
BAROOMPH!
BAM!!
...
IF YOU HAVE AN EXCUSE, LET'S HEAR IT!!!

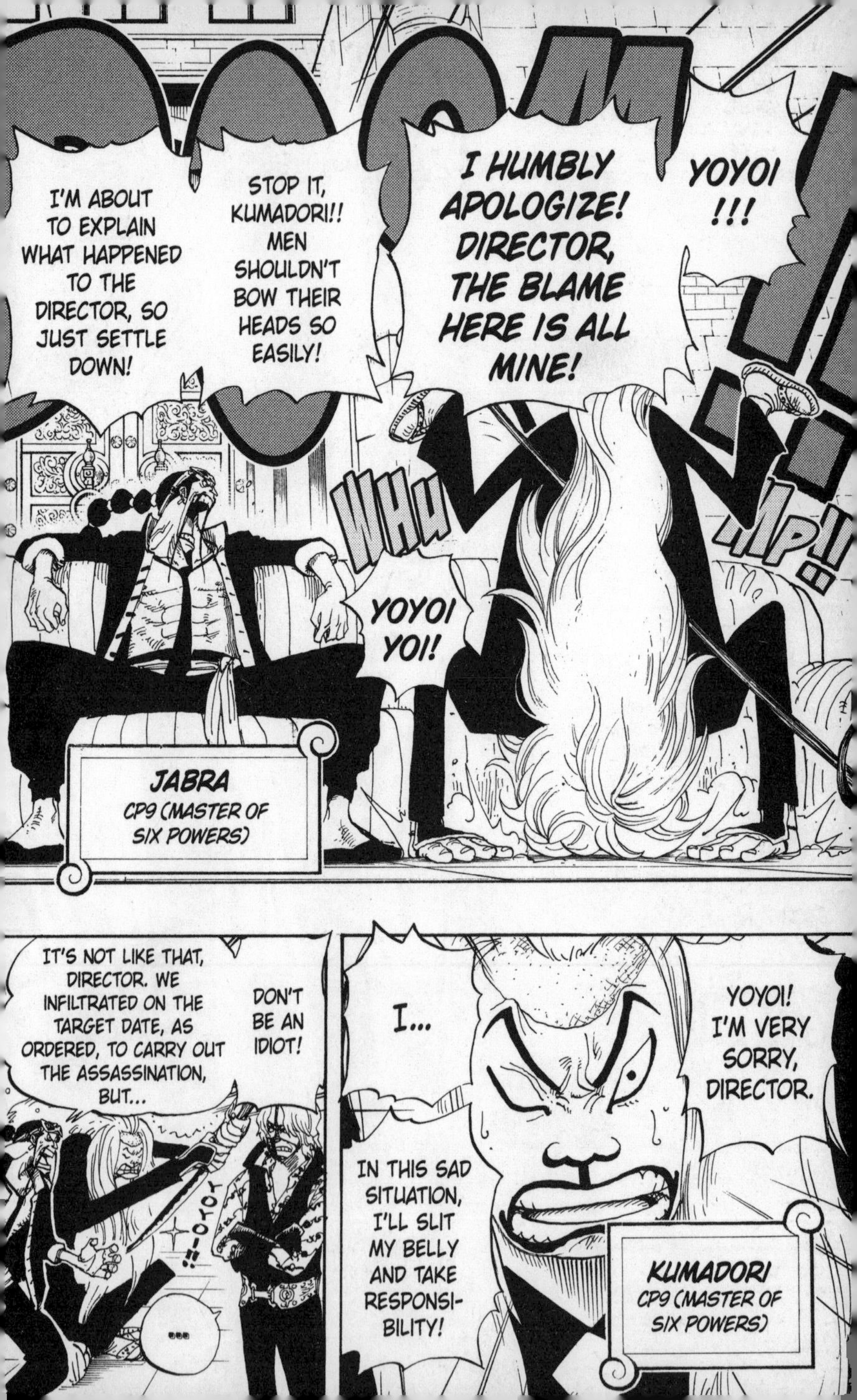
YOYOI !!!
I HUMBLY APOLOGIZE! DIRECTOR, THE BLAME HERE IS ALL MINE!
STOP IT, KUMADORI!! MEN SHOULDN'T BOW THEIR HEADS SO EASILY!
I'M ABOUT TO EXPLAIN WHAT HAPPENED TO THE DIRECTOR, SO JUST SETTLE DOWN!
WHUMP!!
YOYOI YOI!
JABRA
CP9 (MASTER OF SIX POWERS)
YOYOI! I'M VERY SORRY, DIRECTOR.
I...
IN THIS SAD SITUATION, I'LL SLIT MY BELLY AND TAKE RESPONSI-BILITY!
KUMADORI
CP9 (MASTER OF SIX POWERS)
DON'T BE AN IDIOT!
IT'S NOT LIKE THAT, DIRECTOR. WE INFILTRATED ON THE TARGET DATE, AS ORDERED, TO CARRY OUT THE ASSASSINATION, BUT...
YOYOI!!
...

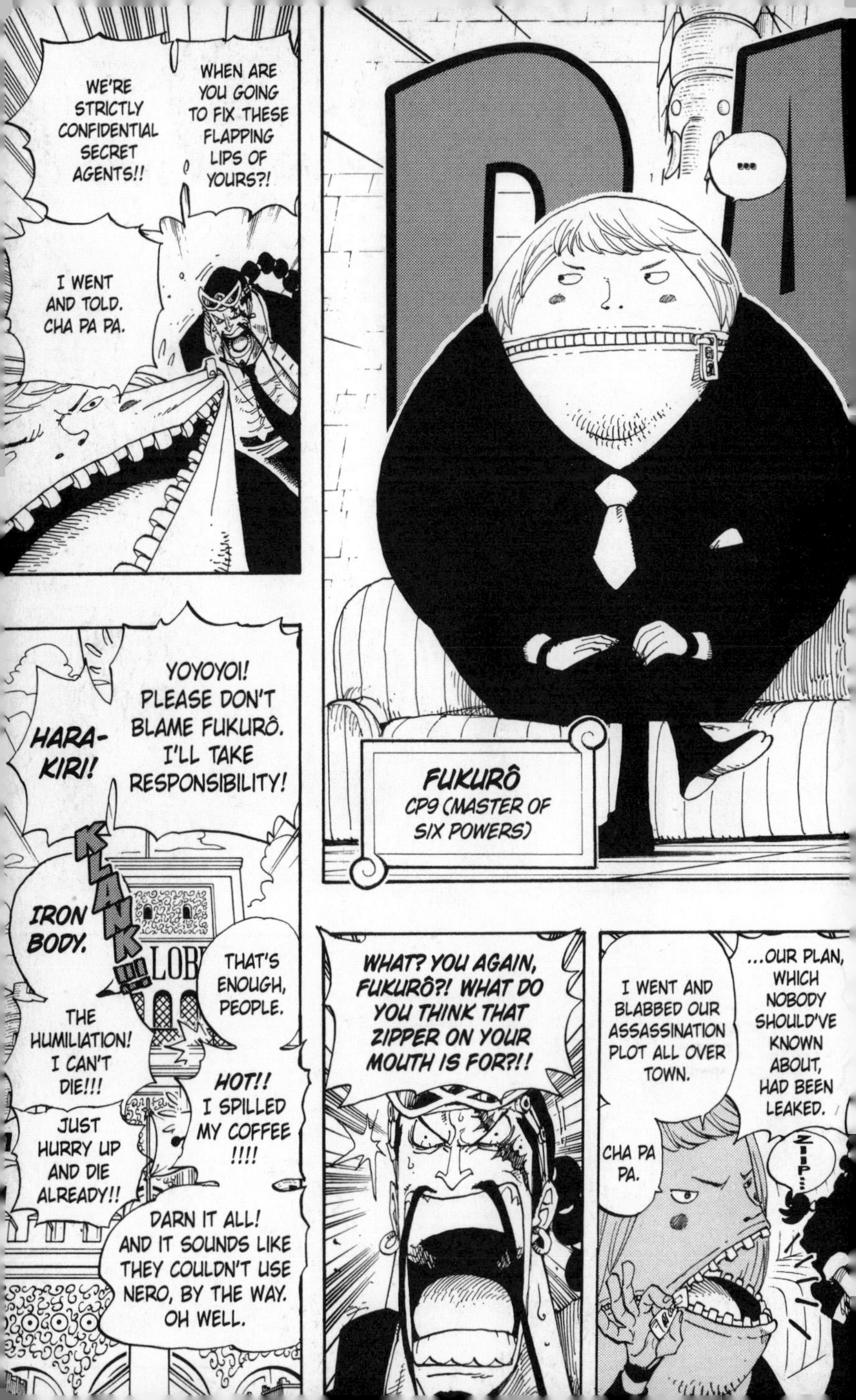

...
FUKURÔ
CP9 (MASTER OF SIX POWERS)
...OUR PLAN, WHICH NOBODY SHOULD'VE KNOWN ABOUT, HAD BEEN LEAKED.
I WENT AND BLABBED OUR ASSASSINATION PLOT ALL OVER TOWN.
ZIIIP...
CHA PA PA.
WHAT? YOU AGAIN, FUKURÔ?! WHAT DO YOU THINK THAT ZIPPER ON YOUR MOUTH IS FOR?!!
WHEN ARE YOU GOING TO FIX THESE FLAPPING LIPS OF YOURS?!
WE'RE STRICTLY CONFIDENTIAL SECRET AGENTS!!
I WENT AND TOLD. CHA PA PA.
YOYOYOI! PLEASE DON'T BLAME FUKURÔ. I'LL TAKE RESPONSIBILITY!
HARA-KIRI!
KLANK
IRON BODY.
LOB
THAT'S ENOUGH, PEOPLE.
THE HUMILIATION! I CAN'T DIE!!!
HOT!! I SPILLED MY COFFEE !!!!
JUST HURRY UP AND DIE ALREADY!!
DARN IT ALL! AND IT SOUNDS LIKE THEY COULDN'T USE NERO, BY THE WAY. OH WELL.

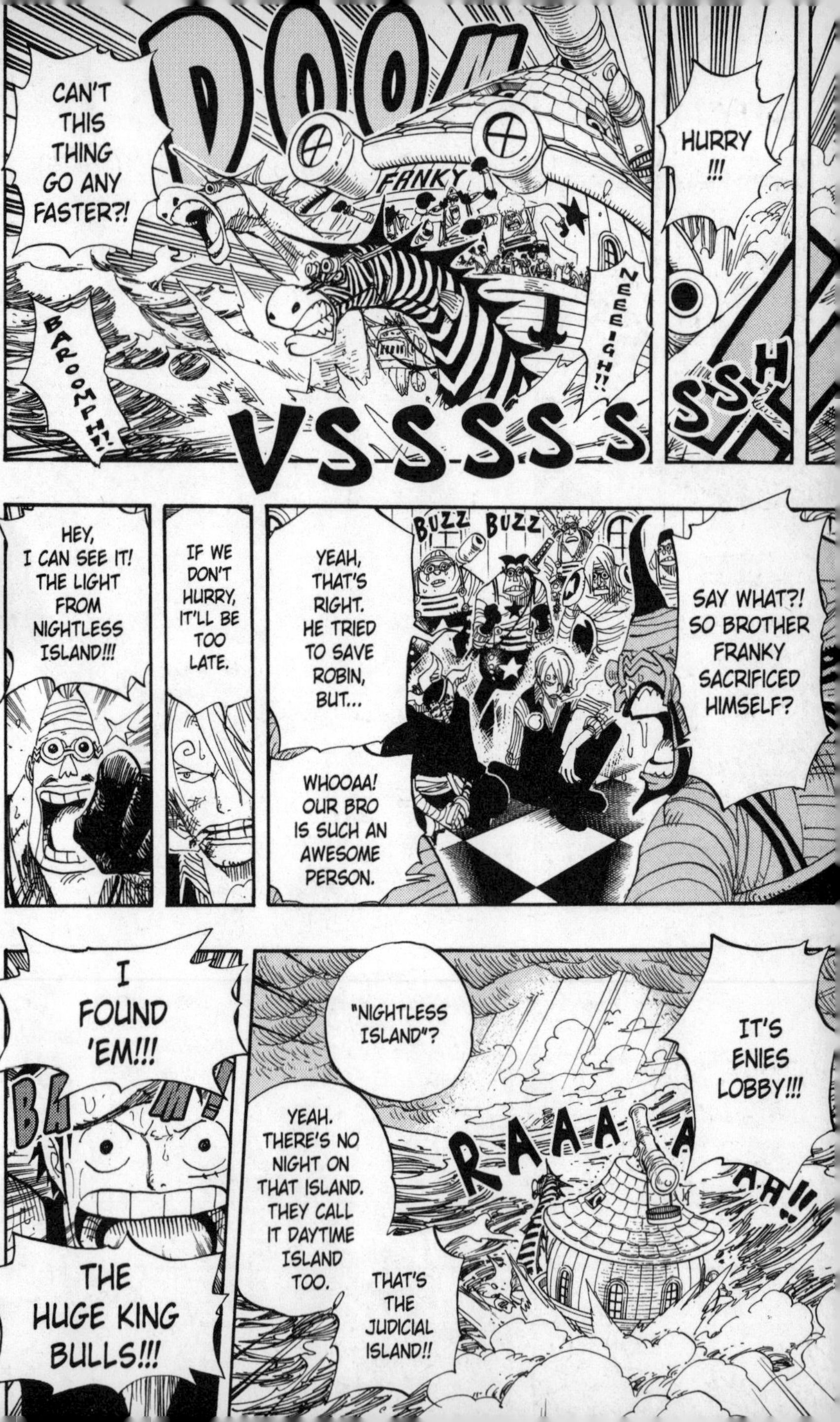
HURRY!!!
SSSH
DOOM
CAN'T THIS THING GO ANY FASTER?!
NEEEIGH!!
BAROOMPH!!
VSSSSS
SAY WHAT?! SO BROTHER FRANKY SACRIFICED HIMSELF?
BUZZ BUZZ
YEAH, THAT'S RIGHT. HE TRIED TO SAVE ROBIN, BUT...
WHOOAA! OUR BRO IS SUCH AN AWESOME PERSON.
IF WE DON'T HURRY, IT'LL BE TOO LATE.
HEY, I CAN SEE IT! THE LIGHT FROM NIGHTLESS ISLAND!!!
IT'S ENIES LOBBY!!!
"NIGHTLESS ISLAND"?
RAAAAAH!!
YEAH. THERE'S NO NIGHT ON THAT ISLAND. THEY CALL IT DAYTIME ISLAND TOO.
THAT'S THE JUDICIAL ISLAND!!
I FOUND 'EM!!!
THE HUGE KING BULLS!!!

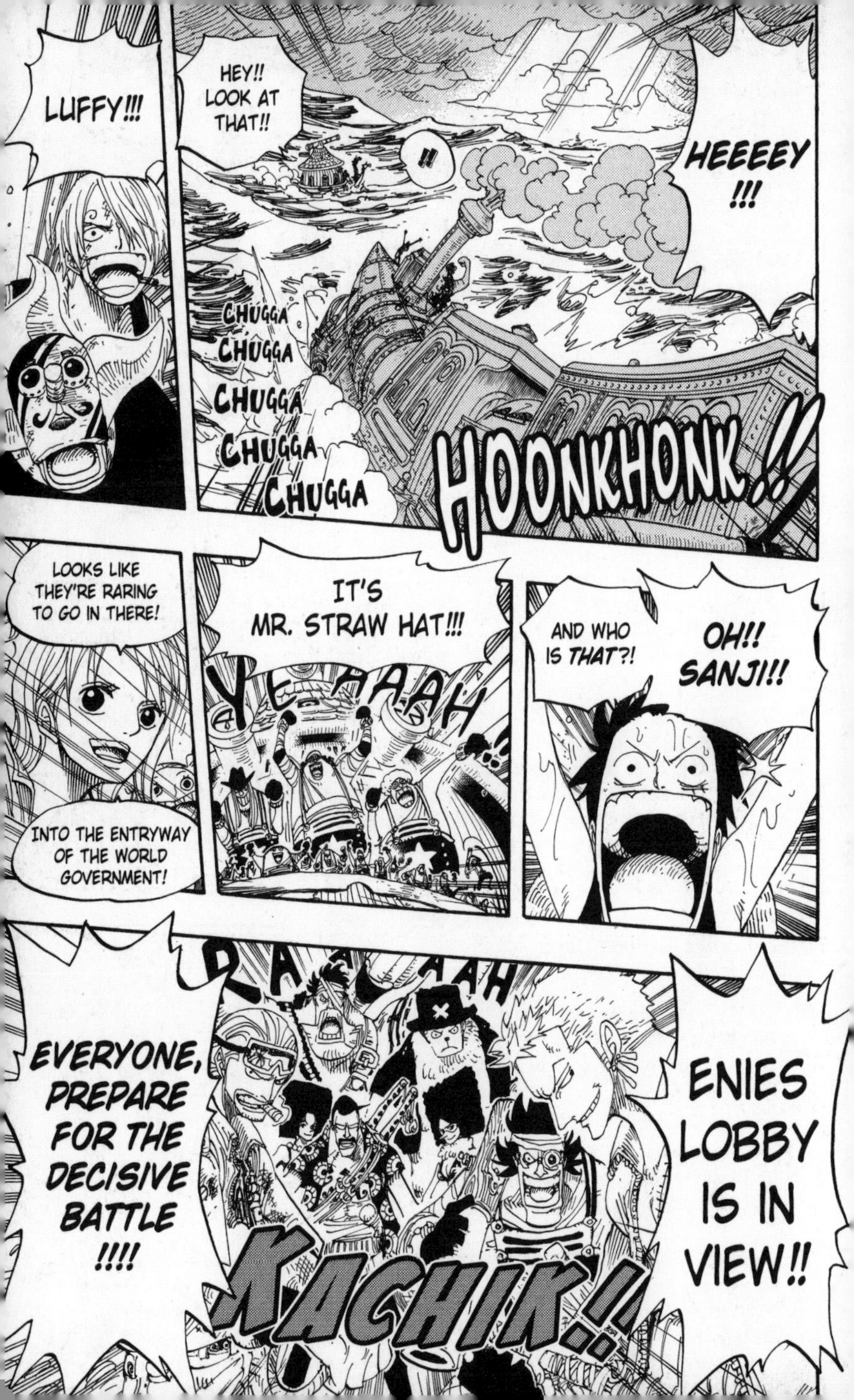
HEEEEY !!!
HEY!! LOOK AT THAT!!
!!
CHUGGA CHUGGA CHUGGA CHUGGA CHUGGA
HOONKHONK!!
LUFFY!!!
OH!! SANJI!!
AND WHO IS THAT?!
IT'S MR. STRAW HAT!!!
YEAAAAH!!
LOOKS LIKE THEY'RE RARING TO GO IN THERE!
INTO THE ENTRYWAY OF THE WORLD GOVERNMENT!
ENIES LOBBY IS IN VIEW!!
DAAAAAH
EVERYONE, PREPARE FOR THE DECISIVE BATTLE !!!!
KACHIK!!

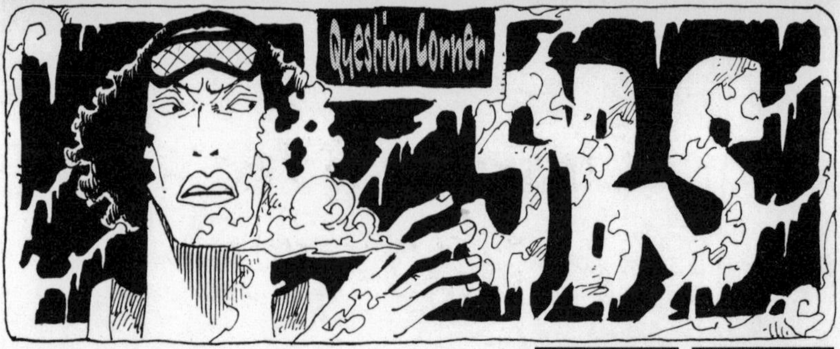
Question Corner

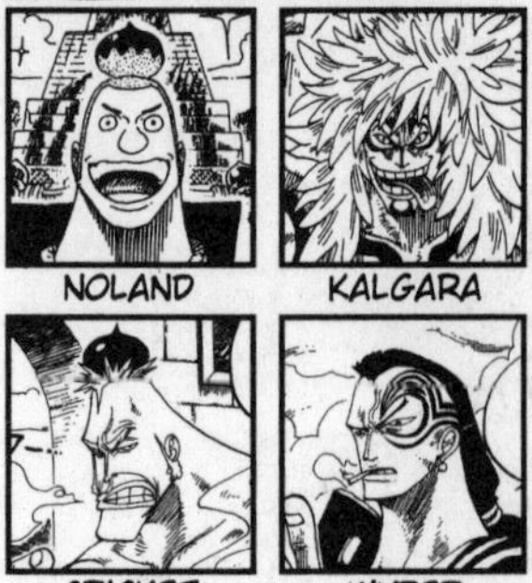
NOLAND KALGARA CRICKET WYPER

Q: I've got a question. Of course this goes for the main story as well, but sometimes the titles of each chapter of *One Piece* bring tears to my eyes. Like the title of chapter 292: "To Meet, Like the Half-Moon Hidden by Clouds." I thought it was just a haiku about the moon, but it also expressed the situation surrounding Jaya Island and the Shandians! I'm a complete sucker for unexpected thrills like that. Oda, which of the chapter titles you've written so far do you like best? I'd like to know.

--Nenza (I also like "The Second Person" and "Isn't it?!"!)

A: Wow! What a careful reader! Having somebody interested enough to read so thoroughly is the highest reward a manga creator could ever hope for. Thank you. You're right about the chapter titles. Sometimes I'm really particular about them. Actually, when I hit on a good title, I do think "Woo-hoo!" etc. But after all, it is just one part of the whole work, and it would be pointless for me to go on and on about how "this title here means this, that and the other," so it's enough for me to know that some people out there are paying attention. I'll keep playing around with concepts in the future, too.

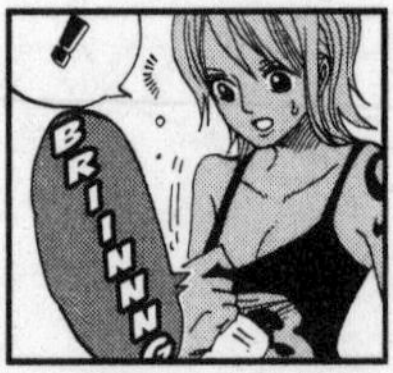
!
BRIINNG

Q: It's time for all good kids to go to bed! (Making sure they're all asleep…) Okay, now Question Corner for adults begins. Oda! In chapter 366, Sanji makes a phone call to Nami; where did Nami pull that baby transponder snail from? Apparently women possess various places where they can hide things. It's been really, really bugging me, and I keep thinking about it, and I can't sleep at night! Think you could give me a hint, Oda? Thanks a ton!

--Casey Keisuke

A: Hey now, this is dangerous territory, y'know?! It's a hidden, unmapped region, y'know?! The hidden Nami Valley?! Once you wander into that, you'll never... POW! Ouch! Something came flying at me! Ah! I'm a good kid, so I've gotta get to bed now! Okay, everybody, see you next volume! SNOORE! POW! Ouch!

Chapter 376:
I GOT IT!

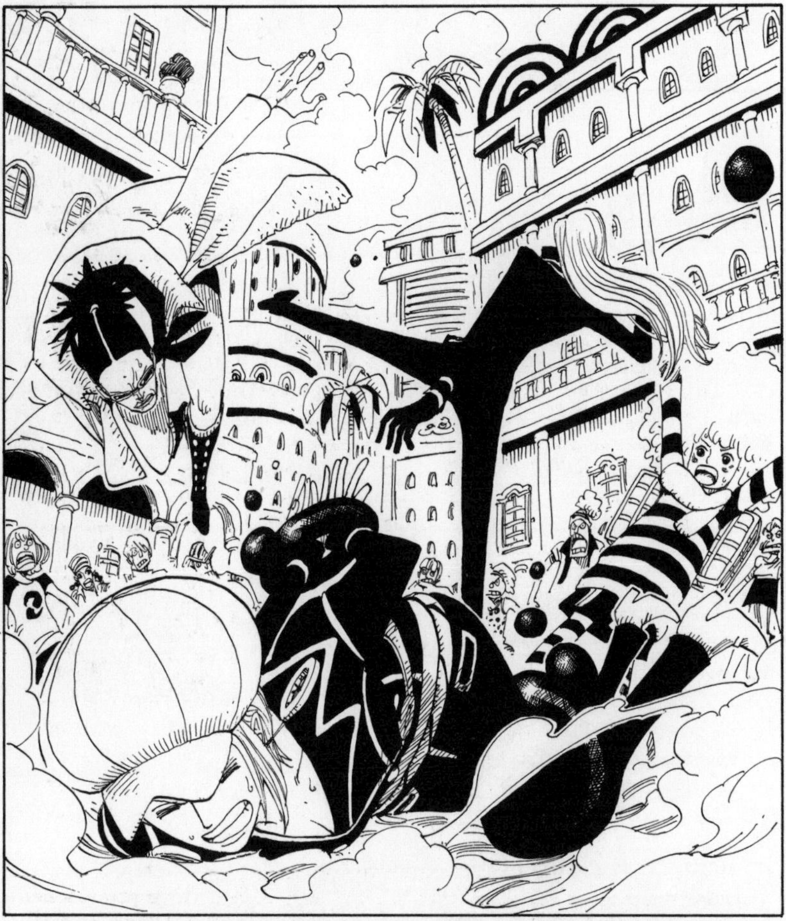

MS. GOLDEN WEEK'S PLAN, A BAROQUE REUNION, VOL. 14:
"HINA STRIKES"

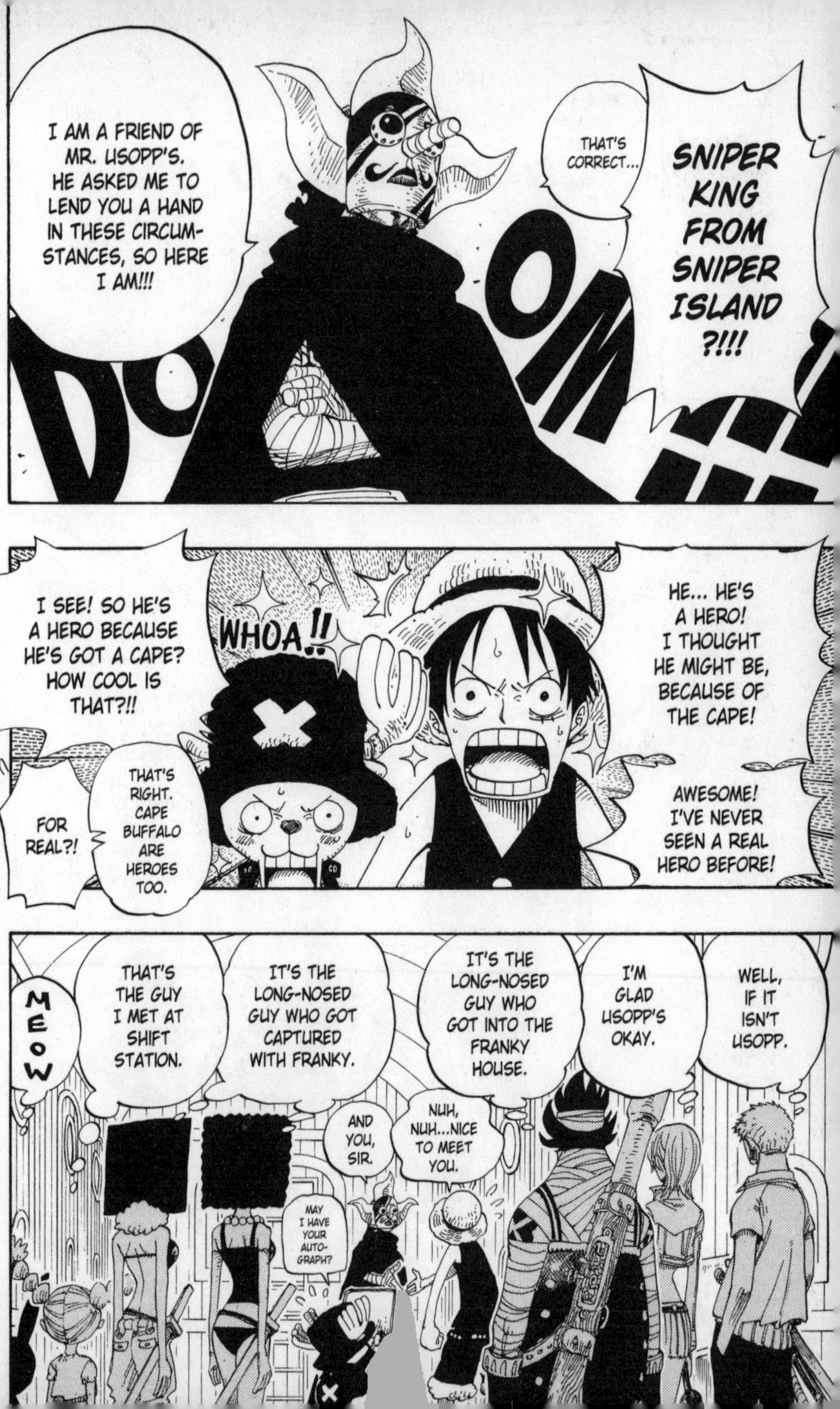
SNIPER KING FROM SNIPER ISLAND?!!!
THAT'S CORRECT...
I AM A FRIEND OF MR. USOPP'S. HE ASKED ME TO LEND YOU A HAND IN THESE CIRCUMSTANCES, SO HERE I AM!!!
DOOM
HE... HE'S A HERO! I THOUGHT HE MIGHT BE, BECAUSE OF THE CAPE!
AWESOME! I'VE NEVER SEEN A REAL HERO BEFORE!
WHOA!!
I SEE! SO HE'S A HERO BECAUSE HE'S GOT A CAPE? HOW COOL IS THAT?!!
THAT'S RIGHT. CAPE BUFFALO ARE HEROES TOO.
FOR REAL?!
WELL, IF IT ISN'T USOPP.
I'M GLAD USOPP'S OKAY.
IT'S THE LONG-NOSED GUY WHO GOT INTO THE FRANKY HOUSE.
NUH, NUH...NICE TO MEET YOU.
AND YOU, SIR.
IT'S THE LONG-NOSED GUY WHO GOT CAPTURED WITH FRANKY.
MAY I HAVE YOUR AUTOGRAPH?
THAT'S THE GUY I MET AT SHIFT STATION.
MEOW

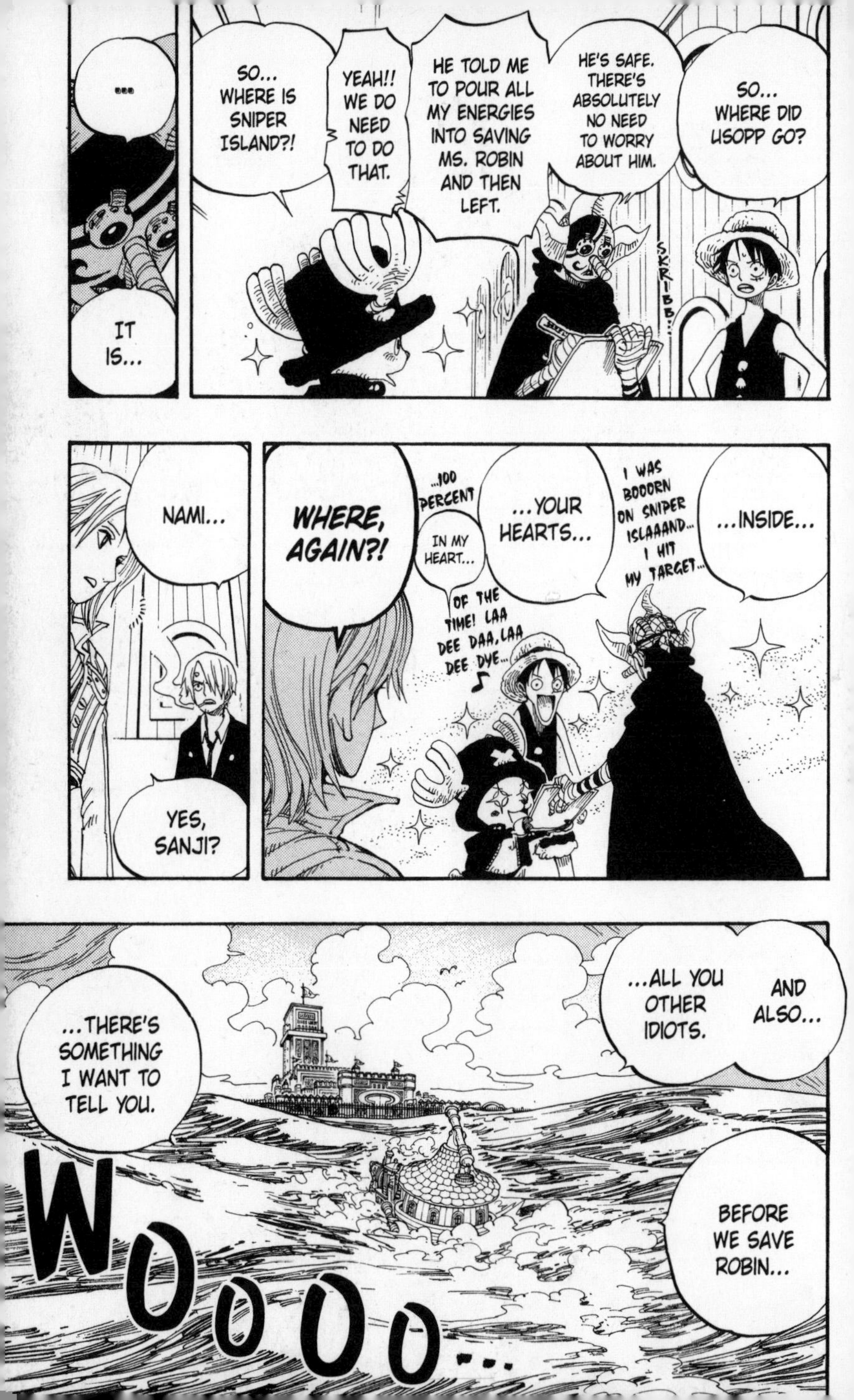
SO... WHERE DID USOPP GO?
HE'S SAFE. THERE'S ABSOLUTELY NO NEED TO WORRY ABOUT HIM.
SKRIBB...
HE TOLD ME TO POUR ALL MY ENERGIES INTO SAVING MS. ROBIN AND THEN LEFT.
YEAH!! WE DO NEED TO DO THAT.
SO... WHERE IS SNIPER ISLAND?!
...
IT IS...
...INSIDE...
I WAS BOOORN ON SNIPER ISLAAAND... I HIT MY TARGET...
...YOUR HEARTS...
...100 PERCENT
IN MY HEART...
OF THE TIME! LAA DEE DAA, LAA DEE DYE...
WHERE, AGAIN?!
NAMI...
YES, SANJI?
AND ALSO...
...ALL YOU OTHER IDIOTS.
BEFORE WE SAVE ROBIN...
...THERE'S SOMETHING I WANT TO TELL YOU.
WOOOOO...

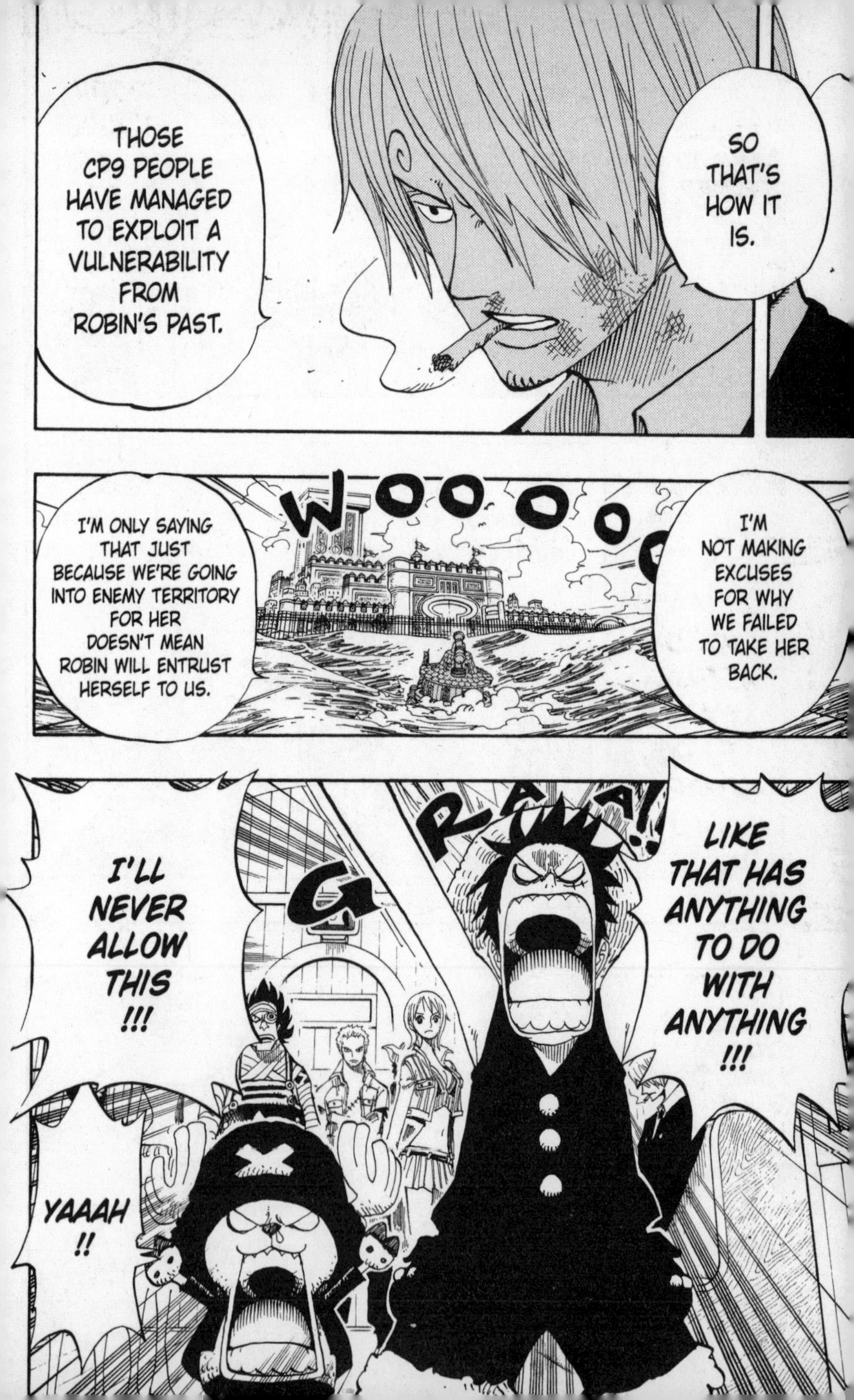
SO THAT'S HOW IT IS.
THOSE CP9 PEOPLE HAVE MANAGED TO EXPLOIT A VULNERABILITY FROM ROBIN'S PAST.
I'M NOT MAKING EXCUSES FOR WHY WE FAILED TO TAKE HER BACK.
WOOOO
I'M ONLY SAYING THAT JUST BECAUSE WE'RE GOING INTO ENEMY TERRITORY FOR HER DOESN'T MEAN ROBIN WILL ENTRUST HERSELF TO US.
LIKE THAT HAS ANYTHING TO DO WITH ANYTHING!!!
GRAA!
I'LL NEVER ALLOW THIS!!!
YAAAH!!

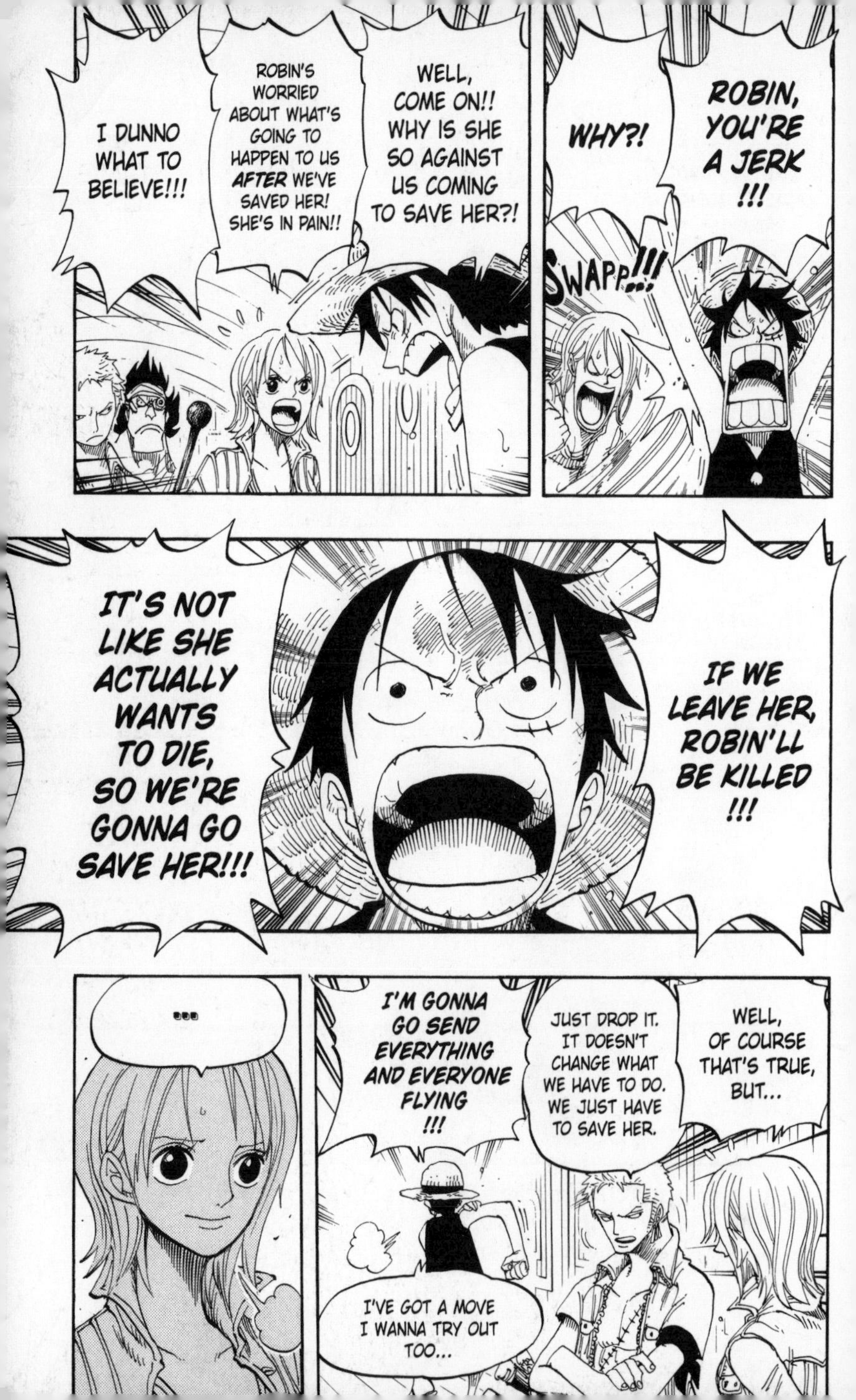
ROBIN, YOU'RE A JERK !!!
SWAPP!!!
WHY?!
WELL, COME ON!! WHY IS SHE SO AGAINST US COMING TO SAVE HER?!
ROBIN'S WORRIED ABOUT WHAT'S GOING TO HAPPEN TO US AFTER WE'VE SAVED HER! SHE'S IN PAIN!!
I DUNNO WHAT TO BELIEVE!!!
IF WE LEAVE HER, ROBIN'LL BE KILLED !!!
IT'S NOT LIKE SHE ACTUALLY WANTS TO DIE, SO WE'RE GONNA GO SAVE HER!!!
WELL, OF COURSE THAT'S TRUE, BUT...
JUST DROP IT. IT DOESN'T CHANGE WHAT WE HAVE TO DO. WE JUST HAVE TO SAVE HER.
I'M GONNA GO SEND EVERYTHING AND EVERYONE FLYING !!!
I'VE GOT A MOVE I WANNA TRY OUT TOO...
...

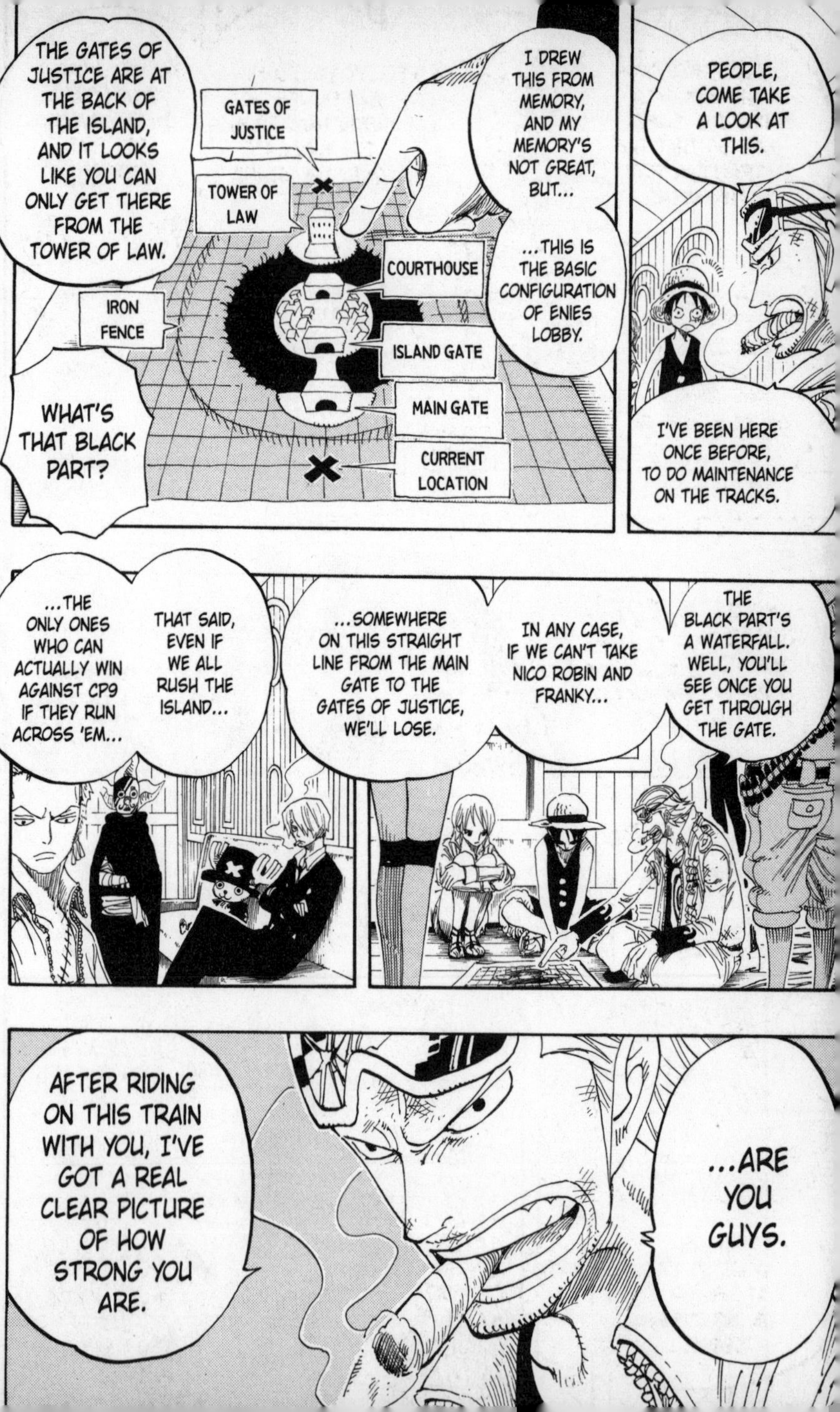
PEOPLE, COME TAKE A LOOK AT THIS.
I'VE BEEN HERE ONCE BEFORE, TO DO MAINTENANCE ON THE TRACKS.
I DREW THIS FROM MEMORY, AND MY MEMORY'S NOT GREAT, BUT...
...THIS IS THE BASIC CONFIGURATION OF ENIES LOBBY.
GATES OF JUSTICE
TOWER OF LAW
COURTHOUSE
ISLAND GATE
MAIN GATE
CURRENT LOCATION
IRON FENCE
THE GATES OF JUSTICE ARE AT THE BACK OF THE ISLAND, AND IT LOOKS LIKE YOU CAN ONLY GET THERE FROM THE TOWER OF LAW.
WHAT'S THAT BLACK PART?
THE BLACK PART'S A WATERFALL. WELL, YOU'LL SEE ONCE YOU GET THROUGH THE GATE.
IN ANY CASE, IF WE CAN'T TAKE NICO ROBIN AND FRANKY...
...SOMEWHERE ON THIS STRAIGHT LINE FROM THE MAIN GATE TO THE GATES OF JUSTICE, WE'LL LOSE.
THAT SAID, EVEN IF WE ALL RUSH THE ISLAND...
...THE ONLY ONES WHO CAN ACTUALLY WIN AGAINST CP9 IF THEY RUN ACROSS 'EM...
...ARE YOU GUYS.
AFTER RIDING ON THIS TRAIN WITH YOU, I'VE GOT A REAL CLEAR PICTURE OF HOW STRONG YOU ARE.

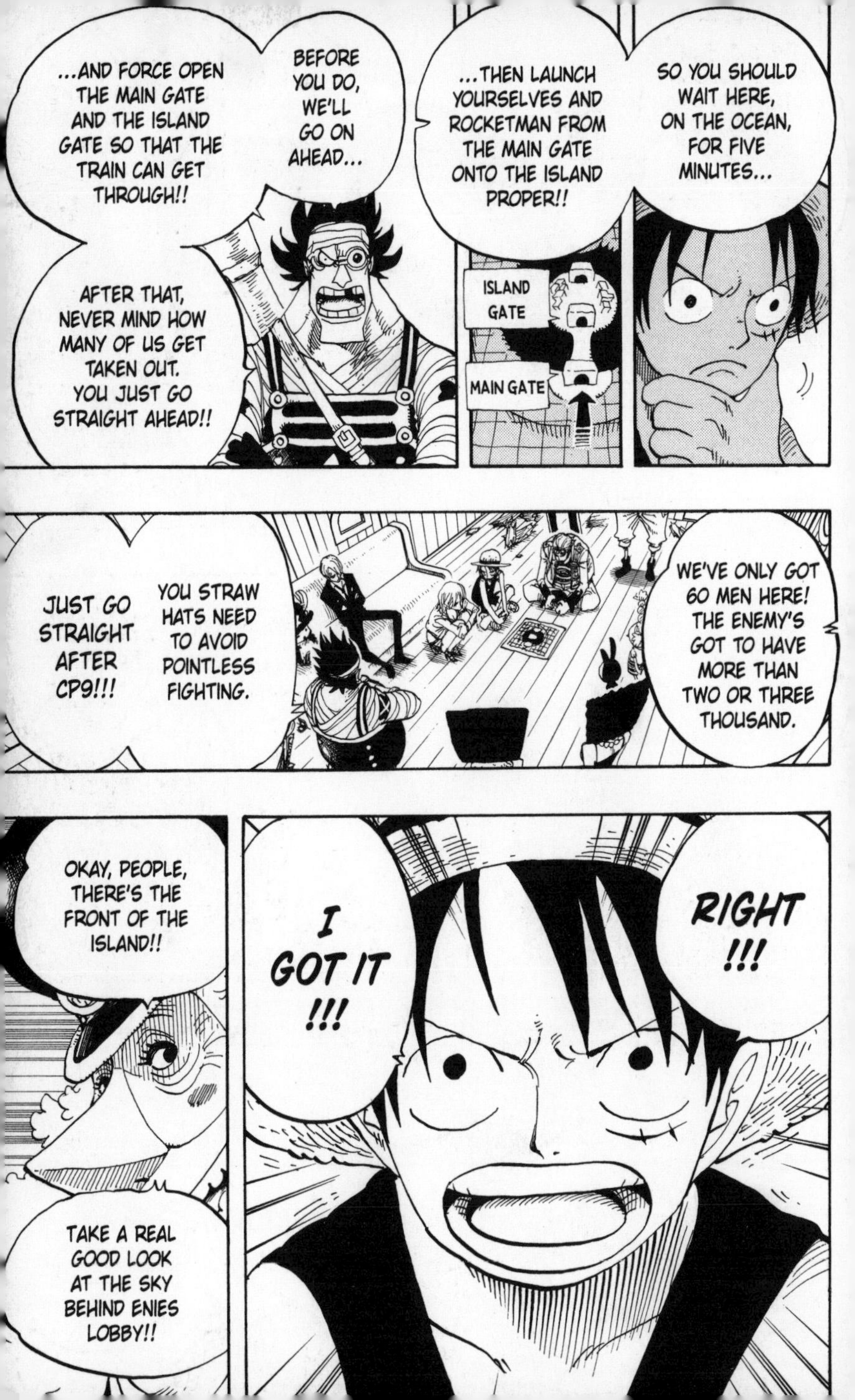
SO YOU SHOULD WAIT HERE, ON THE OCEAN, FOR FIVE MINUTES...
...THEN LAUNCH YOURSELVES AND ROCKETMAN FROM THE MAIN GATE ONTO THE ISLAND PROPER!!
ISLAND GATE
MAIN GATE
BEFORE YOU DO, WE'LL GO ON AHEAD...
...AND FORCE OPEN THE MAIN GATE AND THE ISLAND GATE SO THAT THE TRAIN CAN GET THROUGH!!
AFTER THAT, NEVER MIND HOW MANY OF US GET TAKEN OUT. YOU JUST GO STRAIGHT AHEAD!!
WE'VE ONLY GOT 60 MEN HERE! THE ENEMY'S GOT TO HAVE MORE THAN TWO OR THREE THOUSAND.
YOU STRAW HATS NEED TO AVOID POINTLESS FIGHTING.
JUST GO STRAIGHT AFTER CP9!!!
RIGHT !!!
I GOT IT !!!
OKAY, PEOPLE, THERE'S THE FRONT OF THE ISLAND!!
TAKE A REAL GOOD LOOK AT THE SKY BEHIND ENIES LOBBY!!

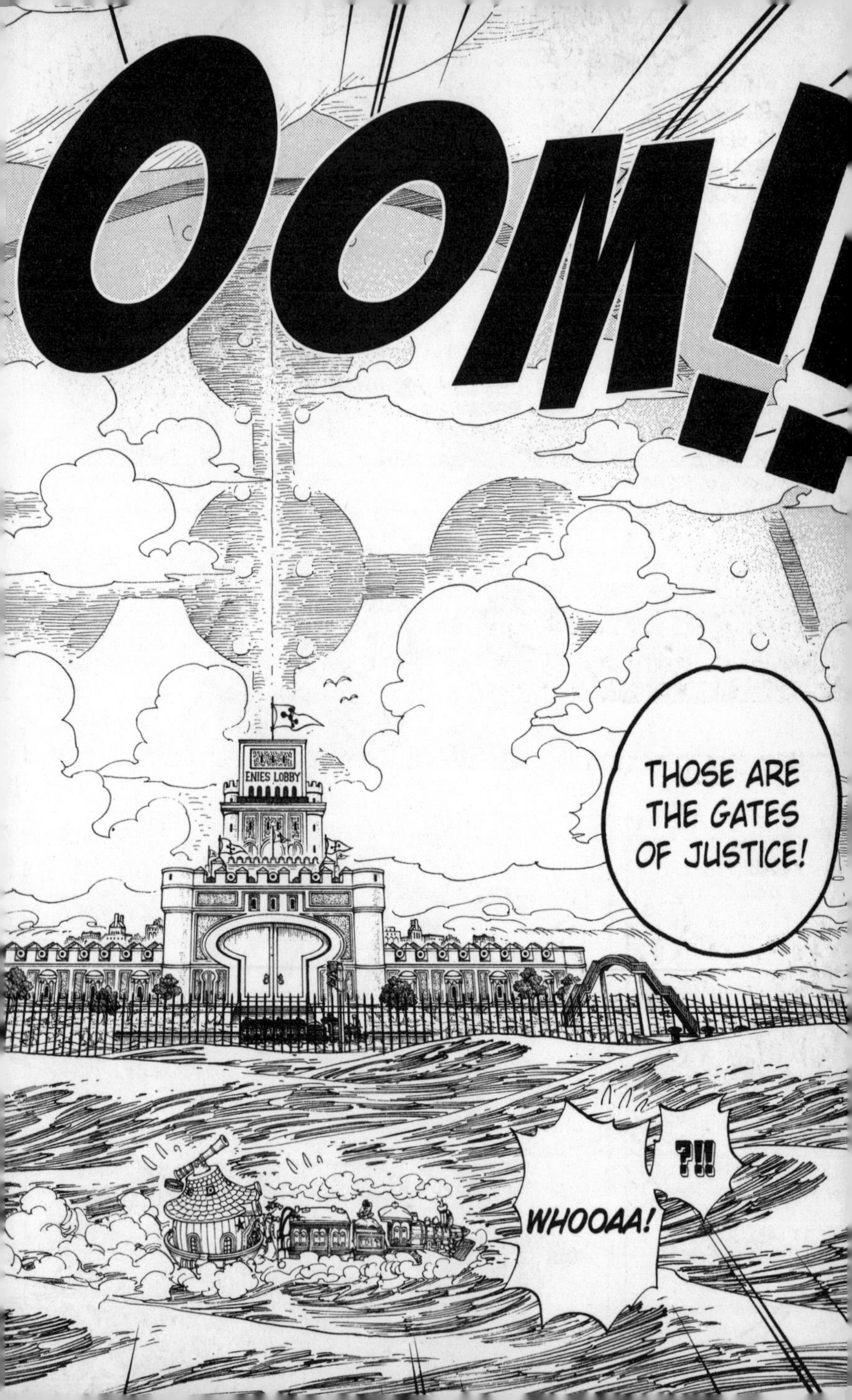
OOM!!
ENIES LOBBY
THOSE ARE THE GATES OF JUSTICE!
?!!
WHOOAA!

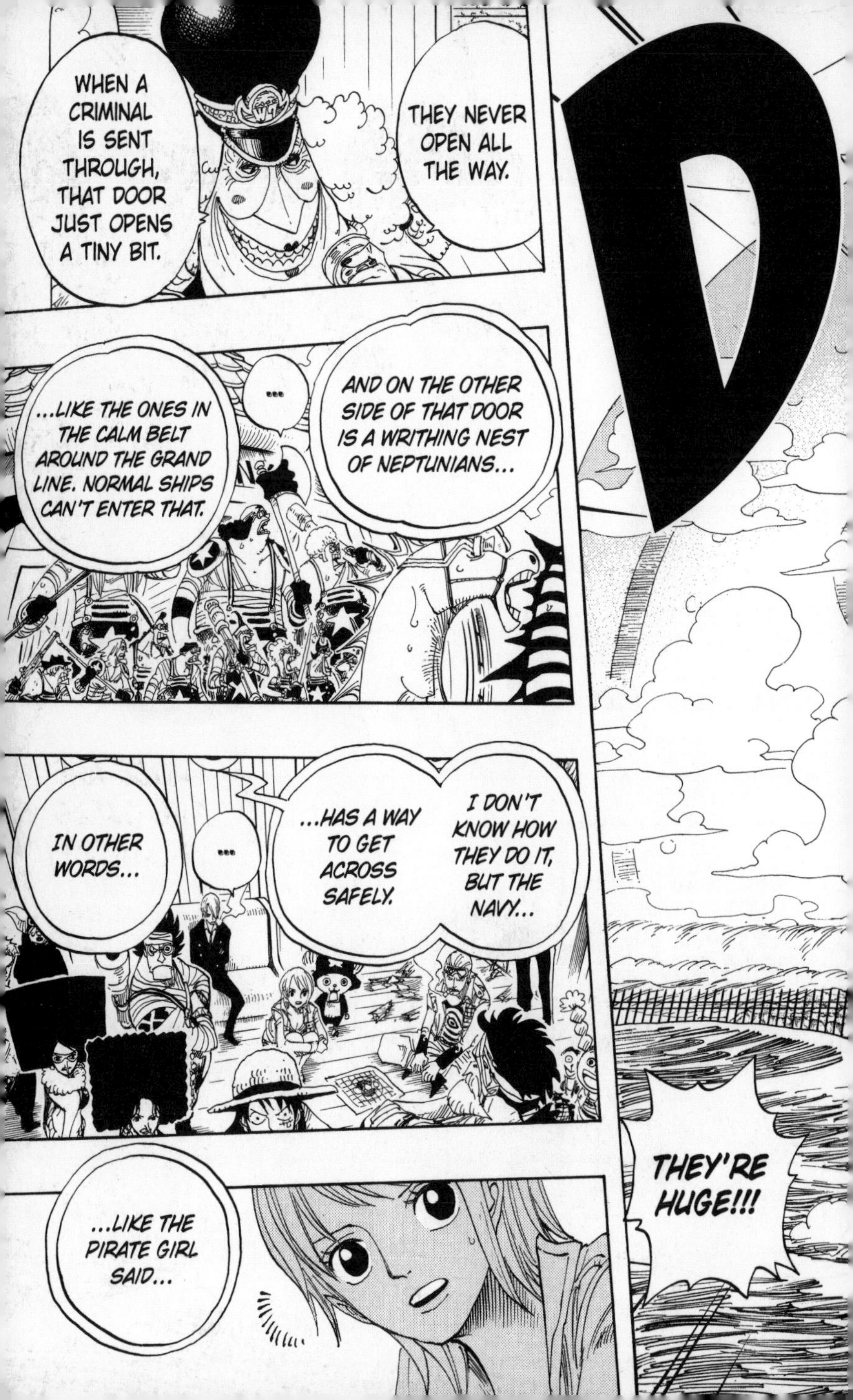
THEY'RE HUGE!!!
THEY NEVER OPEN ALL THE WAY.
WHEN A CRIMINAL IS SENT THROUGH, THAT DOOR JUST OPENS A TINY BIT.
AND ON THE OTHER SIDE OF THAT DOOR IS A WRITHING NEST OF NEPTUNIANS...
...
...LIKE THE ONES IN THE CALM BELT AROUND THE GRAND LINE. NORMAL SHIPS CAN'T ENTER THAT.
I DON'T KNOW HOW THEY DO IT, BUT THE NAVY...
...HAS A WAY TO GET ACROSS SAFELY.
...
IN OTHER WORDS...
...LIKE THE PIRATE GIRL SAID...

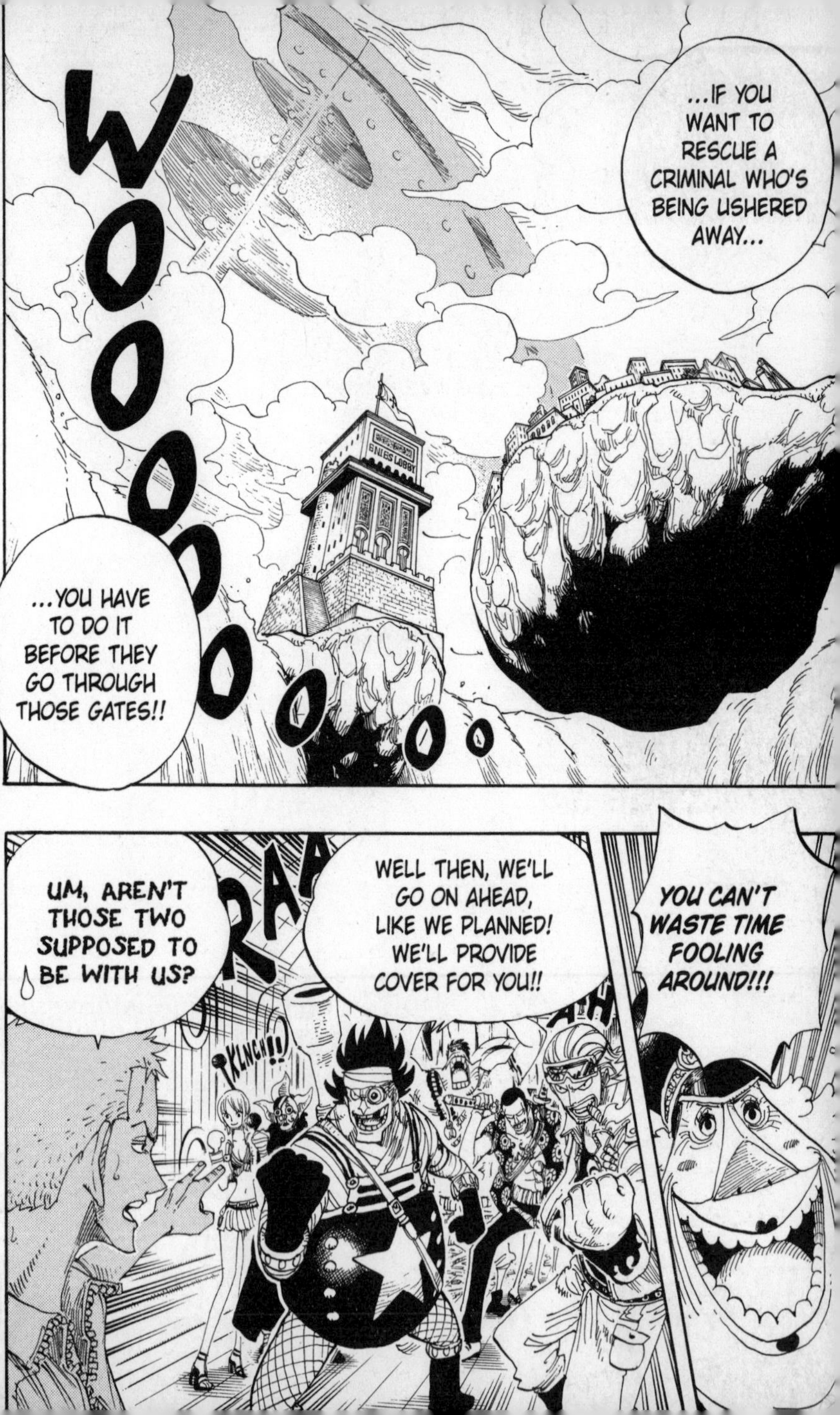
...IF YOU WANT TO RESCUE A CRIMINAL WHO'S BEING USHERED AWAY...
WOOOOOOOO
...YOU HAVE TO DO IT BEFORE THEY GO THROUGH THOSE GATES!!
YOU CAN'T WASTE TIME FOOLING AROUND!!!
WELL THEN, WE'LL GO ON AHEAD, LIKE WE PLANNED! WE'LL PROVIDE COVER FOR YOU!!
UM, AREN'T THOSE TWO SUPPOSED TO BE WITH US?
KLNCH!!

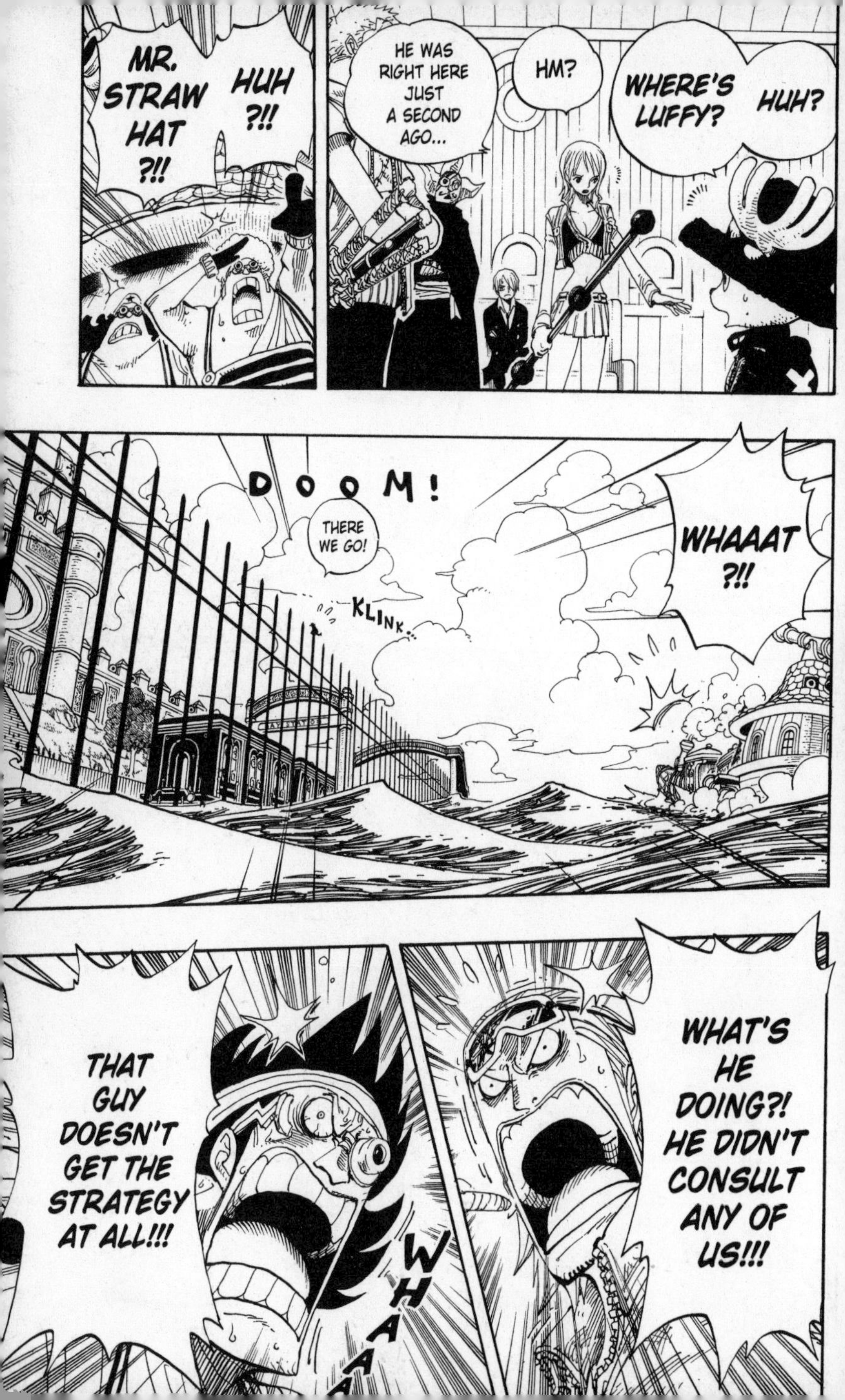
HUH?
WHERE'S LUFFY?
HM?
HE WAS RIGHT HERE JUST A SECOND AGO...
HUH ?!!
MR. STRAW HAT ?!!
WHAAAT ?!!
DOOM!
THERE WE GO!
KLINK...
WHAT'S HE DOING?! HE DIDN'T CONSULT ANY OF US!!!
THAT GUY DOESN'T GET THE STRATEGY AT ALL!!!
WHAAAA

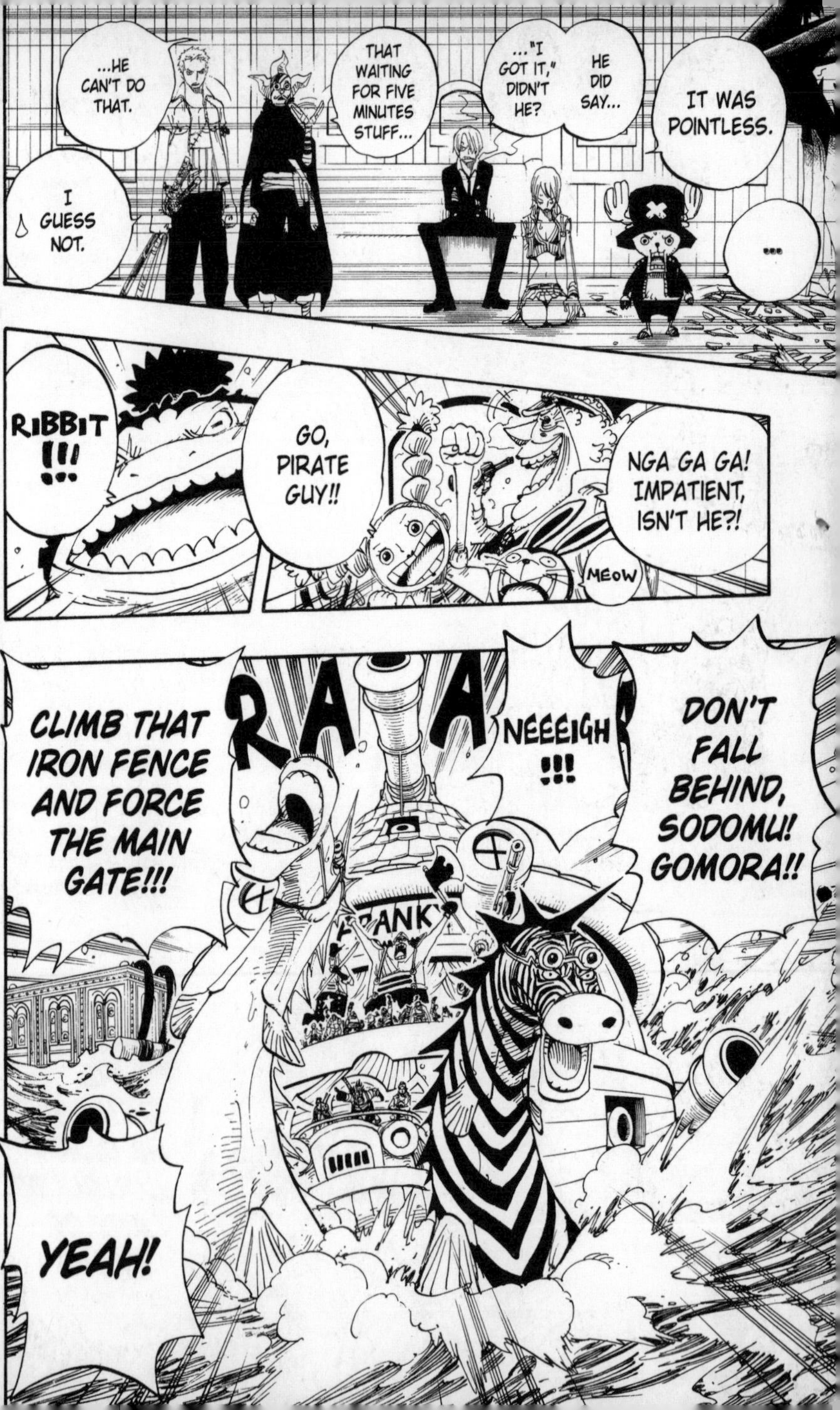
IT WAS POINTLESS.
...
HE DID SAY...
..."I GOT IT," DIDN'T HE?
THAT WAITING FOR FIVE MINUTES STUFF...
...HE CAN'T DO THAT.
I GUESS NOT.
NGA GA GA! IMPATIENT, ISN'T HE?!
MEOW
GO, PIRATE GUY!!
RIBBIT!!!...
DON'T FALL BEHIND, SODOMU! GOMORA!!
NEEEIGH!!!
RAA
CLIMB THAT IRON FENCE AND FORCE THE MAIN GATE!!!
YEAH!

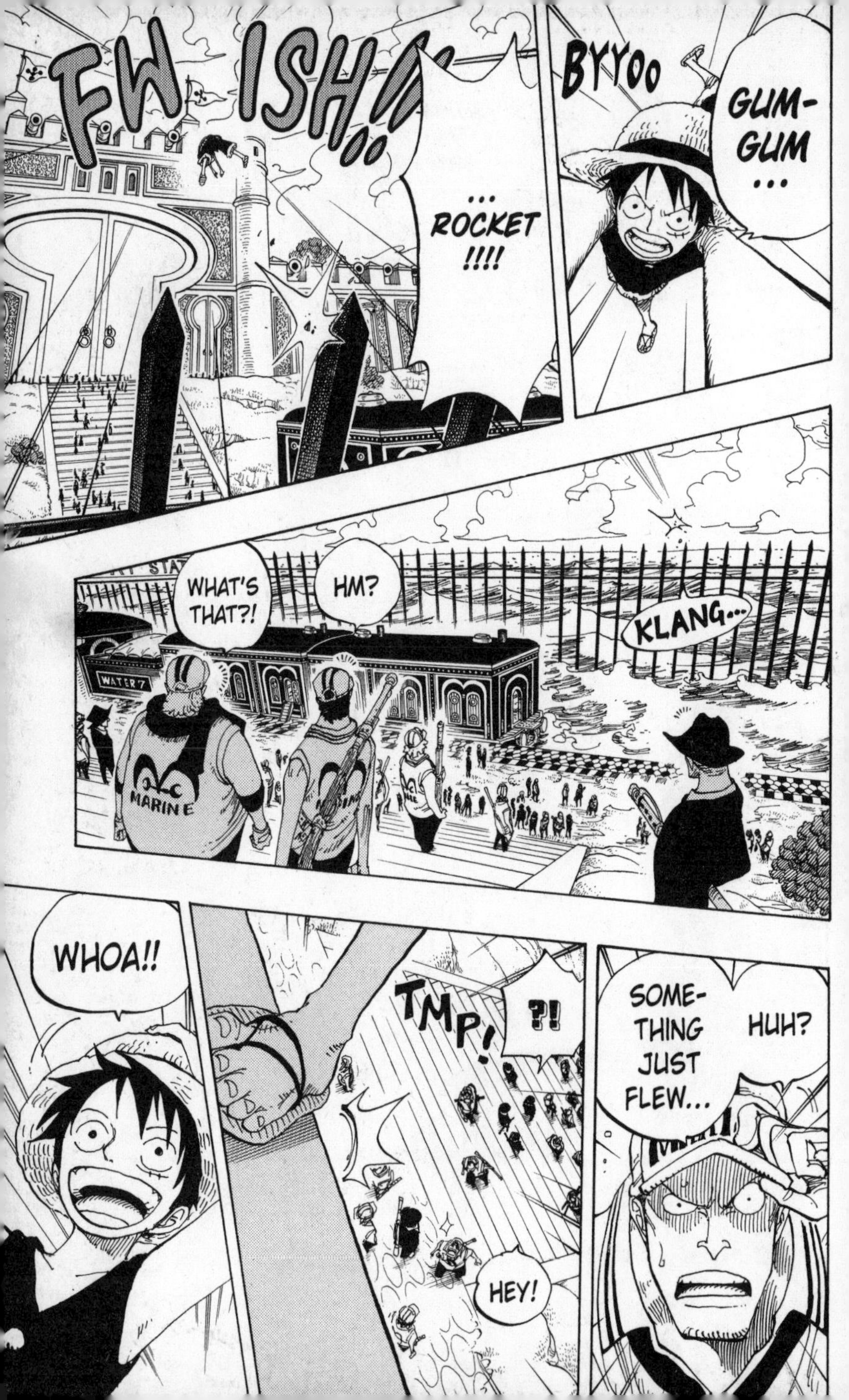
BYYOO
GUM-GUM...
...ROCKET!!!!
FWISH!!
KLANG...
HM?
WHAT'S THAT?!
HUH?
SOME-THING JUST FLEW...
?!
TMP!
HEY!
WHOA!!

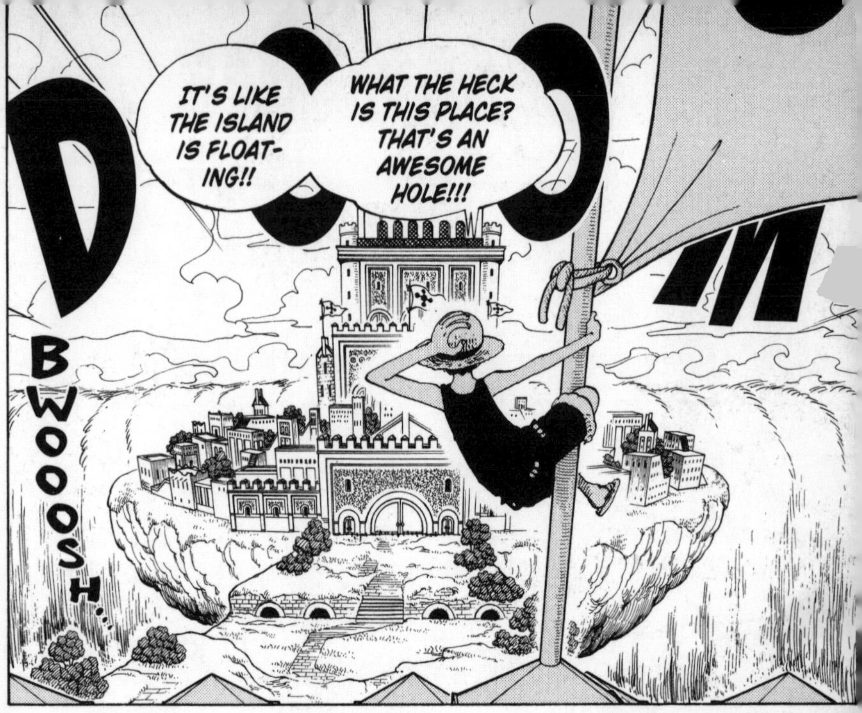
DOOM
WHAT THE HECK IS THIS PLACE? THAT'S AN AWESOME HOLE!!!
IT'S LIKE THE ISLAND IS FLOAT-ING!!
BWOOOSH...

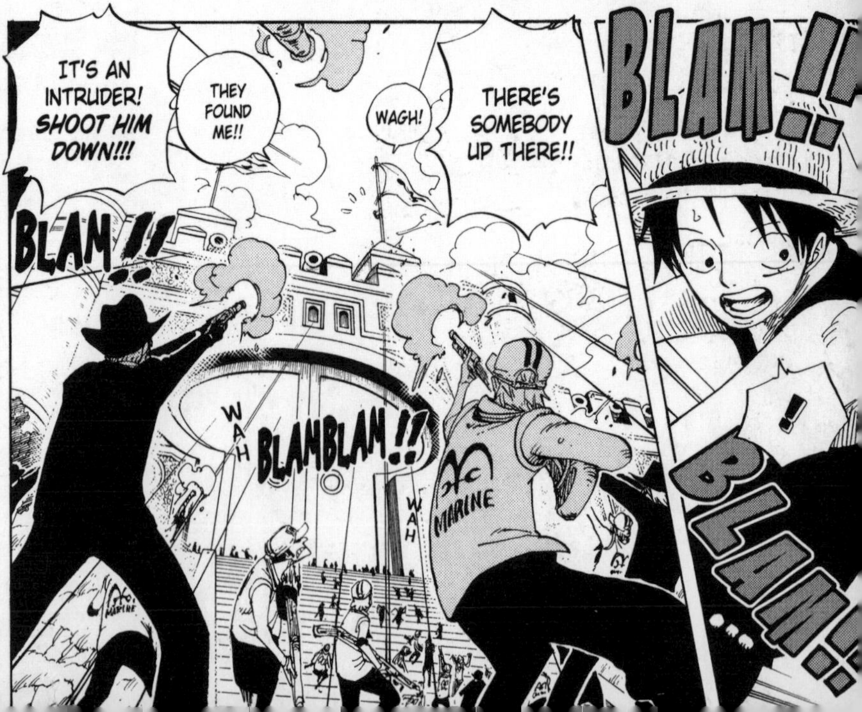
BLAM!!
THERE'S SOMEBODY UP THERE!!
WAGH!
THEY FOUND ME!!
IT'S AN INTRUDER! SHOOT HIM DOWN!!!
BLAM!!
!
BLAM!!
WAH
BLAMBLAM!!
WAH
MARINE

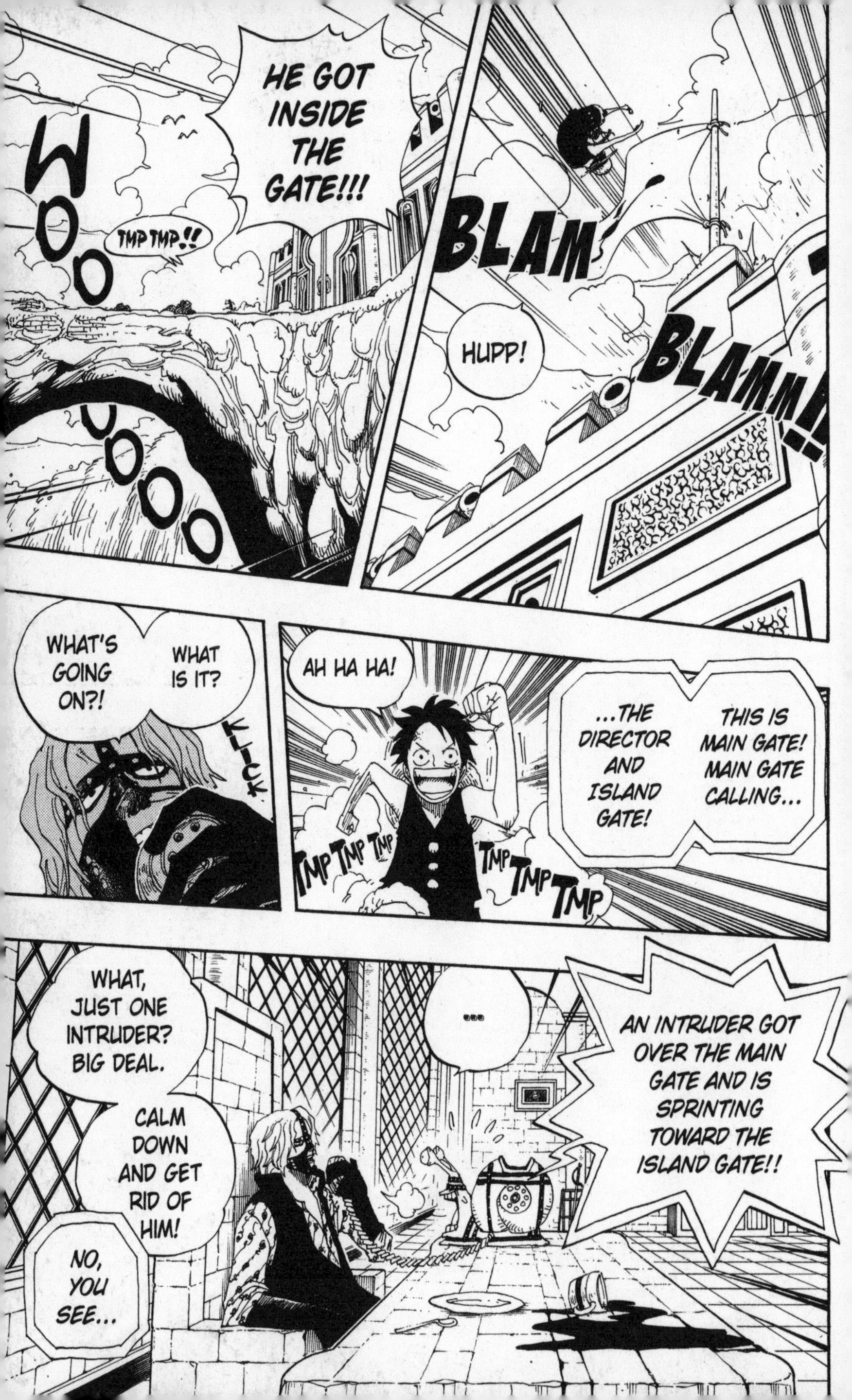
BLAM
HUPP!
BLAMM!!
HE GOT INSIDE THE GATE!!!
WOOOOOOOO
TMP TMP!!
THIS IS MAIN GATE! MAIN GATE CALLING...
...THE DIRECTOR AND ISLAND GATE!
AH HA HA!
TMP TMP TMP
TMP TMP TMP
WHAT IS IT?
WHAT'S GOING ON?!
KLICK
AN INTRUDER GOT OVER THE MAIN GATE AND IS SPRINTING TOWARD THE ISLAND GATE!!
...
WHAT, JUST ONE INTRUDER? BIG DEAL.
CALM DOWN AND GET RID OF HIM!
NO, YOU SEE...

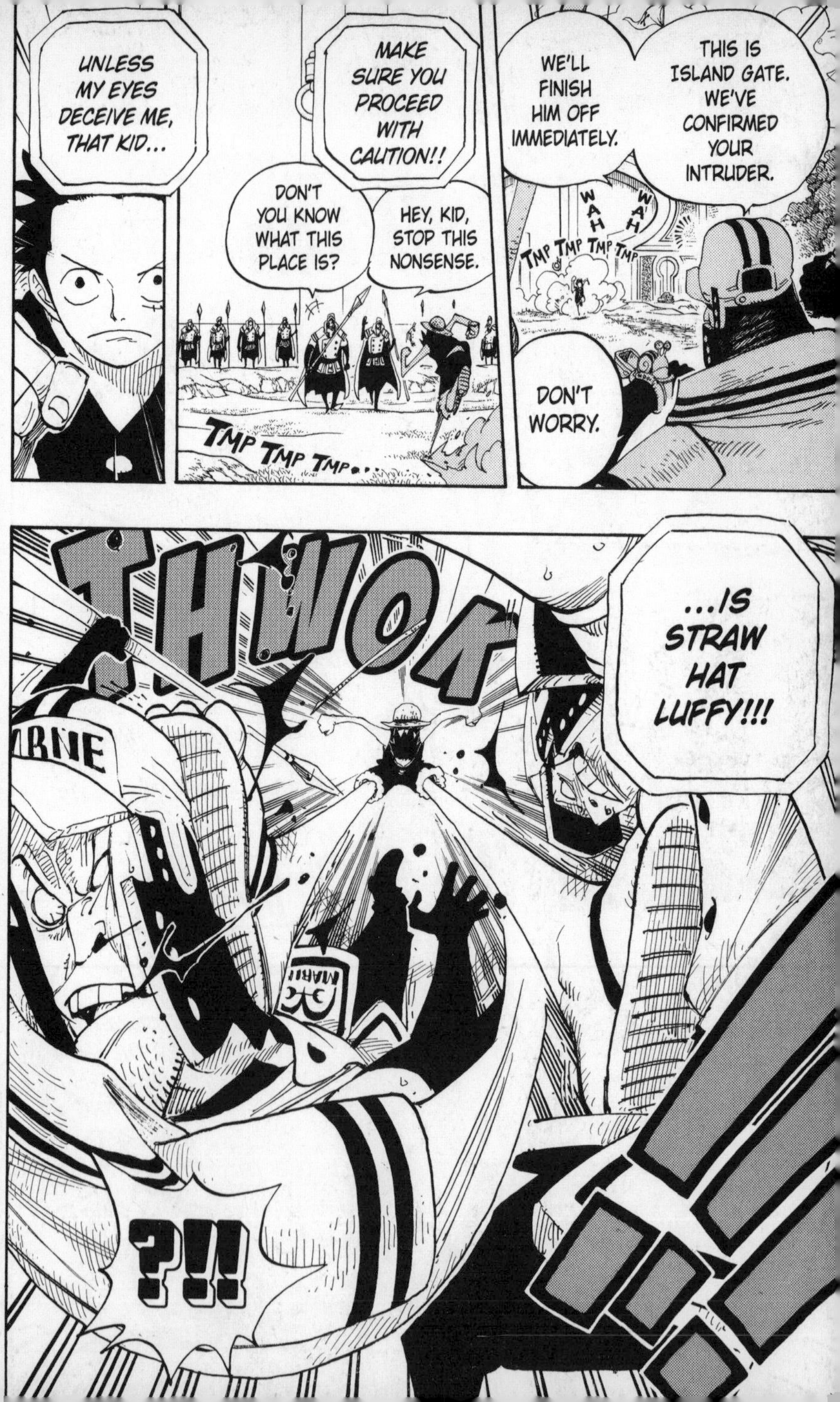
THIS IS ISLAND GATE. WE'VE CONFIRMED YOUR INTRUDER.
WE'LL FINISH HIM OFF IMMEDIATELY.
WAH
WAH
TMP TMP TMP TMP
DON'T WORRY.
MAKE SURE YOU PROCEED WITH CAUTION!!
HEY, KID, STOP THIS NONSENSE.
DON'T YOU KNOW WHAT THIS PLACE IS?
TMP TMP TMP...
UNLESS MY EYES DECEIVE ME, THAT KID...
THWOK
...IS STRAW HAT LUFFY!!!
?!!

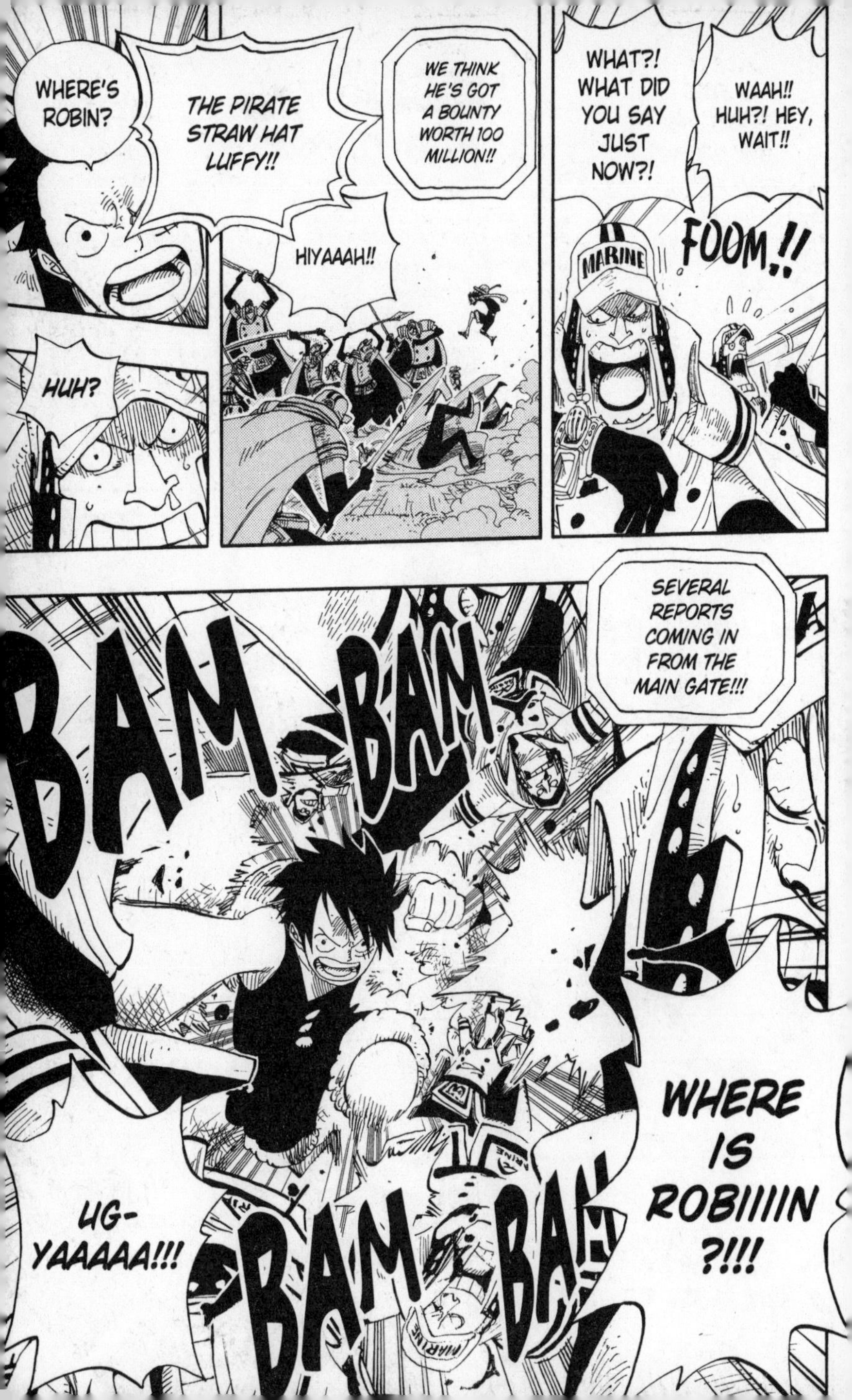
WAAH!! HUH?! HEY, WAIT!!
WHAT?! WHAT DID YOU SAY JUST NOW?!
FOOM!!
MARINE
WE THINK HE'S GOT A BOUNTY WORTH 100 MILLION!!
HIYAAAH!!
THE PIRATE STRAW HAT LUFFY!!
WHERE'S ROBIN?
HUH?
SEVERAL REPORTS COMING IN FROM THE MAIN GATE!!!
BAM-BAM
WHERE IS ROBIIIIN ?!!!
BAM-BAM-BAM
UG-YAAAAA!!!

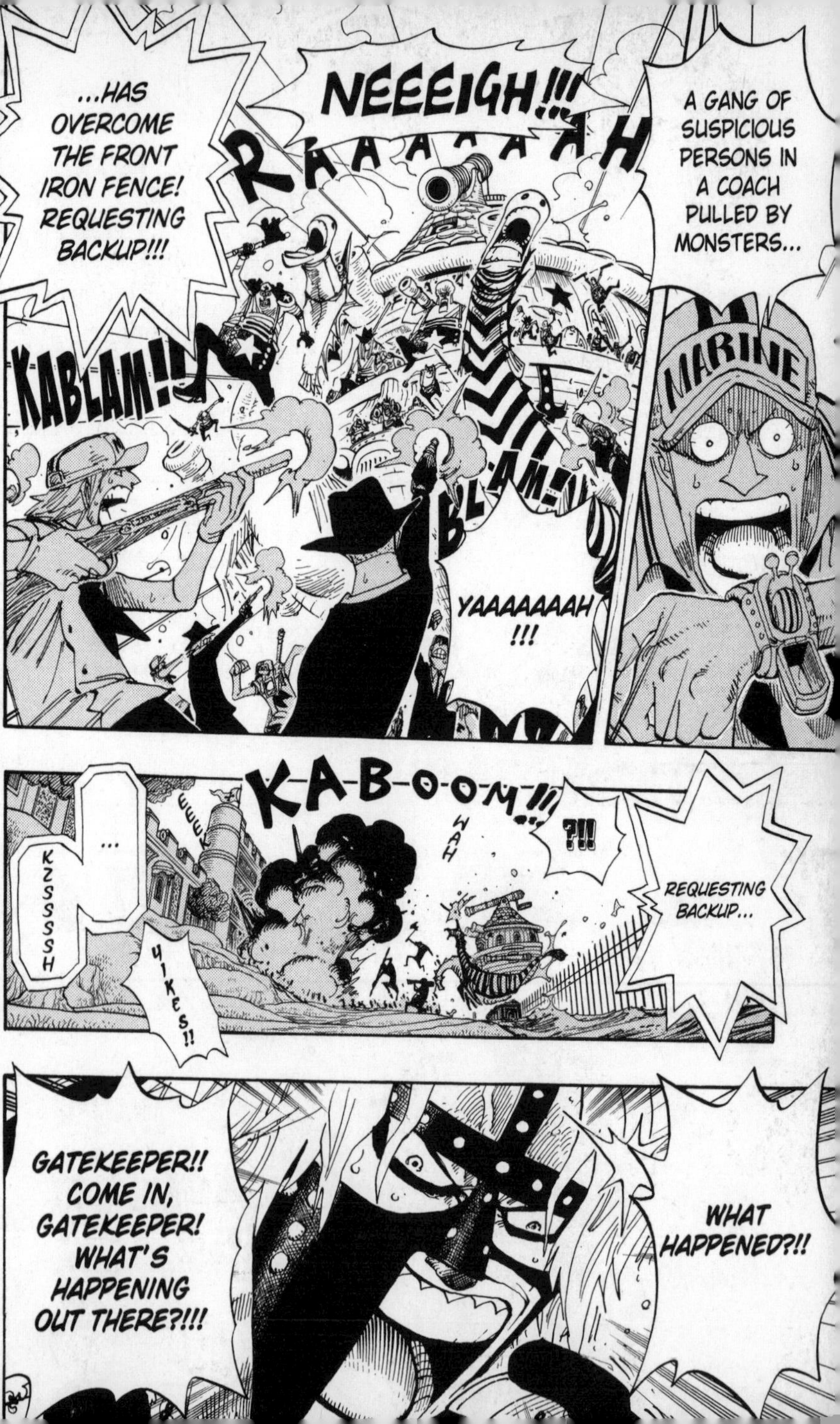
A GANG OF SUSPICIOUS PERSONS IN A COACH PULLED BY MONSTERS...
NEEEIGH!!!
RAAAAAAH
...HAS OVERCOME THE FRONT IRON FENCE! REQUESTING BACKUP!!!
KABLAM!!!
BLAM!!
YAAAAAAAH!!!
REQUESTING BACKUP...
?!!
KA-B-O-O-M!!
WAH
EEEEK
...
KZSSSSSH
YIKES!!
WHAT HAPPENED?!!
GATEKEEPER!! COME IN, GATEKEEPER! WHAT'S HAPPENING OUT THERE?!!!

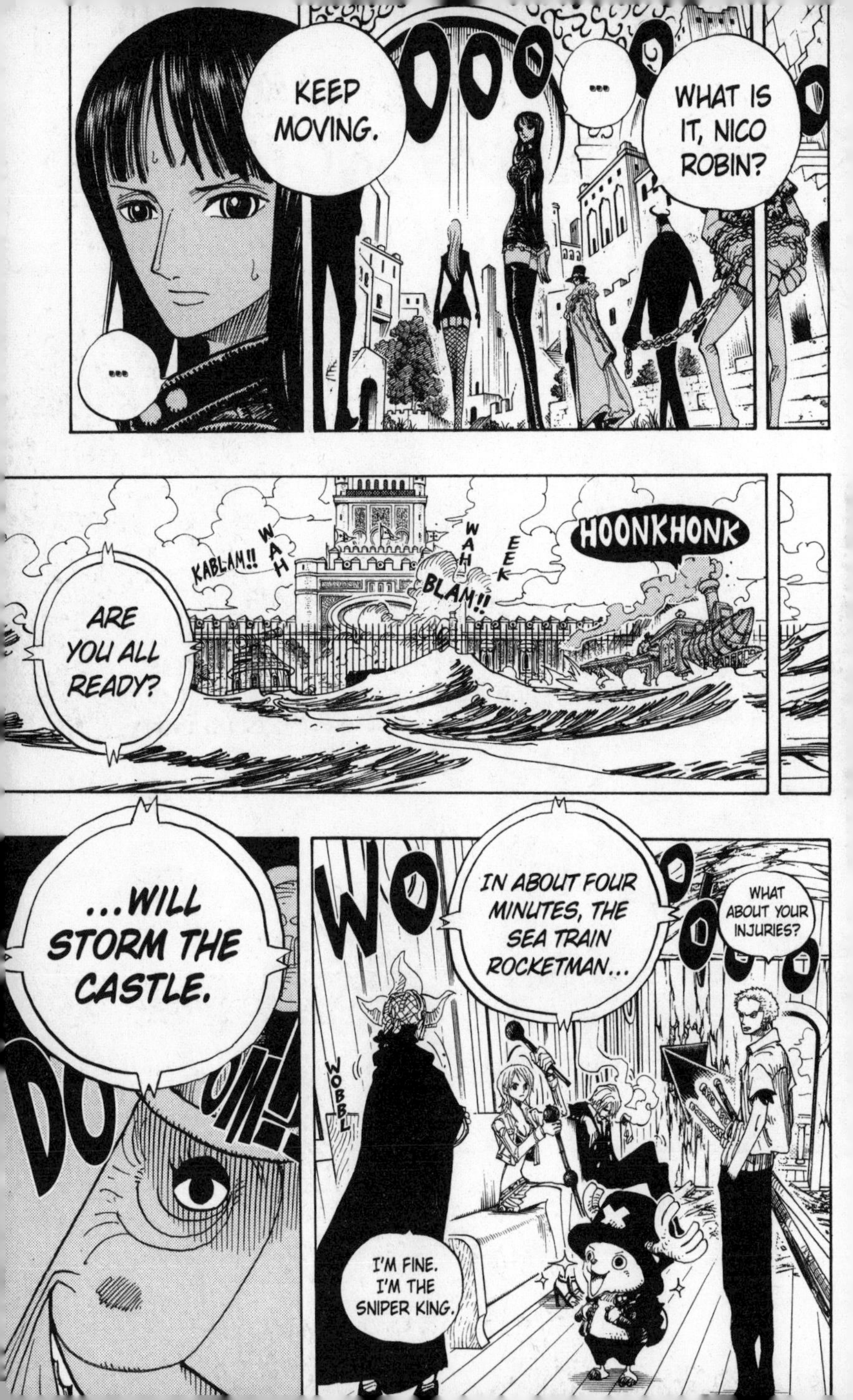
WHAT IS IT, NICO ROBIN?
...
KEEP MOVING.
...
HOONKHONK
EEK
WAH
BLAM!!
WAH
KABLAM!!
ARE YOU ALL READY?
WHAT ABOUT YOUR INJURIES?
IN ABOUT FOUR MINUTES, THE SEA TRAIN ROCKETMAN...
WO
WOBBL
I'M FINE. I'M THE SNIPER KING.
...WILL STORM THE CASTLE.

Chapter 377:
THE BIG SHOWDOWN ON THE JUDICIAL ISLAND!!

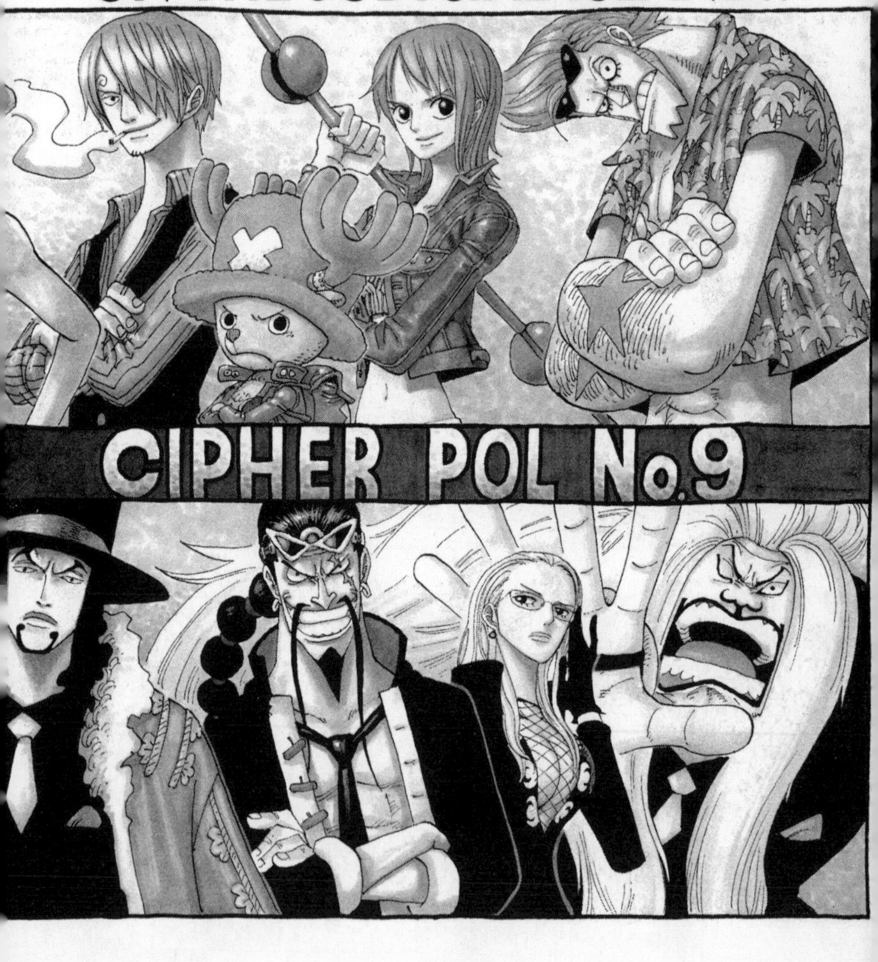
CIPHER POL No.9

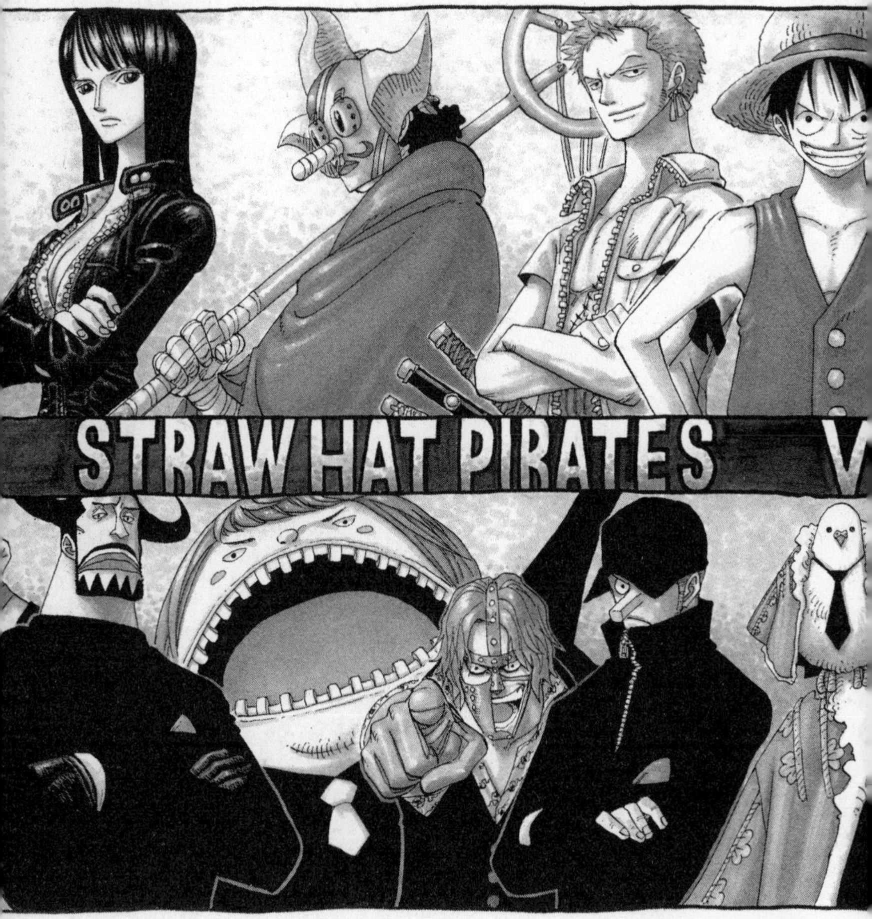
STRAW HAT PIRATES V

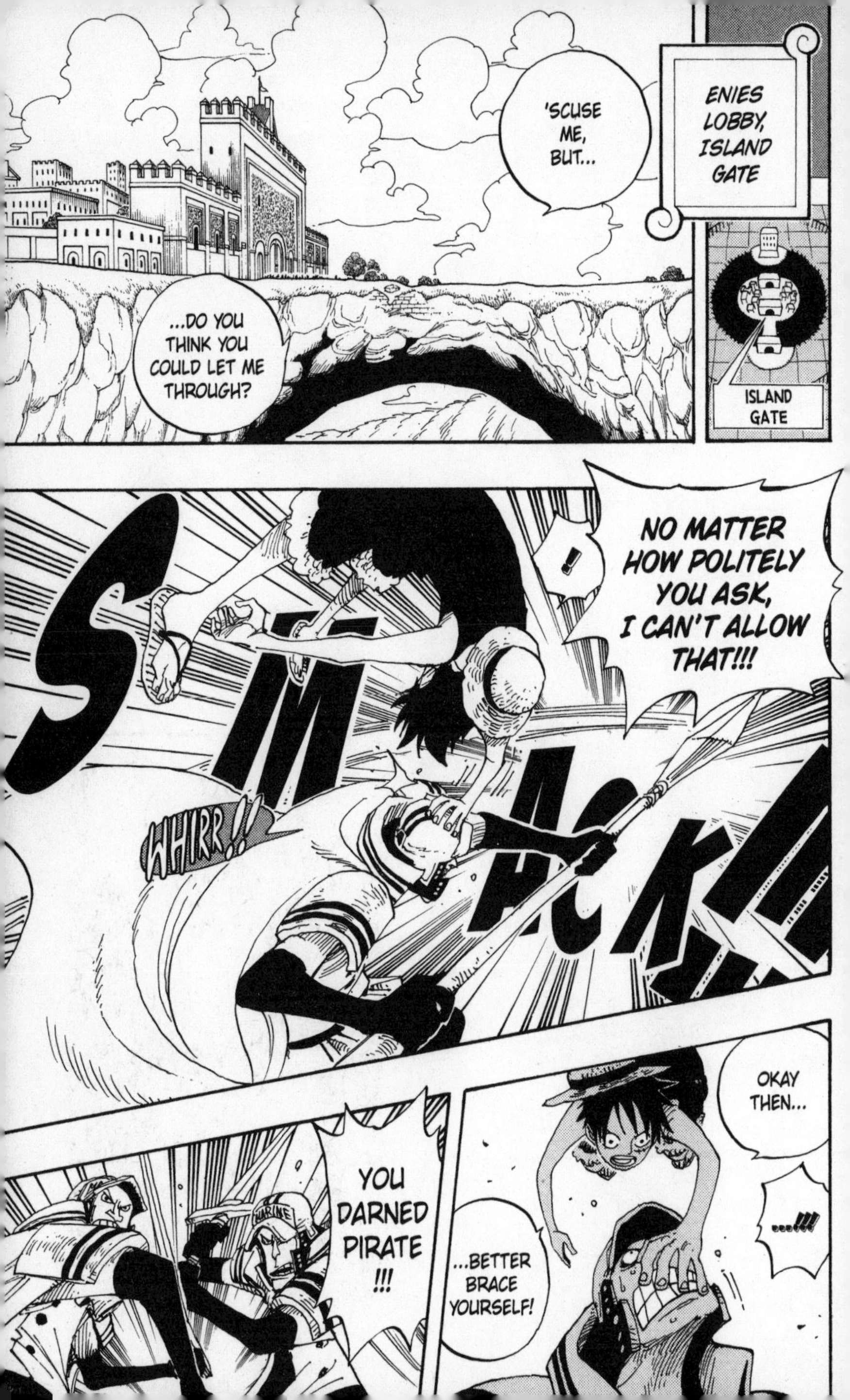
ENIES LOBBY, ISLAND GATE
ISLAND GATE
'SCUSE ME, BUT...
...DO YOU THINK YOU COULD LET ME THROUGH?
!
NO MATTER HOW POLITELY YOU ASK, I CAN'T ALLOW THAT!!!
SMACK!!
WHIRR!!
OKAY THEN...
...!!!
...BETTER BRACE YOURSELF!
YOU DARNED PIRATE!!!
MARINE

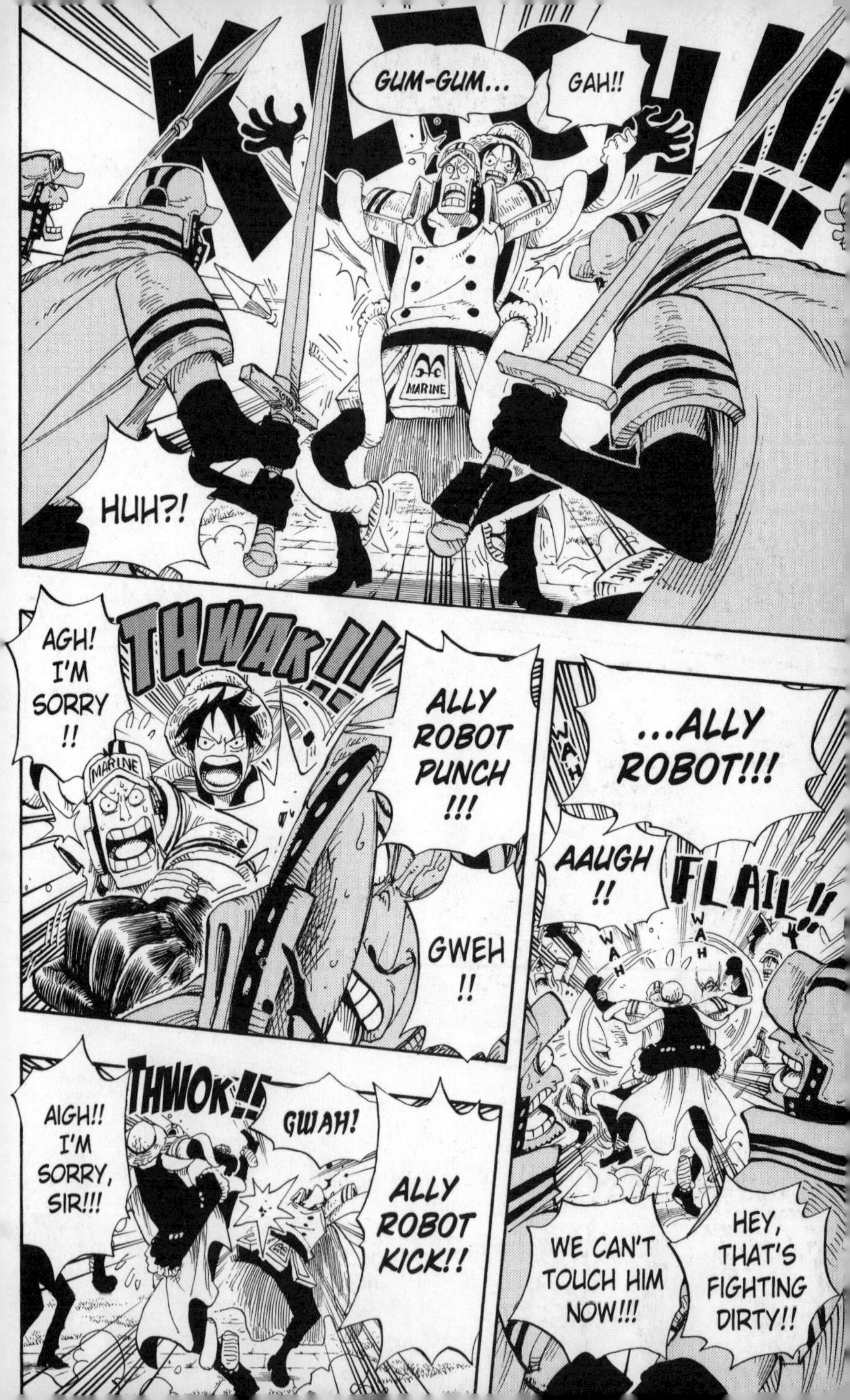
GAH!!
GUM-GUM...
HUH?!
...ALLY ROBOT!!!
AAUGH !!
FLAIL!!
WAH
WAH
WAH
HEY, THAT'S FIGHTING DIRTY!!
WE CAN'T TOUCH HIM NOW!!!
ALLY ROBOT PUNCH !!!
THWAK!!
AGH! I'M SORRY !!
GWEH !!
ALLY ROBOT KICK!!
GWAH!
THWOK!!
AIGH!! I'M SORRY, SIR!!!

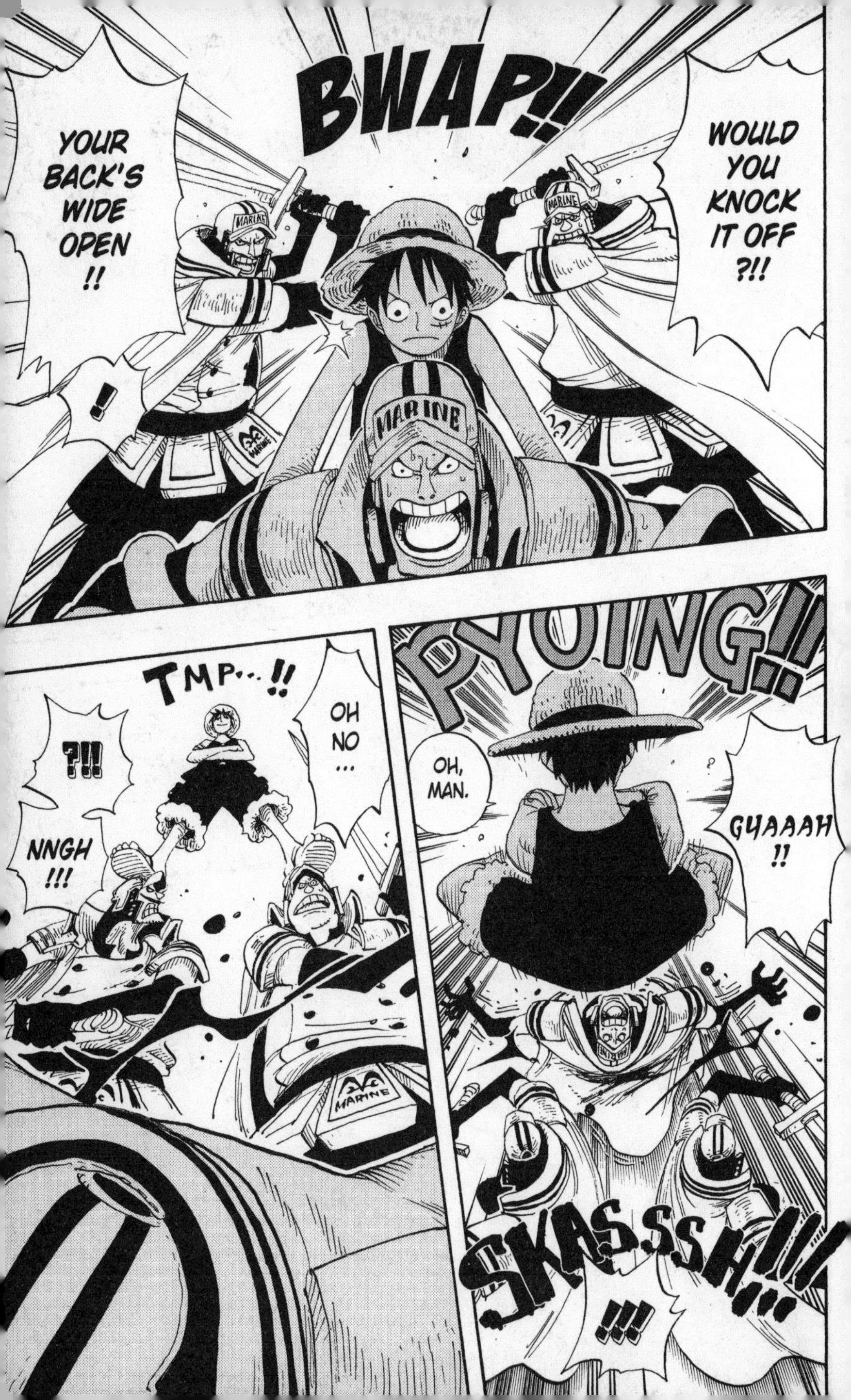
BWAP!!
WOULD YOU KNOCK IT OFF ?!!
YOUR BACK'S WIDE OPEN !!
!
PYOING!!
GUAAAH !!
OH, MAN.
SKASSSH!!!
!!!
OH NO ...
TMP...!!
?!!
NNGH !!!

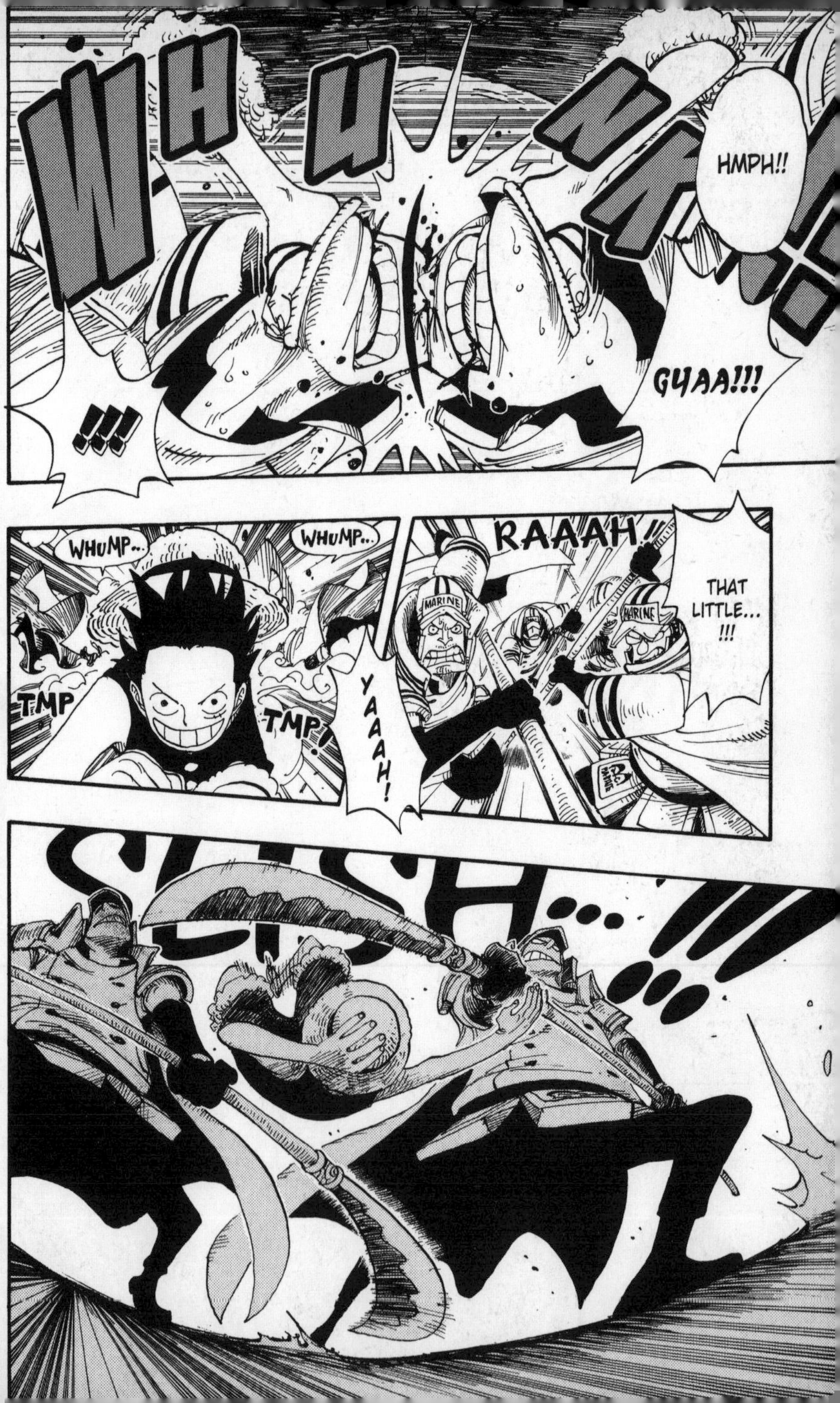

HMPH!!
GUAA!!!
!!!!
THAT LITTLE... !!!
RAAAH!!
YAAAH!
WHUMP...
WHUMP...
TMP!
TMP

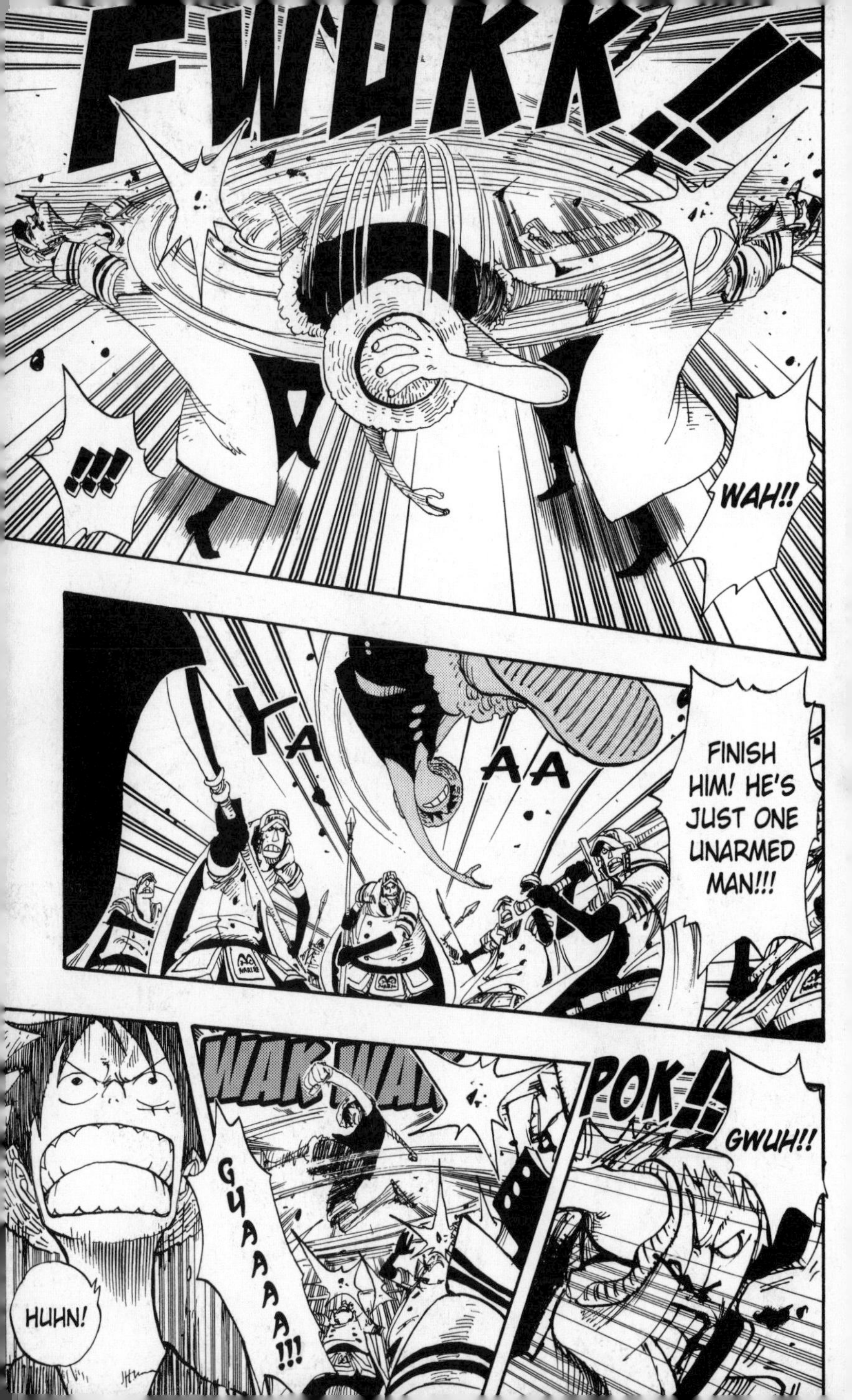
FWUKK!!
WAH!!
!!!
YA AA
FINISH HIM! HE'S JUST ONE UNARMED MAN!!!
GWUH!!
POK!!
WAK WAK
GUAAAAA!!!
HUHN!

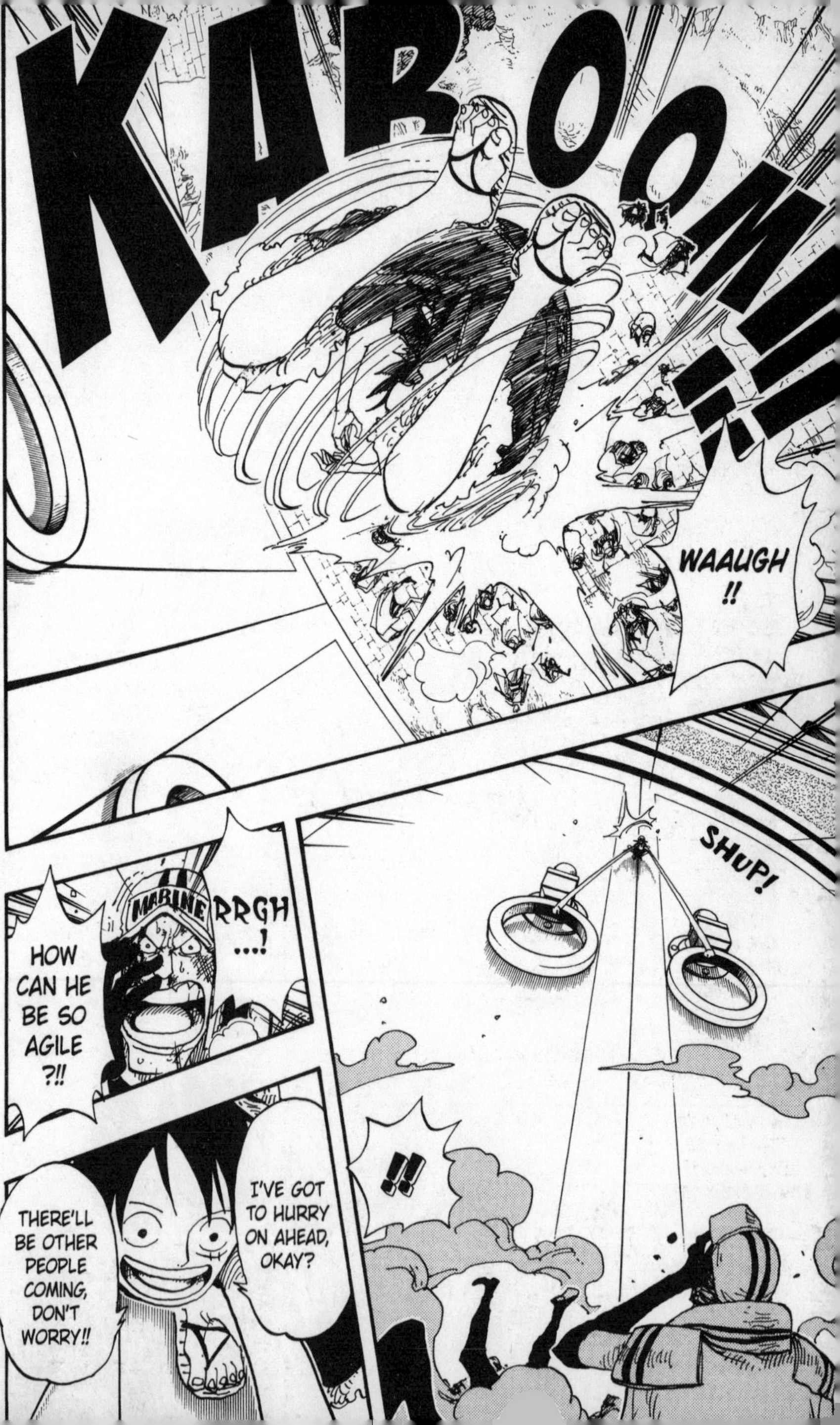
KABOOM!!
WAAUGH!!
SHUP!
!!
RRGH...!
HOW CAN HE BE SO AGILE?!!
I'VE GOT TO HURRY ON AHEAD, OKAY?
THERE'LL BE OTHER PEOPLE COMING, DON'T WORRY!!

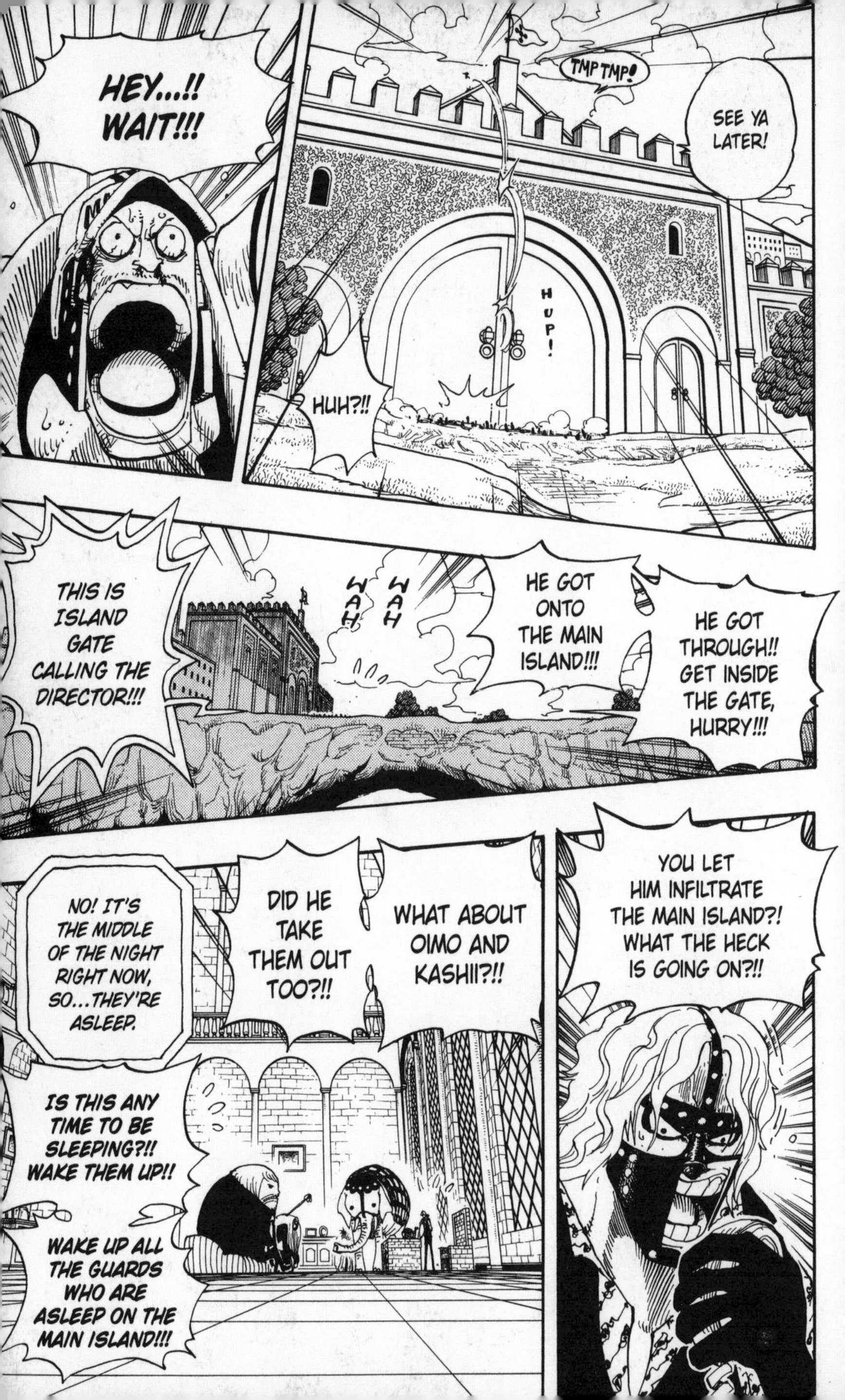
SEE YA LATER!
TMP TMP!
HUP!
HUH?!!
HEY...!! WAIT!!!
HE GOT THROUGH!! GET INSIDE THE GATE, HURRY!!!
HE GOT ONTO THE MAIN ISLAND!!!
WAH WAH
THIS IS ISLAND GATE CALLING THE DIRECTOR!!!
YOU LET HIM INFILTRATE THE MAIN ISLAND?! WHAT THE HECK IS GOING ON?!!
WHAT ABOUT OIMO AND KASHII?!!
DID HE TAKE THEM OUT TOO?!!
NO! IT'S THE MIDDLE OF THE NIGHT RIGHT NOW, SO...THEY'RE ASLEEP.
IS THIS ANY TIME TO BE SLEEPING?!! WAKE THEM UP!!
WAKE UP ALL THE GUARDS WHO ARE ASLEEP ON THE MAIN ISLAND!!!

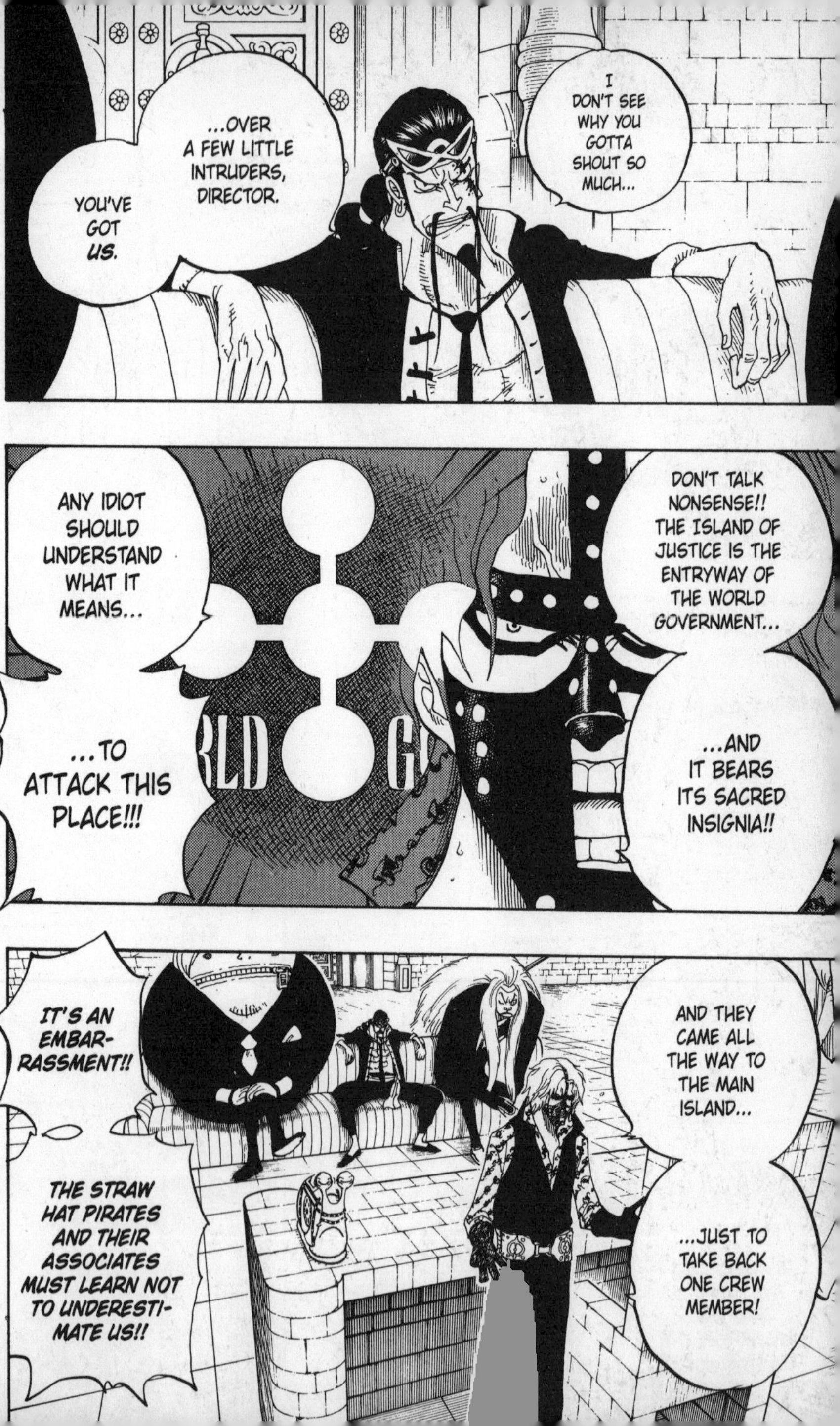
I DON'T SEE WHY YOU GOTTA SHOUT SO MUCH...
...OVER A FEW LITTLE INTRUDERS, DIRECTOR.
YOU'VE GOT *US.*
DON'T TALK NONSENSE!! THE ISLAND OF JUSTICE IS THE ENTRYWAY OF THE WORLD GOVERNMENT...
...AND IT BEARS ITS SACRED INSIGNIA!!
ANY IDIOT SHOULD UNDERSTAND WHAT IT MEANS...
...TO ATTACK THIS PLACE!!!
AND THEY CAME ALL THE WAY TO THE MAIN ISLAND...
...JUST TO TAKE BACK ONE CREW MEMBER!
IT'S AN EMBAR-RASSMENT!!
THE STRAW HAT PIRATES AND THEIR ASSOCIATES MUST LEARN NOT TO UNDERESTI-MATE US!!

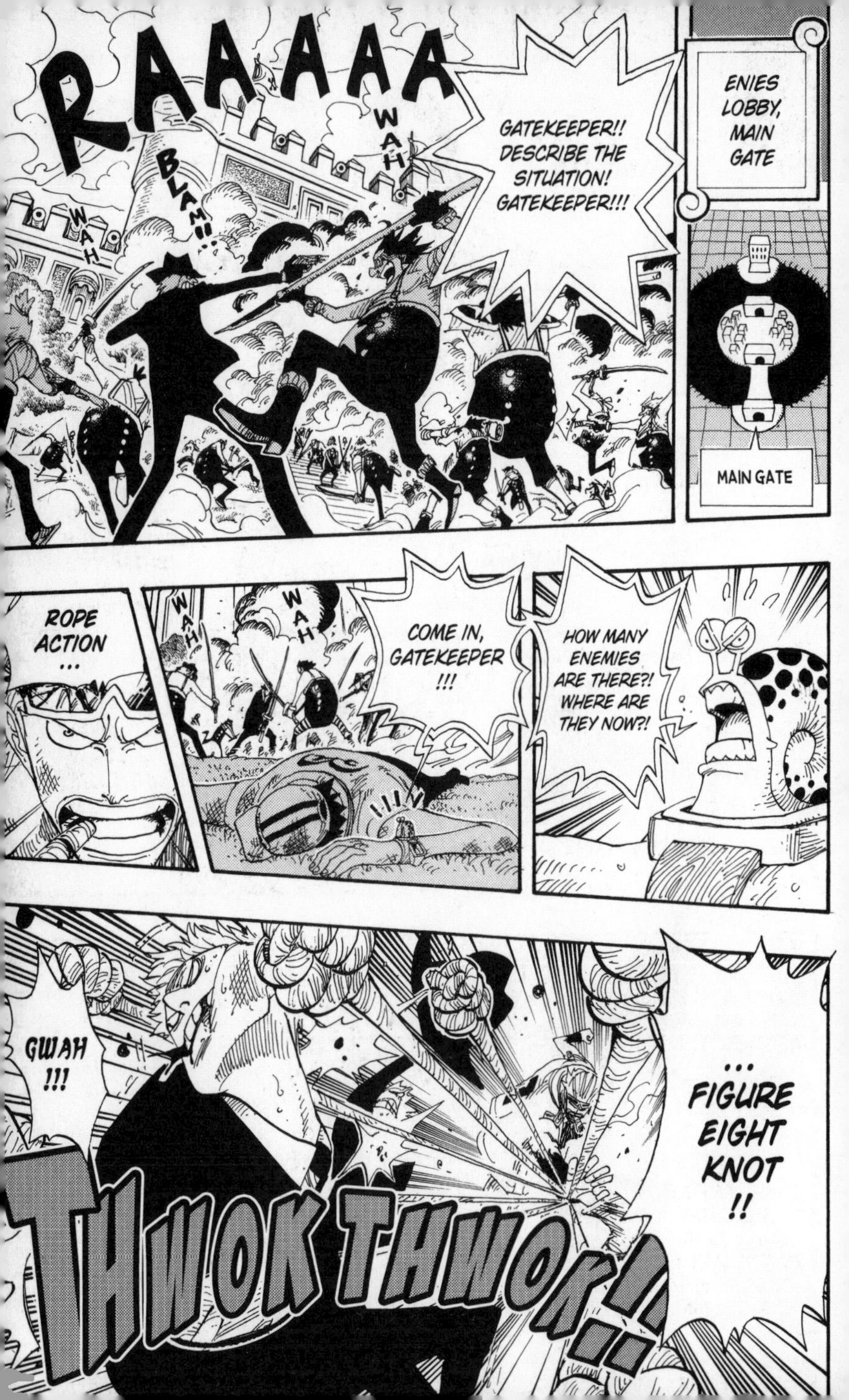
ENIES LOBBY, MAIN GATE
MAIN GATE
GATEKEEPER!! DESCRIBE THE SITUATION! GATEKEEPER!!!
RAAAAA
WAH
BLAM!!
WAH
HOW MANY ENEMIES ARE THERE?! WHERE ARE THEY NOW?!
COME IN, GATEKEEPER!!!
WAH
WAH
ROPE ACTION...
...FIGURE EIGHT KNOT!!
GWAH!!!
THWOK THWOK!!

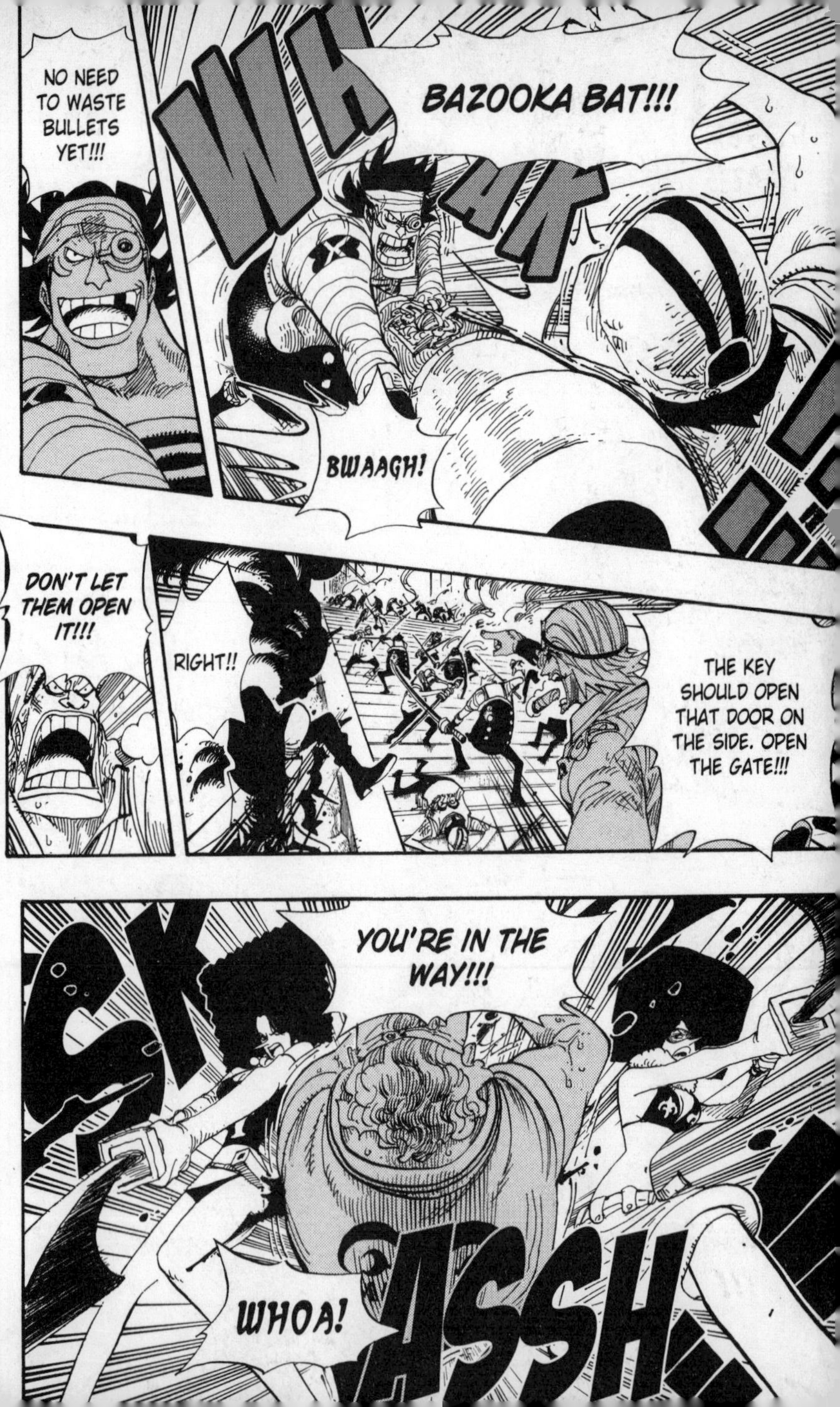
WHAK
BAZOOKA BAT!!!
BWAAGH!
NO NEED TO WASTE BULLETS YET!!!
THE KEY SHOULD OPEN THAT DOOR ON THE SIDE. OPEN THE GATE!!!
RIGHT!!
DON'T LET THEM OPEN IT!!!
YOU'RE IN THE WAY!!!
WHOA!

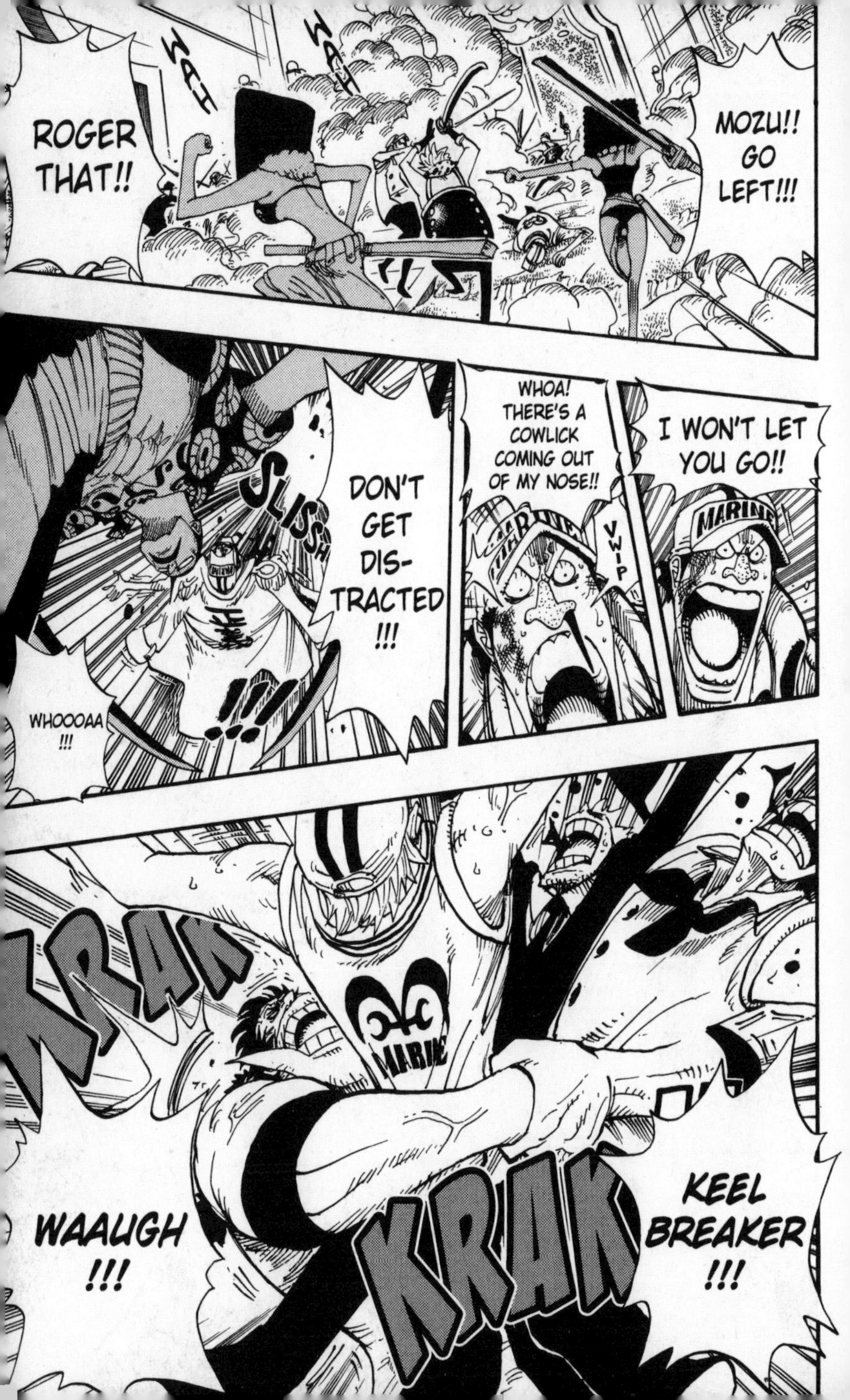
MOZU!! GO LEFT!!!
WACH
WACH
ROGER THAT!!
I WON'T LET YOU GO!!
WHOA! THERE'S A COWLICK COMING OUT OF MY NOSE!!
VWIP
DON'T GET DIS-TRACTED!!!
SLISSH
WHOOOAA!!!
KEEL BREAKER!!!
KRAK
WAAUGH!!!
KRAK

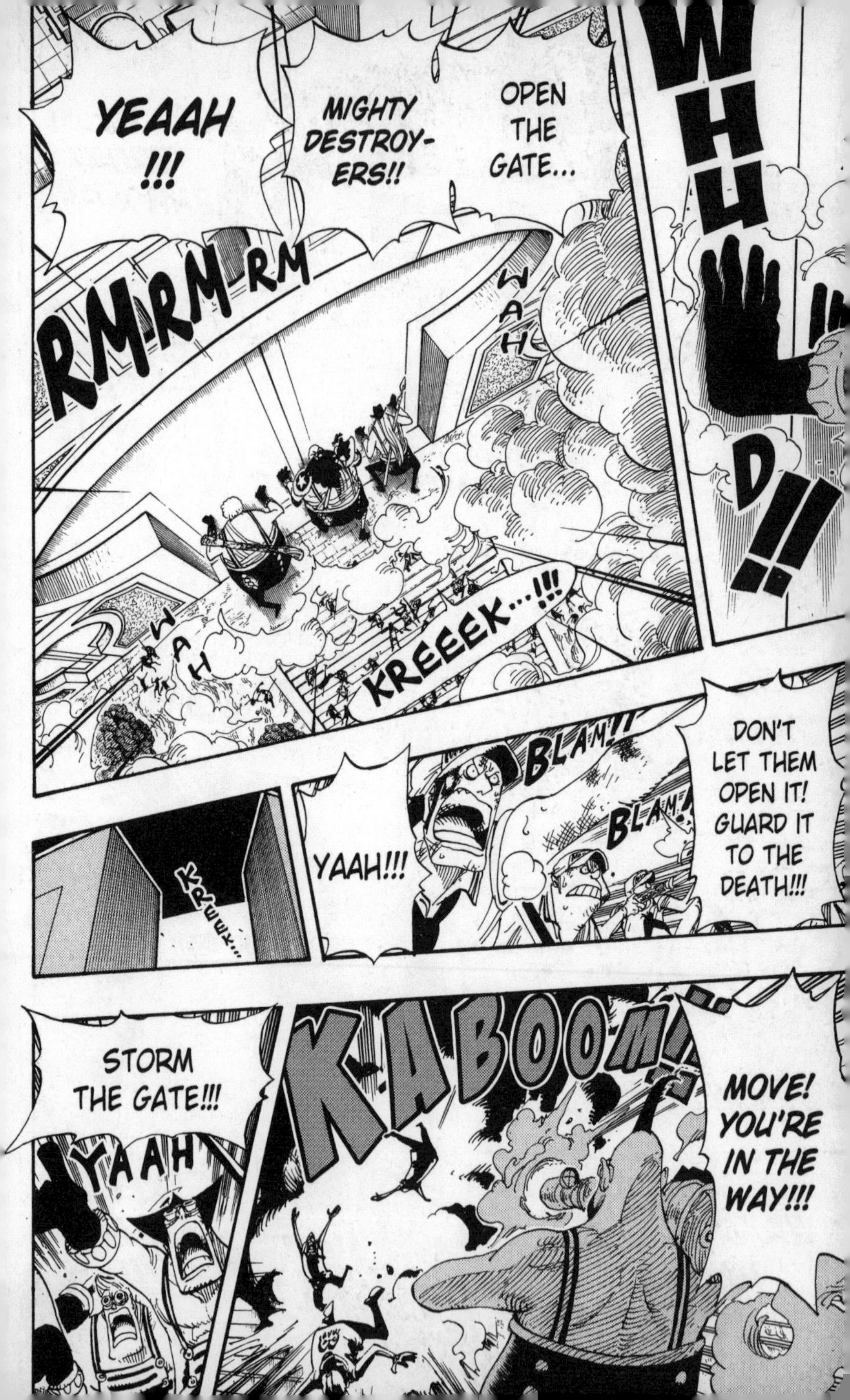
WHUD!!
OPEN THE GATE...
MIGHTY DESTROYERS!!
YEAAH !!!
WAH
RM-RM-RM-RM
KREEEK...!!!
WAH
DON'T LET THEM OPEN IT! GUARD IT TO THE DEATH!!!
BLAM!!
BLAM
YAAH!!!
KREEEK...
MOVE! YOU'RE IN THE WAY!!!
KABOOM!!
STORM THE GATE!!!
YAAH

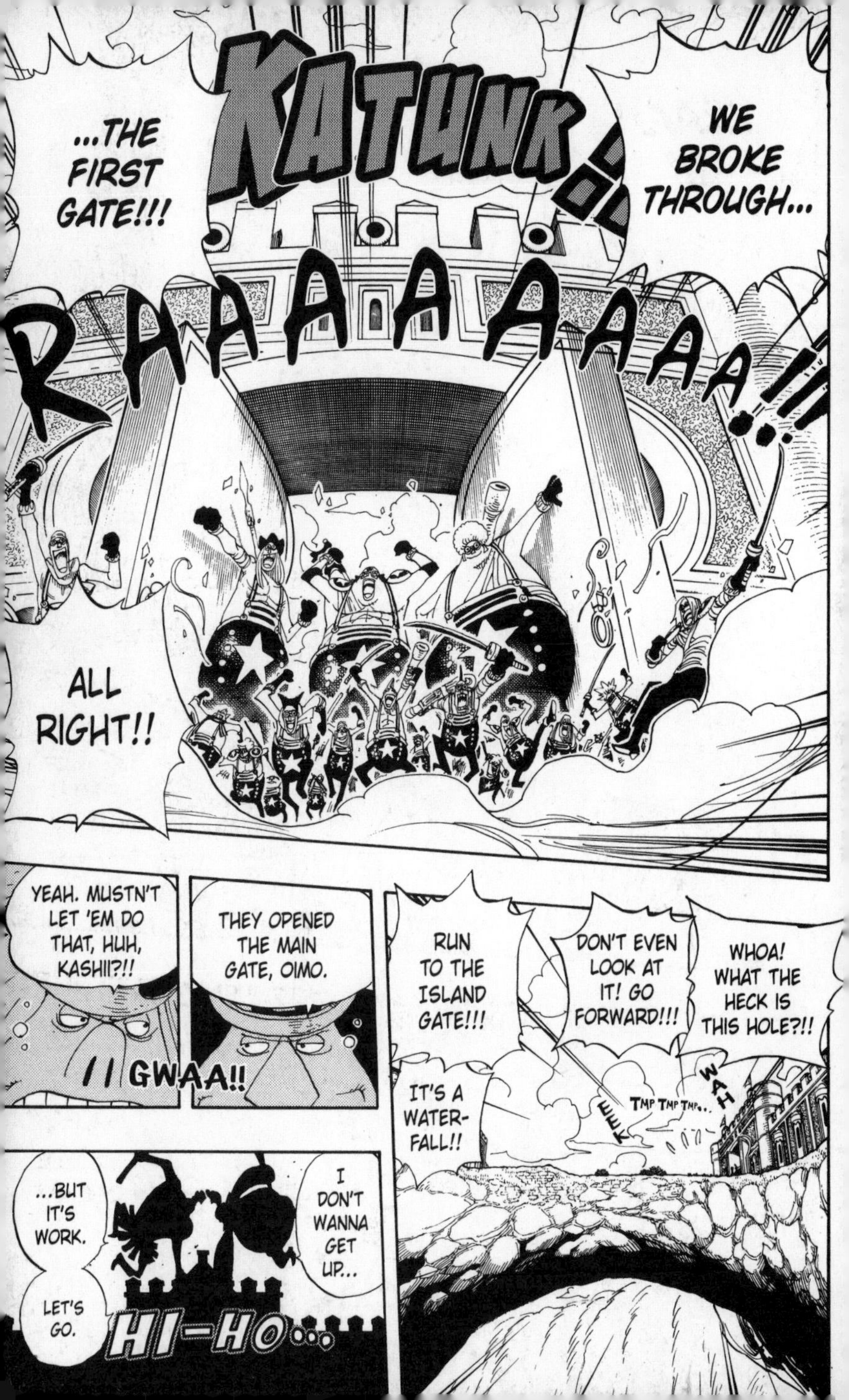
WE BROKE THROUGH...
KATUNK!!
...THE FIRST GATE!!!
RAAAAAAAAAA!!!
ALL RIGHT!!
WHOA! WHAT THE HECK IS THIS HOLE?!!
DON'T EVEN LOOK AT IT! GO FORWARD!!!
RUN TO THE ISLAND GATE!!!
WAH
TMP TMP TMP...
EEK
IT'S A WATER-FALL!!
THEY OPENED THE MAIN GATE, OIMO.
YEAH. MUSTN'T LET 'EM DO THAT, HUH, KASHII?!!
GWAA!!
I DON'T WANNA GET UP...
...BUT IT'S WORK.
LET'S GO.
HI-HO...

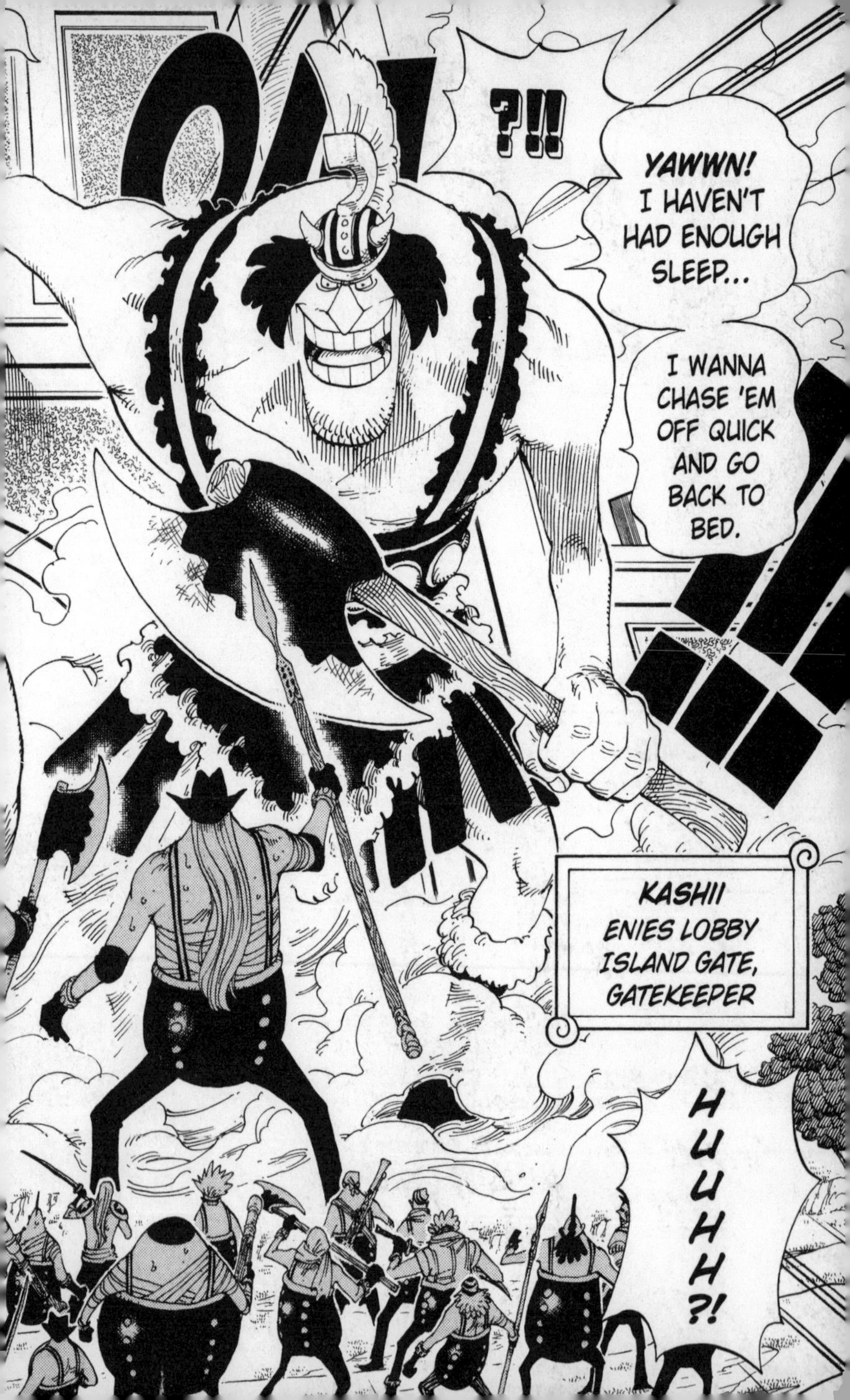

YAWWN! I HAVEN'T HAD ENOUGH SLEEP...
I WANNA CHASE 'EM OFF QUICK AND GO BACK TO BED.
?!!
KASHII
ENIES LOBBY ISLAND GATE, GATEKEEPER
HUUHH?!

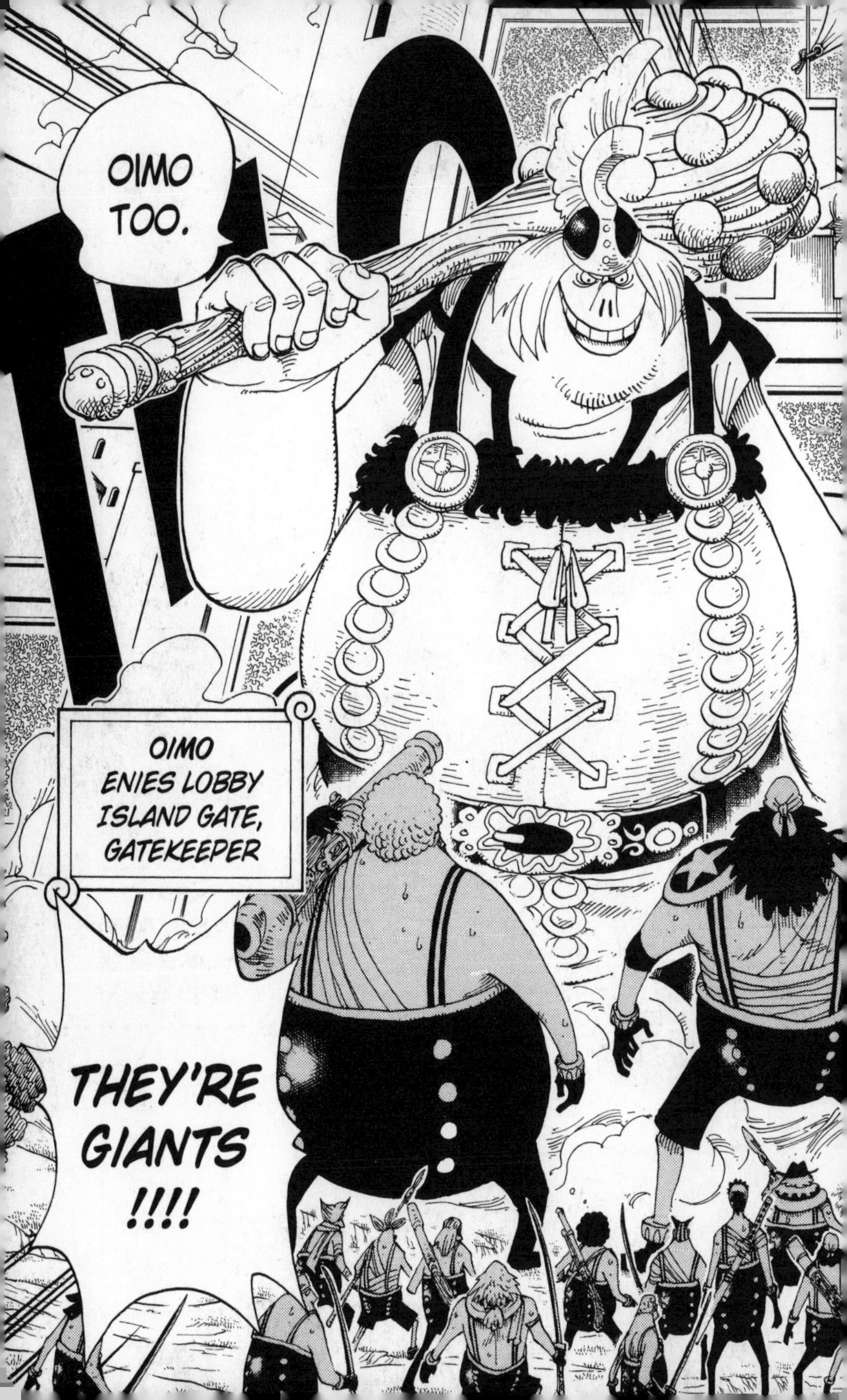
OIMO TOO.
OIMO ENIES LOBBY ISLAND GATE, GATEKEEPER
THEY'RE GIANTS !!!!

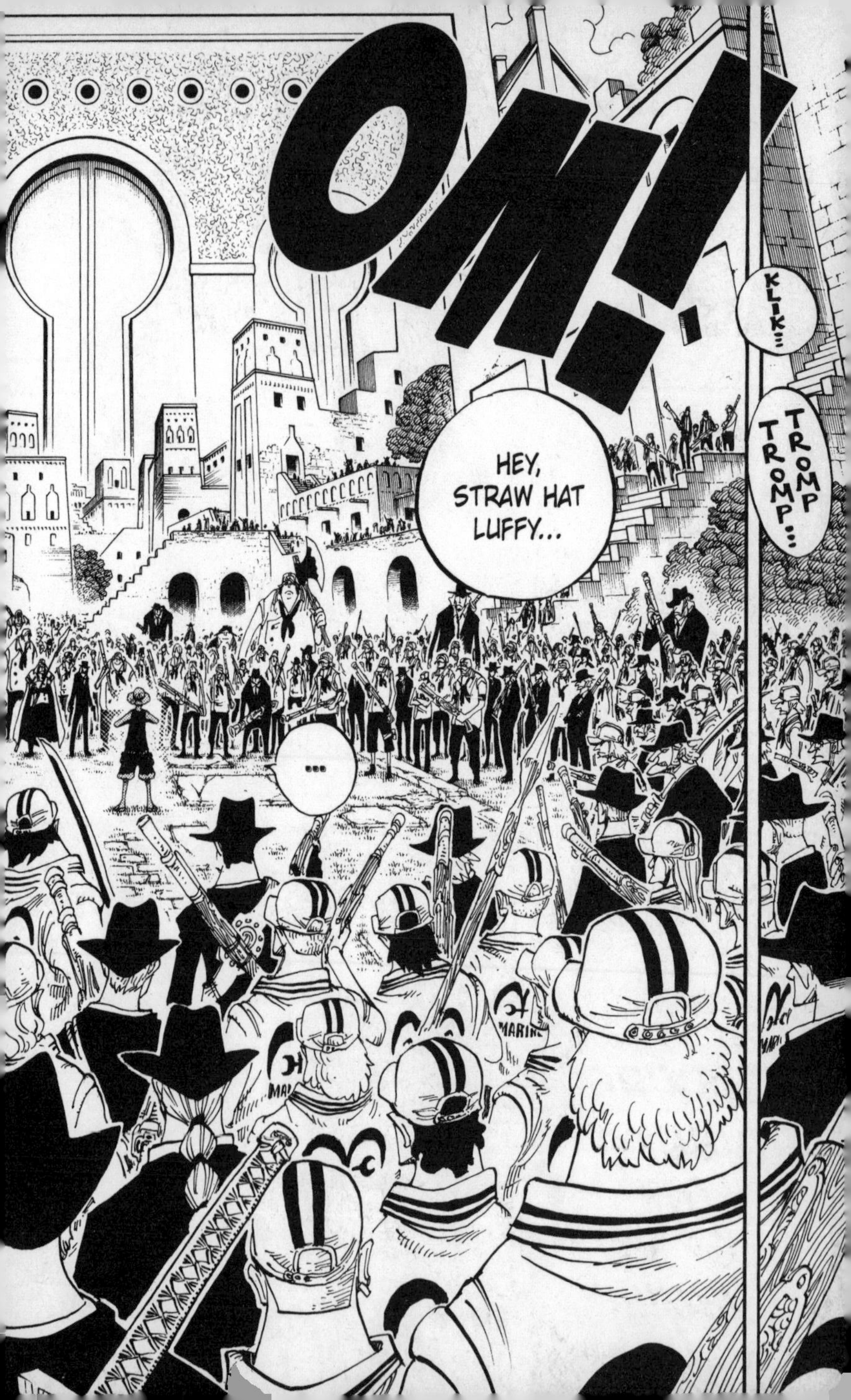
KLIK...
TROMP TROMP...
OH!!
HEY, STRAW HAT LUFFY...
...

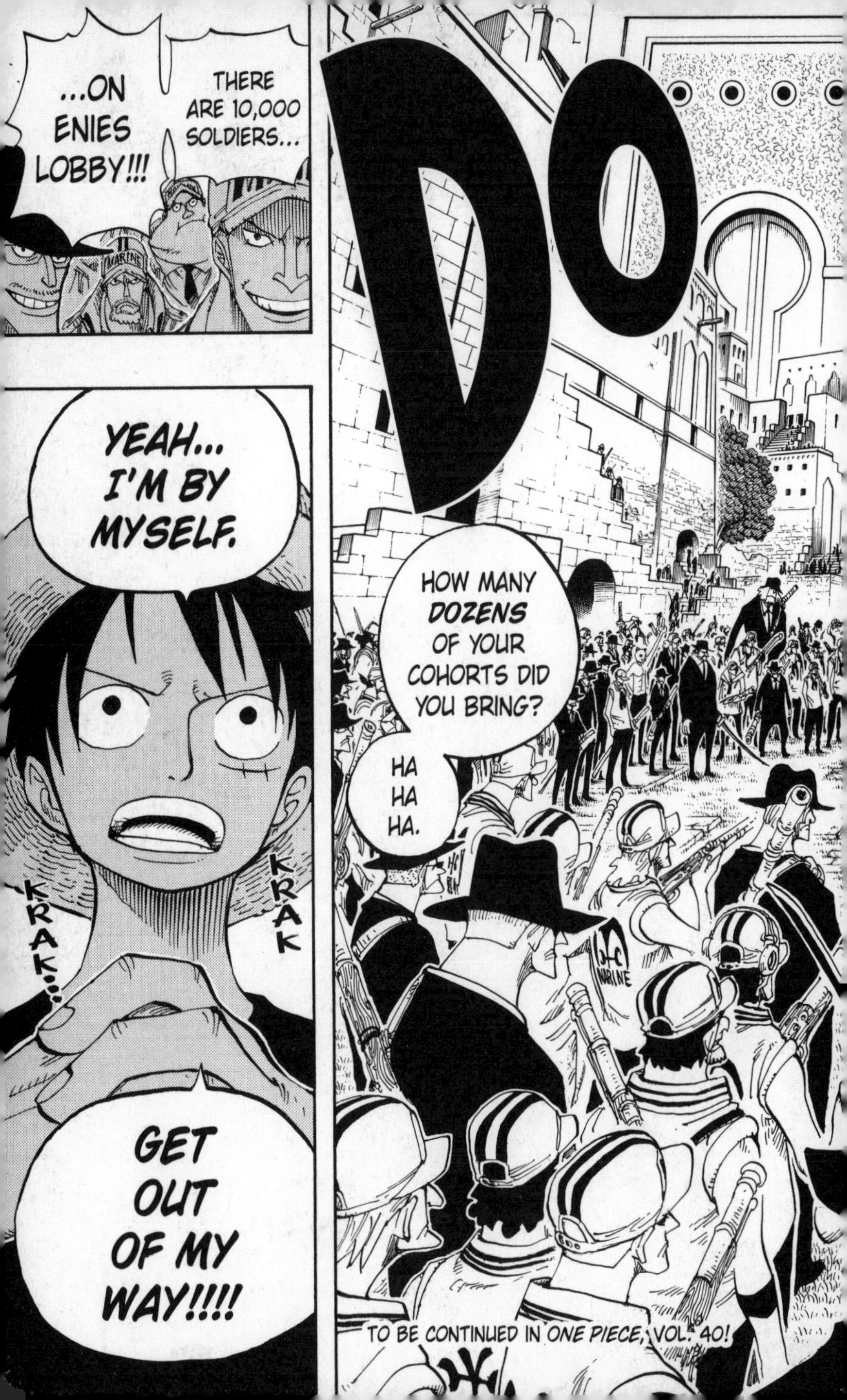
DO
HOW MANY DOZENS OF YOUR COHORTS DID YOU BRING?
HA HA HA.
TO BE CONTINUED IN ONE PIECE, VOL. 40!
THERE ARE 10,000 SOLDIERS...
...ON ENIES LOBBY!!!
YEAH... I'M BY MYSELF.
KRAK
KRAK...
GET OUT OF MY WAY!!!!

COMING NEXT VOLUME:

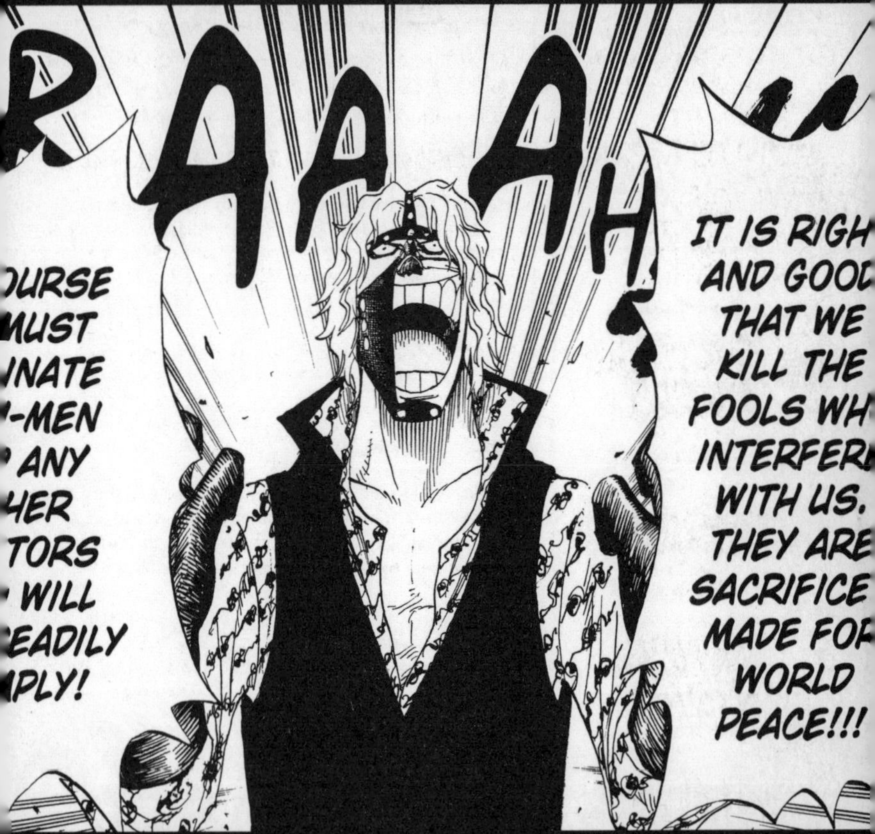
IT IS RIGH AND GOOD THAT WE KILL THE FOOLS WH INTERFERE WITH US. THEY ARE SACRIFICE MADE FOR WORLD PEACE!!!
RAAAAH
OURSE MUST INATE -MEN ANY HER TORS WILL EADILY PLY!

Hankering for a fight, Luffy's got a jump start on the battle to rescue Robin and Franky before they're sentenced by the Navy's court at Enies Lobby. The Straw Hats and the Franky Family band together, but they're in for an epic battle against the side of World Government–style "justice."

ON SALE NOW!

Set Sail with

Read all about **MONKEY D. LUFFY**'s adventures as he sails around the world assembling a motley crew to join him on his search for the legendary treasure **"ONE PIECE."** For more information, check out **onepiece.viz.com**.

EAST BLUE
(Vols. 1-12)
Available now!

See where it all began! One man, a dinghy and a dream. Or rather… a rubber man who can't swim, setting out in a tiny boat on the vast seas without any navigational skills. What are the odds that his dream of becoming King of the Pirates will ever come true?

BAROQUE WORKS
(Vols. 12-24)
Available now!

Friend or foe? Ms. Wednesday is part of a group of bounty hunters—or isn't she? The Straw Hats get caught up in a civil war when they find a princess in their midst. But can they help her stop the revolution in her home country before the evil Crocodile gets his way?!

SKYPIEA
(Vols. 24-32)
Available now!

Luffy's quest to become King of the Pirates and find the elusive treasure known as "One Piece" continues…in the sky! The Straw Hats sail to Skypiea, an airborne island in the midst of a territorial war and ruled by a short-fused megalomaniac!

WATER SEVEN
(Vols. 32-46)
Available from February 2010!

The *Merry Go* has been a stalwart for the Straw Hats since the beginning, but countless battles have taken their toll on the ship. Luckily, their next stop is Water Seven, where a rough-and-tumble crew of shipwrights awaits their arrival!

THRILLER BARK
(Vols. 46-50)
Available from May 2010!

Luffy and crew get more than they bargained for when their ship is drawn toward haunted Thriller Bark. When Gecko Moria, one of the Warlords of the Sea, steals the crew's shadows, they'll have to get them back before the sun rises or else they'll all turn into zombies!

SABAODY
(Vols. 50-54)
Available from June 2010!

On the way to Fish-Man Island, the Straw Hats disembark on the Sabaody archipelago to get soaped up for their undersea adventure! But it's not too long before they get caught up in trouble! Luffy's made an enemy of an exalted World Noble when he saves Camie the mermaid from being sold on the slave market, and now he's got the Navy after him too!

IMPEL DOWN
(from Vol. 54)
Available from July 2010!

Luffy's brother Ace is about to be executed! Held in the Navy's maximum security prison Impel Down, Luffy needs to find a way to break in to help Ace escape. But with murderous fiends for guards inside, the notorious prisoners start to seem not so bad. Some are even friendly enough to give Luffy a helping hand!

SHONEN JUMP

THE WORLD'S MOST POPULAR MANGA

BLEACH

STORY AND ART BY
TITE KUBO

ONE PIECE

STORY AND ART BY
EIICHIRO ODA

Tegami Bachi
LETTER · BEE

STORY AND ART BY
HIROYUKI ASADA

JUMP INTO THE ACTION BY TELLING US WHAT YOU LOVE (AND WHAT YOU DON'T)

LET YOUR VOICE BE HEARD!

SHONENJUMP.VIZ.COM/MANGASURVEY

HELP US MAKE MORE OF THE WORLD'S MOST POPULAR MANGA!

BLEACH © 2001 by Tite Kubo/SHUEISHA Inc.
ONE PIECE © 1997 by Eiichiro Oda/SHUEISHA Inc.
TEGAMIBACHI © 2006 by Hiroyuki Asada/SHUEISHA Inc.

RATED
T
TEEN
ratings.viz.com

VIZ
media
www.viz.com